Beauty and Belief
Aesthetics and religion in Victorian literature

Beauty and Belief

Aesthetics and religion in Victorian literature

Hilary Fraser

Post-Doctoral Research Fellow
University of Western Australia

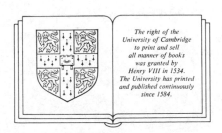

The right of the
University of Cambridge
to print and sell
all manner of books
was granted by
Henry VIII in 1534.
The University has printed
and published continuously
since 1584.

Cambridge University Press

Cambridge
London   New York   New Rochelle
Melbourne   Sydney

Published by the Press Syndicate of the University of Cambridge
The Pitt Building, Trumpington Street, Cambridge CB2 1RP
32 East 57th Street, New York, NY 10022, USA
10 Stamford Road, Oakleigh, Melbourne 3166, Australia

First published 1986

Printed in Great Britain by
the University Press, Cambridge

British Library cataloguing in publication data
Fraser, Hilary
Beauty and belief: aesthetics and religion in Victorian literature.
1. English literature–19th century–History and criticism
2. Religion in literature
I. Title
820.9′382   PR469.R4

Library of Congress cataloguing in publication data
Fraser, Hilary, 1953–
Beauty and belief.
Bibliography: p.
Includes index.
1. English literature–19th century–History and criticism.
2. Aestheticism (Literature)   3. Aesthetics in literature.
4. Religion in literature.   5. Aesthetics, British.   I. Title.
PR468.A33F73   1985   820′.9′008   85–11297

ISBN 0 521 30767 8

Contents

To Rob

Acknowledgements

I should like to thank my supervisor at Oxford, Mr A. O. J. Cockshut, for his guidance during the writing of the thesis on which this book is based. I am very grateful to Stephen Prickett for his thoughtful and detailed comments on how the thesis might be refined and improved upon for publication. Since then, many friends and colleagues have given practical advice, helpful information, and moral support. Max Beloff, John Clarke, George Hughes, and Hartley Slater kindly offered to read chapters of the book during its preparation, and I thank them for their generous help and invaluable suggestions. I should especially like to thank Ray Forsyth for sharing his extensive knowledge of Victorian literature, and for his constructive criticism at every stage of the book's development. I am greatly indebted to Graham Storey, of Trinity Hall, Cambridge, and Alan Robinson, of the University of Lancaster, for reading the manuscript so carefully, pointing out my inaccuracies and omissions, and offering many stimulating ideas of their own. I am also grateful to David Bean, Jan Pritchard, Helen Watson-Williams, and Fay Zwicky for their helpful contributions.

I owe thanks to the University of Western Australia and the University of Buckingham for providing the time and the research facilities which have enabled me to complete the book. Terence Moore, at Cambridge University Press, has given me considerable encouragement and advice, and I thank him for having the imagination to envisage the book that might be quarried from the thesis. I am very grateful to Lee Carter, Caroline Horobin, and Sue Lewis for so patiently and excellently deciphering my manuscript, to Bruce McClintock for his help at the proof stage, and to Pauline Marsh, who has provided valuable assistance in the editing of the text for Cambridge University Press.

Finally, there are those to whom my indebtedness is really inexpressible. I thank my parents for their untiring interest and encouragement throughout my academic career. My husband's quiet confidence and cheerful optimism has made the completion of a long and unwieldy study not only possible but enjoyable. It may seem a poor reward for all his help and support, but it is to Rob that I dedicate this book.

Abbreviations

Arnold	Super	*The Complete Prose Works of Matthew Arnold*, ed. R. H. Super. University of Michigan Press (1960–70).
	Arnold, *Poems*	*The Poems of Matthew Arnold*, ed. Kenneth Allott. Longmans, Green & Co. (1965).
Hopkins	*Journals*	*The Journals and Papers of Gerard Manley Hopkins*, ed. Humphry House and Graham Storey. Oxford University Press (1966 (1st edn, 1959)).
	Letters I	*The Letters of Gerard Manley Hopkins to Robert Bridges*, ed. C. C. Abbott. Oxford University Press (1970 (1935)).
	Letters II	*The Correspondence of Gerard Manley Hopkins and Richard Watson Dixon*, ed. C. C. Abbott. Oxford University Press (1970 (1935)).
	Letters III	*The Further Letters of Gerard Manley Hopkins*, ed. C. C. Abbott. Oxford University Press (1970 (1938)).
	Hopkins, *Poems*	*The Poems of Gerard Manley Hopkins*, ed. W. H. Gardner and N. H. Mackenzie. Oxford University Press (1970 (1918)).
	Sermons	*The Sermons and Devotional Writings of Gerard Manley Hopkins*, ed. Christopher Devlin. Oxford University Press (1967 (1959)).
Pater	*Appreciations* *Essays from the Guardian* *Imaginary Portraits* *Marius* *Miscellaneous Studies* *Plato and Platonism* *The Renaissance*	All these items refer to The Library Edition of *The Works of Walter Pater*. Macmillan (1910).

List of abbreviations

Ruskin	Ruskin, *Works*	*The Works of John Ruskin*, ed. E. T. Cook and Alexander Wedderburn. George Allen (1903–12).
Wilde	Wilde, *Works*	*Complete Works of Oscar Wilde*, ed. Vyvyan Holland. Collins (1966 (1948)).

Introduction

In a disapproving essay on Arnold's and Pater's aestheticised versions of Christianity, T. S. Eliot observes that their persistent and, in his view, misguided identification of art and religion is highly representative of 'one moment in the history of thought and sensibility in the nineteenth century':

The dissolution of thought in that age, the isolation of art, philosophy, religion, ethics and literature, is interrupted by various chimerical attempts to effect imperfect syntheses.[1]

Elsewhere, Eliot locates the central weakness of Victorian poetry in its 'dissociation of sensibility': 'Tennyson and Browning', he says, 'are poets, and they think; but they do not feel their thought as immediately as the odour of a rose.'[2] In the essay on Arnold and Pater he suggests that other Victorian intellectuals were similarly engaged in an unrealistic and futile endeavour to reconstruct an irreparably fragmented aesthetic, philosophical, and religious sensibility. The breadth of his indictment may well lead us to perceive an element of special pleading in Eliot's views, but even setting aside the combined prejudices of Catholic and Modernist orthodoxy of which those views are comprised, Eliot has here identified one of the most prominent and characteristic features of Victorian thought: a proliferation of religio-aesthetic theories designed to reconcile the claims of Christianity and beauty, morality and art.

In their desire to relate aesthetic cognition and judgement to religious and moral values, and the Christian faith to aesthetic experience, the Victorians are entirely traditional. Natural affinities between religion and art have conventionally been perceived in their common endeavour to express and embody non-material ideal truths in a physical form through a common language of myth and symbol. This seemingly natural alliance has traditionally manifested itself both practically and intellectually. In practical terms, religious patronage has enabled the arts to flourish through the centuries, and poetic language, symbols and structures are fundamental to liturgical ceremony, prayer, and aspects of theology. Intellectually, art has been related to religion and morality in a philosophical tradition which spans classical and modern aesthetics.[3] And from Dante to Wordsworth and Keats the greatest moments of European art and culture seem to bear witness to a mysterious affinity between beauty and truth.[4]

This traditional disposition to relate religious and aesthetic experience was unusually pronounced in the nineteenth century. The evocation of religious meaning in the arts was widespread and sustained. In the visual arts, painters as diverse as the Pre-Raphaelite Holman Hunt and the spectacularly melodramatic John Martin took as their subject-matter biblical scenes and invested their art with a peculiarly Victorian religious mysticism. Gothic Revival architecture exploited religious emotion in every pointed arch and soaring pinnacle. Quantities of religious poetry and novels were written.[5] The influence of the arts upon Victorian religion was equally far-reaching. Aesthetic sensibility defined the special character of the Victorian Anglo-Catholic revival, and a new style of 'literary' Catholicism developed among writers such as Coventry Patmore, Aubrey de Vere, Francis Thompson, the Wards and the Meynells. For the extremist ecclesiological Ritualists, attention to elaborate devotional practices came to dominate all other concerns. Poetry came to be accepted by many as the most appropriate way of expressing religious truths, and as the key to the interpretation of Scriptural meaning. The Bible was in the nineteenth century for the first time criticised as a work of literature,[6] while the arts were consistently measured by moral and religious as well as by aesthetic criteria. This all-pervasive, deliberate, and rather self-conscious concern with the relationship between religious and aesthetic experience is indeed the hallmark of the Victorian age.

What then were the cultural and historical conditions which determined such a conspicuous interaction of religion, art, and aesthetics in the period? Eliot was right in pointing to 'something which had happened to the mind of England between the time of Donne or Lord Herbert of Cherbury and the time of Tennyson and Browning',[7] and to bring his perception into historical focus we need to understand that that 'something which had happened' was, of course, Romanticism.

It might legitimately be argued that the Victorians inherited their desire for a unified, integrated consciousness from Coleridge, who believed that the poetic imagination, 'that synthetic and magical power', brings the whole soul of man into activity, with the subordination of its faculties to each other according to their relative worth and dignity.[8]

2

Introduction

If the Victorians inherited their concern with philosophical synthesis from Coleridge, it is arguable that they inherited their characteristic critical rhetoric on the moral uses of poetry from Wordsworth.[9] But in another (Hegelian) sense, we may consider the Romantic legacy to the Victorians as the legacy of an aesthetic in which 'content' has transcended 'form', meaning can no longer be adequately realised in a physical shape, and infinite spiritual subjectivity has attained in itself its own objectivity.[10] Thus, for instance, we find Hegel, in his lectures on aesthetics (first published in 1835) concluding a discussion of 'The Romantic Form of Art' with the prophetic warning that 'we must acquire higher forms for the apprehension of truth than those which art is in a position to supply'.[11]

It is not necessary to be a Hegelian, however, to be aware that the culmination of Romanticism left problems in its wake for succeeding generations. If Coleridge and Wordsworth passed on to their spiritual descendants the fruits of their own philosophical synthesis, they also passed on its attendant problems. The Victorians stood to inherit long-standing problems of perception in Romantic aesthetics, problems which few were able to resolve satisfactorily.

Coleridge was profoundly influenced by Kantian theories of perception, and it has been suggested that Wordsworth, despite his unspeculative leanings, gave imaginative expression to ideas which correspond remarkably closely to ideas current in contemporary German philosophical thought.[12] Coleridge was greatly exercised by the problems raised by transcendental epistemology, especially the question of the dialectic between subject and object in the act of knowing.[13] In *Biographia Literaria* he considers the tension between the subjectivity of perception and the sense of there being an objective 'meaning'. As Coleridge expresses it, it is necessary to find some absolute truth which is 'self-grounded, unconditional and known by its own light', which is 'neither subject nor object exclusively, but which is the identity of both'.[14] The only truth of which this may be said, he argues, is 'I AM', self or self-consciousness:

in this, and in this alone, object and subject, being and knowing, are identical, each involving and supposing the other.[15]

Through the empirical 'I', the absolute 'I AM' may be known. Paradoxically, 'we begin with the I KNOW MYSELF, in order to end with the absolute I AM'.[16]

The transcendental philosophy of Kant and Schelling upon which Coleridge bases his own position claims the act of self-consciousness as the source and principle of all human knowledge, but it also posits that ultimate reality is transcendent, beyond the bounds of our possible knowledge. A central problem of Kantian aesthetics is the unknowability of 'things in themselves':[17] all that is accessible to man is a 'sentiment of Being...lost beyond the reach of thought/And human knowledge'.[18]

The problems raised by the German Idealist philosophers were discussed by Coleridge and given poetic expression by Wordsworth, but essentially passed on unresolved to the Victorians. Some Victorians rose to the challenge and assimilated the implications of Romantic aesthetics into their own philosophical investigations. Others felt vulnerable to and dogged by the problematic dialectic in the act of perception between objective and subjective, 'two of the most objectionable words coined by the troublesomeness of metaphysicians' in Ruskin's view.[19] Subject and object, instead of being identified and synthesised, were naïvely confused, and transcendental truths were confidently, even aggressively asserted. Anyone who wished to become involved in questions relating to the self, nature, perception, and epistemology had to face Kant directly or knowingly retreat from the problems he had raised. Either response would clearly have significant implications for both religious and aesthetic thought.

The Kantian problem of the unknowability of 'things in themselves' flowed into another area of acknowledged mystery in the Victorian period. In his recapitulation of the ideas set forth in *The Origin of Species*, Darwin admits that not everything can be explained in terms of natural selection:

We can to a certain extent understand how it is that there is so much beauty throughout nature; for this may be largely attributed to the agency of selection...How it comes that certain colours, sounds and forms should give pleasure to man and the lower animals, – that is, how the sense of beauty in its simplest form was first acquired, – we do not know any more than how certain odours and flavours were first rendered agreeable.[20]

A question often asked in the Victorian period is 'How should science find beauty?',[21] and many are the attempts to define 'what sort of human, pre-eminently human feeling it is that loves a stone for a stone's sake, and a cloud for a cloud'.[22] Man's aesthetic sense, too, seemed to be beyond the reach of empirical explanation and to need philosophical reinvestigation.

But Darwinism also brought with it other more tangible and immediate problems. The theory of evolution contradicted the very essence of the Paleyan Argument from Design, or Natural Theology, according to which evidence of God's creative hand was found in the ordered perfection of the natural universe. This not only meant that the relationship between God, man and nature was more complex than had hitherto been assumed and needed therefore to be re-evaluated. It also meant effectively for many Victorians that God had disappeared from their world. In this way, combined with the impact of scepticism and German biblical criticism, which seemed simultaneously to undermine the Scriptural foundations of Christianity, Darwin's discoveries contributed to the crisis of faith which beset the Victorians in the mid nineteenth century. The waning power of an embattled Church brought fears of what would take its place as an effective stay against the threat of spiritual and moral anarchy. In this context of the diminishing spiritual authority of the Church, many of the traditional properties and functions of Christianity were transferred to poetry. In its new elevated position, poetry was invested with so many moral and mystical qualities that it became, in the rhetoric of many Victorians, inseparable from religion. As Culture replaced Christianity as the main agency responsible for keeping Anarchy at bay, aesthetic, religious, and moral concepts were inevitably and increasingly identified.

In Chapter 1 of this study I examine how the essential critical assumptions which were to shape the intellectual character of the Victorian age were first developed in the context of the Tractarians' efforts to reform the Church of England. The formation of the Oxford Movement pre-dates the publication of *The Origin of Species* by twenty-six years, yet it was already clear to its members that the Church of England was in a very vulnerable position. It needed to reassert its spiritual authority if it was to defend itself successfully against secular encroachments which it felt to be illegitimate, and it had to make itself generally more attractive in the face of growing criticism and scepticism. What more appropriate way to broaden the appeal of the Church without broadening its doctrinal basis than by making it more 'poetical'?[23] Keble and Newman were both in their different ways profoundly influenced by the English Romantics, and it was their awareness of the significance of Romantic poetry and aesthetics which determined the nature of their transformation of the Church of England.

In Chapter 2 of my study, I pursue the implications of the connections between religious and aesthetic experience which were established in Chapter 1 for a writer whose interests were not only theological but also more significantly literary and more broadly philosophical. Unlike Newman, Hopkins engages directly in an epistemological exploration of the relationship between the self, nature, and God. He achieves a perfect reconciliation of religious and aesthetic ideas in the theory which he calls 'inscape', whereby he confronts and resolves the problematical question of the meeting point of self-consciousness and transcendental reality.

In Chapter 3 I turn to the work of the two most influential critics of the period, Ruskin and Arnold, and explore the way in which art became for them a legitimate medium of aesthetic instruction. But in both cases the moral aesthetic which they so confidently proclaim is confused and dogmatic. Their limitations are directly related to their failure to confront the problematical implications of Kantian theories of perception and epistemology and Darwinian relativism. Retreating from the real issues, both writers try to mediate between a sharp awareness of the self and an equally acute sense of responsibility to a public context of religious and moral values.

Pater and Wilde, on the other hand, deny the notion of the answerability of the artist to his audience, and embrace the subjectivism and relativism which Ruskin and Arnold sought to evade. Wilde, in particular, offers a radical restatement of conventional Victorian ideas concerning the moral function of art. I conclude by examining how Pater and Wilde turn Newman's insight into the aesthetic qualities inherent in the Christian religion on its head in their espousal of a 'religion of art'. I shall also consider the works in which they present the highly aestheticised accounts of Christianity which later so offended Eliot, and attempt to re-evaluate their respective contributions to the Victorian religio-aesthetic debate.

1 Theology: Keble, Newman, and the Oxford Movement

After his conversion to Rome Newman criticised the Church of England for its lack of a proper sense of its own identity:

Nor can it in consequence be said to have any antecedents, or any future; or to live, except in the passing moment. As a thing without a soul, it does not contemplate itself, define its intrinsic constitution, or ascertain its position. It has no traditions; it cannot be said to think; it does not know what it holds, and what it does not; it is not even conscious of its own existence.[1]

Twenty years earlier, however, as an Anglican himself, he had believed that the Anglican Church could be made more self-aware. He conceded that the *via media* had never existed except on paper and had never been reduced to practice,[2] yet along with others he had determined to reform Anglican 'practice', and bring out 'in a substantive form, a living Church of England in a position proper to herself, and founded on distinct principles', 'a living Church, made of flesh and blood, with voice, complexion, and motion and action, and a will of its own'.[3] It was a task doomed to failure, for the Church of England was essentially ambiguous in its foundation and flexible in its forms. It deliberately maintained an ill-defined relationship with secular authority and a 'sort of elasticity' in its Articles.[4] It was, however, only after many years of vigorous campaigning to give the Church of England a degree of consistency that Newman fully comprehended that it was fundamentally and irredeemably inconsistent.

But in the early 1830s it had seemed possible to a group of men in Oxford that they might transform the Church of England. Tractarianism was initiated partly in response to changing relations between Church and State which crucial political developments in the late 1820s and early 1830s implied.[5] As the established church, the Church of England had derived considerable privileges from its alliance with the State. In the early years of the nineteenth century, the concerns of High Church Anglicans, 'the Tories at prayer',[6] were often more political than spiritual, having to do with protecting the property and privileges of the Church of England rather than with the nature of the Church as a religious institution. But by allying itself to a temporal authority the Church necessarily laid itself open to the vicissitudes of time. As long as that secular authority was in the control of Anglicans the question of establishment was relatively unproblematical. But the situation was fundamentally changed by the Repeal of the Test Act in 1828 and Catholic Emancipation in 1829. Once non-Anglicans were allowed to take their place in Parliament the State could no longer be so readily identified with the Church of England.

This was the context in which the outraged High Church response to long overdue reforms of the Irish Church in 1833 should be understood. John Keble's Assize Sermon on 'National Apostasy' preached on 14 July 1833, afterwards hailed by Newman as the inauguration of the Oxford Movement, expressed the alarm felt by High Churchmen at the Irish Church Act and the prospect of further Whig reforms. The reforms instituted by the Act were entirely reasonable and necessary – ten Irish bishoprics were abolished, the revenues of the two wealthiest sees were reduced, sinecures were suppressed, and livings over £300 were taxed – but an important principle was at stake. Without consulting the Church authorities, a civil government, one, moreover, which depended on Catholic and dissenting votes, was interfering with Church affairs. It was clear to Keble, Newman, and other High Churchmen that the Church should look to its long-neglected theology and reassert its sacred authority. It was necessary to restore in the public mind the sense that the Christian ministry possessed a divine authority independent of the State and Establishment.

The theological basis of Anglicanism in the years before the advent of Tractarianism was extremely weak. Wellington's idea of the Church of England as a maker of 'honest men' expressed the limits of most people's understanding of its function and status. The Church was primarily seen as a guide to the moral life. J. A. Froude describes the state of the Church before the 'Oxford Counter-Reformation' thus:

It was orthodox without being theological. Doctrinal problems were little thought of. Religion, as taught in the Church of England, meant moral obedience to the will of God. The speculative part of it was accepted because it was assumed to be true. The creeds were reverentially repeated; but the essential thing was practice. People went to church on Sunday to learn to be good, to hear the commandments repeated for the thousandth time, and to see them written in gilt letters over the communion-table. About the powers of the keys, the real presence, or the metaphysics of doctrine, no one was anxious, for no one thought about them. It was not worth while to waste time over questions which had no bearing on conduct, and could be satisfactorily disposed of only by sensible indifference.[7]

William Palmer, one of the original founders of the Oxford Movement, complained that there was '*no principle in the public mind to which we could appeal*'; an utter ignorance of all rational grounds of attachment to the Church; an oblivion of its spiritual character, as an institution, not of man, but of God; the grossest Erastianism most widely prevalent, especially amongst all classes of politicians'.[8] Palmer, Hurrell Froude, Keble, Newman and later Pusey set themselves the task of exposing and correcting this general ignorance of the true nature of the Church. They began to publish *Tracts for the Times* in which they stressed the apostolical descent of the Church of England as the central article of faith upon which its authority was founded, and explored the real meaning of the beliefs and institutions and Sacraments which had been for so long simply taken for granted.

There were precedents within the High Church in the early years of the nineteenth century for this renewed interest in the doctrines and liturgy of the Church. Clergymen such as Alexander Knox and Thomas Sikes are referred to by Newman, first in an article published in 1839 entitled 'The State of Religious Parties', later in the *Apologia*, as having anticipated the Oxford Movement in their strenuous opposition to the Protestantising tendencies within the Church of England and their desire to maintain the ancient doctrines of the early Church.[9] But such men were exceptional, and by and large the spiritual precursors of the Tractarians might more appropriately be located not among the old 'High and dry' Tory Churchmen, but among the Evangelicals. Newman, like a number of other early Victorian converts to Rome, had himself been an Evangelical in his youth. There are significant affinities between Evangelicalism and Tractarianism, and, as Robert Wilberforce pointed out, the Oxford Movement was a natural consequence of the earlier religious revival:

During the first quarter of the century, men were roused from slumber and wakened to earnestness; the next period gave them an external object on which to expend the zeal that had been enkindled. For it must be observed...that these movements, though distinct, were not repugnant. On the contrary, persons who had been most influenced by the one, often entered most readily into the other...So then the second movement was a sort of consequence of the first.[10]

David Newsome explains in his study of the Evangelical origins of Anglo-Catholicism, *The Parting of Friends*, that the tightest bond between the Evangelicals and the Tractarians in the early years of the Oxford Movement was 'the common pursuit of holiness'.[11] Owen Chadwick sees the 'continuity of piety between the Evangelical movement and the Oxford Movement' in terms of the fact that 'the Evangelicals taught the Oxford men not to be afraid of their feelings', which, as Gladstone observed, in turn affected 'the general tone and tendency of the preaching of the clergy'.[12]

It was hardly surprising that the Tractarians should find the emotional vigour and commitment of Evangelicalism an attractive alternative to the barrenness of the old High Church party. Anglicans had only to look around them at the paucity of the devotional life of their churches to detect other kinds of inadequacy to match the Church of England's theological insufficiencies. Keble describes the spiritual and aesthetic aridity of Anglican practice:

prayers in our churches are few and far between; as for sacramental symbols, such as the first Christians saw around them at all times and in all places, there is not the least thought of such now ...Consequently, men gladly betake themselves to rural charms and pastoral poetry and find in them a very real satisfaction.[13]

Alternatively, of course, they looked to Rome. A disenchanted Newman, writing shortly after his conversion, provides a pertinent rejoinder from his new perspective as a Roman Catholic: 'Poetry is the refuge of those who have not the Catholic Church to fly to and repose upon; the Church itself is the most sacred and venerable of poets.'[14] He describes the state of the Anglican Church which confronted Keble in the early days of the movement:

Now the author of the Christian Year found the Anglican system all but destitute of this divine element, which is an essential property of Catholicism; – a ritual dashed upon the ground, trodden on, and broken piecemeal; prayers, clipped, pieced, torn, shuffled about at pleasure, until the meaning of the composition perished, and offices which had been poetry were no longer even good prose; – antiphons, hymns, benediction invocations, shovelled away; – Scripture lessons turned into chapters; – heaviness, feebleness, unwieldiness, where the Catholic rites had had the lightness and airiness of a spirit; – vestments chucked off, lights quenched, jewels stolen, the pomp and circumstances of worship annihilated; a dreariness which could be felt, and which seemed the token of an incipient Socinianism, forcing itself upon the eye, the ear, the nostrils of the worshipper; a smell of dust and damp, not of incense; a sound of ministers preaching Catholic prayers, and parish clerks droning out Catholic canticles; the royal arms for the crucifix; huge ugly boxes of wood, sacred to preachers, frowning on the congregation in the place of the mysterious altar; and long cathedral aisles unused, railed off, like the tombs (as they were) of what had been and was not; and for orthodoxy, a frigid, unelastic, inconsistent, dull, helpless dogmatic which could give no just account of itself, yet was intolerant of all teaching which contained a doctrine more or a doctrine less, and resented every attempt to give it a meaning, – such was the religion of which this gifted author was, – not the judge and denouncer, (a deep spirit of reverence hindered it,) – but the renovator, as far as it has been renovated.[15]

Keble, according to Newman, 'did that for the Church of England which none but a poet could do: he made it poetical'.[16] I intend to concentrate upon this aspect of the Tractarian ideal, for it prepared the ground for that characteristically Victorian preoccupation with the relationship between religion and art which is the theme of this study. Moreover, an examination of their divergent understanding of the meaning of the poetical helps to explain why Newman became a Roman Catholic and Keble remained an Anglican.

I

As Newman suggested, Keble was well qualified to make the Church of England 'poetical' in that he was a poet whose work was admired by many devout Christians. One of the foremost theologians of his day, he was also unusually involved in the world of the arts. He managed to combine the responsibilities of a country parish with the Chair of Poetry at Oxford, a post he held from 1832 to 1841. Newman too was a poet and literary critic. His poetry was widely read in its time, and, like Keble, he turned his exceptional intellect and critical acumen to aesthetic as well as theological matters. In their own characters, both men seemed to epitomise the personal style which became known as the Oxford *ethos* (the expression was coined by Keble), 'an habitual toning or colouring diffused over all a man's moral qualities, giving the exercise of them a peculiar gentleness and grace'.[17] Indeed, it is hardly surprising that their religious character came to have a profound effect on their views on art and, conversely, their aesthetic awareness shaped their religious thinking.[18]

The literary context within which they wrote had itself recently undergone a significant upheaval. It is a critical commonplace that the Oxford Movement was, in some important respects, a late theological flowering of Romanticism. It is necessary, however, to exercise caution in making generalised claims about the influence of the Romantics on the Oxford Movement theologians. First of all, as the most interesting and challenging modern critics of Romanticism have insisted, 'Romanticism is protean',[19] and therefore all-embracing definitions are liable to be unsatisfactory and tendentious. Secondly, the legacy of Romanticism to Keble and Newman encompasses a wide range of aesthetic, religious, philosophical, and political concerns. 'The Lake School', as Hopkins said, 'expires in Keble and Faber and Cardinal Newman',[20] and there is no doubt that Wordsworth had an important poetic influence on both Keble and Newman and that the poetic theory enunciated in the Preface to the *Lyrical Ballads* helped shape their theories of poetry. But the relationship between Romanticism and Tractarianism went beyond the purely literary. Basil Willey and, more recently, David Newsome and John Coulson have, for example, investigated the similarities between Coleridge's and Newman's philosophical positions, and Stephen Prickett has shown the influence of Wordsworth and Coleridge on the Victorian Church.[21] Thirdly, and perhaps most importantly, the various critical interpretations to which Romanticism has been subject are underpinned by ideological assumptions which are of interest in themselves. Marilyn Butler has drawn attention to the various ways in which succeeding generations of readers and critics have rewritten Romanticism.[22] The Victorians were of course the first to do so and, as will emerge in the course of this study, their perceptions of Romantic writers and of the phenomenon of Romanticism frequently tell us more about the Victorian critic than his purported subject.

Although enthusiastic readers of other Romantic writers too, Keble and Newman were primarily indebted to the writings of Wordsworth and Coleridge in the development of their own theories.[23] A discussion of the relationship between Romanticism and Tractarianism can therefore usefully focus on Keble's and Newman's appropriations and divergences from ideas expressed in Wordsworth's and Coleridge's poetry and prose works.[24] Both Keble and Newman felt that in general terms Romantic poetry had inaugurated 'the spiritual awakening of spiritual wants' in the Church of England.[25] Both acknowledged that their poetic predecessors had paved the way for a Christian revival by opening men's hearts and making them more receptive to faith. But Keble and Newman were clearly interested in different aspects of Wordsworthian and Coleridgean critical theory, and it is instructive to follow the different preoccupations of their literary criticism into their theological writings.

Among the Romantic poets, Wordsworth was Keble's greatest mentor. In Lecture XVI of the Oxford *Lectures on Poetry* Keble says that as fire is kindled by fire, 'so is a poet's mind kindled by contact with a brother poet'.[26] Wordsworth certainly fulfilled this role for Keble. Keble was first introduced to his poetry by John Taylor Coleridge, a fellow undergraduate at Corpus Christi, and made his acquaintance in 1815. He derived great comfort from Wordsworth's poetry and, like Newman, he believed that it had inaugurated a spiritual awakening. Keble leaves us in no doubt of his indebtedness and admiration by dedicating his *Lectures on Poetry* to Wordsworth in the highest terms[27] and hailing him as 'easily the first of modern poets'.[28] He takes the last stanza of Wordsworth's 'Anecdotes for Fathers' as the motto of *Lyra Innocentium*, a book which devotes itself to the Wordsworthian theme of the wisdom and sanctity of childhood. And in Keble's essay on 'Sacred Poetry' Wordsworth is again cited to support the claim that true sacred poetry must reflect a poet's sustained general tone of thought.

But more important than specific acknowledgements are the constant echoes of Wordsworth's and Coleridge's aesthetics in Keble's own poetry and critical writings. Keble's literary criticism largely offers a restatement and expansion of Wordsworth's Preface to the *Lyrical Ballads*. Indeed, as Marilyn Butler, citing M. H. Abrams, points out, although Wordsworth's Preface may be seen as having inaugurated a new idea of poetry as expressive of the poet's emotions, and as essentially intuitive and subjective, 'the doctrine is complete and widely accepted only for the generation *after* "the English Romantics"', by which time 'a thoroughgoing dogma of the mysterious, subconscious origin of art' has been developed.[29] Keble is also concerned in his poetry and literary criticism with the function of sacramental, symbolic, and allegorical modes of expression. We may find parallels with Wordsworth's poetry in this respect too, but we should not overlook important differences. Wordsworth may be loosely described as a sacramental poet, but although in his later years he tried in *The Excursion* and his *Ecclesiastical Sonnets* to write Christian poetry, and 'practised a kind of theological surgery' when he altered the 1805 text of *The Prelude*,[30] in his earlier poetry he had not attempted to provide his intuitive sense of the divine in nature with a dogmatic or conceptual foundation. In these early poems, instead of expressing the traditional Christian triangular pattern of God, nature, and the soul, the whole scheme was demythologised: the divine role receded, and the psychology of the poet's mind became the focus of his artistic effort.[31] Although deeply spiritual, Wordsworth was non-committal in his early poetry as to his exact religious beliefs.[32] This may be explained by the fact that religion, for the early Wordsworth, was connected with his sense of the noumenal; knowledge of the transcendental was confined to a mystical intuition of nature's types and symbols. Coleridge, however, accused Wordsworth of being a semi-atheist and referred to his 'vague, misty rather than mystic, confusion of God with the world'.[33] In fact, in this respect, Keble's interest in sacramental symbol coincides much more significantly with Coleridge's more orthodox ideas about nature as the symbolic language of God, as expressed in his *Lectures on Revealed Religion* and poems such as 'Religious Musings', 'Frost at Midnight' and 'The Destiny of Nations' written in the 1790s, and his statements on symbolism in *The Statesman's Manual*, published in 1816.[34]

Coleridge was, nevertheless, himself aware of an inner conflict between the claims of Christian orthodoxy and the mythopoeic imagination. In his poem entitled 'The Eolian Harp', written in 1795, the speaker's imaginative speculations about nature are checked by his wife's reproving orthodoxy:

> And what if all of animated nature
> Be but organic Harps diversely fram'd,
> That tremble into thought, as o'er them sweeps
> Plastic and vast, one intellectual breeze,
> At once the Soul of each, and God of all?
> But thy more serious eye a mild reproof
> Darts, O beloved Woman! nor such thoughts
> Dim and unhallow'd dost thou not reject,
> And biddest me walk humbly with my God.
> Meek Daughter in the family of Christ!
> Well hast thou said and holily disprais'd
> These shapings of the unregenerate mind;
> Bubbles that glitter as they rise and break
> On vain Philosophy's aye-babbling spring.[35]

Sara's orthodox anxieties anticipate the kinds of reservations about Coleridge that Newman later expressed when he described him as

a very original thinker, who, while he indulged a liberty of speculation which no Christian can tolerate, and advocated conclusions which were often heathen rather than Christian, yet after all instilled a higher philosophy into inquiring minds than they had hitherto been accustomed to accept. In this way he made trial of his age, and succeeded in interesting its genius in the cause of Catholic truth.[36]

Newman's attitude towards Coleridge was clearly ambivalent, but he was certainly influenced by Coleridgean theories of the imagination, perception, language, and form. As John Coulson has argued, Newman was particularly concerned to develop Coleridge's insights into the

14

symbolic possibilities of language and the nature of assent, as elucidated in *Biographia Literaria*, the *Lay Sermons*, and *Aids to Reflection*.[37] He also stresses the parallels between Coleridge's and Newman's shared interest in the relationship between the sacramental origin of the Church and its empirical reality.[38] In *On the Constitution of the Church and State*, the last of his works to be published in his lifetime, Coleridge explores this question in the context of his discussion of the relation of Church and State. *On the Constitution of the Church and State* was published in 1830 in response to precisely the same circumstances that precipitated the formation of the Oxford Movement. The specific issue it addressed was Catholic Emancipation in 1829,[39] the implications of which were only confirmed by the subsequent Whig reforms which led to the formation of the Oxford Movement. Coleridge does not advocate a unitary concept of Church and State in his work, as does Thomas Arnold in his *Principles of Church Reform* published three years later,[40] and to this extent at least Newman would have agreed with him. But in other important respects their conclusions are very different. Coleridge's Church, although he does not say so specifically in *On the Constitution of the Church and State*, is essentially Protestant.[41] For Coleridge, Protestantism is more appropriate than Catholicism to the demands of democratic representative government and a National State, in that it stresses the individual and national as opposed to universal loyalties. Coleridge's vision of an interdependent relationship between Church and State demanded a Protestant basis, whereas Newman's premise in determining the viability of Anglican 'practice' in the 1830s was as emphatically Catholic.

Both Keble and Newman may, then, be said to be in a qualified sense developing Wordsworthian and Coleridgean ideas about poetry, symbolism, and the nature of faith, but they may also be perceived as reacting against the personalising and secularising tendencies of Wordsworth's and Coleridge's works. Both Keble and Newman distrusted Coleridge's speculative tendencies and philosophical conclusions, and judged his and Wordsworth's claims for the poetic imagination and their shared concept of symbolism to be worthless without the sanctions of Christian Revelation, dogmatic formulation, and the historical Church.[42] Keble feared that people might be satisfied with the spiritual meagreness of their creeds and fail to move beyond them to the higher claims of Christianity: 'the mysteries of divine Truth supplied the place of poetry among our forefathers, while now the present generation readily forgoes that higher wisdom, satisfied as it would seem with that poetry which is but a shadow of it'.[43] The Oxford

Movement theologians' relationship with their immediate literary predecessors was, as for so many Victorian writers, an uneasy and ambiguous one. Indubitably influenced as Newman and Keble were by Coleridge and Wordsworth, they represented the very principles of demythology and individualism against which the Tractarians took up arms in defence of their Church.

II

Keble's theory of poetry and its place in the divine scheme was first outlined in his review of Copleston's *Praelectiones Academicae* in the *British Critic* of 1814, and later in his essay on 'Sacred Poetry' written for the *Quarterly Review* of 1825. He had time to formulate these ideas more completely during his years as Professor of Poetry at Oxford, and his more mature views are to be found in the *Lectures on Poetry* and in his review of Lockhart's *Memoirs of the Life of Sir Walter Scott*.[44]

Keble was intrigued by the experience of the 'poetic' in ways which anticipate Hopkins' later fascination with the experience of inscape: 'Certain landscapes...certain combinations of the colours and forms of nature – strike the intelligent observer as poetical, he can hardly tell how or why.'[45] For Keble, a poetic epiphany lifts one out of one's normal state of insensitivity and leads one 'to shape even trivial actions by reference to an archetype beyond the reach of man'.[46] We realise a divine order and purpose through the intuition of religious and moral associations, rather than the direct instruction of religion and ethics: 'It is enough that we feel by an instinct, no matter how attained, that there *is some* leading idea, some *moral* in what we see, could we anyhow discern it.'[47] When nature represents the indirect expression of a state of mind or an engrossing feeling or an intuition of the divine, then it is 'poetical'. In fact, anything which elevates the mind into a state of heightened awareness is 'poetical'.

Keble's clearest definition of poetry is found in his review of the *Life of Sir Walter Scott*: 'Poetry is the indirect expression in words, most appropriately in metrical words, of some overpowering emotion, or ruling taste, or feeling, the direct indulgence whereof is somehow repressed.'[48] Similarly, in the first of his Oxford Lectures Keble describes how poetry provides an emotional outlet and affords relief to strong currents of thought and feeling through their verbal expression in a higher medium than everyday language can offer. Borrowing Wordsworth's terms, he stipulates in Lecture XXII that poetry must be the 'spontaneous outburst of the poet's inmost feeling' and in Lecture IV characterises poets as 'spontaneously moved by impulse', describing how they 'resort to composition for relief and solace of a burdened or over-wrought mind'. In Lecture XXIV he identifies as the essential requirement for poetry the fact that 'everything should flow from a full heart'.[49]

The emotionalism of Keble's poetic theory clearly owed a great deal to Wordsworth's poetics and to the renewed emphasis on powerful religious feelings encouraged by the Evangelical Revival. In this respect too, although his sacramentalism places him firmly in the Platonic tradition, he was also indebted to Aristotle,[50] for, like Aristotle, Keble saw an analogy between emotional catharsis of the soul and physical purgation of the body. According to this theory, repressed emotion is dangerous, a form of insanity, to which poetry brings healing relief by its controlled expression. Keble found a curiously ambiguous function of expression and control in the formal aspects of poetry, for example, in metrical rhythm:

On the one hand, it shapes out a sort of channel for wild and tumultuous feelings to vent themselves by; feelings whose very excess and violence would seem to make the utterance of them almost impossible, for the very throng of thoughts and words, crowding all at once to demand expression.[51]

In this sense, poetic metre determines 'in some one direction, the overflow of sentiment and expression, wherewith the mind might otherwise be fairly oppressed'. Yet it also throws 'a kind of veil over those strong or deep emotions, which need relief but cannot endure publicity'.[52] Poetry offers a structurally controlled form of self-expression which reconciles the apparently incompatible demands of relief and reticence. The poet can utter thoughts in verse which he 'would have shrunk from setting down in the language of conversation', the metrical form thereby functioning both as 'a vent for eager feeling, and a veil of reserve to draw over them'.[53] Indeed, in all the arts there is some regulating principle comparable to poetical metre, which mitigates the subjectiveness of the artist's vision, allows him to express his enthusiasm and passion in accordance with his natural reserve, and makes the work of art accessible to an audience.

Allegory is another technique cited by Keble as meeting the demands of expression and concealment. It serves equally as a check to the poet's fancy, a veil of concealment from the ignorant, and a means of magnifying significance for the perceptive mind. He praised the delicacy of Spenser's disposition as reflected in his choice of the allegorical mode.[54] For Keble, there was an inherent similarity between reserve in poetry and mysticism in religion,[55] and the poet, through his use of ideas, images, similes, and poetic forms, should, he thought, stimulate religious and moral associations in the imagination of the reader, because 'if there be any one term which comprises in itself all the peculiar pleasures of poetry...it is association'.[56]

This definition of poetry can be extended to other art forms, to architecture, sculpture, painting, and music, indeed, to any cause, occasion, or expression of sublimity.[57] According to Keble all the arts are linked by the common denominator of feeling, although each expresses it in a different way. Thus, 'what is called the poetry of painting simply consists in the apt expression of the artist's own feeling',[58] while

we need not spend much time in considering how far Poetry enters into Music: for it is universally allowed that they are twin-sisters, and just as an echo reproduces and returns from afar the human voice, so Poetry and Music alike give back the subtle turns and changes of the mind.[59]

Thus in Keble's aesthetic theory the emphasis shifts from classic post-Aristotelian criticism – genres classified according to criteria such as the subject of the poem, how it is imitated, its form and rhetoric – to the poet himself and the emotions he expresses through poetry.[60] Since Keble sees poetry as consisting of a controlled emotional outburst, delight in poetry depends upon sympathy for the author's particular disposition as well as for his subject-matter and his formal treatment of it. Similarly, Keble's conception of the sublimity of the function of poetry made it impossible for him to distinguish between the poet and the man in the exercise of criticism. Hence his disapproval of some of the greatest poets whose moral defects he felt were manifested in their poetry.

In place of the traditional poetic classifications Keble substituted his own theory of Primary and Secondary Poets.[61] He distinguished between the Primary Poet who 'spontaneously moved by impulse, resort[s] to composition for relief and solace of a burdened or over-wrought mind',[62] whose poetry is the absolutely sincere expression of 'the overflowing warmth of his own natural feelings, kindled by circumstances in which he was himself placed',[63] and the Secondary Poets, who 'imitate the ideas, the expression, and the measures of the former',[64] in short, those who work themselves up to an 'artificial glow'[65] of pseudo-poetic feeling. Among the class of Secondary Poets Keble includes, as well as clever imitators, those who are genuinely stirred by a powerful emotion or a tumultuous passion, but for whom such a feeling is merely transient, inspiring only a brief burst of lyrical utterance. It was a vital principle that 'the feelings the writer expresses should appear to be specimens of his general tone of thought, not sudden bursts and mere flashes of goodness'.[66] There had to be a sense of moral consistency. Keble's categorisation of Primary and Secondary Poets depends upon the distinction between 'settled tastes' and 'present feelings'.[67] The poet whose quietly held but strong and permanent feelings last a lifetime is considered far worthier of respect than one whose enthusiasms are changeable. Keble even characterises poetic genres in terms of the poetic personality: dramatic and narrative forms express a poet's *ethos*, or long-term character traits, while the lyric, elegy, and satire indicate *pathos*, short, intense, overpowering feeling.[68]

Thus for Keble poetry depends upon a tension between personal emotion and reserve, and employs veiled self-expression to bring relief and healing to poet and audience alike. But such a catharsis depends upon the assertion of 'truth'.[69] And 'truth' is a loaded word for Keble, as it is for other writers considered in this study, in that it involves both aesthetic authenticity – truth of sincere feelings, truth of representation – and religious truths, divine Revelation.

III

Newman's sympathy with Wordsworthian and Coleridgean poetics is implicit in his essay 'Poetry, with reference to Aristotle's Poetics'.[70] Curiously, he ignores Aristotle's conception of catharsis which so influenced Keble, instead concentrating upon the necessity of seeing dramatic composition as 'a free and unfettered effusion of genius' rather than 'an exhibition of ingenious workmanship'.[71] Newman underlines the poetic force of 'the characters, sentiments, and diction', as opposed to Aristotle's insistence on the supremacy of plot in tragedy.[72] He concurs with Wordsworth and Coleridge in preferring the suggestive, allusive, and expressive qualities in poetry to classical ideals of clarity and form. Despite this reservation, however, Newman accepts wholeheartedly Aristotle's view that the nature of poetry consists in the representation of an idea created in the mind, whilst the metrical garb is 'but the outward development of the music and harmony within'.[73] His conception of the centrality of the poet's mind coincides with the Wordsworthian concern with poetic 'genius' and the 'growth of a poet's mind'. The subjectivism of this theory of poetic creativity is tempered by an insistence that poetry should be 'the utterance of the inward emotions of a right moral feeling', seeking a purity and truth not to be found in real life.[74] In critical as well as religious terms

Newman required a system of values based on a higher authority than the self, and demanded objective standards of excellence in literature to complement the idiosyncrasies of genius. A superficial reading of this essay on poetry may appear to invalidate my earlier stress on his concern for form. He proposes that poetry exists independently of composition and agrees with Keble that poetry is not limited to the written form. He implies almost that the spirit of poetry suffers when it is given a material form. Composition is necessary to the poet's desire to communicate his vision, but it is not intrinsic to poetry. The poem itself is an 'accessory', 'no essential part of poetry, though indispensable to its exhibition', 'the artificial part', 'dexterity', 'accomplishment' – hence Newman's disparagement of Aristotle's insistence on a 'laboured and complicated' plot.[75]

This is not to say that Newman advocated anarchic formlessness in art, rather that he had a Romantic and not a classical conception of form. He believed that structure or 'plot' happened naturally in that it was 'breathed' out of the poet's mind, and disapproved of an excessive concern with the formal elaboration of this initial inspiration. The poet's inspiration, like Old Testament prophecy, is a complete experience, perfectly structured even before it takes a literary form. Structure cannot be divorced from the poet's feelings and imagination, and the mind itself is a living organic whole.

In his lecture entitled 'Literature' Newman stresses the subjectivity of literature: 'speech, and therefore literature, which is its permanent record, is essentially a personal work...Literature expresses, not objective truth, as it is called, but subjective; not things, but thoughts.'[76] Hence style is essentially the image of an author's mind: inner thought and outward expression exist in an inevitably binding relationship: 'Thought and speech are inseparable from each other. Matter and expression are parts of one: style is a thinking out into language.'[77] Newman conceived of literature as the reflection of a man's moral and social nature, his conscience and heart.[78] Literature was the formal representation of an idea created in the mind, the delineation of 'that perfection which the imagination suggests, and to which as a limit the present system of Divine Providence actually tends'.[79]

Since the merit of literature for Newman, as for Keble, depends upon the innate moral balance of the poet's mind, it gains in beauty as the poet approximates to moral perfection:

Poetry...cannot be separated from its good sense, or taste, as it is called; which is one of its elements. It is originality energising in the world of beauty; the originality of grace, purity, refinement, and good feeling. We do not hestiate to say, that poetry is ultimately founded on correct moral perception; that where there is no sound principle in exercise there will be no poetry; and that on the whole (originality being granted) in proportion to the standard of a writer's moral character will his compositions vary in poetic excellence.[80]

Newman believed that the composition and movement of the mind is mirrored in the symbolic structure of the language which expresses it. The Coleridgean conception of a harmonious organic unity in the mind demanded a correspondingly original rhetoric. This is realised by Newman in his own intensely personal style. It is seen in his patterned orchestration of themes, in his exploitation of the dramatic, in his use of rhythm and climax, in his original and complex use of metaphor, and above all in the autobiographical structure of his writings. His theology demands a fusion of personal and polemical, and in all his writings, most particularly in the *Apologia*, Christian apology expresses itself through spiritual autobiography. Such a rhetorical mode is a necessary philosophical consequence of his theory of the nature of literature.[81] Newman's own style realises the literary ideal he propounds in his lecture on 'Literature':

while the many use language as they find it, the man of genius uses it indeed, but subjects it withal to his own purposes, and moulds it according to his own peculiarities...the very pulsation and throbbing of his intellect, does he image forth, to all does he give utterance, in a corresponding language, which is as multiform as this inward mental action itself and analogous to it, the faithful expression of his intense personality, attending on his own inward world of thought as its very shadow:...his thought and feeling are personal, and so his language is personal.[82]

Newman's theory of style, articulated so consummately in this essay and in the essay on 'Poetry', is entirely consonant with his theory of biography as 'a narrative which impresses the reader with the idea of moral unity, identity, growth, continuity, personality'.[83] Literary style and biography are mutually dependent because they both aim to express the inner essence of a character through the medium of living language. Hence Newman chose to write not a history of ideas in answer to Kingsley's challenge, but an autobiography: he chose to bare not just his intellect to the world, but his soul. The organic style of the *Apologia* is a literary recreation of his own psyche.[84] In a letter to Henry James Coleridge, dated 8 May 1865 he writes, 'it is not theology that Catholics want, but literature treated as Catholic authors cannot help treating it', and of his own lectures on the Turks he says, 'it is *secular* history written by a Catholic'.[85]

Newman clearly conceives of man's mental capacity as an active, energising and assimilating force in the act of perception:

The intellect of man . . . energises as well as his eye or ear, and perceives in sights and sounds something beyond them. It seizes and unites what the senses present to it; it grasps and forms what need not have been seen or heard except in its constituent parts. It discerns in lines and colours, or in tones, what is beautiful and what is not. It gives them a meaning and invests them with an idea. It gathers up a succession of notes into the expression of a whole, and calls it a melody; it has a keen sensibility towards angles and curves, lights and shadow, tints and contours. It distinguishes between rule and exception, between accident and design. It assigns phenomena to a general law, qualities to a subject, acts to a principle, and effects to a cause. In a word, it philosophizes; for I suppose Science and Philosophy, in their elementary idea, are nothing else but this habit of *viewing*, as it may be called, the objects which sense conveys to the mind, of throwing them into a system, and uniting and stamping them with one form.[86]

Newman's terms are strikingly similar to Coleridge's descriptions of the imagination, and it is not surprising that Newman refers to this very faculty in describing man's relationship to his world: 'the world overcomes us, not merely by appealing to our reason, or exciting our passions, but by imposing on our imagination'.[87]

In transmitting his imaginative being to the world, a writer has to work through the medium of language. Newman sees language as a creative poetic medium which moulds itself to the subject of its expression. It is the vehicle of our living imaginative consciousness and must share in its growth and development. It also demands a living imaginative response from the reader, because the medium of communication colours the knowledge it transmits to the perceiving mind. Thus metrical composition, for example, stimulates mental powers into action, and prevents a merely passive reception of images and ideas.[88] Newman describes the mind's slow unravelling of the meaning of images, its growth of understanding and ability to cross the barriers of language and metaphor; how words hold untold riches of meaning which unfold with man's awareness and disclose themselves gradually to the mind's perception:

Revelation, as a Manifestation, is a doctrine variously received by various minds, but nothing more to each than that which each mind comprehends it to be. Considered as a Mystery, it is a doctrine enunciated by inspiration, in human language, as the only possible medium of it, and suitably, according to the capacity of language; a doctrine *lying hid* in language, to be received in that language from the first by every mind, whatever be its separate power of understanding it; entered into more or less by this or that mind, as it may be; and admitting of being apprehended more and more perfectly according to the diligence of this mind and that. It is one and the same, independent and real, of depth unfathomable, and illimitable in its extent.[89]

Newman is speaking specifically of Revelation, but he might have discussed a work of imaginative literature in the same way. For both Newman and Keble, their aesthetic discourse is fundamentally related to their theology.

IV

Newman and Keble were anticipated by Wordsworth and Coleridge, again, in their tendency to relate religious and aesthetic principles. For Wordsworth, beauty played a partially moral role in poetry as it did in landscape. He looked forward to a general adoption of his poetic principles, for thereby 'a class of Poetry would be produced well adapted to interest mankind permanently, and not unimportant in the multiplicity, and in the quality of its moral relations'.[90] In his exposition of poetic theory Wordsworth frequently drew analogies between poetic creation and religious experience. He believed that there were affinities 'between religion – whose element is infinitude... submitting herself to circumscription, and reconciled to substitutions; and poetry – ethereal and transcendent, yet incapable to sustain her existence without sensuous incarnation'.[91] Wordsworth found the basis of both religion and poetry in instinctive feeling, for he believed that faith compensated for the 'deficiencies of reason' in religion, while poetry was 'passionate for the instruction of reason'. Poetry was the best medium for the expression of religious ideas, in that 'the concerns of religion refer to indefinite objects, and are too weighty for the mind to support them without relieving itself by resting a great part of the burthen upon words and symbols'.[92]

However, it was really Coleridge who developed these ideas into a comprehensive philosophy and who explored the deep and reciprocal relationship between poetry and religion.[93] In *The Statesman's Manual*, Coleridge suggests that poetic expression, in that it is not confined by the restraints of scientific knowledge, is the appropriate language of religious discourse. The Scriptures are

the living *educts* of the Imagination; of that reconciling and mediatory power, which incorporating the Reason in Images of the Sense, and organizing (as it were) the flux of the Senses by the permanence and self-circling energies of the gives Reason, birth to the system of symbols, harmonious in themselves, and consubstantial with the truths, of which they are the *conductors*.[94]

Scriptural language is free from 'the hollowness of abstractions'. It is a language of Symbol, and Symbol

is characterized by a translucence of the Special in the Individual or of the General in the Especial or of the Universal in the General. Above all by the translucence of the Eternal through and in the Temporal. It always partakes of the Reality which it renders intelligible; and while it enunciates the whole, abides itself as a living part of that Unity, of which it is the representative.[95]

As the manifestation of the infinite within the finite, poetry symbolises the religious experience of reality: Christian awareness of the divine is a 'poetic' revelation of the whole universe. Coleridge's theology is informed by his aesthetic principles, and his views on art and aesthetics depend as surely on his idea of religion as 'the consideration of the Particular and Individual...but of the Individual, as it exists and has its being in the Universal'. Hence his belief that 'in all the ages and countries of civilization Religion has been the parent and fosterer of the Fine Arts, as of Poetry, Music, Painting, &c. the common essence of which consists in a similar union of the Universal and the Individual'.[96] Like the Cambridge Neo-Platonists, Coleridge thought of Christianity and the Church in terms appropriate to a work of art. His account of the nature of faith, conscience, and man's moral being as poetical, sacrosanct, beyond the bounds of human understanding, provided the crucial foundations upon which the Tractarians could build their theology.

Keble and Newman saw literature and religion as parallel influences on life and were constantly linking the two, finding analogies between religious experience and the artistic and cultural imagination. We have seen how Keble feared that men would find in poetry an alternative to Christianity. While an Anglican, Newman characterised poetry as a kind of religious experience in itself:

the taste for poetry of a religious kind has in modern times in a certain sense taken the place of the deep contemplative spirit of the early Church... as if our character required such an element to counterbalance the firmer and more dominant properties in it...Poetry then is our mysticism; and so far as any two characters of mind tend to penetrate below the surface of things, and to draw men away from the material to the invisible world, so far they may certainly be said to answer the same end; and that too a religious one.[97]

As an Anglican, Newman felt with Keble that, since the modern Church had abandoned the symbolical language and rites of the early mystical

Church and had instead embraced a literal format, men had to turn to poetry to satisfy their spiritual wants and feelings. Certainly Keble's Oxford *Lectures on Poetry* suggest that he accorded to poetry a high spiritual status. In a letter to Sir J. T. Coleridge, he outlines a plan for the lectures which will work out 'the relation between [the art of poetry], and practical goodness, moral and religious'.[98] His belief in the divine nature of poetry is the starting-point of his whole theory. Poetry is the divinely inspired interpreter of the Word of God, and the subject is approached with religious awe. His task is 'most serious, well nigh sacred', and poetry has the dignity of a Sacrament. Religion and poetry are at one in demanding the same temper of mind and providing a framework for the articulation of man's strongest feelings and a means to the attainment of highest truth.

In his discussion of the relationship between religion and poetry, Keble finds two levels of connection: historical and symbolical. Historically, he argues, poetry has frequently paved the way for new developments in religion. In the *Lectures on Poetry* he draws upon his knowledge of the Old Testament, Hebrew poetry, and the classics to support his argument that there has rarely been a religious revival without a poetic precursor, a 'noble order of poetry'. He claims

we shall not readily find an instance of any state, provided indeed it enjoy the advantage of a stable law and morality, which has changed its existing religious belief for a more serious and holier creed, unless the tone of its favourite poets has first undergone a change.[99]

Just as the Hebrew prophets and poets prepared man's mind for Christian revelation, so too the Greek and Latin poets prepared men 'to welcome the pungent flavour of the heavenly doctrine'.[100] The early Christian poets prepared the way for religious developments, while the same principle applied in English literature where Shakespeare and Spenser led the way for the Caroline Revival by lifting men's minds 'to piety and religion: for each of them always tests what can be seen by reference to a standard of heavenly truth, whether he is treating of the deeds and affairs of men or the splendid charm of earth and sky'.[101] Keble brought his argument up to the present by showing how the Romantic poets had paved the way for a Christian Revival by creating an awareness of the unity of the individual and his universe, and by opening men's eyes to the transcendental symbolised in the world around them.

Newman too believed that there was a historical basis to the relationship between art and religion. Thus he suggests that the Oxford Movement itself represented a reaction from the dry and superficial character of the religious teaching and literature of the last generation, or century, and as a result of the need which was felt both by the hearts and the intellects of the nation for a deeper philosophy, and as the evidence and as the partial fulfilment of that need, to which even the chief authors of the then generation had borne witness.[102]

He then goes on to praise Scott and Coleridge for spiritually preparing the way for a religious regeneration. Certainly his own experience suggested that inspired works of religious literature were the likeliest means of attracting converts.[103]

Elsewhere Newman concentrated on the broader historical relationship between religion and art. His lecture on 'Christianity and Letters', written after his conversion to Rome, outlines the growth of civilisation, and then shows how Christianity coalesced and cooperated with this civilisation.[104] He draws many parallels between Christianity and civilisation. Thus he finds a similarity in their organisation, in that both developed continuously, without break, from their first beginnings. Both, too, are built upon unchanging ideas, principles, doctrines, and writings. Christianity looks to inspired works of Scripture, the Lives of the Saints, the Catechism, the Articles of faith. Civilisation rests upon the authority of the great classical authors. Homer was the first apostle of civilisation. Hence, it is unnatural to deny the interdependence of religion and culture, especially as it is so comprehensively and perfectly embodied in the Church of Rome:

The grace stored in Jerusalem, and the gifts which radiate from Athens, are made over and consecrated in Rome...Rome has inherited both sacred and profane learning; she has perpetuated and dispensed the traditions of Moses and David in the supernatural order, and of Homer and Aristotle in the natural. To separate these distinct teachings, human and divine, which meet in Rome, is to retrograde; it is to rebuild the Jewish Temple and to plant anew the groves of Academus.[105]

As David Delaura points out in his *Hebrew and Hellene in Victorian England*, Newman's Christian humanism is 'at once religious and literary': he defines culture as much in religious as in secular terms, and even traces an 'Apostolic Succession' in culture. He asserts the historical unity of the classical intellectual heritage and Christianity, presenting what Dwight Culler has described as an 'image of Civilization as a great, distinct, and objective fact...co-extensive with Christianity and more than coeval in point of time'. The total conception is of a Christian civilisation capable of satisfying 'the permanent ethical and aesthetic needs of man'.[106]

In this way Newman agrees with Keble as to the significance of the historical relationship between the cultural development of art and the spiritual development of Christianity. He similarly endorses Keble's belief in the existence of a more profound symbolic relationship between poetry and religion, 'a hidden tie of kinship'[107] contained in their shared linguistic and metaphorical structure: 'poetry...supplies a rich wealth of similes whereby a pious mind may supply and remedy, in some sort, its powerlessness of speech'.[108] Both men believed that sacred truths find their most satisfactory expression in the recondite imagery and allusive suggestiveness of art forms. They felt that poetry gives imaginative life to religion as religion transports the imagination to spiritual spheres. Poetry is the best vehicle of religious utterance because it reveals itself through a symbolical structure: it re-enacts, as it were, the processes of religious experience, of Revelation, and understanding through faith by analogy. Thus the theological tension between the idea of a transcendent Creator and God as omnipresent love can only be sustained by an emotional and imaginative medium such as poetry. For only poetry can retain the paradox and mirror the religious experience of the mystery of the divine nature in its symbolic mode of presentation.

Newman's faith in art as the most appropriate vehicle for expressing religious truth was always accompanied, however, by an awareness of the dangers of equating the aims of religion and art.[109] He had a passionate interest in music and was transported to spiritual ecstasy by the divine import of this most abstract and perfect of the arts: 'music... is the expression of ideas greater and more profound than any in the visible world, ideas which centre, indeed, in Him whom Catholicism manifests, who is the seat of all beauty, order, and perfection whatever'.[110] He marvels at how the musician 'sweeps the strings and they thrill with an ecstatic meaning'.[111]

Yet alongside his eulogy of music, as of the other arts, Newman warns that it can lose sight of its proper object. Whilst he claims that all the fine arts should be the handmaidens of religion, he warns at the same time of the danger that art may usurp its place, pursuing earthly ends of its own, and thus becoming independent of the religious experience whose expression should be its true purpose. Furthermore, even when it deals with religious matters, art can subject them to its own ends.[112] Music, for instance, can glory in its own gift rather than in the expression of ideas more profound than any in the visible world.[113] The fine arts, in Newman's view, should not dominate religion in this way but should remain subservient to it. And as far as literature in particular was concerned, he liked, according to his biographer, Wilfred Ward, 'nothing the general tendency of which he did not regard as making for righteousness'.[114] His greatest fear was that man's sense of the beautiful would become a substitute for true faith, that he would cease to distinguish between different scales in the hierarchy of beauty:

Your cities are beautiful, your palaces, your public buildings, your territorial mansions, your churches; and their beauty leads to nothing beyond itself. There is a physical beauty and a moral: there is a beauty of person, there is a beauty of our moral being, which is natural virtue; and in like manner there is a beauty, there is a perfection, of the intellect... The artist puts before him beauty of feature and form; the poet, beauty of mind; the preacher, the beauty of grace.[115]

For Newman, the preacher, it was not enough to assert, as Ruskin was later to do, that 'as all lovely art is rooted in virtue, so it bears fruit of virtue, and is didactic in its own nature... it is didactic chiefly by being beautiful'.[116]

However, provided the religious objective remains central, Newman believes that art makes religious truths more accessible, not only because it uses a language of symbol and metaphor, but also because it represents the same sort of organic unity and consistency as Christianity itself. Newman adopts an explanation similar to that of Coleridge, who, in accounting for the power of works of the imagination 'to bring the whole soul of man into activity', ascribed it to our concrete response to the poem as a unified whole – a response distinct from but compatible with our response to the poem's component parts.[117] In the same way, for Newman, our response to the Church is both to its wholeness and to its component parts. The complex aesthetic unity of a poem is analogous to the unique divine unity of the Church. This parallelism of structural organisation, of wholeness and consistency of form, fired Newman's imagination and inspired him to develop his distinctive theory of the relationship between religion and art.

Keble too saw the Church as responding to the needs of the human mind as an integrated organic unity. It is Holy, in its aim of converting men's lives through a national Church; it is Catholic, universal and yet supplying the visible unity of the one Church, it is Apostolic, because it has undergone organic development analogous to the human mind in the continuity of its Apostolic Succession. The component parts of traditional Christianity – the prayers, the Sacraments, the Scriptures, the priesthood – conjoin and integrate, and together contribute to the developing whole of Christianity.[118] In this way, both Keble and Newman found they could follow through artistic principles of structure, unity, and development into their thinking about the Church.

For Newman, imagination is the foremost instrument of religious perception and is analogous to belief because it represents that instinctive reaching for truth which, in Newman's philosophy of faith, always exists alongside intellectual assent.[119] Faith and imagination are interdependent because belief is itself an act of the 'illative' imagination. The imagination perceives physical order in the material world just as it perceives the presence of God: it makes sense of and draws meaning from the world. However, in the case of religion, imagination is endorsed by Revelation, and then goes on to clothe it with poetry to engage the assent of man's innermost self: 'the testimony borne to truth by the mind itself'.[120] Hence the literary and theological traditions have to work in concord, for theology cannot be separated from imaginative utterance without impairing its function of persuading men to embrace divine truths imaginatively.

In *An Essay in Aid of a Grammar of Assent*, when he attempts to define the role of conscience in the apprehension of God, Newman compares the workings of the conscience to our sense of the beautiful:

Conscience too, considered as a moral sense, an intellectual sentiment, is a sense of admiration and disgust, of approbation and blame: but it is something more than a moral sense; it is always, what the sense of the beautiful is only in certain cases; it is always emotional. No wonder then that it always implies what that sense only sometimes implies; that it always involves the recognition of a living object, towards which it is directed.[121]

Conscience 'is the creative principle of religion, as the Moral Sense is the principle of ethics'.[122] We should follow the pattern set by modes of sensory perception in order to understand God, for 'if the impressions which His creatures make on us through our senses oblige us to regard those creatures as *sui generis* respectively, it is not wonderful that the notices which He indirectly gives us of His own nature are such as to make us understand that He is like Himself and like nothing else'.[123]

Thus conscience as a means of moral perception has affinities with aesthetic apprehension and taste, although the comparison requires qualification:

As we have naturally a sense of the beautiful and graceful in nature and art, though tastes proverbially differ, so we have a sense of duty and obligation, whether we all associate it with the same particular actions or not. Here, however, Taste and Conscience part company: for the sense of beautifulness, as indeed the Moral Sense, has no special relations to persons, but contemplates objects in themselves; conscience, on the other hand, is concerned with persons primarily, and with actions mainly as viewed in their doers, or rather with self alone and one's own actions, and with others only indirectly and as if in association with self. And further, taste is its own evidence, appealing to nothing beyond its own sense of the beautiful or the ugly, and enjoying the specimens of the beautiful simply for their own sake; but conscience does not repose on itself, but vaguely reaches forward to something beyond self, and dimly discerns a sanction higher than self for its decisions, as evidenced in that keen sense of obligation and responsibility which informs them.[124]

Newman distinguishes between taste and conscience, yet he perceives a distinct relationship between sense-perception and divine Revelation. Here, he specifically compares the perception of God to the methods of sensory perception:

This may be fitly compared to the impressions made on us by the senses. Material objects are real, whole, and individual; and the impressions which they make on the mind, by means of the senses, are of a corresponding nature, complex and manifold in their relations and bearings, but, considered in themselves, integral and one. And, in like manner, the ideas which are granted of Divine Objects under the Gospel from the nature of the case and because they are ideas, answer to the originals so far as this, that they are whole, indivisible, substantial, and may be called real, as being images of what is real. Objects which are conveyed to us through the senses stand out in our minds, as I may say, with dimensions and aspects and influences various, and all of these consistent with one another, and many of them beyond our memory or even knowledge, while we contemplate the objects themselves; thus forcing on us a persuasion of their reality from the spontaneous congruity and coincidence of these accompaniments, as if they could not be creations of our minds, but were the images of external and independent beings. This of course will take place in the case of the sacred ideas which are the objects of our faith. Religious men, according to their measure, have an idea or vision of the Blessed Trinity in Unity, of the Son Incarnate, and of His Presence, not as a number of qualities, attributes and actions, not as the subject of a number of propositions, but as one and individual, and independent of words, like an impression conveyed through the senses.[125]

Revelation, then, is of an objective truth perceived through an impression which has the same inner authenticity as sense impressions. This is where Newman's idea of the 'illative' sense comes into play. This may be defined as man's capacity to draw certainties from evidence that can only be probable.[126] It employs the mind's capacity to impose something of itself upon objective fact, to step beyond the evidence and create a whole greater than the constituent parts taken separately.[127] 'Such a living *organon* is a personal gift, and not a mere method or calculus',[128] since it is dependent upon the individual mind of the perceiver. Certitude, then, in matters of faith as well as of sense-perception, 'is not a passive impression made upon the mind from without, by argumentative compulsion, but...an active recognition of propositions as true'.[129] For Newman, the ultimate test of truth remained the testimony borne by the mind itself.

In *An Essay in Aid of a Grammar of Assent*, Newman cites the clarification of the object of faith as the main purpose of the supernatural dispensations of religion. Therefore, since Revelation is poetical, devotional works must imitate divine poetry if they are to fire the religious imagination:

And as the exercise of the affections strengthens our apprehension of the object of them, it is impossible to exaggerate the influence exerted on the religious imagination by a book of devotions so sublime, so penetrating, so full of deep instruction as the Psalter, to say nothing of other portions of the Hagiographa.[130]

Newman objected to Arnold's suggestion that the Bible should be viewed primarily as literature.[131] He agreed that the Bible addressed mankind on many levels because its method is symbolical rather than literal. The essential difference for Newman is that the ultimate criterion in judging the truth of a religious symbol lies in the authority of the Church, whereas interpretative assumptions, in the case of a work of art or literature, are dependent upon culture, and are therefore culturally variable. With these important reservations, Newman's view of the Scriptures as working on a poetical level should not be overlooked. As Stephen Prickett points out, the Scriptures carried for him the concreteness and inner truth of 'real assent', as opposed to, or rather complementing, the abstract generalisation of theological propositions, in the same way as 'true poetry is a spontaneous outpouring of thought ...whereas no one becomes a poet merely by the canons of criticism'.[132] The Scriptures are 'poetical' in that they appeal not to man's intellect alone but also to his imagination.

Any effective theological writing, then, must consist of more than a series of arguments: it must inspire the same imaginative response as a work of art, and ultimately as God Himself. As a theologian, Newman's first concern was to produce works of literature, since his success as an apologist was, according to his own theory, dependent upon his ability to evoke an imaginative response. In the best of his works his literary style unites his imagination and his intellect, and invests the tightest theological definitions with the qualities of a work of art. Newman himself remains the most convincing proof of his own philosophy of Christian expression.

Newman's and Keble's poetics owed much to their religious

temperaments. They transposed moral and religious principles into the field of aesthetics, until poetry itself came to mean something wider than its usual definition, implying a whole style of mental activity. It was no longer a term merely related to specific art forms; instead, it was seen as a creative process closely allied to metaphysical revelation. In this sense, poetry, or poetic terminology, can be taken up again and brought back to religion so that it may illuminate through analogy some aspect of divine Revelation. Keble and Newman transformed their aesthetic concerns into Tractarian theology. They came to regard the Church as 'that new language which Christ has brought us',[133] providing a suitably poetic medium for God's poetic revelation of Himself to man.

V

One can find in Keble's work several correlations between his poetic preoccupations and his views on specific religious ceremonies and observances. His interest in the cathartic function of poetry, its ability to unburden the mind and the soul, is directly related to his belief in the healing power of prayer or, even more pertinently, of confession. Keble frequently regretted that auricular confession was not obligatory in the Anglican Church,[134] probably for the same reason as Goethe, who complained that 'Protestantism has given the individual too much to carry...Nowadays a burdened conscience must carry that burden all by itself, and thereby lose the strength to come into harmony with itself again. People ought never to have been deprived of oral confession.'[135] We find too in Keble's theological writings an anti-rationalist interest in the mystical which suggests affinities with Wordsworth and Coleridge. He regretted the absence of a sense of mystery in the Protestant Church:

is it not a reproach frequently cast upon the orthodox and Catholic side in theological debate, that the sincerest among them are led, not by reason, but by feelings akin to poetical ones; and on the other hand, is there not an instinct which causes the youthful and ardent mind to shrink from utilitarian or rationalistic error, previous to accurate examination, as being essentially cold and unpoetical?[136]

The most original aspect of Keble's religious writing was his theological adaptation of Wordsworth's and Coleridge's awareness of the poetical in the natural world.

Wordsworth and Coleridge were fundamentally concerned with the relationship between the natural world and 'things in themselves'. They shouldered the metaphysical responsibility of restoring the experience of participation in nature and the spiritual revelation it afforded to the individual whose universe had become fragmented by the advance of rationalist philosophy. Wordsworth, in particular, emphasised the value of living experience rather than intellectual enquiry. He saw a profound connection between human sentiments and natural objects, a relationship which, if nurtured, would deepen man's understanding of spiritual truths and strengthen his capacity for feeling. Emotional response to sublimity in nature inspires a desire for something better, and leads to knowledge of divine reality. Man has only to look at the wonder of creation, Wordsworth proposes, in order to feel faith in God.

God's presence is evident in the world of nature, but the responsibility of interpretation devolves on the mind of man. Wordsworth believed in a mystical analogy between mind and nature. The poet 'considers man and nature as essentially adapted to each other, and the mind of man as naturally the mirror of the fairest and most interesting qualities of nature'.[137] In drawing lessons from nature, the mind plays an active role in transforming pure sensual perception of natural truth:

> Moreover, each man's Mind is to herself
> Witness and judge; and I remember well
> That in life's every-day appearances
> I seemed about this time to gain clear sight
> Of a new world – a world, too, that was fit
> To be transmitted, and to other eyes
> Made visible; as ruled by those fixed laws
> Whence spiritual dignity originates,
> Which do both give it being and maintain
> A balance, an ennobling interchange
> Of action, from without and from within;
> The excellence, pure function, and best power
> Both of the object seen, and eye that sees.[138]

Wordsworth proclaimed the active creativity of the human mind and showed that the imagination had a capacity for firing the potential spiritual energy lying latent in natural objects. The mind, itself an active, unified, organic whole, can perceive a unifying vision of reality. The result is an ideal state of universal harmony of mind and matter, a world of correspondences and analogies, a universe that is essentially 'poetic', alive with divine imagery and energy, linking man to nature. It is an apocalyptical vision of nature, an aesthetic of landscape, charged, as Hopkins would say, with symbolical manifestations of the divine. Thus Wordsworth arrived at the traditional Christian and Platonic conclusion of a mystical interpretation of the world of nature. He even derived an understanding of how the Christian values what he sees as an 'imperfect shadowing forth' of what he is incapable of seeing. But all this was via the unorthodox route of dependence upon the powers of human imagination.

Coleridge, too, believed that a proper appreciation of the beauties of the natural world expanded and transformed the soul of the observer. Throughout his work he celebrates nature as the symbolic language of God. His religious views of the 1790s, in particular, attest to a strong sense of the sacramental in nature. In the first of his 1795 *Lectures on Revealed Religion*, for example, he writes:

The Omnipotent has unfolded to us the Volume of the World, that there we may read the Transcript of himself. In Earth or Air the meadow's purple stores, the Moons mild radiance, or the Virgins form Blooming with rosy smiles, we see pourtrayed the bright Impressions of the eternal Mind.[139]

And among the fragments of theological lectures of the same period, we find:

The noblest gift of Imagination is the power of discerning the *Cause* in the *Effect* a power which when employed on the works of the Creator elevates and by the variety of its pleasures almost monopolizes the Soul. We see our God everywhere – the Universe in the most literal Sense is his written language.[140]

In his poetry of the same period he is similarly preoccupied with the presence of 'the Great/Invisible (by symbols only seen)'.[141] He refers, in 'Frost at Midnight', to 'The lovely shapes and sounds intelligible/Of that eternal language which thy God/Utters', and in 'The Destiny of Nations' he recommends the Platonic gospel that we learn 'The substance from its shadow':

> For all that meets the bodily sense I deem
> Symbolical, one mighty alphabet
> For infant minds;[142]

and, as we have seen, his later statements on symbolism in *The States-man's Manual* depend upon an acknowledgement of 'the translucence of the Eternal through and in the Temporal'.[143]

The idea of a colloquy between the mind of man and the natural landscape was of course no Romantic invention. Coleridge, for example, was familiar with works by Akenside, Berkeley, and Paine, all of whom express the idea of nature as the symbolic language of God.[144] And the idea has a much longer history. The inherent distinction in the Bible between the apparent order of things open to human comprehension and the hidden order of the providential first cause gave birth to the traditional Christian concept of the *liber naturae*, a world of symbols to be interpreted as evidence of a divine creator. However, in the poetry of Wordsworth and Coleridge, the sacramentalism of nature was given vital new expression.

The poetic insights of Coleridge and Wordsworth were further corroborated by Keble's reading of earlier Christian thinkers, particularly the writings of the Church Fathers and Bishop Butler. He rediscovered in their works Plato's idea of two worlds, only in 'an infinitely higher sense': 'and thus did the whole scheme of material things, and especially those objects in it which are consecrated by scriptural allusion, assume in their eyes a sacramental or symbolical character'.[145]

Newman wrote in the *Apologia* that Butler's philosophy was recast for him in *The Christian Year*. Butler's purpose in *The Analogy of Religion*[146] was to give philosophical confirmation to the principles of religion by comparing them with the principles of the natural world. His conception of the correspondence between the world of nature and the world of the spirit was instrumental in formulating Keble's own philosophy. Keble was influenced by many of Butler's ideas, such as the principle of probability upon which Faith depends, and the idea of a God-given moral sense, but the most characteristic and influential of Butler's theories was his concept of the analogy between the natural and supernatural worlds.[147] In the *Analogy* Butler appealed to man's natural affection for types and parables, a fondness nurtured by biblical tradition. He maintained that all knowledge of God remained analogical, and could therefore only result in probability, rather than scientific certainty. This theory was attractive to one so repelled by the march of the rationalistic spirit as Keble.

Butler's philosophy itself corroborated the theological speculations of the early Church Fathers, to whom Keble looked as the representatives of the true Catholic Church. The Fathers had achieved a perfect synthesis of their religion and their sacramental interpretation of nature and life, a synthesis which had slipped away from later generations of Christians, until it was finally destroyed by rationalism. Keble hoped to reinstate the whole outlook of the Church Fathers by publishing a new edition of their writings, and so the *Library of the Fathers* came into being. As an introduction to it, Keble published *Tract Eighty-Nine*, which justifies the mysticism of the Fathers and vindicates their sacramental reading of life, demonstrating the Scriptural foundations of the allegorical world view. Mysticism was the equivalent of poetry for the Church, and unless we read the symbols sensitively, in the manner of the Fathers, we cannot penetrate the profounder truths. In the poem for Trinity Sunday in *The Christian Year* Keble quotes St John: 'If I have told you earthly things, and ye believe not, how shall ye believe, if I tell you of heavenly things?', and then appeals to God:

Help us, each hour, with steadier eye
To search the deepening mystery
The wonders of Thy sea and sky.[148]

For Keble, the Fathers moved from one level of mysticism into another, 'from allegorizing the word of God, to spiritualizing His works'.[149]

Keble was not the first nineteenth-century thinker to respond to the allusive, metaphorical and symbolic exegetical methods of the early Church. Coleridge had in *The Statesman's Manual*, as we have seen, discussed the Scriptures as imaginative works, and in later life he vigorously promoted the reading of the Bible as a work of literature.[150] It is in this tradition that Keble, in *Tract Eighty-Nine*, discusses the Fathers' allegorical interpretation of the Old Testament and their detection of a figurative Christian meaning throughout. The Fathers had turned the whole process of biblical exegesis into a systematic critical process. In *Tract Eighty-Nine*, Keble quotes from Origen's account of the threefold nature of their exegetical method, whereby they discerned a literal, a moral, and a spiritual level of meaning in the Scriptures. Keble distinguishes three parallel levels in the Fathers' symbolic interpretation of nature: poetical, or simple instructive thinking in images; moral, that is providing guidance for human life and conduct; and mystical, by which he means the theological set of symbols authorised by God himself which the Fathers deduced from the external world.[151]

Having interpreted God's message allegorically, the Fathers understood the role of allegory in all life and poetry. They preached a doctrine of reserve, claiming that the sanctity of truth about God, in the Scriptures for example, was preserved by its mystical exposition – through symbol the truth was veiled from abuse by unbelievers: 'the chosen vehicle for the most direct divine communications has always been that form of speech which most readily adopts and invites such imagery; *viz.* the Poetical'.[152] In his essay entitled 'Sacred Poetry', Keble draws our attention to the virtues of allegory as a spiritual stimulant:

a good deal surely is to be gained from the mere habit of looking at things with a view to something beyond their qualities merely sensible; to their sacred and moral meaning, and to the high association they were intended to create in us. Neither the works nor the word of God; neither poetry nor theology; can be duly comprehended without constant mental exercise of this kind. The comparison of the Old Testament with the New is nothing else from beginning to end.[153]

Keble urged a revival of the figurative world view of the Fathers, of the universe as a living representation of God's presence. He feared that, without this consciousness of divine Revelation, Christianity would lay itself open to the insidiously undermining influence of the rationalistic, scientific spirit.

The most disquieting thing about the state of the Church of England for Keble was its indifference to sacramental grace. By denying sacramental truth he felt that the Church was denying belief in divine Revelation. Since the Church was dependent upon a sacramental system representing the mystical Body of Christ, vindication of the Sacraments was a first priority, and so he set about re-educating men as to their true significance.

The existence of a sacramental system is dependent upon the Incarnation of Christ. The Incarnation was 'the means as well as the token, so the entire sacrament, of the redemption of our nature',[154] and as such it is a constantly recurring theme in Keble's sermons and poetry:

Christ's life and His miracles are promises of the great miracles to come, namely the Sacraments. Since the burial of Christ the whole earth has been the place where He lay for a time, and His mark is on all material things.[155]

He constantly reminds his congregation that Christ has been present ever since the Incarnation, reviving the belief that Christ 'is near at hand. You have but to lift up your eyes and look, and behold Jesus Christ visibly set forth, crucified among you. He is in His Church; He is in His Scriptures; He is in your prayers; He is most especially in His Sacraments.'[156] The earth, having once been the scene of Christ's birth and death, is transformed and transcendentalised. The transposition of the properties of the higher nature to the lower was complete from the time Christ took on a human form:

> Thenceforth, to eyes of high desire,
> The meanest things below,
> As with a seraph's robe of fire
> Invested, burn and glow.[157]

Keble believed, like Wordsworth, that the world must be translated in terms of the divine, not dissected by the reason. In *Tract Eighty-Nine*, he cites St Ambrose: 'it is not, therefore, by the nature of the elements, but by the nature of Christ, who hath done all according to His will, abounding in the fullness of His Godhead, that we are to order our thoughts of what was made, and our inquiries into that which nature could bring about'.[158] Keble expands this idea and offers a lyrical interpretation of the origin and nature of the Holy Sacraments. On the hypothesis, derived from Wordsworth and reworked in the Oxford *Lectures on Poetry*, that poetry is the expression of an overflowing mind, Keble concludes that each person has his own poetry, a personal set of associations appropriate to his own individual make-up. Therefore, he suggests:

May it not, then, be so, that our Blessed Lord, in union and communion with all His members, is represented to us as constituting, in a certain sense, one great and manifold Person, into which, by degrees, all souls of men, who do not cast themselves away, are to be absorbed? and as it is a scriptural and ecclesiastical way of speaking, to say, Christ suffers in our flesh, is put to shame in our sins, our members are part of Him; so may it not be affirmed that He condescends in like manner to have a Poetry of His own, a set of holy and divine associations and meanings wherewith it is His will to invest all material things?[159]

In the introduction to his edition of Hooker, Keble proposes as 'silently pervading the whole language and system of the Church' a theory that from the whole universe of material objects symbolising different aspects of God, the Church chose certain forms and actions which she deliberately incorporated into an orderly system of ceremonies which, wherever they might be performed, would constitute a perpetual sacrifice. And so the Blessed Sacraments of the Church were a concentration and intensification of the general sacramental significance of nature.

Since the Incarnation was the central doctrine of Christianity, the Sacrament which commands most reverence is the Real Presence of Christ in the Holy Eucharist. The clearest statement of Keble's personal belief and of the devotion he hoped to arouse in the Anglican Church is found in his work *On Eucharistical Adoration*. Having rather defensively argued that the worship of Christ in any form would surely not be forbidden but rather sanctioned,[160] he goes on to illustrate the moral and devotional compulsion of adoration:

Christ's Person is in the holy Eucharist by the presence of His Body and Blood therein. From which, as will be seen, it follows, by direct inference, that the Person of Christ is to be adored in that Sacrament, as there present in a peculiar manner, by the presence of His Body and Blood.[161]

He explains by analogy how we understand the nature of Christ's presence: 'as we know the soul of a man, which we cannot see, to be present by the presence of his living body, which we can see, so the presence of that Bread and Wine is to us a sure token of the Presence of Christ's Body and Blood'.[162] He knew he was treading on dangerous ground when he declared his belief in a corporeal Presence[163] and he was careful to qualify this and thereby protect himself against charges of 'gross carnal belief' by specifying that it was a Presence only for the purposes of the Sacrament. Yet he could not accept the restrictive definition advanced by Protestants. He dismissed their use of the term 'Real Presence' as absurd since, in their sense, it could only mean a 'real absence'. Instead of confining the area of admissible doctrine to the Thirty-nine Articles, Keble wanted to expand the meaning of the Incarnation to cover all Eucharistical matters.

The Holy Eucharist is the climax of the whole unified system of Sacraments which Keble reinstated in the Anglican consciousness. He wrote extensively about the Sacraments of the Church, such as matrimony, confirmation and baptism. For example, baptism was a God-given grace which rescues us from our fallen fragmented state and endows us with a 'moral sense', illuminating not only the nature of right and wrong, but also the sacramental nature of the universe, by enabling us to perceive divine analogies.[164] But above all Keble is noted for his expansion of the signification of the term 'Sacrament' to cover a wide range of religious categories: thus, not only is the Church sacramental, being invested with God's divine associations as His mystical Body, but also man's moral sense and symbolical sense. Working from the original dogmatic definition of sacramentalism, he extends the term beyond the realms of the Church to include the world of nature, though always keeping God as the end and object of the mystical analogy. Thus, by simultaneously extending the Christian sense of sacramentalism and giving orthodox definition to the Wordsworthian, Keble created an innovatory aesthetic theory of sacramentalism.

As Stephen Prickett points out, it is only in terms of a shared 'broad vision' that Keble may be said to be Wordsworthian. There is little in the style or content of *The Christian Year* to recall Wordsworth's theory of poetic diction or of the truth of the simple rustic life.[165] And although Keble may be said to share Wordsworth's vision of a 'poetic' universe, Keble's Tractarian analogising is in important ways quite different from the natural religion of Wordsworth's poetry. There are, of course, frequent examples of the simple interplay between nature and the mind in Keble's work which display a Wordsworthian sensibility:

When men are moved by strong feeling...it would be strange if they did not twist everything in the direction in which their own thoughts are running. So the flight of birds, the appetite of chickens, the accidental words of bystanders, seem divinely inspired to accord with and answer to the secret feelings of their minds. Nothing is too insignificant, nothing too haphazard to be fastened upon as an augury.[166]

But instead of simply intuitively experiencing the presence of God through the world, Keble gives his analogical theory of nature a theological basis. He shows that the sacramental principle in religion may be extended to nature, because whenever man's mind is incited by God to see the supernatural in any good or beautiful action or object, then his experience is comparable to the giving and receiving of Christian sacramental grace. In *The Christian Year*, Keble celebrates God's message throughout creation as symbolic corroboration of Christian Revelation. In the poem for Septuagesima Sunday, he writes:

> The works of God above, below,
> Within us and around,
> Are pages in that book, to show
> How God himself is found.

Keble's verses are Wordsworthian in their description of a natural world that is alive with divine significance, but he goes further in claiming that the lessons of nature may only be understood by 'Pure eyes and Christian heart'. He is always an Anglican clergyman, writing for Christian readers. It is important for Keble to define the real object of his intimations, and in his writings, unlike Wordsworth's, the analogies are traced back to their specific divine counterparts. Thus, the sky is like the Maker's love, the sun like the Light of the world, the moon like the Church which reflects its rays, the stars the Saints above, the trees the Saints below, and so on.[167]

In his recent study of Victorian devotional poetry, G. B. Tennyson points to a further quality in Keble's nature poetry which distinguishes it from the Wordsworthian mode. Keble's joy in nature, he says, 'usually draws forth somber reflections on the imperfections of this world as a consequence of original sin' in a way which anticipates 'the sadder and more elegiac character of so much Victorian nature poetry as compared with Romantic'.[168] Keble's poems frequently express an acute awareness of how man's sinful nature obscures his perception of the divine in nature, which is quite unlike the delight in nature which we commonly find in Wordsworth's works.

Wordsworth is reputed to have remarked, somewhat ambiguously, that *The Christian Year* was so good that he wished he could have written it himself so that he could have written it better.[169] In fact, during the very period in which the poetry of *The Christian Year* was written, Wordsworth was composing what we might think of as his version of that volume, his series of *Ecclesiastical Sonnets*. The *Ecclesiastical Sonnets* trace the history of Christianity in Britain from its first introduction up until the nineteenth century. Not only do they suggest an interest in the development of the historical Church, which parallels the Tractarians' theological investigations into the continuity of Anglicanism with the early Church, but they also explore aspects of the sacramental ceremony of the Church. There are sonnets, for example, on 'The Liturgy' and 'Sacrament', and on 'Baptism', 'Confirmation', and 'The Marriage Ceremony', which show a new interest in the Church as an institution. It is clear that Wordsworth's poetry took a theological turn in the years from about 1820, when the first of these sonnets was written. But are they really preaching the same gospel as Keble's? The epigraph to *Ecclesiastical Sonnets* tells us that 'A verse may catch a wandering Soul, that flies/Profounder Tracts, and by a blest surprise/Convert delight into a Sacrifice.' His own talents, in contrast to Keble's, lie more with 'verse' than with 'Profounder Tracts' and with 'delight' rather than 'Sacrifice', and for all that his later nature poetry is more decidedly Christian than his earlier pantheistic poetry, he is inclined to settle for nature's teachings and for a secular 'sabbath of the heart'[170] in preference to the doctrines and consolations of the Church.

Keble, on the other hand, points to the world about us specifically as an aid to meditation on Christ: 'we are taught to make every part of life, every scene in nature, an occasion – in other words, a topic – of devotion'.[171] The correspondence between the natural object and the spirit, between the world and the soul, exists independently of man's figurative interpretation of it. The mind does not 'half-create' what it perceives, and the mystical message that nature gives is not a mere 'poet's dream'.[172] Instead he asserts the objective truth of natural sacramentalism. Creation becomes a magnificent array of symbols bearing a solemn and sacramental significance, attesting to God's permanent presence in the world among men. Through his understanding of the moral function of all created things man is able to participate in supernatural truth.

In this way, Keble pinned down Wordsworth's natural sacramentalism to a strict definition of the sacrament as a material object created for the purpose of revealing God's presence. Hence the sacrament in nature was taken to perform a function analogous to the Holy Sacraments of the Church. With the authority of the early Church Fathers and Bishop Butler before him, he synthesised the specific and the general applications of sacramentalism into a unified system of divine Revelation. Anything in the world that brought man into communion with God by symbolising one of His attributes was a Sacrament. This is extremely important for the understanding of Keble's poetical theories because, through such symbolism, poetry itself, in that it consists of outwardly visible forms and inward truths, and in that the poetic image works by a process of analogy, achieves sacramental significance.

VI

When we turn to Newman we find a similar sacramental awareness.[173] In his essay on 'Poetry, with reference to Aristotle's Poetics', Newman defines the creative vision of the religious mind:

It is the charm of the descriptive poetry of a religious mind, that nature is viewed in a moral connexion. Ordinary writers, for instance, compare aged men to trees in autumn – a gifted poet will in the fading trees discern the fading men.[174]

The ability to see a 'moral connexion' in nature denotes a sacramental understanding of the universe. Through such an understanding man's aesthetic appreciation of the beauty of the world becomes integrated into his moral and intellectual apprehensions, all his faculties conspiring to create a comprehensive vision of truth. We have seen in Keble how the 'sacramental system', taken in its wider sense, came to include the objective facts of Christian Revelation, dogma, and liturgy, tempered by a strong personal note, dependent upon an intimate relationship with the personal, ever-living Christ. Many of Newman's sacramental beliefs can be traced to Keble's influence, including his understanding of the Sacraments of the Church as special cases of a general rule: the 'Holy Church in her sacraments' is after all only 'a symbol of those heavenly facts which fill eternity'.[175] In the *Apologia*, Newman describes how Keble's *Christian Year* invoked in him the idea of the world as a symbol or economy of the *invisibilia*. He learned from Keble 'the doctrine that material phenomena are both the types and the instruments of real things unseen'.[176]

The main source of his idea of sacramental analogy was Butler. Newman warmly acknowledges his debt in the *Apologia*.[177] He was further inspired by his reading of the early Church Fathers:

Some portions of their teaching, magnificent in themselves, came like music to my inward ear, as if the response to ideas, which, with little external to encourage them, I had cherished so long. These were based on the mystical or sacramental principle, and spoke of the various Economies or Dispensations of the Eternal. I understood them to mean that the exterior world, physical and historical, was but the outward manifestation of realities greater than itself. Nature was a parable: Scripture was an allegory: pagan literature, philosophy, and mythology, properly understood, were but a preparation for the Gospel.[178]

Newman's reading of the Fathers and Butler, combined with the intellectual milieu and religious temper of contemporary Oxford, nurtured his growing sacramental sense and fed a natural inclination to see the world as full of types and symbols of God, as a mirror of divine order and unity:

All that is seen, – the world, the Bible, the Church, the civil polity, and man himself, – are types, and, in their degree and place, representatives and organs of an unseen world, truer and higher than themselves.[179]

The relationship between the physical and moral systems became clear to him as it had to Keble. Like Keble, he recognised the principle of reserve at work in divine typology. Nature, a complex array of imagery, both hides and reveals: 'what a veil and curtain this world of sense is! beautiful, but still a veil'.[180] Again following Keble's example, he applied the pattern of divine Revelation as a principle of all religious communication. He too felt that the imagery of the Old Testament, no less than the Sacraments of the New, was an indispensable vehicle of our understanding of God incarnate who addressed not only our mind but also our conscience, will, emotional sympathy, and poetic imagination. Any attempt to reduce the whole economy of God's Revelation would be to sacrifice truth and the richness of allusion to clarity, and the result would be far removed from the spirit of Christianity.

Certainly language alone could not transmit the essence of moral truth, a truth which, in his view, 'cannot be adequately explained and defended in words at all. Its views and human language are incommensurable. For, after all, what *is* language but an artificial system adapted for particular purposes, which have been determined by our wants?'[181] As Revelation consists of a series of isolated and incomplete truths which are mysteriously interrelated rather than comprising a complete revealed system,[182] analogy, symbol, and metaphor are the most appropriate vehicles for communicating the living idea of Christianity. Moreover:

When the mind is occupied by some vast and awful subject of contemplation, it is prompted to give utterance to its feelings in a figurative style; for ordinary words will not convey the admiration, nor literal words the reverence which possesses it.[183]

The imaginative barrenness of logical argument in theological debate, which has drained words of their rich poetry of associations, and has 'starved each term down till it has become the ghost of itself',[184] increases the need for a more poetic religious language. Dogmatic formulations are only a part of the living, growing whole of Christianity, a straitjacket of philosophic language about an inarticulate spiritual experience. They must be balanced by poetry, by channels for the natural relief of 'devotional and penitential emotions',[185] by the rites and ceremonies of Catholic ritual. The Church needs its own metaphorical and symbolic structure if it is to survive as a living idea. If the imagination is to seize upon and realise the being of God, then the Church must address itself to that perceiving imagination lest its doctrines remain lifeless and meaningless. Only the Catholic Church, for Newman, lives through its symbols and Sacraments and makes Christ accessible 'to our imaginations, by His visible symbols'.[186]

Sacramental awareness, then, was an important element in Newman's view of the world and of the Church, but his emphasis was different from Coleridge's and Wordsworth's, and even from Keble's. In the proof of Christian doctrine, the analogy of the world merely provided confirmation of the truth of Revelation which was the real basis of religious conviction for Newman. Awareness of God came primarily from within. Only with that inner faith did the natural world assume divine significance. The Argument from Design is no longer relevant for a post-evolutionary world. When Newman looks around him objectively at the world of nature, his senses can perceive only God's absence:

I look out of myself into the world of men, and there I see a sight which fills me with unspeakable distress. The world seems simply to give the lie to that great truth, of which my whole being is so full; and the effect upon me is, in consequence, as a matter of necessity, as confusing as if it denied that I am in existence myself. If I looked into a mirror, and did not see my face, I should have the sort of feeling which actually comes upon me, when I look into this living busy world, and see no reflexion of its Creator. This is, to me, one of the great difficulties of this absolute primary truth, to which I referred just now. Were it not for this voice, speaking so clearly in my conscience and my heart, I should be an atheist, or a pantheist, or a polytheist when I looked into the world. I am speaking for myself only; and I am far from denying the real force of the arguments in proof of a God, drawn from the general facts of human society, but these do not warm me or enlighten me; they do not take away the winter of my desolation, or make the buds unfold and the leaves grow within me, and my moral being rejoice. The sight of the world is nothing else than the prophet's scroll, full of 'lamentation and mourning, and woe'.[187]

Natural law does not always seem to confirm the existence of God. Although accepting the doctrine that the pattern of God's presence and order extends to all His created works, he cannot follow the tradition of Christian visionaries and embrace this truth with imaginative fervour. The physical world seems to give the lie to the divine truth, and therefore he can only give a 'notional', not a 'real' assent to it:

This established order of things, in which we find ourselves, if it has a Creator, must surely speak of His will in its broad outlines and its main issues. This being laid down as certain, when we come to apply it to things as they are, our first feeling is one of surprise and (I may say) of dismay, that His control of the world is so indirect, and His action so obscure... What strikes the mind most forcibly and so painfully is, His absence (if I may so speak) from His own world.[188]

His dismay foreshadows that of Hopkins in the 'terrible sonnets':

Why does not He, our Maker and Ruler, give us some immediate knowledge of Himself? Why does He not write His Moral Nature in large letters upon the face of history, and bring the blind tumultuous rush of its events into a celestial, hierarchical order?[189]

Newman gave three sermons, as Hopkins wrote a poem, around the text from Isaiah 45:15, 'Verily thou art a God who hidest thyself.'

Even if one could accept the post-evolutionary world as the ordered reflection of the divine, Newman argues the inadequacy of the Argument from Design as a basis for a religious system. As he says in *The Idea of a University*, Revelation refers to circumstances which did not arise until long after the natural creation of heaven and earth, and it was in this interim period that moral evil entered into the world. Hence nature has little to say about moral law.[190] Natural theology represents a very small part of religious truth, and can tell us nothing of Christianity because the natural world existed before anything else took place.[191] It can tell us only of laws, not of miracles, the essence of the idea of Revelation. Natural religion had to await its completion and fulfilment in Christianity. For Newman, 'Revelation begins where Natural Religion fails.'[192] They are 'two independent witnesses on one and the same question', namely that:

the Revealed system is rooted deep in the natural course of things, of which it is merely the result and completion; that his Saviour has interpreted for him the faint or unbroken accents of Nature; and that in them, so interpreted, he has, as if in some old prophecy, at once the evidence and the lasting memorial of the truths of the Gospel.[193]

And so Newman in a sense reverses the Wordsworthian procedure of divine comprehension, as we see from a letter to William Robert

Brownlow, 13 April 1870, in which he says 'I believe in design because I believe in God; not in a God because I see design.'[194] Newman opposes the unintelligibility of nature to its illumination by faith. Faith alone equips us to respond to a world which proceeds not according to a rational principle of cause and effect, but according to the mysterious system of Providence.[195]

The respect for the emotional life inculcated in him in his early years as an Evangelical remained with Newman when his religious loyalties changed. For Newman, the life of the feelings became the justification not only of his own being, but also of his God. As Hopkins did later, Newman based his proof of the existence of God upon the knowledge of his own existence, or from the faculty of conscience which is inseparable from that existence:

Conscience is the essential principle and sanction of Religion in the mind. Conscience implies a relation between the soul and something exterior, and that, moreover, superior to itself; a relation to an excellence which it does not possess, and to a tribunal over which it has no power.[196]

Again, a Wordsworthian preoccupation, this time the stress on the authenticity of the inner life, takes a theological turn; the moral principle of right and wrong inherent in the function of conscience becomes the means of comprehending a moral governor.[197] Nevertheless Newman's faith in the existence of God is realised immediately and from within. He attains knowledge of the ultimate objective truth, the truth of God's existence, through a highly subjective mode of vision in which reality and meaning are determined by his own mind and conscience.

The essence of Newman's religious philosophy is that belief is neither simply an intellectual exercise, nor an intuitive feeling: it is a complex act of spiritual perception whereby a man's diverse faculties are brought into play:

Belief...being concerned with things concrete, not abstract, which variously excite the mind from their moral and imaginative properties, has for its object not only objectively what is true, but inclusively what is beautiful, useful, admirable, heroic; objects which kindle devotion, rouse the passions, and attach the affections; and thus it leads the way to actions of every kind, to the establishment of principles, and the formation of character, and is thus again intimately connected with what is individual and personal.[198]

An organic, vital mind is unlikely to be aroused to the same comprehensiveness of belief by an appeal based on logic and directed to the intellectual faculty alone. 'Deductions', Newman says, 'have no power of persuasion':

> The heart is commonly reached, not through the reason, but through the imagination, by means of direct impressions, by the testimony of facts and events, by history, by description. Persons influence us, voices melt us, looks subdue us, deeds inflame us. Many a man will live and die upon a dogma: no man will be a martyr for a conclusion.[199]

And to make his point that 'Logic makes but a sorry rhetoric with the multitude' the more forcibly, he urges 'first shoot round corners, and you may not despair of converting by a syllogism'.[200]

Newman's diatribes against rationalism have often been distorted or exaggerated. Hopkins rebuked Coventry Patmore for taking too literally the oft-quoted text, 'man is not a reasoning animal; he is a seeing, feeling, contemplating, acting animal'.[201] The text is meant to be a paradox, he argued, and is not to be taken altogether seriously. Obviously the text is an overstatement of Newman's anti-rationalist position. Perhaps he would have been misinterpreted less had he said, 'Man is *not simply* a reasoning animal.' In his writings about reason he wanted to show that reason could not be an adequate substitute for faith, or indeed for any more comprehensive view of human nature. He does not disparage human reason as such, within its own limitations – indeed, 'it is the way to faith'.[202] In his own experience, he became intellectually convinced by Roman Catholicism before he abandoned himself to complete belief: witness his desire, 'may I have only one tenth part as much faith as I have intellectual conviction where the truth lies'.[203] He finds dubious the sort of religious conviction that rests upon no logical foundations: 'few minds in earnest can remain at ease without some sort of rational grounds for their religious belief; to reconcile theory and fact is almost an instinct of the mind'.[204] Yet reason must not be considered as the way to God, for human reason since the Fall is imperfect. At all events, faith does not live by the same processes of deduction and methods of proof as reason: faith has 'its life in a certain moral temper', whereas 'argumentative exercises are not moral; Faith, then, does not afford the same method of proof as Reason':[205]

> Faith is influenced by previous notices, prepossessions, and (in a good sense of the word) prejudices; but Reason, by direct and definite proof. The mind that believes is acted upon by its own hopes, fears, and existing opinions.[206]

Yet while faith is a principle distinct from reason, it is also in another sense a legitimate 'exercise of Reason',[207] because it proceeds from premises to conclusions. Faith, then, preserves the normal rational process, but adds new perspectives by giving it moral, subjective, and 'spiritual' dimensions. For Newman, as a Catholic, the reasoning faculty can only operate once a groundwork of faith has been established. This initial basis of faith relies upon a process of implicit reasoning leading to an act of fiduciary assent:

Faith is the reasoning of a religious mind, or of what Scripture calls a right or renewed heart, which acts upon presumptions rather than evidence, which speculates and ventures on the future when it cannot make sure of it.[208]

There is a sense in Newman's mind of a fusion of the intellectual faculty with a belief based upon certainty of feeling. He has the same capacity as John Donne for generating emotional enthusiasm through the processes of logical reasoning: the very act of reason is an emotional experience authenticating itself through the feelings.

In *An Essay in Aid of a Grammar of Assent*, Newman analyses the mutual dependence of faith and reason in religious understanding and assent, and coins the terms 'real' and 'notional' assent respectively in an attempt to define the experience. First he examines the dual nature of our response to the dogmatic formulations of the Church:

A dogma is a proposition; it stands for a notion or for a thing; and to believe it is to give the assent of the mind to it, as standing for one or for the other. To give a real assent to it is an act of religion; to give a notional, is a theological act. It is discerned, rested in, and appropriated as a reality, by the religious imagination; it is held as a truth, by the theological intellect.[209]

Newman draws a psychological distinction between the active 'life and force' that is the property of real assent, and the more passive acquiescence of notional assent. He asks:

Can I attain to any more vivid assent to the Being of God, than that which is given merely to notions of the intellect? Can I enter with a personal knowledge into the circle of truths which make up that great thought? Can I arise to what I have called an imaginative apprehension of it? Can I believe as if I saw?[210]

The combination of an abstract understanding of the ideas represented by the word 'God', with an insight into 'His own nature' which is 'like Himself and like nothing else'[211] – an intimation of God's innate 'selfhood' – characterises man's religious sense of God. The dual nature of God, abstract divinity on the one hand and incarnate presence on the other, lies at the root of Newman's theory of assent. He traces 'the process by which the mind arrives, not only at a notional, but at an imaginative or real assent to the doctrine that there is One God, that is, an assent made with an apprehension, not only of what the words of the proposition mean, but of the object denoted by them'.[212] Newman shows the importance of ritual in realising the power of dogma, in transforming notional into real assent to the nature of God:

Consider the services for Christmas or Epiphany; for Easter, Ascension, and (I may say) pre-eminently Corpus Christi; what are these great Festivals but comments on the words, 'The Son is God'? Yet who will say that they have the subtlety, the aridity, the coldness of mere scholastic science? Are they addressed to the pure intellect, or to the imagination? do they interest our logical faculty, or excite our devotion?[213]

The theory of real and notional assent can of course be applied to other modes of perception and understanding. Newman shows that one's appreciation of the riches of classical authors matures from a purely notional to a real assent as one moves from childhood into adulthood.[214] But his first concern was to provide in this psychological philosophy of apprehension a 'solution of the common mistake of supposing that there is a contrariety and antagonism between a dogmatic creed and vital religion'.[215] His own spiritual history, his movement from the vital Evangelical faith of his youth into the dogmatic folds of Roman Catholicism, gave him grounds for believing that, on the contrary, the two aspects of faith were mutually supportive and enriching:

in religion the imagination and affections should always be under the control of reason. Theology may stand as a substantive science, without the life of religion; but religion cannot maintain its ground without theology. Sentiment, whether imaginative or emotional, falls back upon the intellect for its stay, when sense cannot be called into exercise; and it is in this way that devotion falls back upon dogma.[216]

In this way, Newman conceives of a Church which reconciles and harnesses together the respective demands of subjective feeling and objective truth. He remained wary of the characteristic Protestant religious style consisting 'not in knowledge, but in feeling or sentiment', and opposed the tendency whereby 'conscience has become a mere self-respect'. He feared that the law of the self was taking over from belief in an objective religious and moral law.[217] Newman wanted something beyond personal insight, something independent of his own being. Hence he always preached against the principle of private judgement, and looked towards the authority of the Church. He turned to Catholicism as the upholder of the objective truth of Revelation, of Christianity as 'a revelation which comes to us as a revelation, as a whole, objectively, and with a profession of infallibility'.[218]

One of the aspects of the Roman Catholic Church which commands most respect from Newman is the scope it gives to energy of intellect, to the creative, progressive interplay between the subject and object, the individual and authority:

> Every exercise of Infallibility is brought out into act by an intense and varied operation of the Reason, from within and without, and provokes again a re-action of Reason against it;...Catholic Christendom is no simple exhibition of religious absolutism, but it presents a continuous picture of Authority and Private Judgement alternately advancing and retreating as the ebb and flow of the tide; – it is a vast assemblage of human beings with wilful intellects and wild passions, brought together into one by the beauty and majesty of a Superhuman Power.[219]

There are many examples in Newman's writings not only of 'wilful intellect' but also of 'wild passion', or at least of the depth of his religious feelings, examples which suggest his emotional and aesthetic attraction to the Roman Church over the Anglican:

> In 1838 I illustrated it by the contrast presented to us between the Madonna and Child, and a Calvary. I said that the peculiarity of the Anglican theology was this, – that it 'supposed the Truth to be entirely objective and detached, not' (as the Roman) 'lying hid in the bosom of the Church as if one with her, clinging to and (as it were) lost in her embrace, but as being sole and unapproachable, as on the Cross or at the Resurrection, with the Church close by, but in the background'.[220]

The Roman Catholic Church, that is to say, has, in Newman's view, greater emotional and spiritual resources than the Church of England. While still an Anglican, he wrote, 'She alone, amid all the errors and evils of her practical system, has given free scope to the feelings of awe, mystery, tenderness, reverence, devotedness, and other feelings which may be especially called Catholic.'[221] For Newman, the demands of subjectivism and of objective truth are equally vital, and finally only the Catholic Church could meet these apparently incompatible needs: 'the Catholic, and he alone, has within him that union of external, with internal notes of God's favour'.[222]

Newman's theological writings are less preoccupied with Wordsworth's and Coleridge's 'sacramentalism' than with their conceptions of the human mind as a unified, organic whole, and of the act of perception as an energising creativity, finding an answering harmony in the objects of perception. Hence, for Newman, religion, like university education, his other main concern, had to answer to the harmony of aspects embodied in the human mind. Christianity should be considered as an analogy of the mind, a counterpart of ourselves. For Newman, only Roman Catholicism expressed the balanced harmony, consistency of development, inclusiveness of purpose, which characterised man's own nature. At the same time, only the Catholic Church provided fit expression of the organic unity of the Godhead for which it was the earthly representative and symbol.

As we have seen, Newman came to regard the theology of the Roman Catholic Church as more satisfactory than that of the Church of England. He viewed theology as an organising principle. He believed that man's religious imagination seized upon and contemplated individual facets of Revelation, and his theological sense shapes these disparate, highly individualised revelations into a comprehensive whole. In this way, the systematised whole is the object of notional assent, while its separate propositions are the objects of real assent.[223] Hence, our understanding of the mystery of the Holy Trinity is a complex accumulation of real assents to the separate natures of God the Father, God the Son, and God the Holy Ghost, held together by a general acceptance of the dogma of the Three in One:

Religion has to do with the real, and the real is the particular; theology has to do with what is notional, and the notional is the general and systematic. Hence theology has to do with the dogma of the Holy Trinity as a whole made up of many propositions; but Religion has to do with each of those separate propositions which compose it, and lives and thrives in the contemplation of them. In them it finds the motives for devotion and faithful obedience; while theology on the other hand forms and protects them by virtue of its function of regarding them, not merely one by one, but as a system of truth.[224]

Coleridge had applied this theory of the method of apprehension more generally in *Biographia Literaria*:

In order to obtain adequate notions of any truth, we must intellectually separate its distinguishable parts; and this is the technical *process* of philosophy. But having done so, we must then restore them in our conceptions to the unity, in which they actually co-exist; and this is the *result* of philosophy.[225]

Like Coleridge, Newman believes in the importance of experiencing unities rather than things in isolation.[226] All unities and knowledge of unities derive from the notion of an equilibrium of functions within the individual mind, making for the associated sensibility to external unities. Hence, the world is seen as a system of modal parallels, each reflecting and responding with its own unity of being to the integrated wholeness of everything else in the world. Newman sought a holistic ideal in the harmony of all human attributes, and in all his writings about the nature of the human mind and intellect, this hankering after some organising principle is at work. In the Oxford University *Sermons* and *The Idea of a University* he articulates his theory of the intellect as 'enlargement or expansion of mind...a wise and comprehensive view of things', engaged in looking at things relatively: 'this enlargement consists in the comparison of the subjects of knowledge one with another', 'the movement onwards, of that moral centre':

a comprehensive mind...implies a connected view of the old with the new: an insight into the bearing and influence of each part upon each other; without which there is no whole, and could be no centre. It is the knowledge, not only of things, but of their mutual relations. It is organized, and therefore living knowledge.[227]

The act of perception itself, or the illative sense, reflects the harmony and integration of the perceiving mind by unifying the contradictory and separate images before it, and acts thereby as a power which realises or forms ideas:

It is the peculiarity of the human mind, that it cannot take an object in, which is submitted to it, simply and integrally. It conceives by means of definition or description; whole objects do not create in the intellect whole ideas, but are, to use a mathematical phrase, thrown into series, into a number of statements, strengthening, interpreting, correcting each other, and with more or less exactness approximating, as they accumulate, to a perfect image.[228]

Human perception, then, can bring contrary aspects into harmony, can make connections, see relations, apprehend its object completely.[229]

Since for Newman faith may be thought of as a directed act of perception, the same principles apply. Hence, we apprehend God by a 'complex act of intuition',[230] bringing into play all the integrated diversity of our mental faculties. Newman stresses the principles of totality and of idiosyncrasy at work in each human mind in his own subjective apprehension of divine truth, the involvement of the 'whole man' in the act of cognition. Faith, coming to a world of incomprehensible formlessness with a right mind, invests that world with its own integration and harmony.

Moving outwards from the organic unity of the perceiving mind through the process of perception, concerned with imposing a unified structure upon the object perceived, Newman was interested in the unity and consistency of those bodies created for man's intellectual and

Theology

spiritual welfare, whose principal function is to organise the individuality of each of its members into one body: namely the universities, and the Catholic Church. Newman wished to redefine an ideal of totality, comprehensiveness, and inclusiveness, to re-evoke the truth of antecedent unity. Here too the model of organisation was the harmonious unity of the mind of man. His thought process, moving from the mind outwards, works from level to level by a series of parallels and correspondences – the parts constantly being referred to the whole, and the whole to the parts. Language is capable of expressing the particular unity both of the subjective mind and of the objective fact; metaphorically, the forms of language express the forms of ideas, objects and perceptions, and stimulate the mind's understanding.

Newman thought of education as an equilibrium of disciplines answering to an inner equilibrium of mental faculties: as he illustrated in *An Essay in Aid of a Grammar of Assent*, 'a right moral state of mind germinates or even generates good intellectual principles'.[231] His central concern was with the idea of what Pater called a 'universal commonwealth of mind':[232]

Truth is the object of Knowledge of whatever kind; and when we inquire what is meant by Truth, I suppose it is right to answer that Truth means facts and their relations, which stand towards each other pretty much as subjects and predicates in logic. All that exists, as contemplated by the human mind, forms one large system or complex fact, and this of course resolves itself into an indefinite number of particular facts, which, as being portions of a whole, have countless relations of every kind, one towards another. Knowledge is the apprehension of these facts whether in themselves, or in their mutual positions and bearings.[233]

Newman insists upon the integrated unity of knowledge as the premise for his argument in the educational treatises:

all knowledge forms one whole, because its subject-matter is one; for the universe in its length and breadth is so intimately knit together, that we cannot separate off portion from portion, and operation from operation, except by a mental abstraction.[234]

The lectures collected under the title of *The Idea of a University defined and illustrated* were intended to show that no one branch of knowledge could be removed from the curriculum without detriment to the whole. Indeed, Newman's role in the founding of the Catholic University of Ireland to which these lectures refer derived from his conviction that there was no satisfactory establishment of learning for Roman Catholics. Neither a secular education nor its alternative offered by Catholic seminaries, a theological one, provided a satisfactory educational system, for neither offered the complete spectrum of learning needed to attain the sort of comprehensive knowledge he so respected. In the lectures, Newman shows that theology should be included in a university course, since it is a major element in universal knowledge, and since it corresponds to an important part of man's mental framework. He proceeds to demonstrate theology's compatibility with those areas of knowledge which seem to be most out of sympathy with it. *The Idea of a University* is a consummate justification of the principle of unity and harmony in knowledge and hence in the ideal educational system.

Within such a system, each subject is in itself an integrated harmonious whole. We have seen how Newman perceived theology as moulding the diverse individuality of faith into a system of dogma. Faith remains incomplete without the discipline of a rigorously exacting theology. The discipline of the moral life, the sovereignty of conscience, circumscribes the individual's religious being; theological doctrine defines that of the community of Christians. Newman describes how theology exhibits perfect precision and consistency:

I speak of one idea unfolded in its just proportions, carried out upon an intelligible method, and issuing in necessary and immutable results; ... after all, in all times and places, where it is found, the evolution, not of half-a-dozen ideas, but of one.[235]

Newman conceives of Christian Revelation, of God's grace, as essentially an organising energy, 'a quickening, renovating, organizing principle', which has not only 'new created the individual', but also joined him to the Christian community, to the body of a Church which itself shows a structural unity and a historical continuity:

Each one of us has lit his lamp from his neighbour, or received it from his fathers, and the lights thus transmitted are at this time as strong and as clear as if 1800 years had not passed since the kindling of the sacred flame.[236]

VII

Hitherto we have concentrated on integrated unity spatially, in a given experience or object at a moment of time; but inherent in the idea of organic energy which pervades Newman's theories of structural organisation is the principle of growth, movement, development, that is of linear unity, viewed historically. Newman's doctrine of development was an acknowledgement of the nineteenth-century demand for a historical perspective. His ideas of growth and development were essential both to his understanding of himself, as we see from the

Apologia, and to his vision of mankind as a whole. In his lecture 'Christianity and Letters' he describes the idea of civilisation as a process of growth and assimilation of culture:

Looking, then, at the countries which surround the Mediterranean Sea as a whole, I see them to be, from time immemorial, the seat of an association of intellect and mind, such as to deserve to be called the Intellect and Mind of the Human Kind. Starting as it does and advancing from certain centres, till their respective influences intersect and conflict, and then at length intermingle and combine, a common Thought has been generated, and a common Civilization defined and established.[237]

This concept of man's progress as a living growth impinges upon every human action and manifests itself in everything in the world, in every human faculty. Thus the principle of development is at work in the growth of the mind's capacity to appreciate literature[238] and in the fact that the Bible 'is written on the principle of development'. In his lecture on 'Literature', Newman finds parallels between the historical development of literature, the growth of a nation, and the personal development of the individual man.[239] The Wordsworthian pre-occupation with the growth of the mind combined in his work with nineteenth-century historicism. He believed that any form of development must be as complex as the mind in which it grew, must be subject to the same laws of growth and development. Human development, centred upon the growth of his own mind, was a constant source of wonder and fascination to Newman:

For myself, it was not logic then that carried me on; as well might one say that the quicksilver in the barometer changes the weather. It is the concrete being that reasons; pass a number of years, and I find myself in a new place; how? the whole man moves; paper logic is but the record of it.[240]

It is in Newman's *Essay on the Development of Christian Doctrine* that the theory of development is most significantly expounded. And it was whilst writing this book, in which he proves to his own satisfaction that the Roman Catholic Church is the true heir to the early Christian Church, that Newman finally decided to be converted. The *Essay on the Development of Christian Doctrine* centres upon the growth of the human mind in history and within each individual's spiritual development. The holy Scriptures did not determine doctrine once and for all, but 'were intended to create an idea, and that idea is not in the sacred text, but in the mind of the reader'. This incomplete doctrine then 'expands in his heart and intellect, and comes to perfection in the course of time'.[241] Developments are 'the spontaneous, gradual and ethical growth...of existing opinions'.[242] The character of the Catholic Church is formed not by the strict and systematic imposition of authority, but by means of a growth, socially, 'over a large mental field'. Under the guiding authority of the Church, 'implicit faith becomes explicit'.[243] In writing about the development in ideas, Newman centres his argument upon the growth of the universal and individual mind:

Let one such idea get possession of the popular mind, or the mind of any set of persons, and it is not difficult to understand the effects which will ensue. There will be a general agitation of thought, and an action of mind both upon itself and upon other minds.[244]

The idea expands and becomes complex and confused until finally some definite form of doctrine emerges, itself inspiring many different individual views, 'till the idea in which they centre will be to each mind separately what at first it was only to all together'. It will enter into relations with other doctrines and facts, and will be defined in relation to these other systems:

Thus in time it has grown into an ethical code, or into a system of government, or into a theology, or into a ritual, according to its capabilities; and this system, or body of thought, theoretical and practical, thus laboriously gained, will after all be only the adequate representation of the original idea, being nothing else than what that very idea *meant* from the first, – its exact image as seen in a combination of the most diversified aspects, with the suggestions and corrections of many minds, and the illustration of many trials.[245]

In this way, an idea which originated in the minds of individuals develops into a body of dogmatic statements: the change takes place from implicit awareness to explicit formulation, 'till what was an impression in the Imagination has become a system or creed in the reason'.[246] Church history could no longer be regarded as an external sequence of events and ideas, but as a process inseparable from the growth of the minds that articulated and fostered those ideas. *An Essay on the Development of Christian Doctrine* is the story of the spiritual, moral, and mental growth of mankind: since it takes place in the minds of the recipients, it cannot remain fixed and immutable, but is ever dynamically evolving, within the absolute boundaries of revealed truth. The forms are variable, but the essence is unchanging and provides a stem of unity. The principle of development gave personality and consistency to Christianity,[247] and it was therefore important that, over the whole course of development, the doctrine maintained identity of nature, identity of essential tendencies, and identity of laws of growth. Newman believed that although religious expression changed, although a complex system of forms and economies had evolved, although the original idea had been defined and redefined almost beyond recognition, nevertheless, in the Church the 'principles of the doctrine of Christ' gave an internal consistency to the historical mutations of Christian dogma and ceremony. The facts of Revelation are not simply evidence of the truth of the revelation, but the media of its impressiveness. The life of Christ brings together and concentrates truths concerning the chief good and the laws of our being, which wander idle and forlorn over the surface of the moral world, and often appear to diverge from each other. It collects the scattered rays of light, which, in the first days of creation, were poured over the whole face of nature, into certain intelligible centres, in the firmament of the heaven, to rule over the day and over the night, and to divide the light from the darkness.[248]

Christ is the essential figure of formulation and harmony in Newman's thought. Revelation is all about Christ, the man, with His own character and individuality, not simply about moral and theological principles: 'the philosopher aspires towards a divine *principle*; the Christian, towards a *Divine Agent*'. Newman defines Christian philosophy as a 'method of personation', which is 'carried throughout the revealed system'.[249] The idea of the Church is identified explicitly with the person of the living Christ, the Christ who, for Hopkins, 'rides time, like riding a river'.[250] The Church was properly the Body or Form of Christ, symbolising His unique harmony of aspects.

When Newman considered the different sections of the Church in the 1830s, this organically unifying personation of Christ was not evident in any but the Roman Catholic Church. Nowhere else could he find that character and unity which Christ's presence determined. He considered the Evangelical religion:

I observed upon its organization; but on the other hand it had no intellectual basis; no internal idea, no principle of unity, no theology. 'Its adherents', I said, 'are already separating from each other; they will melt away like a snowdrift.'[251]

He felt that a lack of form, of one central fulcrum of order, Christ's presence, and one system of dogmatic statement, characterised the Anglican Church in general:

We have a vast inheritance, but no inventory of our treasures. All is given us in profusion; it remains for us to catalogue, sort, distribute, select, harmonize, and complete. We have more than we know how to use; stores of learning, but little that is precise and serviceable; Catholic truth and individual opinion, first principles and the guesses of genius, all mingled in the same works, and requiring to be discriminated.[252]

Newman attempted to reform the Anglican Church, trying to strengthen its spiritual basis and its consistency. But his efforts to put the Church on a more satisfactory intellectual basis served only to expose the very deficiencies he was attempting to remedy. His *Lectures on Difficulties of Anglicans* is a record of these discoveries of Anglican inconsistency. A book addressed to the remnants of the Oxford Movement, it warns them to seek life not in semblance but in the reality of the Catholic faith. As in *An Essay on the Development of Christian Doctrine*, Newman applies the principle of 'life' as a test of doctrinal truth, and concludes that the Anglican Church counterfeits life, shows no powers of growth, no 'activity of principle'. No longer a 'body politic of any kind', it has lapsed into a 'department of government'. Newman poignantly recalls the shock of first realisation that the Anglican Church has no historical or doctrinal coherence. What is left, he asks, once the poetry, a false accoutrement, is stripped away?

Thus it is that students of the Fathers, antiquarians, and poets, begin by assuming that the body to which they belong is that of which they read in time past, and then proceed to decorate it with that majesty and beauty of which history tells, or which their genius creates...But at length, either the force of circumstances or some unexpected accident dissipates it; and, as in fairy tales the magic castle vanishes when the spell is broken, and nothing is seen but the wild heath, the barren rock, and the forlorn sheep-walk: so is it with us as regards the Church of England, when we look in amazement on that we thought so unearthly, and find so commonplace or worthless. Then we perceive that aforetime we have not been guided by reason; but biassed by education, and swayed by affection.[253]

Its unity and personality gone, the Church of England can no longer hope to excite the feelings.[254] One of the basic conditions of personality is self-awareness, and this was manifestly absent in the Church of England. Newman believed that the final position in the process of doctrinal development was not reached by blind mechanical evolution, but through a concurrent process in the human reason. Parallel to the development of doctrine there should be a growth of understanding of why these principles emerge. The Church of England had no centre of consciousness around which to develop a proper theological insight. Despite his efforts to give it such an identity, Newman was forced to admit to Manning that the claims he had been making for his Church lacked substance:

Our blanket is too small for our bed...we are raising longings and tastes which we are not allowed to supply – and till our bishops and others give scope to the development of Catholicism externally and wisely, we *do* tend to make impatient minds seek where it has ever been, in Rome.[255]

These words are taken from a letter written before his conversion, about the problem of Tractarian defections to Rome. Even at this stage, Newman was becoming aware that the Church of Rome exhibited the consistency and consciousness of its own identity that the Church of England so clearly lacked. It was a consistency and identity upheld by the doctrine of infallibility:

the very idea of revelation implies a present informant and guide, and that an infallible one; not a mere abstract declaration of truths not known before to man, or a record of history, or the result of an antiquarian research, but a message and a lesson, speaking to this man and that.[256]

Christianity has many faces, many moods, and Newman began to see that a stem of authority was necessary to hold these many perspectives and shapes into a unified whole: 'for Christianity has many aspects: it has its imaginative side, its philosophical, its ethical, its political; it is solemn, and it is cheerful; it is indulgent, and it is strict; it is light, and it is dark; it is love, and it is fear'.[257] Just as all these emotional aspects play off against each other, so do the many and various Catholic doctrines complement and reflect each other:

The Catholic Doctrines...are members of one family, and suggestive, or correlative, or confirmatory, or illustrative of each other. In other words, one furnishes *evidence* to another, and all to each of them; if this is proved, that becomes probable; if this and that are both probable, but for different reasons, each adds to the other its own probability.[258]

The Church is an equilibrium of functions, regulated by theology.[259] Newman viewed the family of believers united in the Church in the same way. He justified the Catholic body and the common forms of Catholic life in the face of the claims of individuality by showing how God stressed an image or idea of Himself first of all in the individual and how then 'that Image, cherished and worshipped in individual minds, becomes a principle of association, and a real bond of those subjects one with another, who are thus united to the body by being united to that Image'.[260] Newman saw in God a principle of unity both for the individual and for the body of the Church to which he belonged. He recognised in the Catholic Church the principle that 'each individual man must be in his own person one whole and perfect temple of God, while he is also one of the living stones which build up a visible religious community'.[261]

For Newman, religious language demanded the same sort of response as poetic language, in that the objects of faith were themselves symbolic forms. Many religious assertions are linguistically similar to poetic assertions in demanding a response to metaphor and symbol. Newman came to believe that the interrelationship of images and Sacraments, the order of words, all had a poetic meaning in the Catholic Church alone. Thus, in *Loss and Gain*, Willis expresses the sacramental beauty of the Mass:

It is not a mere form of words, – it is a great action, the greatest action that can be on earth. It is, not the invocation merely, but, if I dare use the word, the evocation of the Eternal. He becomes present on the altar in flesh and blood, before whom angels bow and devils tremble. This is that awful event which is the end, and is the interpretation, of every part of the solemnity. Words are necessary, but as means, not as ends; they are not mere addresses to the throne of grace, they are instruments of what is far higher, of consecration, of sacrifice. They hurry on, as if impatient to fulfil their mission. Quickly they go, the whole is quick; for they are all parts of one integral action...Each in his place, with his own heart, with his own wants, with his own thoughts, with his own intention, with his own prayers, separate but concordant, watching what is going on, watching its progress, uniting in its consummation; – not painfully and hopelessly following a hard form of prayer from beginning to end, but like a concert of musical instruments, each different, but concurring in a sweet harmony, we take our part with God's priest, supporting him, yet guided by him.[262]

Newman saw the symbol of the Holy Catholic Church as the actual body of Christ in the world, the means of encountering Christ through outward forms of Sacrament. This conception of the Church as an idea or symbol, an organic whole, requires from us a similar organic and unified response, a conception which brings all aspects of religion and of the believer into a unifying focus. The essence of a Catholic's response to his Church is that it is to a living unity, complex of apprehension and definition, which demands the same response as poetry. Hence the Catholic faith cannot be received passively by men, 'but it becomes an active principle within them, leading them to an ever-new contemplation of itself, to an application of it in various directions, and a propagation of it on every side'.[263]

For Newman, the source of this organic unity in the Catholic Church is that it is the living symbol of Christ's presence: every celebration of Mass, every sacramental sign, is in recognition of the presence of Christ. Man's response is to a personal unity, not simply to an objective theological system.[264] God's Revelation is uniquely personal, and evokes the response of the believer's own personal unity. The unity of the Catholic Church is ultimately derived from the unity of the personality of Christ, of which it is the symbol and body. The various aspects of the Church may be reconciled, Newman suggests, by analogy with the unity of the three offices of Christ:

He is Prophet, Priest, and King; and after His pattern, and in human measure, Holy Church has a triple office too; not the Prophetical alone and in isolation,...but three offices, which are indivisible, though diverse, viz. teaching, rule, and sacred ministry.[265]

Such a description of the Church allows us to respond to it as an organic unity of persons through whom the verifying presence of Christ is transmitted.

Thus, for Newman, Roman Catholicism is 'poetical' because our response and assent to it resembles the complexity of our response to the aesthetic unity of a poem and because it is an imaginative act involving the whole personality. Finally, only Roman Catholicism can offer such a 'principle of association', can represent this powerful cohesion between all its various but complementary aspects. The contrast between the poetry of Catholicism and the prosaic nature of Protestantism is sharply made in Newman's essay on Keble, in which he describes the Church of England before the Oxford Movement tried to inject some poetry into it. However, the attempt failed, because only Catholicism 'has that within her which justifies' her high claims against the temporal power: 'she merely acts out what she says she is'.[266]

In great poetry Newman believed the external forms must reflect and express the beauty of the inner soul. If there is discordance, if the externals elaborate artificially upon a feeble inner truth, then it suffers as poetry. The same is true of the Christian religion. Newman disparages that aesthetic attraction to Catholicism which is supported by no deeper, more serious conviction:

Catholic truths and rites are so beautiful, so great, so consolatory, that they draw one on to love and admire them with a natural love, as a prospect might draw them on, or a skilful piece of mechanism. Hence men of lively imagination profess this doctrine or that, or adopt this or that ceremony or usage, for their very beauty-sake, not asking themselves whether they are true, and having no real perception or mental hold of them. Thus too they will decorate their churches, stretch and strain their ritual, attempt candles, vestments, flowers, incense, and processions, not from faith, but from poetical feelings.[267]

Such an attraction to Catholicism is merely cheap aesthetic self-indulgence:

It is in vain to discourse upon the beauty, the sanctity, the sublimity of the Catholic doctrines and worship, where men have no faith to accept them as divine. They may confess their beauty, sublimity, and sanctity, without believing them; they may acknowledge that the Catholic religion is noble and majestic: they may be struck with its wisdom, they may admire its adaptation to human nature, they may be penetrated by its tender and winning conduct, they may be awed by its consistency. But to commit themselves to it, that is another matter.[268]

In *Loss and Gain* Newman depicts a number of what he calls 'Tractarians *improper*...whose religion lay in ritualism or architecture, and who "played at Popery" or at Anglicanism'.[269] Stress on one aspect of Christianity at the expense of other more important doctrines destroys the harmony of true poetical response. Newman says, 'it is one thing to desire fine churches and ceremonies, (which of course I did myself), and quite another thing to desire these and nothing else'.[270] In *An Essay on the Development of Christian Doctrine*, he quotes Guizot:

[Religion] assumes many other forms beside that of a pure sentiment; it appears a union of doctrines, of precepts, of promises. This is what truly constitutes religion; this is its fundamental character; it is not merely a form of sensibility, an impulse of the imagination, a variety of poetry.[271]

With more sincerity than the Ritualists, the Anglicans of the High Church party, Newman among them, had yet, in his view, tried to appropriate the trimmings of Catholicism without its soul. They had decorated their churches in the same way, they had adopted Catholic vestments, and beautified the external forms of their religion: 'but it is like feeding on flowers, unless you have that objective vision in your faith, and that satisfaction in your reason, of which devotional exercises and ecclesiastical appointments are the suitable expression'. Newman was forced to concede that the 'poetry' which the Tractarians had attempted to give their Church was inconsistent with its essential character:

It is well to have rich architecture, curious works of art, and splendid vestments, when you have a present God; but O! what a mockery, if you have not! If your externals surpass what is within, you are, so far, as hollow as your evangelical opponents who baptize, yet expect no grace.[272]

Protestantism, therefore, failed for Newman as a 'poetic' religion, because of the basic incompatibility of its elaborately revived external ceremonies and its eminently unpoetical spirit. Newman never discounted the importance of poetry and imagination in his discussions of the nature of religion, for he was convinced of the poetic nature of Revelation itself, how it shaped our imaginations into a new awareness of the world and its beauty, and its history:

Revealed Religion should be especially poetical – and it is so in fact. While its disclosures have an originality in them to engage the intellect, they have a beauty to satisfy the moral nature. It presents us with those ideal forms of excellence in which a poetical mind delights, and with which all grace and harmony are associated. It brings us into a new world – a world of overpowering interest, of the sublimest views, and the tenderest and purest feelings. The peculiar grace of mind of the New Testament writers is as striking as the actual effect produced upon the hearts of those who have imbibed their spirit. At present we are not concerned with the practical, but the poetical nature of revealed truth. With Christians, a poetical view of things is a duty, – we are bid to colour all things with hues of faith, to see a Divine meaning in every event, and a superhuman tendency. Even our friends around are invested with unearthly brightness – no longer imperfect men, but beings taken into Divine favour, stamped with His seal, and in training for future happiness. It may be added, that the virtues peculiarly Christian are especially poetical – meekness, gentleness, compassion, contentment, modesty, not to mention the devotional virtues.[273]

It becomes clear that Newman believed the subjective inner life of the Christian shaped images of Revelation as it did forms of Church ritual. Newman's was a highly aestheticised vision of religion and of the Catholic Church in particular. He invested Christianity and morality with beauty, richness, imagination and poetry. He eulogised the 'beauty of our moral being', and 'the beauty of grace'.[274] Finding the principles of organic growth and structural unity common to Christianity and poetry, Newman assumed a direct parallel between religious and aesthetic experience, and proposed that the Christian religion be viewed as a work of art. He took up an aesthetic model to show his philosophy of religious form and Christian history. Religious formulas themselves came to take on a perennial power and beauty. The Catholic Church itself became poetical:

Poetry, as Mr. Keble lays it down in his University Lectures on the subject, is a method of relieving the over-burdened mind; it is a channel through which emotion finds expression and that a safe, regulated expression. Now what is the Catholic Church, viewed in her human aspect, but a discipline of the affections and passions? What are her ordinances and practices but the regulated expression of keen, or deep or turbid feeling, and thus a 'cleansing', as Aristotle would word it, of the sick soul? She is the poet of her children; full of music to soothe the sad and control the wayward – wonderful in story for the imagination of the romantic; rich in symbol and imagery, so that gentle and delicate feelings, which will not bear words, may in silence intimate their presence or commune with themselves. Her very being is poetry; every psalm, every petition, every collect, every versicle, the cross, the mitre, the thurible, is a fulfilment of some dream of childhood, or aspiration of youth. Such poets as are born under her shadow, she takes into her service; she sets them to write hymns, or to compose chants, or to embellish shrines, or to determine ceremonies, or to marshal processions; nay, she can even make schoolmen of them, as she made St. Thomas, till logic becomes poetical.[275]

VIII

It would seem possible, then, to explain Newman's conversion to Rome as essentially 'poetic'. Yet, I would argue, it is equally plausible to explain Keble's decision to remain an Anglican in 'poetic' terms. The apparent paradox, and their different solutions, may be explained by the fact that they conceived of the 'poetic' in different ways. Keble's response to the poetry of the Church was more personal, more quietly intimate, more 'English' than Newman's. Newman's was both more emotionally flamboyant and more detached and intellectual. Their respective attitudes to Rome reflected this.

The Church of Rome in the middle years of the nineteenth century had a rather different style from that of the modern Roman Catholic Church. It was extremely baroque and Italianate, and certainly very far removed from the spirit of the Oxford ethos. It is significant that whereas most of the High Anglican architecture of the period was built in the Gothic style, Victorian Roman Catholic architecture was normally baroque. Many English converts to Rome felt oddly dislocated. Often the only way they could fuse their faith with an English tradition was to look back to the Catholic Church in England in the Middle Ages. This explains the beleaguered tone of much of Pugin's writing. He was fighting a losing battle to restore the architecture, and with it the ritual and liturgy, of English medieval Catholicism. The problematical nature of his position is illuminated in a letter Newman wrote to Lisle Phillipps in 1848, after he had met Pugin in Rome.[276] The two men clashed in their architectural views, but this was symptomatic of a more fundamental disagreement. Pugin, Newman says, implied 'that he would as soon build a mechanics' institute as an Oratory', which, given the contempt in which Pugin held mechanics' institutes, provided a radical point of contention between the two converts. Newman had joined the Oratorians, a post-medieval order, in 1845, and began to involve himself in setting up oratories in England with as much vigour as Pugin engaged in medieval revivalism.

Both Pugin's deprecation of oratories and Newman's response throw light on the question of why Newman was converted and why Keble was not. Pugin's position gives some insight into the difficulty for an Englishman with strong emotional attachments to his native traditions of going over to Rome at that time. He certainly passed the rest of his life in neither one camp nor the other, devoting his last ten years to the writing of 'An Apology for the Separated Church of England', a position surely more paradoxical than that of those Tractarians who still believed in a *via media*.

Newman, on the other hand, responded to the Roman style of architecture with enthusiasm, preferring it to the native Gothic style. Describing a church he visited in Milan in 1846 just after his conversion, he wrote:

It is like a Jesuit Church, Grecian and Palladian – and I cannot deny that, however my reason may go with Gothic, my heart has ever gone with Grecian. I loved Trinity Chapel at Oxford more than any other building. There is in the Italian style such a simplicity, purity, elegance, beauty, brightness, which I suppose the word 'classical' implies, that it seems to befit the notion of an Angel or Saint. The Gothic style does not seem to me to typify the sanctity or innocence of the Blessed Virgin, or St. Gabriel, or the lightness, grace, and sweet cheerfulness of the elect as the Grecian does.[277]

On the same day, he wrote in similarly glowing terms of St Fidelis:

It has such a sweet, smiling, open countenance – and the altar is so gracious and winning, standing out for all to see, and to approach. The tall polished marble columns, the marble rails, the marble floor, the bright pictures, all speak the same language. And a light dome crowns the whole. Perhaps I do but follow the way of elderly persons, who have seen enough that is sad [in] life to be able to dispense with officious intentional sadness – and as the young prefer autumn and the old spring, the young tragedy and the old comedy, so in the ceremonial of religion, younger men have my leave to prefer Gothic, if they will but tolerate me in my weakness which requires the Italian.[278]

When he established the Birmingham Oratory in 1848 its architectural style conformed with these orthodox tastes. The Oratory adopted the Roman vestments too, and, indeed, as Wilfred Ward confirms, 'his own personal taste in devotion was always far more in sympathy with the Continental forms than was that of the old Catholics'.[279]

Newman's own difficulties in leaving the Church of England and Oxford should not be underestimated. His own accounts of his feelings, in the *Apologia* and elsewhere, are deeply moving. Shortly before his conversion, he wrote home from Rome to a friend about the lingering doubts that still persisted: 'Of course I could not make use of a *feeling* as an argument, yet I confess that sometimes when I am hard pressed, I feel that there is a little fortress in the background quite unsuspected by the enemy, namely recollections of Oxford.'[280] Two interesting points emerge from this. First of all, his 'feeling' of regret takes a clear second place behind 'argument'. Secondly, it is specifically, and, one suspects, exclusively Oxford that he regrets, rather than Anglicanism.

Throughout his religious development, Newman's allegiances were always to Oxford, and to the early Christian Church. He had never really felt much in common with the great Anglican divines of the seventeenth century.

Keble, on the other hand, felt much closer to his Anglican roots. He very clearly belonged to the tradition of Laud, Hooker, and George Herbert. His style was always recognisably Church of England and it is entirely appropriate that Keble College in Oxford is built in Gothic Revival style. His own parish church at Hursley, designed by William Butterfield, was a fine example of High Victorian Gothic. His feelings of attachment to the Church of England had a much more fundamental basis in his personality as well as in his theology. He differed from Newman also in putting a great deal more emphasis on the life of the feelings, in his writings on both poetry and theology. His own feelings were not powerful enough to lead him to Rome, but they were entirely adequate as a reason for staying in the Church of England. Poetry, if we recall his view of it, permitted among other things, for Keble, the expression of the logically inconsistent: it allowed paradox, ambiguity, and this was one of its great virtues.

Newman wrote persuasively about the feelings as a basis for poetry and for belief, but finally he was more impressed by a different 'poetic' quality – a quality of unity and consistency, which is essentially intellectual. Shortly before his conversion he wrote to Faber, 'Really I have a great repugnance at mixing religions or worships together, it is like sowing the field with mingled seed. A system is a whole; one cannot tell the effect of one part disjoined from the rest...I do not like decanting Rome into England; the bottles may break.'[281] Newman finally found it impossible to ignore the contradictions of the High Anglican position. He found no comfort in a *via media* which lacked consistency: 'It was beautiful and religious, but it did not even profess to be logical.'[282] Seduced as he was by the 'beautiful' and the 'religious', the essential quality of the 'poetic' for Newman was finally consistency, and only the Church of Rome could offer him that. For Keble, on the other hand, the 'beautiful and religious' nature of Anglicanism gave adequate grounds for intellectual compromise, and he chose to remain loyal to the Church of England.

2 Epistemology and perception: Gerard Manley Hopkins

It is customary to consider Hopkins' theory of inscape as *sui generis*, the philosophy of a solitary mystical and poetical visionary. Its fusion of Parmenidean, Platonic, and Scotist concepts with a distinctive and innovative aesthetic is indeed unique, reflecting the virtual isolation of Hopkins, as a Jesuit priest, from the mainstream of Victorian letters. Yet, in that it represents an attempt to relate ideas about beauty, art, and religion into one comprehensive philosophy, the idea of inscape places Hopkins very centrally in the post-Romantic religio-aesthetic tradition which defines Victorian aesthetic thought. Keble and Newman were both poets and critics of poetry, yet the main focus of their intellectual effort and achievement was religious. Hopkins dedicated his life to a religious vocation, but his distinction for the modern reader is as a poet and literary theorist. All three men pursued a philosophical synthesis which would incorporate their religious commitment and their passion for art. If Keble and Newman as a result 'made the Church of England poetical', then Hopkins just as convincingly made the figure of Christ fundamental to his theories about perception, beauty, and poetry.

There is in the large body of literature on Hopkins a dogged critical emphasis on the conflict between his exaggerated conscience and priestly vocation on the one hand and his poetical genius and intense vulnerability to beauty on the other. Certainly an acute tension existed between the 'priest' and the 'poet' in him, a tension which undeniably broke down at crucial points in his life. From letters that he wrote to his friend Richard Watson Dixon we may infer that he felt prohibited by his religious vocation from seeking fame as a poet through publication: 'for genius attracts fame and individual fame St. Ignatius looked on as the most dangerous and dazzling of all attractions'.[1] It was an inhibition which led, in times of spiritual crisis, inevitably to stultifying frustration:

> Only what word
> Wisest my heart breeds dark heaven's baffling ban
> Bars or hell's spell thwarts. This to hoard unheard,
> Heard unheeded, leaves me a lonely began.[2]

But actually, from quite early in his career, even apart from his deliberate attempts at an intellectual reconciliation of his faith and his appreciation of beauty, it is clear that these two aspects of his life are subtly related rather than being thus radically divided. In a poem written in 1866, 'The Habit of Perfection', ascetic renunciation of the sensuous world is couched in language which could itself scarcely be more sensuous:

> O feel-of-primrose hands, O feet
> That want the yield of plushy sward,
> But you shall walk the golden street
> And you unhouse and house the Lord.[3]

And the burden of the poem is that the beauty embodied in the religious life surpasses, rather than excludes, that beauty which is merely sensuous. In a less serious but similar vein, he writes to an Oxford friend in the same year, 'the Sussex downs are seductive, as Pater says, if there is a church'.[4] More significantly, amongst the reasons he offers his father in October 1866 for his conversion to Roman Catholicism is 'an increasing knowledge of the Catholic system, which only wants to be known in order to be loved – its consolations, its marvellous ideal of holiness, the faith and devotion of its children, its multiplicity, its array of saints and martyrs, its consistency and unity, its glowing prayers, the daring majesty of its claims'.[5] And throughout his writings as a Catholic runs an awareness of kinds of beauty which transcend the physical yet may be acknowledged in aesthetic terms: beauty of mind and character, and of the soul;[6] Christ's beauty;[7] 'God's *better* beauty, grace'.[8]

Hopkins was a great theoriser. He delighted in attempting to explain, both to himself and to his friends, things as diverse as effects of nature, derivations of words, how poems scanned. He embarked upon theories not only in those areas in which we would expect him to speculate – poetic diction, rhetoric, aesthetics, theology – but also in music, philology, and metaphysics. It is not at all surprising therefore that a theory began to emerge from his natural inclination to find a compatibility between aesthetics and religion. It is puzzling, however, that, given his intellectual rigour and perseverence, Hopkins nowhere wrote one central comprehensive philosophical formulation of his theory of inscape. The critic is hence obliged himself to construct the theory from hints to be found in Hopkins' various writings on beauty, religion, philosophy and art. This necessary but artificial separation of the ideas from their context carries with it the danger that the critic may be tempted to raid Hopkins' work in such a way as to suggest that it is more of a piece than it actually is. Hopkins' intellectual history is problematical, and his work does not represent a coherent and consistent intellectual position. But if it is questionable to attempt to isolate and define a theory of inscape, it is nevertheless possible to examine how it naturally evolved from Hopkins' characteristic attitudes and preoccupations.

Two basic questions emerge from the rich fund of disparate material on inscape in Hopkins' writings which seem to be central to the genesis of the theory. Why do some things in nature and in our experience suddenly strike us as special and in some way significant? And if we are to explain why they are special in terms of their affording some intimation of the divine, then what exactly is the relationship between the natural object or experience and God?

For Hopkins, nature was sacramental in that it was symbolic of a divine creator. Even in a world explained by evolution, a world in which 'all nature is mechanical', he maintained that 'mechanics contains that which is beyond mechanics'.[9] Yet he was anxious to find a more intellectually satisfying explanation for sacramental analogy than had hitherto been given. In the sacramental and Romantic poetical traditions and in Kant's philosophical Idealism alike, the link between appreciation of the beauty of the natural world and knowledge of divine purposiveness depended on a leap of faith based entirely on a subjective feeling or intuition of sublimity. But when Hopkins found himself making correlations between visual and moral or metaphysical qualities he questioned the manner and meaning of his own perceptive process. In a diary entry, he recalls how, in the Sheldonian Theatre in Oxford, he remarked of the crowd assembled before him:

the short strokes of eyes, nose, mouth, repeated hundreds of times I believe it is which gives the visible law: looked at in any one instance it flies. I could find a sort of beauty in this, certainly character – but in fact that is almost synonymous with finding order, anywhere.[10]

His awareness of his own failure to understand and articulate the true nature and meaning of the shock and wonder he himself felt in the face of certain unique experiences of beauty led him to seek a personal and original sacramental explanation for aesthetic experience.

The problem with sacramental views of nature before Hopkins began to develop his theories, and the reason why he found them so unsatisfactory, was that they did not seem to offer a specifically Christian concept of nature. For the sacramental poets who came before him, such as Vaughan, Traherne, and Wordsworth, the natural world simply showed evidence of a divine creator. Vaughan, for example, addresses himself to

> ...thou immortal light and heat,
> Whose hand so shines through all this frame,
> That by the beauty of the seat,
> We plainly see who made the same.[11]

In this scheme, Christ is perceived only as a Mediator.[12] Wordsworth's moonlit vision as he climbed Snowdon similarly has a profoundly religious but not specifically Christian sacramental significance:

> ...it appeared to me the type
> Of a majestic intellect, its acts
> And its possessions, what it has and craves,
> What in itself it is, and would become.
> There I beheld the emblem of a mind
> That feeds upon infinity...
> ...a mind sustained
> By recognitions of transcendent power,
> In sense conducting to ideal form,
> In soul of more than mortal privilege.[13]

Natural sacramentalism of this kind takes no account of circumstances which took place after the creation of heaven and earth – the coming of evil, sin, and suffering into the world, for example, Christ's Incarnation, miracles, the Redemption – in fact, it takes no account of the essential facts of Christian Revelation.[14]

Hopkins' contribution to the sacramental tradition was to consider nature as expressive of Christ incarnate as well as of God the creator, of the 'redemptive strain' as well as the 'creative strain'. Christ incarnate, the physical manifestation of God, represented for Hopkins, in His selfhood, the pattern, the inscape, to which all created forms aspire. The distinctiveness of certain forms, of certain experiences of beauty, was explained by their resemblance to the uniqueness of Christ's inscape. In this way, inscape became the common denominator of religious, aesthetic, and poetic experience alike. Christ represented the ultimate inscape, and through His Incarnation the principles of perfect physical and moral beauty, love, and sacrifice became manifest in the created world. Hopkins' awareness of Christ as the divine archetype of created beauty, as the nub of his theory of inscape, enabled him to merge his love of beauty and poetic creativity with his religious commitment. In his theory of inscape, and in the philosophical interests that stem from this, Hopkins made the crucial link between perception, expression, and religious belief which was the foundation of a highly sophisticated and unique religio-aesthetic theory.

I

Hopkins' journals largely consist of painstakingly accurate recordings of the activities of the natural world, accompanied by exquisite Ruskinesque sketches of its minutiae. In 1863, he wrote to his friend Baillie:

I am sketching (in pencil chiefly) a good deal. I venture to hope you will approve of some of the sketches in a Ruskinese point of view: – if you do not, who will, my sole congenial thinker on art?[15]

In 1857, when Ruskin first published *The Elements of Drawing*, in which he urges all young apprentice artists to recover 'the *innocence of the eye*'[16] and search out pure organic form in landscape, Hopkins was twelve years old, falling exactly into the age group for which the guide was intended. It seems likely that Hopkins was familiar with the work, for as an undergraduate he uses the same terms to describe the artist who did not 'go to nature' as one whose 'eye had not been trained to look severely at things apart from their associations, *innocently* or *purely* as painters say'.[17] He also explains how 'when the innocent eye of the uneducated or of children is spoken of in art it is understood that their sense is correct, that is that they are free from fallacies implying some education, but not that it is strong or definite'.[18] There are a number of explicit references in Hopkins' letters and journals which indicate a familiarity with *Modern Painters* and other works by Ruskin. Although he often betrays some irritation with Ruskin both as critic and philosopher – 'Ruskin often goes astray';[19] of his criticism of Whistler, 'Ruskin was wrong about him, & did him great injustice';[20] and in general, 'Ruskin, it seems to me, has the insight of a dozen critics, but intemperance and *wrongness* undoes all his good again'[21] – he nevertheless numbers him among 'the true men'.[22] He admires him as one 'whose whole powers have been devoted to criticism, powers which in their line are perhaps equal to those of the men whose works he criticises'.[23]

A glance at Hopkins' sketches reveals his aesthetic discipleship, and the journals as a whole show him responding to Ruskin's elevation of the minute recording of natural phenomena to the status of art. He fastened upon Ruskin's love of 'Nature's self' and sought to express, through a close investigation of the organic forms of nature, the peculiar delight aroused by particular experiences of nature, the result being a characteristically Ruskinian combination of painstaking scientific investigation and passionate response:

I think I have told you that I have particular periods of admiration for particular things in Nature; for a certain time I am astonished at the beauty of a tree, shape, effect etc., then when the passion, so to speak, has subsided, it is consigned to my treasury of explored beauty, and acknowledged with admiration and interest ever after, while something new takes its place in my enthusiasm. The present fury is the ash, and perhaps barley and two shapes of growth in leaves and one in tree boughs and also a conformation of fine-weather cloud.[24]

Many of his precise studies can be traced directly back to the methods advocated in Ruskin's chapters on 'Of Truth of Vegetation' and 'Of Truth of Clouds' in volume one of *Modern Painters* (1843). In his diaries and sketch books he recorded distinctive effects of light and sound patterns. But most significantly of all he was like Ruskin in his fascination with the relationship between permanent form and transient effect.

His preoccupation with nature in flux, his attempts to catch fleeting impressions of beauty, embodied most distinctly in cloudscapes, rainbows and sunsets, show a remarkable affinity with Ruskin.[25] His chief concern seems to be to 'catch' or 'hold' the fleeting beauty of nature – cloud formations, sunsets, storms, and rainbows. These nature notes are but one manifestation of Hopkins' lifelong grapple with the sense of flux, with the knowledge that 'life and time are always losing, always spending, always running down and running out'.[26] And this was an age, of course, when consciousness of flux was the more acute with the discovery of evolution. Later, in his great poem about a world defined by time and dissolution, 'That Nature is a Heraclitean Fire', Hopkins finds comfort in the Resurrection:

> Enough! the Resurrection,
> A heart's-clarion! Away grief's gasping, | joyless days, dejection.
> Across my foundering deck shone
> A beacon, an eternal beam. | Flesh fade, and mortal trash
> Fall to the residuary worm; | world's wildfire, leave but ash:
> In a flash, at a trumpet crash,
> I am all at once what Christ is, | since he was what I am, and
> This Jack, joke, poor potsherd, | patch, matchwood, immortal diamond,
> Is immortal diamond.[27]

Perhaps it was in the spirit of Eliot's 'Because I do not hope to turn again'[28] that Hopkins chose Catholicism as a means of rescue from an equally acute sense of spiritual flux, although in fact he found the life of a Jesuit priest to be one of constant physical upheaval. He wrote to his friend Robert Bridges, 'permanence with us is gingerbread permanence: cobweb, soapsud, and frost-feather permanence'.[29]

Hopkins' acute awareness of flux was also nurtured by his association with Walter Pater at Oxford. In his memoir of Hopkins, Robert

Bridges notes that he 'enjoyed the sympathetic tuition of Walter Pater'.[30] Hopkins' letters and diaries testify to the frequency and importance of his meetings with Pater between 1865 and 1867. In 1865 he wrote an essay for Pater with the title 'The Origin of our Moral Ideas'.[31] On 2 May 1866 he writes, 'Coaching with W. H. Pater this term. Walked with him on Monday evening last, April 30. Fine evening bitterly cold. "Bleak-faced Neology in cap and gown": no cap and gown, but very bleak'.[32] On 31 May 1866, he notes, 'Pater talking two hours against Xtianity.'[33] On 17 June 1868 he writes, 'To lunch with Pater, then to Mr Solomon's studio and the Academy',[34] by which it appears that through Pater Hopkins came into contact with some of the notable aesthetes of the day. He talks of staying with Pater in Sidmouth during the summer vacation.[35] Years later, Hopkins recalls 'when I was at Oxford Pater was one of the men I saw most of'.[36] Their friendship continued for many years after Hopkins graduated. In 1878 he wrote to Bridges, 'It was pleasing and flattering to hear that Mr. Pater remembers and takes an interest in me',[37] and later on in that year, during a visit to Oxford, he dined with Pater.[38]

The extent of Pater's influence as Hopkins' mentor is difficult to assess because he was only beginning to write seriously for the reviews while Hopkins was under his tutelage. 'Diaphaneitè' was first published in July 1864, followed by his essay on Coleridge in 1866, and by the more famous essay on Winckelmann in January 1867. His first book, *Studies in the History of the Renaissance*, was not published until 1873, and indeed most of his important work was produced after Hopkins had left Oxford. Nevertheless the germ of his later writings is there in his early essays, and it seems fair to assume that Pater would have discussed his developing aesthetic theories with a student as exceptional as Hopkins, the 'Star of Balliol'.

Like Ruskin, Pater encouraged the development of visual awareness as a means of enhancing the inner life of the individual. The Paterian ideal is 'a quickened, multiplied consciousness'[39] through an intensification of the perceptive faculty. Through 'a continual analysis of facts of rough and general observation into groups of facts more precise and minute'[40] it is possible to discern and relate to a moral pattern which is not fixed and absolute – he makes this point very forcefully in his essay on Coleridge – but shifting and relative. For the individual in a post-evolutionary world the faculty for discerning truth is 'recognised as a power of distinguishing and fixing delicate and fugitive detail'.[41]

Yet within the unarguably shifting world of the 1860s Hopkins noticed that there are certain forms which have a great hold on the mind and are always reappearing and seem imperishable...while every day we see designs both simple and elaborate which do not live and are at once forgotten; and these things are inexplicable on the theory of pure chromatism or continuity – the forms have in some sense or other an absolute existence.[42]

In his journals Hopkins was particularly concerned to delineate these forms. He was fascinated by the structure and unity of the things he observed in nature: 'I saw the wholeness of the sky and the sun like its ace';[43] 'In watching the sea one should be alive to the oneness which all its motion and tumult receives from its perpetual balance and falling this way and that to its level.'[44] His attraction to images of unity is reflected in a delight in curvature and fanshapes:[45] 'Grey clouds in knops. A curious fan of this kind of cloud radiating from a crown, and covering half the sky.'[46] Describing a pair of ashes, he says:

I saw how great the richness and subtlety is of the curves in the clusters, both in the forward bow mentioned before and in some most graceful hangers on the other side: it combines somewhat-slanted outward strokes with rounding.[47]

And again:

I watched the great bushes of foam-water, the texture of branchings and water-spandrils which makes them up. At their outsides nearest the rock they gave off showers of drops strung together into little quills which sprang out in fans.[48]

The foot of the Rhone glacier seemed to him to be 'shaped like the fan-fin of a dolphin'.[49]

Hopkins developed a refined appreciation for form, composition, colour-shading, and balance. He worked to discover the 'organisation' of the oak tree[50] and the 'law' of its leaves.[51] Elsewhere he observes:

The clouds were repeatedly formed in horizontal ribs. At a distance their straightness of line was wonderful...the ribs granulated delicately the splits fretted with lacy curves and honeycomb work, the laws of which were exquisitely traced.[52]

Elsewhere again, he describes minutely and sketches the 'composition' of the furze bloom,[53] parallel banks of cloud, 'parallel straight lapwaves' around a barge,[54] how 'on the Common the snow was channelled all in parallels by the sharp driving winds'.[55] He notes evidence of order and pattern in two stars which are 'such counterparts that each seems the reflection of the other in opposite bays of the sky and not two distinct things'.[56] Hopkins had discovered a concrete world about him which, in the vital unity of its lines and curves, all seemingly mastered by some inherent energy, seemed a reflection of an ideal divine order beyond. The patterned order of the universe seemed to provide evidence of the divine hand of creation:

All the world is full of inscape and chance left free to act falls into an order as well as purpose: looking out of my window, I caught it in the random clods and broken heaps of snow made by the cast of a broom.[57]

But Hopkins was not content with explaining the extraordinary experiences of nature as a simple reflection of divine order. He probed further into the workings of the perceptive process to try to discover the meaning of such experiences. He faced the question of the exact relationship between observer and observed at every turn. He was fascinated by the complexities of perception, by the fact that 'what you look hard at seems to look hard at you',[58] by the way subject and object sometimes seem to drift into each other:

Drops of rain hanging on rails etc. seen with only the lower rim lighted like nails (of fingers). Screws of brooks and twines. Soft chalky look with more shadowy middles of the globes of cloud on a night with a moon faint or concealed. Mealy clouds with a not brilliant moon. Blunt buds of the ash. Pencil buds of the beech. Lobes of the trees. Cups of the eyes. Gathering back the lightly hinged eyelids. Bows of the eyelids. Pencil of eyelashes. Juices of the eyeball. Eyelids like leaves, petals, caps, tufted hats, handkerchiefs, sleeves, gloves. Also of the bones sleeved in flesh. Juices of the sunrise. Joins and veins of the same. Vermilion look of the hand held against a candle with the darker parts as the middles of the fingers and especially the knuckles covered with ash.[59]

Here the eyes of the perceiver are bound up, through metaphor, shape, and sound, with the sensuous reality of the scene: the juices of the eyeball with the drops of rain, the juices of the sunrise; the cups of the eyes with the globes of cloud, the lobes of the trees; the pencil of eyelashes with the blunt buds of the ash, the pencil buds of the beech; bows of the eyelids, lightly hinged, with leaves, petals.

In his journal entries he constantly relates the things of nature to human features: 'Yew-trees, like ears, in hedges';[60] 'the mouthed centre of a violet';[61] 'parallel spines' of 'vertebrated' clouds;[62] the three stages of the Rhone glacier as 'the heel, instep, and ball or toes of a foot';[63] the 'continuous eyebrow curves' of clouds.[64] Pathetic fallacy maybe, but such metamorphoses of nature, while idiosyncratic, point to a serious exploration of the relationship between man and the nature he observes. Man is, essentially, 'Earth's eye, tongue' and 'heart',[65] and the human features which he finds there are not only reflections of himself as subject. They are in some way related to Christ. The process is described most completely in one of Hopkins' mature poems, 'Hurrahing in Harvest', in which the extended harvest metaphor unites the earth, the heavens, the perceiver, and Christ:

> Summer ends now; now, barbarous in beauty, the stooks rise
> Around; up above, what wind-walks! what lovely behaviour
> Of silk-sack clouds! has wilder, wilful-wavier
> Meal-drift moulded ever and melted across skies?
>
> I walk, I lift up, I lift up heart, eyes,
> Down all that glory in the heavens to glean our Saviour;
> And, éyes, heárt, what looks, what lips yet gave you a
> Rapturous love's greeting of realer, of rounder replies?
>
> And the azurous hung hills are his world-wielding shoulder
> Majestic – as a stallion stalwart, very-violet-sweet! –
> These things, these things were here and but the beholder
> Wanting; which two when they once meet,
> The heart rears wings bold and bolder
> And hurls for him, O half hurls earth for him off under his feet.[66]

But what is the philosophical basis of such an experience as this poem describes? And how did it develop?

Hopkins' studies in Greek theories of perception at Oxford sharpened his philosophical understanding of this collaboration of subject and object in the act of perception.[67] The theory of perception that he began to develop was, like classical models, dynamic and threefold. The process involved for him the physical fact of the object in all its complexity, the sensuous cognition of this object, and finally the more complete perception of it, whereby the mind, the reacting self, responded in its own way, even imposing something of itself on to the object.

The shifting perspectives of the second of the two sonnets 'To Oxford' is an interesting example of the creative imagination at work in sense perception. As the observer changes his position with respect to the chapel wall he is contemplating, he describes how the appearance of the wall alters accordingly, 'as falsified/By visual compulsion':

> Thus, I come underneath this chapel-side,
> So that the mason's levels, courses, all
> The vigorous horizontals, each way fall
> In bows above my head, as falsified
> By visual compulsion, till I hide
> The steep-up roof at last behind the small
> Eclipsing parapet; yet above the wall
> The sumptuous ridge-crest leave to poise and ride.[68]

However, although this is a literally justified shift in some sense, in that the perceiver has changed his perspective by moving, it is not founded solely on the visual perception of the apparent change in the architectural line of the building. Hopkins, the subject in this very personal tribute to Oxford, was strongly attracted to the Gothic style in architecture,[69] and his mind needed only a hint from the senses to spark off a small imaginative flight in which he fancied the chapel transformed. Hopkins' perception itself invoked his more general attitudes, tastes, and convictions.

As a student at Oxford, Hopkins was influenced not only by classical theories of perception, but also by more recent continental thinkers. Hopkins did not himself read German philosophy,[70] but he certainly had access to Kantian and Hegelian theories of perception and aesthetics through his closest friend, Robert Bridges, and his teacher, Walter Pater, both of whom were significantly influenced by German philosophical ideas.[71] His tutor at Balliol, moreover, was the English Idealist philosopher T. H. Green, a man whom Hopkins liked and admired.[72] T. H. Green, best known for his exposition of Kant and Hegel and his criticism of Hume's philosophy, was preparing his work 'Popular Philosophy in its Relation to Life' during the period when he taught Hopkins. In it, he suggests that philosophy can learn from 'evangelical religion' and from 'the deeper views of life which the contemplative poets originated'. His view of Wordsworth as one who looked not 'within his own breast' to 'read what he was', but to 'the open scroll of the world, of the world, however, as written within and without by a self-conscious and determining spirit'[73] may well have played an influential role in the development of Hopkins' own epistemological investigations into the relationship between the self and a world informed by the principle of selfhood.

Hopkins himself was an enthusiastic reader of Wordsworth's mystical nature poetry, which gave imaginative and intuitive expression to ideas systematically developed by Coleridge and the German Romantic philosophers. Of Wordsworth's 'Ode: Intimations of Immortality', for example, he said:

There have been in history a few, a very few men, whom common repute, even where it did not trust them, has treated as having had something happen to them that does not happen to other men, as having *seen something*...human nature in these men saw something, got a shock;... in Wordsworth when he wrote that ode human nature got another of those shocks, and the tremble from it is spreading...I am, ever since I knew the ode, in that tremble.[74]

He also read *Biographia Literaria,* in which Coleridge virtually restates Kant's transcendental method,[75] and would have been familiar with Coleridge's reassertion of the imagination as the supreme mental power, and his belief in the 'absolute identity of subject and object, which it calls nature, and which in its highest power is nothing else than self-conscious will or intelligence'.[76] He would also have considered the implications of a divinity perceived as 'the infinite I AM'.[77] Humphry House, noting certain similarities between Coleridge and Hopkins, has suggested that Hopkins may even have had access to Coleridge's notebooks through his friendship with Ernest Hartley Coleridge at Highgate School and Oxford.[78]

Hopkins' concern with the relationship between subject and object in the act of perception coincides significantly with Kant's critical method, and his philosophical investigations into the relationship between the mind and empirical experience in the act of knowledge. By means of his 'Copernican Revolution' Kant modified the view of the English empirical philosophers, that knowledge begins with an understanding of experience, proposing instead that an understanding of the mind must come first, for 'objects must conform to our knowledge'.[79] He believed that 'though all our knowledge begins with experience, it does not follow that it all arises out of experience'.[80] He saw the mind not as the passive recipient of impressions, but as an active, synthesising faculty which 'half-creates what it perceives' by imposing its own categories of the understanding on nature, so that only under those categories, which are themselves independent of sense experience, can it apprehend things: 'We can know *a priori* of things only what we ourselves put into them.'[81] In the *Critique of Pure Reason* Kant emphasises the role of the imagination in the formation of knowledge, describing it as 'an active faculty for the synthesis of the manifold data of sense perception'.[82] Kant distinguishes between two kinds of imagination: the empirical, or 'reproductive' imagination, and the transcendental or 'productive' imagination. The empirical imagination has to do with everyday perceptive processes and the identification of categories. The transcendental imagination has a constructive function. It is active and creative. This is the imagination of the creative artist.[83] For Kant, the transcendental function of imagination is 'a necessary ingredient of perception itself' and the indispensable mediator between sensibility and understanding.[84] Kant's belief in the creativity of sense-perception, and its relationship with imagination, developed so positively in the poetry of Wordsworth and the theoretical writings of Coleridge, remained a vital preoccupation for Hopkins, writing in 1864:

It was a hard thing to undo this knot.
The rainbow shines, but only in the thought
Of him that looks. Yet not in that alone,
For who makes rainbows by invention?
And many standing round a waterfall
See one bow each, yet not the same to all,
But each a hand's breadth further than the next.
The sun on falling waters writes the text
Which yet is in the eye or in the thought.
It was a hard thing to undo this knot.[85]

An interesting parallel to this is to be found in Duns Scotus' theory of the sensuous perception of spiritual reality.[86] He suggests that there is an important connection between sensation and the innate memory.[87] According to Scotus, the senses respond to a real object outside the mind, yet the response is at the same time the expression of something which already exists in the mind. The object, as it were, strikes independently the senses and the intellect. Innate knowledge, embedded in the intellectual memory, provides a context for immediate sensation. Scotus goes on to postulate an original spiritual object which makes the mind start knowing, as indeed does Hopkins, but it seems that to this point at least they conceive of the processes of perception in a similar way.

Kant's characteristic doctrine, as embraced by the English Romantic poets, is that ultimate reality is transcendent, beyond the reach of empiricism and pure reason.[88] The world that we perceive and seem to understand is not the noumenon, the world in itself, but only the world as phenomenon, a world of appearances. Kant argues that the reality of the noumenon cannot be known by pure reason:

All our intuition is nothing but the representation of appearance...As appearances, they cannot exist in themselves, but only in us. What objects may be in themselves...remains completely unknown to us.[89]

The Romantic intuition of there being something mysterious beyond our experience which we nevertheless know to fulfil our humanity, must, because such truths cannot be known, remain suggestive abstraction. Hence the symbolic power of nature in Wordsworth's poetry:

I felt the sentiment of Being spread
O'er all that moves and all that seemeth still;
O'er all that, lost beyond the reach of thought
And human knowledge, to the human eye
Invisible, yet liveth to the heart.[90]

Yet Hopkins, an intrepid theoriser, strove to understand and articulate the true nature of beauty and the perceptive process, and its relationship with the transcendental.

Kant, in his third Critique, the *Critique of Judgement*, identified a fundamental problem in aesthetic judgement. How can an avowedly subjective expression of experience, as the aesthetic sense certainly is, claim the objective validity that the idea of judgement implies? How can the immediate pleasure of aesthetic experience be justified in terms which would command universal assent?[91] This is the very question to which Hopkins addresses himself in his most interesting undergraduate essays, his earliest attempts to distinguish theoretically subjective response from objective fact.

II

In his undergraduate essays Hopkins set out to prove that our subjective responses to beauty are based on a perception of objective relations, that 'Beauty therefore is a relation, and the apprehension of it a comparison.'[92] In his essay 'On the Signs of Health and Decay in the Arts', written in 1864, Hopkins identifies the original cause of our sense of the beautiful as comparison, and suggests that comparison is inseparable from thought. He finds four dimensions within the concept of comparison: of existence with non-existence; of a thing with itself in the continuance of its laws; of two or more things together; and of finite with infinite.[93] A few years later, in 1870, Hopkins describes a sunset in terms of these different kinds of comparison:

A fine sunset: the higher sky dead clear blue bridged by a broad slant causeway rising from right to left of wisped or grass cloud, the wisps lying across; the sundown yellow, moist with light but ending at the top in a foam of delicate white pearling and spotted with big tufts of cloud in colour russet between brown and purple but edged with brassy light. But what I note it all for is this: before I had always taken the sunset and the sun as quite out of gauge with each other, as indeed physically they are, for the eye after looking at the sun is blunted to everything else and if you look at the rest of the sunset you must cover the sun, but today I inscaped them together and made the sun the true eye and ace of the whole, as it is. It was all active and tossing out light and started as strongly forward from the field as a long stone or a boss in the knop of the chalice-stem: it is indeed by stalling it so that it falls into scape with the sky.[94]

In this extraordinary attempt to describe and explain the spectacular beauty of the sunset, Hopkins identifies the contrast of the causeway of cloud with the dead clear blue of the sky, the internal relations of colour-shading in that causeway of colour, the relation of the sunset with the sun, and the finite phenomenon of the sun setting within an infinite skyscape.

In his undergraduate essay 'The Origin of our Moral Ideas' he considers the possibility of analogy between beauty and moral excellence, both in terms of distinctions between the subjective and the objective, and in terms of the comparative process which both demand:

Beauty lies in the relation of the parts of a sensuous thing to each other, that is in a certain relation, it being absolute at one point and comparative in those nearing it or falling from it. Thus in those arts of which the effect is in time, not space, it is a sequence at certain intervals – elementary at least. These arts are instanced as being nearest to morality, since action lies in time. Does then morality lie in a relation between acts or (otherwise) the parts of action? Is it a sequence of action?[95]

In 'On the Origin of Beauty: A Platonic Dialogue', two kinds of beauty are postulated – transitional beauty, measured in time, which he terms 'chromatic beauty', and abrupt beauty, measured spatially and structurally, which he calls 'diatonic beauty'. Under these two headings Hopkins is able to categorise different art forms and to characterise different techniques used in art:

The division then is of abrupt and gradual, of parallelistic and continuous, of intervallary and chromatic, of quantitative and qualitative beauty. The beauty of an infinite curve is chromatic, of a system of curves parallelistic; of deepening colour or of a passing from one colour into another chromatic, of a collocation of colours intervallary; of the change of note on the string of a violin or in a strain of wind chromatic, of that on the keys of a piano intervallary. Art of course combines the two kinds of beauty; some arts have more of the one, some of the other.[96]

The essay 'On the Origin of Beauty', along with his other undergraduate exercises, clearly provides a pertinent theoretical commentary on the way Hopkins' own ideas about poetry were developing. It reveals, for example, his own preference for the abrupt, the parallelistic, the diatonic, which is such a characteristic feature of his mature poetry. In fact, the essay as a whole describes many recognisable techniques of Hopkins' developed idiosyncratic style. For example, the Professor of Aesthetics persuades his student Hanbury that beauty depends upon the existence of a fine tension between regularity and irregularity of form, a tension which Hopkins himself later exploits to an extreme degree by deviating from conventional rhyming and metrical patterns with a boldness, even recklessness, which yet never quite destroys the structure. Yet while the avowed purpose of this essay, as of the others, is to 'explain' beauty and the aesthetic experience by invoking the firm objective principles upon which it rests, few readers can dismiss Hanbury's persistent doubt as readily or as confidently as the Professor of Aesthetics:

'Well', said [Hanbury], 'I must own, with all my wish for the logical ground I spoke of in discussions of taste, I feel it very unworthy to think that beauty resolves itself into a relation. However, it may be that the particular kind of beauty in a chestnut-fan, which seems after all a geometrical sort of thing, may be explained as you say, and you seem to have pulled it to pieces to exhibit that, so that I am either convinced or I really do not know what to say to the contrary; but I am sure there is in the higher forms of beauty – at least I seem to feel – something mystical, something I don't know how to call it. Is not there now something beyond what you have explained?'

'Oh! my dear friend, when one sets out with *a priori* notions – I am afraid I have lost the only chance of a disciple I ever had.'[97]

'On the Origin of Beauty: A Platonic Dialogue' is so conspicuously dependent on the aesthetic principles expounded by Ruskin in *Modern Painters*[98] that we might be forgiven for presuming that Hanbury is alluding to a similarly Ruskinian correlation between natural beauty and the divine. But, as I have suggested, the essay also addresses itself to the Kantian problem of the paradox of demanding objective explanations in the matter of taste. In which case, Hanbury's intuition of 'something mystical' in the higher forms of beauty, if given a Kantian interpretation, would suggest something rather different: a transcendental reality lying beyond the bounds of thought.

But it was exactly in order to explain this sense of the mystical, to explore *why* it is that there are on the scale of beauty certain forms which 'have a great hold on the mind', that Hopkins embarked upon the creation of his philosophy of inscape and instress. They were concepts which he hoped would illuminate why the perceptions of certain experiences of certain moments should so elevate the spirit. He wished to articulate his experiences of objects, their revelation of striking individual essences, to express the unique relationship between himself as subject and the object of his perception, to define the personal quality of that greeting, and to represent the unity of the whole experience.

In his quest for understanding of the perceptual process, Hopkins speaks, in some notes he wrote on the Greek philosopher Parmenides, of the necessity for there being a 'bridge', a 'stem of stress between us and things to bear us out and carry the mind over: without stress we might not and could not say/Blood is red/but only/ This blood is red/ or/the last blood I saw was red/.' And later in the notes he says:

Parmenides will say that the mind's grasp – ...the foredrawing act – that this is blood or that that blood is red is to be looked for in Being, the foredrawn, alone, not in the thing we named blood or the blood we worded as being red.[99]

So what is this 'stem of stress between us and things'? Hopkins seems to suggest that it lies in our recognition of the shared yet distinctive selfhood, the thisness of things in nature, a recognition made possible by our own self-awareness. This is described in 'As kingfishers catch fire':

> As kingfishers catch fire, dragonflies draw flame;
> As tumbled over rim in roundy wells
> Stones ring; like each tucked string tells, each hung bell's
> Bow swung finds tongue to fling out broad its name;
> Each mortal thing does one thing and the same:
> Deals out that being indoors each one dwells;
> Selves – goes itself; *myself* it speaks and spells,
> Crying *What I do is me: for that I came.*[100]

The things of nature are paradoxically united by their very distinctiveness, by the fact that they share a quality of selfhood. Elsewhere, in the poem 'Pied Beauty', Hopkins explores a similar paradox – that the dappled variousness of nature all stems from God, 'whose beauty is past change'.[101]

Significantly, it is in the notes on Parmenides, and in connection with the idea of there being a 'bridge' or a 'stem of stress between us and things', that we find Hopkins first using the terms 'inscape' and 'instress'. First of all, Hopkins defines the Parmenidean text 'Being is and Not-Being is not' in his own terms as signifying that 'all things are upheld by instress and are meaningless without it'. He then goes on:

But indeed I have often felt when I have been in this mood and felt the depth of an instress or how fast the inscape holds a thing that nothing is so pregnant and straightforward to the truth as simple *yes* and *is*.[102]

From this, then, it seems that instress is something within the observed object which provokes a deep-felt response, while inscape is that which defines its shape, protects its form. Through the act of perception, by way of the energy of the 'stem of stress' between the object and the subject, one inscape responds to another, for 'the way men judge in particular is determined for each by his own inscape'.[103] Hopkins' reverence for the selfhood of all created things calls forth an emotional response from within him – a response which is uniquely his. Appreciation of inscape brings new insight into the patterned logic of an object as created being, and forges a link between perceiver and perceived. The idea of inscape was implicit in his early descriptions of a world of imperishable forms at fixed distances from one another in a scale of being. The nature journals are full of descriptions of unforgettable types, described in terms of their inscape: plants 'with strongly inscaped leaves';[104] 'Sycamores grew on the slopes of the valley, scantily leaved, sharply quained and accidented by perhaps the valley winds, and often most gracefully inscaped'; [105] 'saw trees in the river flat below inscaped in distinctly projected, crisp, and almost hard, rows of loaves, their edges, especially at the top, being a little fixed and shaped with shadow'.[106]

Hopkins' description of a mass of bluebells suggests the complexity of his response:

It was a lovely sight. – The bluebells in your hand baffle you with their inscape, made to every sense: if you draw your fingers through them they are lodged and struggle/with a shock of wet heads; the long stalks rub and click and flatten to a fan on one another like your fingers themselves would when you passed the palms hard across one another, making a brittle rub and jostle like the noise of a hurdle strained by leaning against; then there is the faint honey smell and in the mouth the sweet gum when you bite them. But this is easy, it is the eye they baffle. They give one a fancy of panpipes and of some wind instrument with stops – a trombone perhaps. The overhung necks – for growing they are little more than a staff with a simple crook but in water, where they stiffen, they take stronger turns, in the head like sheephooks or, when more waved throughout, like the waves riding through a whip that is being smacked – what with these overhung necks and what with the crisped ruffled bells dropping mostly on one side and the gloss these have at their footstalks they have an air of the knights at chess. Then the knot or 'knoop' of buds some shut, some just gaping, which makes the pencil of the whole spike, should be noticed: the inscape of the flower most finely carried out in the siding of the axes, each striking a greater and greater slant, is finished in these clustered buds, which for the most part are not straightened but rise to the end like a tongue and this and their tapering and a little flattening they have make them look like the heads of snakes.[107]

His experience of inscape is extraordinarily multidimensional. It is richly sensuous, 'made to every sense' moreover: the feel, taste, smell of bluebells is powerfully and unmistakably evoked through simile; their form is painstakingly described. The description is fancifully associative. The convergence of sense impressions is suggested by the comparisons with panpipes and bells and trombones, with tongues and with snakes. The dignity of the bluebells, their suggestiveness of a more perfect realm, is implied in their 'air of the knights at chess'. They are subjected to scientific scrutiny also. Hopkins observes physical differences between the bluebell growing wild and in a vase. Above all he examines and explains their composition, the secret of their overwhelming loveliness. Instress seems to carry within itself two ideas. On the one hand it is the energy within the object which determines its being, the force which holds up its design or inscape. Thus, Hopkins says of a skyscape, 'The blue was charged with simple instress, the higher, zenith sky earnest and frowning, lower and more light and sweet.'[108] When describing Ely Cathedral, Hopkins notices 'the all-powerfulness of instress in mode and the immediateness of its effect'.[109] Without the stem of instress, inscape must collapse. In his journal, Hopkins recalls how he once woke from a nightmare and felt a terrible sensation of slackness:

The feeling is terrible: the body no longer swayed as a piece by the nervous and muscular instress seems to fall in and hang like a dead weight on the chest.[110]

And he describes death thus:

all that energy or instress with which the soul animates and otherwise acts in the body is by death thrown back upon the soul itself.[111]

The other idea contained within the concept of instress is that of the stress which an object brings to bear externally on the observer – the actual intuition whereby the inscape of the object is realised in the mind. Indeed, 'instress' frequently becomes a verb in the journals. Elsewhere, Hopkins concentrates on the actual passage of the sense of inscape to the observing mind, as in this description of bluebells:

and a notable glare the eye may abstract and sever from the blue colour/of light beating up from so many glassy heads, which like water is good to float their deeper instress in upon the mind.[112]

Within the one concept of instress, by means of this dual theory, Hopkins succeeds in maintaining the autonomy of the object through recognition of the spring of its unity, while yet actualising it still further in the mind of the participating observer who responds to an intuition of being.

III

In a journal entry for 3 August 1872, Hopkins wrote:

At this time I had first begun to get hold of the copy of Scotus on the Sentences in the Baddely library and was flush with a new stroke of enthusiasm. It may come to nothing or it may be a mercy from God. But just then when I took in any inscape of the sky or sea I thought of Scotus.[113]

It was a discovery which was to prove integral to Hopkins' subsequent aesthetic and intellectual development. The confirmation and authentication of his own insights by this venerable medieval philosopher gave Hopkins the impetus he needed to find a metaphysical and theological basis for his early theories of inscape and instress.

Christopher Devlin, in an illuminating essay on the influence of Duns Scotus on Hopkins' philosophical development,[114] shows how Hopkins' 'Notes on the history of Greek Philosophy etc' and 'All words mean either things or relations of things' and 'Parmenides', written in 1868 and hence his last writings on ideogenesis before encountering Scotus, explore a number of themes which are later to be corroborated and refined by his reading of Scotus. In general, Hopkins found in Scotus support for his own espousal of intuitive and sensory experience. In the notes on words, Hopkins distinguishes between the 'inchoate word' and the 'conception',[115] and in doing so echoes Scotus' distinction between 'knowing confusedly' and 'understanding distinctly'.[116] Both recognised the value of intuitive knowledge as a crucial prerequisite to abstract knowledge. Similarly, Hopkins found confirmation in Scotus for his own faith in the epistemological significance of sensory experience.[117]

But it is in the matter of the object of intuitive and sensory knowledge that Hopkins' ideas coincide most significantly with those of Scotus. As Devlin explains it, in Scotus' theory of knowing, the distinction between nature and individuality is more important than any other opposition, and it is represented in the process of abstractive knowing by two levels of consciousness which Scotus calls the 'first act' and the 'second act'. Devlin defines them thus:[118] the 'first act' of a being is that it exists with its various faculties; when that being, a man for example, actualises his human faculties by acts of seeing, thinking, willing, and so on, he is in 'second act'. The 'first act' is the specific form, in this case human nature, exercising an innate knowledge. The 'second act' is the striving of the individual to appropriate and adapt this power of knowing, it is the selfhood imposing its *haecceitas* (thisness) on the common nature and seeking definition and differentiation both for itself and for the other objects which belong to the common nature: 'every being which is in first act finds its ultimate perfection in its second act, through which it is united to that which is best for it'.[119] Insight, which is intuitive and sensory, is the expression of the 'first act' when it is just on the point of becoming the 'second act': it catches universal nature in the very act of individualising itself.[120] Scotus seems to suggest that before abstraction takes place and isolates the individual from the pattern, it is possible to be momentarily aware of nature evolving as a pattern of sense qualities in the very instant that we are aware of the individual that is both cause and climax of the evolution.[121] And this phenomenon Scotus calls the *species specialissima*, a term which implies a concurrent awareness of the thing as species and as individual.

This idea is as vital to inscape as it was to the *species specialissima*. In 'The Windhover', for example, inscape occurs with the intuition of the point when the nature of the bird first manifests itself in individuality. The octave presents the commanding physical being of the bird; the distinctive sweep of its wing movements, the nobility, 'the achieve of, the mastery of the thing'. Having detailed the particularity of the bird and of the response it inspires, Hopkins then goes on in the beginning of the sestet to consider the abstract qualities which the bird represents, and how they yield, 'buckle', as abstractions in the face of their vivid representation in a particular bird. The universal categories that the bird embodies collapse and synthesise in the distinctive individuality of its inscape:

> Brute beauty and valour and act, oh, air, pride, plume, here
> Buckle![122]

The bird is both a unique entity in itself and the carrier of universal and essential truth. Inscape, then, involves an immediate insight into the created nature of a thing, and a recognition of sharing in that created nature, at the same time as it involves a recognition of shared individuality. The medium of this contact is inscape, the *species specialissima*:

For the phenomenal world (and the distinction between men or subjects and things without them is unimportant in Parmenides: the contrast is between the one and the many) is the brink, limbus, lapping, run-and-mingle/of two principles which meet in the scape of everything – probably Being, under its modification or siding of particular oneness or Being, and Not-being, under its siding of the Many. The two may be called two degrees of siding in the scale of Being. Foreshortening and equivalency will explain all possible difference. The inscape will be the proportion of the mixture.[123]

Aware of the importance of individuality to both Hopkins and Scotus, critics have too readily identified 'inscape' with *haecceitas*. But Devlin alerts us to the problems of making such a correlation.[124] The word *haecceitas* is used by Scotus to represent the principle of individuation. In his discussion of universals, he demonstrates the principle of formal objective distinction by saying that although the physical nature of an object is inseparable from its *haecceitas*, its thisness, or principle of individuation, there is a formal objective distinction between nature and *haecceitas*.[125] As Frederick Copleston explains it, *haecceitas* appears to be neither matter, nor form, nor the composite thing. Without conferring any further qualitative determination than sealing the being as *this* being, it is a positive entity, the final reality of matter, form, and the composite thing.[126] If we accept *haecceitas* as the ultimate intelligible factor beneath the generic and the specific, the basis of individuality that differentiates a being from all other beings and brings it home with immediacy to our consciousness, then there would seem to be a very close correlation between *haecceitas* and inscape. Yet it is clear that Hopkins does not identify inscape with *haecceitas*, for, aware that the distinction between nature and *haecceitas* is fundamental to Scotist philosophy, he uses 'natures' and 'inscapes' as analogous terms, in opposition to 'selves':

For in the world, besides natures or essences or 'inscapes' and the selves, supposits, hypostases, or, in the case of rational natures, persons/ which wear and 'fetch' or instance them, there is still something else – fact or fate.[127]

Instead, Hopkins himself mentions 'Scotus's *ecceitas*' in relation to his own theory of moral pitch, or *arbitrium*:

So also *pitch* is ultimately simple positiveness, that by which being differs from and is more than nothing and not-being, and it is with precision expressed by the English *do* (the simple auxiliary), which when we employ or emphasise, as 'he said it, he did say it', we do not mean that the fact is any more a fact but that we the more state it. . . So that this pitch might be expressed, if it were good English, *the doing* be, *the doing* choose, *the doing* so-and-so in that sense. Where there was no question of will it would become mere fact; where there is will it is free action, moral action. And such 'doing-be', and the thread or chain of such pitches or 'doing-be's' prior to nature's being overlaid, is self, personality; but it is not truly self: self or personality then truly comes into being when the self, the person, comes into being with the accession of nature.

Is not this pitch or whatever we call it then the same as Scotus' *ecceitas*?[128]

This is the moral pitch of conscious and active response to God's stress expressed in the use of the emphatic auxiliary in 'I did say yes/O at lightning and lashed rod'.[129]

Devlin suggests that the most fundamental connection between Hopkins and Scotus is to be found in Scotus' idea that the process of 'being created' is the same as the substance of 'created being',[130] and Hopkins' identification of this notion with his own concept of stress in the essay on Parmenides. For both men, behind all forms of evolving nature is something which transcends all categories and species yet includes all created things. We may discern its operation first and foremost within our own selves, for the finite human soul has a natural desire for the infinite, from which arises a confused idea of 'being', which lies somewhere between infinity and finitude. Our introspective awareness enables us to form a concept of being. In his essay on Parmenides, Hopkins takes the text 'Being is and Not-Being is not' and, as we have seen, translates it into his own terms of inscape and instress. There must be, he argues, behind our perception of the fact of inter-subjectivity, some concept of universal being.

This brings us back full circle to Hopkins' central concern with the process of perception, and to our definition of his concept of inscape. Alan Heuser, tracing the word back to its Greek, Latin and Old English roots, finds an etymological link between its aesthetic and religious connotations. 'Inscape', he suggests, derives from Latin *scapus*, Greek *skapos*, meaning 'shaft of a column/tongue of a balance/flower stalk, stem', while Old English ȝesceap translates as 'creation, creature/make, structure/decree, destiny'. Hence he concludes that Hopkins' word 'inscape' means 'created form held fast by evidence of creative power'.[131] It remains to be seen how exactly the idea of inscape, with its aesthetic sense of uniqueness and beauty of form, was bound up for Hopkins with the divine.

IV

Hopkins found himself stimulated by his reading of Scotus in 1872 perhaps only as a result of a more significant watershed in his life some six years earlier. On 28 August 1866, Hopkins, then twenty-two years old, wrote to the Rev. Dr John Henry Newman expressing his wish to be converted to Roman Catholicism as the 'only consistent position'.[132] It was a decision which was to prove crucial to the development of his aesthetic theories – indeed, he wrote to his friend Baillie in September 1865 'of the difference the apprehension of the Catholic truths one after another makes in one's views of everything'.[133]

Hopkins entered the Society of Jesus in 1868 and during the years of his novitiate became thoroughly instilled with the meditative methods of St Ignatius as prescribed by the *Spiritual Exercises*. The standard meditative exercise consists of three main stages.[134] As a prelude, the meditator imagines the corporeal place as a vivid concrete setting for his meditation. By a process of allegorical thinking, he feels the theological issue as part of a living dramatic scene. Such 'composition of place, seeing the spot' is a prerequisite of intellectual analysis of the problem and subsequent understanding, whereupon the reformed soul is lifted up to speak with God, Christ, or the Virgin in colloquy. The art of meditation fosters among those who practise it a power of intense concentration on some object which focuses the soul and the consciousness. It creates a central habitual mode of thinking whereby the devout individual quite naturally finds the transcendental in the world around him. With the encouragement of the *Spiritual Exercises* Hopkins sought the final link in the chain which would explain the ecstatic joy that the instress of nature's inscapes gave him. Indeed, his theories are articulated primarily in his commentary on the *Spiritual Exercises*.

The Incarnation of Christ, the act in which human and divine meet, was the focus of Hopkins' Christianity:

our lives, and particularly those of religious, as mine, are in their whole direction, not only inwardly but most visibly and outwardly, shaped by Christ's. Without that even outwardly the world could be so different that we cannot even guess it. And my life is determined by the Incarnation down to most of the details of the day. Now this being so that I cannot even stop it, why should I not make the cause that determines my life, both as a whole and in much detail, determine it in greater detail still and to the greater efficiency of what I in any case should do, and to my greater happiness in doing it?[135]

Once again Hopkins' reading of Scotus was to have a decisive effect on the development and sophistication of his own idiosyncratic theory of the Incarnation. Scotus maintained that in God's original design Christ would have come to a sinless world in order to demonstrate his love for God – in other words that the Incarnation was not contingent upon sin, and was not primarily for the purpose of redemption.[136]

Scotus' theory of the Incarnation was integral to Hopkins' own theory of the Great Sacrifice, which in turn led to the fulfilment of the inscape theory. While meditating on the 'Three Sins' as part of the *Spiritual Exercises*, Hopkins suddenly understood the real meaning of the Incarnation. He saw the coming of Christ into the world as a voluntary sacrifice to God. He shared St Paul's great insight into the mind of Christ,[137] and this inspiration gave him something on which to model his own beliefs and his ideas about the meaning of creation:

being in the form of God...he thought it nevertheless no snatching-matter for him to be equal with God, but annihilated himself, taking the form of a servant;...and then being in the guise of man humbled himself to death, the death of the cross. It is this holding of himself back, and not snatching at the truest and highest good, the good that was his right, nay his possession from a past eternity in his other nature, his own being and self, which seems to me the root of all his holiness and the imitation of this the root of all moral good in other men.[138]

Christ's descent into creation was for Hopkins not primarily as a reparation for sin, but an act of love, and as such all created nature was dependent upon it – the world was created for the purpose of revealing Christ's adoration of the Father. This idea may be discerned in several of Hopkins' sermons, notably the Liverpool trilogy, 'The Kingdom of God', and the sermon 'The Feast of the Precious Blood':

Reigning in heaven he could not worship the Father, but when he became man and entered upon his new nature the first thing he did in it was to adore God in it... Christ no sooner found himself in human nature than he blessed and hallowed it by saluting his heavenly Father, raising his new heart to him and offering all his new being to his honour. That offering was accepted, but he was told that the sacrifice must be accomplished on the cross of shame.[139]

In his commentary on the *Spiritual Exercises*, applying this idea to human psychology, Hopkins shows how this original design moulds our consciousness so that we are able to regard the world as it was originally intended alongside the world of actuality. The original design, he suggests, continues to inspire the ideal of human nature in spite of the Fall of man, and makes possible the operation of divine grace and the response of man's free will.

In 1878, Hopkins came across the works of Marie Lataste, and was influenced by her theory of the two 'movements' given to the world by God: by the first design, the creative strain, men are moved according to their natures; by the second, the redemptive strain, men act as free agents, according to their exercise of free will. Hopkins copied out the following from her writings:

L'homme vient de Dieu et doit retourner à Dieu. Il y a deux mouvements en l'homme: de son être créé par Dieu vers l'existence et de son être existant vers Dieu. Ces deux mouvements sont donnés à l'homme par Dieu; et par ces deux mouvements, l'homme, s'il le veut, retournera infailliblement à Dieu. Je dis s'il le veut, parce que l'homme peut changer la direction de ce mouvement...

Aujourd'hui, tout homme reçoit, comme au commencement, le premier mouvement, qui le lance dans la vie; mais le second mouvement, qui relance l'homme vivant vers Dieu, ne lui est plus donné avec le premier mouvement. Le second mouvement le lance vivant dans la mort; mais je suis là pour ressaisir l'homme par le baptême et le remettre sur le chemin qui mène à Dieu. Alors tout est réparé: l'homme est régénéré; il marchera, s'il le veut, vers Dieu ou retournera à Satan dont je l'ai délivré; il marchera dans la vérité ou le mensonge.[140]

In the fifth exercise, 'A Meditation on Hell', Hopkins seems to echo this idea when speaking of the fallen angels and men:

[The strain or tendency towards being, towards good, towards God] must go on after their fall, because it is the strain of creating action as received in the creature and cannot cease without the creature's ceasing to be. On the other hand the strain or tendency towards God through Christ and the great sacrifice had by their own act been broken, refracted, and turned aside, and it was only through Christ and the great sacrifice that God has meant any being to come to him at all.[141]

God is present in nature in two ways: His creative design exists alongside Christ's redemptive inscape in nature and, more pointedly, in the moral life of humanity.

Hopkins connects the idea of the two strains in creation with Scotus' theory of the Incarnation and his distinction between nature and personality to form his own theory of the Great Sacrifice, henceforth the focal point of his speculative energies. Had man never sinned, Christ's Incarnation would have been the natural fulfilment of the creative strain, and man's mind would have been harmoniously at one with God. However, as a result of the Fall, man's natural values became perverted and Christ had to refocus them by his redemptive suffering. Henceforth, the world became identified with sacrifice:

It is as if the blissful agony or stress of selving in God had forced out drops of sweat or blood, which drops were the world, or as if the lights lit at the festival of that 'peaceful Trinity' through some little cranny striking out lit up into being one 'cleave' of the world of possible creatures.[142]

For Hopkins, these two visions of the world, the original design, and the reality of man's sin and Christ's redemption, coexist in a kind of moral counterpoint:

Suppose God shewed us in a vision the whole world inclosed first in a drop of water, allowing everything to be seen in its native colours; then the same in a drop of Christ's blood, by which everything whatever was turned scarlet, keeping nevertheless mounted in the scarlet its own colour too.[143]

As Alan Heuser explains it, as well as finding the 'unity of creative source' in nature, Hopkins found that all created things were completed by 'unity of redemptive destiny' in the ideal human nature of Christ incarnate. The essential nature or idea of every creature is hence one with the created nature of Christ, and sensuous intuition of common nature is drawn to Christ as its innate type. Henceforth, the instress of nature's inscapes, 'the fixed type between natural form and essential idea', was a means for a vision of Christ. Inscape became a re-enactment of the Incarnation.[144] This is literally the burden of the nun's experience in 'The Wreck of the Deutschland'.[145] 'The cross to her she calls Christ to her, christens her wild-worst Best', and in so doing 'Read the unshapeable shock night/And knew the who and the why'. The nun is specifically identified with the Virgin Mary,[146] and seen, through her recognition of Christ in the inscape of the storm, and her utterance of the cry, as conceiving him anew. Christ is tangibly present to her in the storm:

> But how shall I...make me room there:
> Reach me a...Fancy, come faster –
> Strike you the sight of it? look at it loom there,
> Thing that she...There then! the Master,
> *Ipse*, the only one, Christ, King, Head.

In the poem, Hopkins uses the nun's experience of the reincarnation of Christ in the storm as a symbolic illustration of his earlier evocation of Christ's mysterious presence in nature:

> Not out of his bliss
> Springs the stress felt
> Nor first from heaven (and few know this)
> Swings the stroke dealt –
> Stroke and a stress that stars and storms deliver,
> That guilt is hushed by, hearts are flushed by and melt –
> But it rides time like riding a river
> (And here the faithful waver, the faithless fable and miss).

> It dates from day
> Of his going in Galilee;
> Warm-laid grave of a womb-life grey;
> Manger, maiden's knee;
> The dense and the driven Passion, and frightful sweat...

The whole poem offers a 'justification of the ways of God to men' by showing how the storm is symbolic of Christ's crucifixion as the stars are of his beauty. The nun's recognition and acceptance of Christ's inscape in the storm allows her to participate not only in His suffering, but in His redemption. It allows Hopkins' interpretation of God's role in His 'sea-romp' as 'martyr-master', and of the fatal storm as 'A released shower, let flash to the shire, not a lightning of fire hard-hurled'. In 'The Wreck of the Deutschland' we are invited to 'Grasp God, throned behind/Death', to allow Christ, 'Our passion-plungèd giant risen', to 'easter in us', and frequently in Hopkins' mature poems we

find images of the redemption of Christ imprinted on nature. In
'God's Grandeur':

> ...though the last lights off the black West went
> Oh, morning, at the brown brink eastward, springs –
> Because the Holy Ghost over the bent
> World broods with warm breast and with ah! bright wings.[147]

The cycles of nature bear witness to the Resurrection: morning follows
the blackest night, Spring follows Autumn. The Great Sacrifice is
rescued by 'the Resurrection/A heart's-clarion', and the recognition
of Christ's Resurrection leads to understanding and acceptance of
personal redemption, of the miraculous paradox that 'This Jack, joke,
poor potsherd, | patch, matchwood, immortal diamond,/Is immortal
diamond'.[148]

The illumination of the Great Sacrifice set the seal to Hopkins'
theory of inscape, spiritualised his aesthetic philosophy, and intellectually authorised the sanctification of sensory experience that we find, for
example, in his vision of 'God's utterance of Himself' at St Winifred's
Well:

The strong unfailing flow of the water and the chain of cures from year to
year all these centuries took hold of my mind with wonder at the bounty
of God in one of His saints, the sensible thing so naturally and gracefully
uttering the spiritual reason of its being...and the spring in place leading
back the thoughts by its spring in time to its spring in eternity: even now
the stress and buoyancy and abundance of the water is before my eyes.[149]

Henceforth, both the beauty and the specific essence, the dignity, even
the danger of created things could be explained by their derivation from
their likeness to some aspect of the divine essence. For Hopkins, as
Hillis Miller explains, all things are created in Christ, who is the model
of all things made. He is the common nature who contains in Himself
all natures. Yet Christ is uniquely individual, in that He possesses a
whole specific nature. Normal human beings are individuals because
they are differentiated from the species of humanity as a whole: Christ
is individual because His humanity is a perfect whole species by itself.
Yet the individual created natures all partake in the perfect human–divine
nature of Christ. Inscapes are versions of the whole nature of Christ:
they participate directly in and are completed by the ideal human
nature of Christ.[150] Christ is the ultimate inscape, the personification
and perfection of created nature. Hence the joy Hopkins felt in the
perception of natural forms – for they were no less than a medium
through which he could instress Christ:

God's utterance of himself in himself is God the Word, outside himself
is this world. This world then is word, expression, news of God. Therefore
its end, its purpose, its purport, its meaning, is God and its life or work
to name and praise him.[151]

Christ, like the things of nature, had His inscape, His 'law' to be
understood. He too was there to be instressed. Instress of Christ could
be intuitive, and it seems that for Hopkins this was the natural response
once he had understood Christ as the defining principle of inscape:

As we drove home the stars came out thick: I leant back to look at them
and my heart opening more than usual praised our Lord to and in whom
all that beauty comes home.[152]

and:

I do not think I have ever seen anything more beautiful than the bluebell
I have been looking at. I know the beauty of our Lord by it. It[s inscape]
is [mixed of] strength and grace, like an ash [tree].[153]

Sometimes it was simply a question of 'gleaning' Him from, or 'wafting
Him out of' nature.[154] Sometimes He seemed actually to be physically
present: 'And the azurous hung hills are his world-wielding shoulder/
Majestic'.[155] At times, Hopkins spontaneously uses imagery that recalls
Christ, as in his description of an aurora:

It gathered. . .a knot or crown, not a true circle, of dull, blood-coloured
horns and dropped long red beams down the sky on every side, each
impaling its lot of stars.[156]

And sometimes inscape of Christ came quite unexpectedly and raided
hidden emotional reserves within him. More than once in his journals he
recalls how he was moved to tears, 'Not seeing in my reason the traces
of an adequate cause for such strong emotion.'[157]

V

With his discovery of the redemptive strain in nature and the Great
Sacrifice Hopkins' interests shifted from the presence of Christ's
inscape in nature to the completion of that design, through stress and
instress, in man. He found an identifiable moral strain in inanimate
nature. In 'The Windhover', for example, the sacrifice of Christ is
seen imprinted like a physical law on the lowliest forms in nature:

> . . .shéer plód makes plough down sillion
> Shine, and blue-bleak embers, ah my dear,
> Fall, gall themselves, and gash gold-vermilion.[158]

There is much in Hopkins' nature writings that corresponds to the resilience of Ruskin's little mountain flower whose beauty lies in the fact that it struggles to survive in a place where no other vegetation could grow.[159] Despite man's efforts to 'sear, blear, and smear' the natural world, it manages to retain its integrity:

> And for all this, nature is never spent;
> There lives the dearest freshness deep down things.[160]

But nature is inarticulate. It has to await interpretation by man. This is the burden of the poem entitled 'Ribblesdale':

> Earth, sweet Earth, sweet landscape, with leavès throng
> And louchèd low grass, heaven that dost appeal
> To, with no tongue to plead, no heart to feel;
> That canst but only be, but dost that long –
>
> Thou canst but be, but that thou well dost; strong
> Thy plea with him who dealt, nay does now deal,
> Thy lovely dale down thus and thus bids reel
> Thy river, and o'er gives all to rack or wrong.
>
> And what is Earth's eye, tongue, or heart else, where
> Else, but in dear and dogged man? – Ah, the heir
> To his own selfbent so bound, so tied to his turn,
>
> To thriftless reave both our rich round world bare
> And none reck of world after, this bids wear
> Earth brows of such care, care and dear concern.[161]

Here, ironically, man is so self-absorbed, so incognisant of 'him who dealt', that it is he who is 'earthbound' and Earth who pleads and cares.

However, man's potential for the glorification of God through the imitation of Christ's example is infinitely greater:

> The sun and the stars shining glorify God. They stand where he placed them, they move where he bid them. 'The heavens declare the glory of God.' They glorify God, *but they do not know it.* The birds sing to him, the thunder speaks of his terror, the lion is like his strength, the sea is like his greatness, the honey like his sweetness; they are something like him, they make him known, they tell of him, they give him glory, but they do not know they do, they do not know him, they never can...But AMIDST THEM ALL IS MAN...Man was created. Like the rest then to praise, reverence, and serve God; to give him glory. He does so, even by his being, beyond all visible creatures:...But man can know God, *can mean to give him glory.* This then was why he was made, to give God glory and to mean to give it.[162]

This, the most active instress of Christ, evolves from the recognition that the deliberate stress from God is a call which demands a violent

and, if necessary, self-sacrificing response from the human spirit. Such
is the theme of 'The Wreck of the Deutschland'. First of all God exerts
stress, offers grace:

For grace is any action, activity, on God's part by which, in creating or
after creating, he carries the creature to or towards the end of its being,
which is its selfsacrifice to God and its salvation. It is, I say, any such
activity on God's part; so that so far as this action or activity is God's it is
divine stress, holy spirit, and, as all is done through Christ, Christ's
spirit; so far as it is action, correspondence, on the creature's it is *actio
salutaris*; so far as it is looked at *in esse quieto* it is Christ in his member
on the one side, his member in Christ on the other. It is as if a man said:
That is Christ playing at me and me playing at Christ, only that it is no
play but truth; That is Christ *being me* and me being Christ.

Having received God's grace, then, the will must respond:

For there must be something which shall be truly the creature's in the
work of corresponding with grace: this is the *arbitrium*, the verdict on
God's side, the saying Yes, the 'doing-agree'...[163]

When speaking of the will, Hopkins distinguishes between 'that which
decides action in us, *arbitrium*' and 'the faculty which is affected well or
ill towards things, *voluntas*'. The *arbitrium* he terms the 'faculty at
pitch', the *voluntas* the 'faculty at splay'.[164] Again he draws distinctions
between nature and individuality:

the self...supplies the determination, the difference, ...the nature...
supplies the exercise, and in these two things freedom consists.[165]

Elsewhere he terms these 'affective will' (*voluntas*) and 'elective will'
(*arbitrium*). The *arbitrium*, the moral will, acts its part after Christ,
responds with love to God's grace, a fact which Hopkins stresses by
making 'justice' a verb in the sestet of 'As kingfishers catch fire', in
which he pays homage to man's inscape:

> I say more: the just man justices;
> Keeps gráce: thát keeps all his goings graces;
> Acts in God's eye what in God's eye he is –
> Chríst. For Christ plays in ten thousand places,
> Lovely in limbs, and lovely in eyes not his
> To the Father through the features of men's faces.[166]

Devlin alerted us to the fallacy of equating inscape too simply with
Scotus' *haecceitas*, on the grounds that inscape represents a tension
between specific nature and individuality. A similarly strong, yet
modified sense of self is maintained in Hopkins' religious philosophy.
His sense of the selfhood of God's creatures is nowhere more striking
than in man, nature's 'clearest-selvèd spark'. Man's inscape, that which

makes him unique among God's creatures, is that he can be like Christ in terms of his character: he has a moral life, and a religious life, he can praise God, and 'can mean to give him glory'. This is the inscape of man as species. Within the type, however, each man has also his own unique sense of self, a sense which Hopkins attempts to articulate in his notes on the *Spiritual Exercises*:

I find myself both as man and as myself something most determined and distinctive, at pitch, more distinctive and higher pitched than anything else I see; I find myself with my pleasures and pains, my powers and experiences, my deserts and guilt, my shame and sense of beauty, my dangers, hopes, fears, and all my fate, more important to myself than anything else I see...when I consider my self being, my consciousness and feeling of myself, that taste of myself, of *I* and *me* above and in all things, which is more distinctive than the taste of ale or alum, more distinctive than the smell of walnutleaf or camphor, and is incommunicable by any means to another man (as when I was a child I used to ask myself: What must it be to be someone else?). Nothing else in nature comes near this unspeakable stress of pitch, distinctiveness, and selving, this self-being of my own. Nothing explains it or resembles it, except so far as this, that other men to themselves have the same feeling. But this only multiplies the phenomena to be explained so far as the cases are like and do resemble. But to me there is no resemblance: searching nature I taste *self* but at one tankard, that of my own being. The development, refinement, condensation of nothing shews any sign of being able to match this to me or give me another taste of it, a taste even resembling it.[167]

But it is significant that this is taken from an argument for the existence of a creator. Hopkins finds the ultimate objective reality of God through his very sense of self. And this is true, in a larger sense, of his whole philosophy. His own selfhood, and his sense of the selves of natural things, brings access to the divine self:

the tendency in the soul towards an infinite object comes from the *arbitrium*. The *arbitrium* in itself is man's personality or individuality and places him on a level of individuality in some sense with God; so that in so far as God is one thing, a self, an individual being, he is an object of apprehension, desire, pursuit, to man's *arbitrium*.[168]

In accordance with the prominence Hopkins gives to the selfhood of the things of nature, to the selfhood of man, and to his own personal sense of self, Hopkins conceives of God as the supreme self. In this the most original aspect of his theory of inscape, Hopkins finds in God's inscape, 'Christ, *Ipse*, the only one', the qualities of uniqueness, physical and moral beauty, and praise, which we recognised as comprising the inscapes of man and nature, only in an infinitely higher sense. In Christ, the ultimate pattern of personality, man may encounter, through a consciousness of his own individuality, the personality of God:

> The Trinity made man after the image of their one nature but they redeem him...by bringing into play with infinite charity their personality. Being personal, they see as if with sympathy the play of personality in man below them, for in his personality his freedom lies and this same personality playing in its freedom not only exerts and displays the riches and capacities of his one nature...but unhappily disunites it, rends it, and almost tears it to pieces. One of them, therefore makes himself one of those throng of persons, a man among men, by charity to bring them back to that unity with themselves which they have lost by freedom and even to bring them to a union with God which nothing in their nature gave them.[169]

Hopkins explains the entire Christian story in terms of personality, and in so doing makes the principle of personality, of selfhood, of inscape, central to his aesthetic, and the cornerstone of his religious philosophy. At the core of things is the very personality of Christ, his 'burl of being', 'and for every man there is his own burl of being, which are all "by lays" or "by falls" of Christ's and of one another's'.[170]

Through his insight into the selfhood of the incarnate Christ, Hopkins finds an objective authority for the subjective experience of inscape, and in so doing solves long-standing problems of perception in Romantic aesthetics. The essence of the poetry of Wordsworth and of the epistemological systems of Kant and Coleridge is self-consciousness. Kant's aesthetic and teleological writings share the subjective Idealism of his metaphysical doctrines. He attempts in his three Critiques to show that, although we can only know the world from our own limited perspective, our knowledge claims, moral judgements, and judgements of taste have universal validity. Our knowledge of nature, for example, depends upon the 'transcendental unity of apperception',[171] a unified self-conscious experience, which itself derives from something beyond our experience. Kant believed that positive knowledge of the soul is not possible by means of pure reason, because the transcendental is essentially unknowable. We cannot, then, know ourselves as noumena through pure reason. He suggests, though, that it may be possible to discover, by means other than pure reason,

> a spontaneity through which our reality would be determinable, independently of the conditions of empirical intuition. And we should also become aware that in the consciousness of our existence there is contained something *a priori*, which can serve to determine our existence – the

complete determination of which is possible only in sensible terms – as being related, in respect of a certain inner faculty, to a non-sensible intelligible world.[172]

But Kant never really satisfactorily identifies that 'something *a priori*' which determines and individuates the selfhood of things. Kant was a theist. He believed that the universe was governed by moral laws, but he rejected orthodox expressions of dogma, and in particular belief in the Incarnation of God. Hopkins transforms Kantian subjective Idealism, as he transformed the sacramental poetic tradition, by making it Christocentric. He seizes upon that self-consciousness which is so definitive of Kant's method and, in the theory of inscape, unites it with the principle of divine immanence. Through the medium of inscape, Hopkins perceives the transcendental self not only as the bridge between selves in the act of perception, but as a distinct noumenal thing, in the form of a universal spirit of being, in which the objects of the phenomenal world participate. And, again through the experience of inscape, Hopkins identifies the transcendental self, or the inscape of each created thing in nature, with Christ, the supreme self, who determines the principle of individuation in the world. In this way, Hopkins succeeds in maintaining a dialectic between an intense, and avowedly subjective, sense of the individuality of nature, and an equally strong sense of objective meaning guaranteed by God's immanence.

VI

Many of Hopkins' poems have an experience of inscape as their subject: 'The Wreck of the Deutschland' re-enacts the inscape of Christ in the mystical experiences of Hopkins and the tall nun; 'The Windhover' and 'Hurrahing in Harvest' describe the inscape of Christ through the beauty of nature; 'As kingfishers catch fire' is about the selving of all God's creatures; and 'Binsey Poplars' is about how nature's inscapes are destroyed by man. A prose account of the content of these poems might give us some understanding of what Hopkins meant by inscape. But the idea of inscape is just as crucial to an understanding of their form and style.[173]

In a much-quoted letter to his friend Robert Bridges, in defence of the eccentricities of his own poetic style, Hopkins wrote:

No doubt my poetry errs on the side of oddness...But as air, melody, is what strikes me most of all in music and design in painting, so design, pattern or what I am in the habit of calling 'inscape' is what I above all aim at in poetry. Now it is the virtue of design, pattern, or inscape to be distinctive and it is the vice of distinctiveness to become queer. This vice I cannot have escaped.[174]

A poem sustains an inscape in itself. Hence the importance of the qualities of originality and uniqueness that Hopkins attaches to the work of art. For Hopkins, poetry is the creation of a pattern of words which is so highly wrought that it cannot resemble any other word-shape.[175] A poem must have its distinctive self-taste, must represent the one set of words that alone can utter a particular experience.

From his early undergraduate essay 'Poetic Diction', written in 1865, to his lectures on rhetoric given at Manresa House, Roehampton, from 1873 to 1874, Hopkins argued that structure is essential to the definition of poetry. In a short fragment on 'Poetry and Verse', probably written in 1874, he specifically describes poetry in terms of inscape:

Poetry is speech framed for contemplation of the mind by the way of hearing or speech framed to be heard for its own sake and interest even over and above its interest of meaning. Some matter and meaning is essential to it but only as an element necessary to support and employ the shape which is contemplated for its own sake. (Poetry is in fact speech only employed to carry the inscape of speech for the inscape's sake – and therefore the inscape must be dwelt on...)[176]

This is not an early expression of 'art for art's sake' doctrines, although it may be easily confused with such ideas. Rather, Hopkins is claiming the defining principle of poetry, as opposed to simple speech or prose, to be its structure. That which distinguishes it is its inscape. In this way, verse became for Hopkins the inscape of spoken sound. The unity of art, its structural principles, were linked to the revelation of inscape.

In his lecture notes on rhetoric, Hopkins recalls a principle he enunciated earlier in 'On the Origin of Beauty: A Platonic Dialogue' when he maintains that a degree of deviation from the regular structure of verse does not detract from its unity. His own poetic anonymity in the delivery of these lectures makes the self-justification inherent in his argument none the less poignant:

All intermittent elements of verse, as alliteration, rhyme. It should be understood that these various means of breaking the sameness of rhythm, and especially caesura do not break the unity of the verse but the contrary; they make it organic and what is organic is one. All the parts of water are alike but the parts of man's body differ and man's individuality is marked but the individual being a waterdrop has is gone when it falls into water again. And in everything the more remote the ratio of the parts to one another or the whole the greater the unity if felt at all...[177]

It is significant that individuality, or distinctiveness, and form, the two most important aesthetic principles of inscape, are brought together here in a discussion of the structural parts of poetry.

For purposes of definition, Hopkins declared that the meaning of a poem was of secondary importance to its form. Yet his stress on form is often linked to the meaning of a poem. In his essay 'Poetic Diction', having proposed that 'the artificial part of poetry...reduces itself to the principle of parallelism' in rhyme, metre, assonance, alliteration, and rhythm, he continues:

> Now the force of this recurrence is to beget a recurrence or parallelism answering to it in the words or thought and, speaking roughly and rather for the tendency than the invariable result, the more marked parallelism in structure whether of elaboration or of emphasis begets more marked parallelism in the words and sense. And moreover parallelism in expression tends to beget or passes into parallelism in thought.[178]

Hopkins made a similar observation in the notes he made on words in his 'Notes on the history of Greek Philosophy' three years later:

> The further in anything, as a work of art, the organisation is carried out, the deeper the form penetrates, the prepossession flushes the matter, the more effort will be required in apprehension, the more power of comparison, the more capacity for receiving that synthesis of (either successive or spatially distinct) impressions which gives us the unity with the prepossession conveyed by it.[179]

But it is with the unit on which poetry is based, the word, that Hopkins concerns himself mainly in both the essay 'Poetic Diction' and the notes 'All words mean either things or relations of things'. In the latter, he tries to discriminate between the different kinds of meaning that a word has. He begins by saying that all words 'mean' things, and that, in addition to its definition in the form of its vocal expression, and its application to concrete things, 'to every word meaning a thing and not a relation belongs a passion or prepossession or enthusiasm which it has the power of suggesting or producing'.[180] This prepossession of feeling, which he links with the 'form' or 'soul' of the word, suggests a connotative meaning of some mystical energy which first gave the word meaning in relation to reality. Pursuing the question of the way a word corresponds with reality, he perceives the word as 'the expression, *uttering* of the idea in the mind'. Words recreate for Hopkins the singular or specific qualities of phenomena as they are experienced. Each word is witness to a dynamic interplay of mind and world.[181] As such, consciousness depends upon verbal expression:

To be and to know or Being and thought are the same. The truth in thought is Being, stress, and each word is one way of acknowledging Being and each sentence by its copula *is* (or its equivalent) the utterance and assertion of it.[182]

Words bring about a kind of incarnation. The realisation of a thing in a word engenders a selving both in the concrete thing to which it refers and in the utterer.

If we return to 'The Wreck of the Deutschland', this is exactly the significance of the tall nun's cry 'O Christ, Christ, come quickly':

> For so conceivèd, so to conceive thee is done;
> But here was heart-throe, birth of a brain,
> Word, that heard and kept thee and uttered thee outright.[183]

In the context of the poem, the word is 'Christ', and she words it 'how but by him that present and past,/Heaven and earth are word of, worded by?' Yet it is hard to avoid the conclusion that all utterance, and therefore all meaning for Hopkins stems from God's expression of himself:

God's utterance of himself in himself is God the Word, outside himself is this world. This world then is word, expression, news of God.[184]

So for Hopkins the idiosyncrasy of his own diction, the many eccentricities of his language, may be related to the fact that the soul of their utterance is Christ, God's utterance of himself.

The great artist, he believed, can express his distinctiveness without lapsing into 'd——d subjective rot'.[185] In his great poem on artistic genius, 'Henry Purcell', he praises 'so arch-especial a spirit as he was,' who, 'whereas other musicians have given utterance to the moods of men's minds...has, beyond that, uttered in notes the very make and species of man as created both in him and in all men generally':

> Not mood in him nor meaning, proud fire or sacred fear,
> Or love or pity or all that sweet notes not his might nursle:
> It is the forgèd feature finds me; it is the rehearsal
> Of own, of abrúpt sélf there so thrusts on, so throngs the ear.[186]

Purcell, inscaped in his music, expresses in his distinctive genius the generic beauty of humanity.[187] Elsewhere, Hopkins wrote, 'each poet is like a species in nature...and can never recur'.[188] As such, the inscape of the poet/genius is the closest human approximation to Christ, whose humanity was a perfect whole species unto itself. Just as Christ, possessing a whole human nature, is selved in His distinctive inscape, so human genius is the inscape of human nature.

In his theory of inscape, then, Hopkins managed to accommodate his acute self-awareness, his aesthetic sensibility, and his poetry within the bounds of his faith. Yet the true picture is sometimes distorted by the critical effort to systematise a poet's thought, and it must be said that, although the philosophy of inscape that we can piece together from Hopkins' writings is very convincing intellectually, the synthesis did not always hold up for him in practice. One has only to look at the 'terrible' sonnets, and at some of the letters he wrote in the last years of his life, to see a man racked with self-criticism and spiritual pain.

We can distinguish two different yet related problems. We are struck first of all by his general sense of inadequacy, by a spiritual depression which seemed at times to overcome him and to destroy his sense of the purposefulness of his life. It is clear that his understanding of inscape did not always give him the faith and support he needed. This is perhaps due to the simple fact that Hopkins' religious criteria were so very rigorous. He made extraordinary demands upon himself, both as a priest and as a poet, and he made similar demands upon his God. Not only his religion, but his whole style of participating in the world required considerable strength and energy, resources which he could not always call upon. In a journal entry, he describes walking home from Blackburn to Stonyhurst College:

From Blackburn I walked: infinite stiles and sloppy fields, for there has been much rain. A few big shining drops hit us aslant as if they were blown off from eaves or leaves. Bright sunset: all the sky hung with tall tossed clouds, in the west with strong printing glass edges, westward lamping with tipsy bufflights, the colour of yellow roses. Parlick Ridge like a pale goldish skin without body. The plain about Clitheroe was sponged out by a tall white storm of rain. The sun itself and the spot of 'session' dappled with big laps and flowers-in-damask of cloud...But we hurried too fast and it knocked me up...In fact, being unwell I was quite downcast: nature in all her parcels and faculties gaped and fell apart, *fatiscebat*, like a clod cleaving and holding only by strings of root. But this must often be.[189]

As a metaphor for his whole life, with its sensitivity, its grand unity of vision, yet its vulnerability and fragility, this diary entry is perhaps the most eloquent passage Hopkins ever wrote.

Secondly, there is the problem of his sense of the inappropriateness for a Jesuit priest of writing poetry. According to Ignatian and Scotist principles, poetry is a thing of beauty without entitive value. It does not represent a proper dedication of the self to God, but is what Scotus would have called a 'morally indifferent' act. For Hopkins, this was true of all beauty that was not 'given back' to God, for beauty is like primal innocence, 'A strain of the earth's sweet being in the beginning/In

Eden garden',[190] untested, inactive, morally indifferent. Hopkins for one had to pass beyond it:

> What do then? how meet beauty? | Merely meet it; own,
> Home at heart, heaven's sweet gift; | then leave, let that alone.
> Yea, wish that though, wish all, | God's better beauty, grace.[191]

Hopkins was not always able to assimilate his individuality, his distinctiveness as a poet, to the religious character or 'nature' that he had assumed. At times his rebel self provoked in him a soured sense of personality, of 'helpless loathing',[192] a foretaste of perdition:

> I am gall, I am heartburn. God's most deep decree
> Bitter would have me taste: my taste was me;
> Bones built in me, flesh filled, blood brimmed the curse.
>
> Selfyeast of spirit a dull dough sours. I see
> The lost are like this, and their scourge to be
> As I am mine, their sweating selves; but worse.[193]

His sense of his failure of will, his failure to submit his personality to God's service, was certainly one cause of the spiritual anxiety he experienced increasingly in the last years of his life.

This points to an unresolved paradox in Hopkins' synthesis of religious and aesthetic experience. The theory of inscape, founded on the paradoxical nature of Christ, conjoins an aesthetic which prizes above all else the principle of selfhood with a faith which demands submission and self-sacrifice. Hopkins' uniquely original poetic style, with its extraordinary fusion of self-expression and discipline, can be seen as a brilliant illustration of inscape. But are we, and was Hopkins, intellectualising away the real meaning of the violence of his poetic language by explaining it only as a necessary and desirable function of inscape in art? Is it more legitimate to interpret his characteristically tense and strenuous rhythms as symptomatic of repression?

There can be few readers of Hopkins' poetry who do not find his style excessively convoluted at times, to the point of becoming obscure, or even absurd. Hopkins did not need Bridges to point out that his distinctiveness of style might easily err into oddness. He wrote to his friend and critic, 'I find myself that when I am tired things of mine sound strange, forced, and without idiom, which had pleased me well enough in the fresh heat of composition.'[194] In fact, while inscape remains the dominating principle of his poetry, in many of his critical comments on literature, Hopkins explores the inevitable problems associated with originality and individuality in art. He is alert not only to critical conservativeness in the reader, but to the ease with which a poet may lapse into what he calls 'Parnassian', and write in a language which, although distinctively his, is more like self-parody than inspiration.[195] Again, the general principle is reinforced by an awareness of his own poetic tendencies in his concern with 'licence', with how far a poet may bend the rules in matters of rhyme, rhythm, and grammar.[196] Hopkins felt there should be a proper balance in poetry between its uniquely personal inspirational qualities, and its objective rhetorical principles. Inspiration, 'that fine desire that fathers thought', is abundant in English poetry, he claimed, 'but its rhetoric is inadequate'.[197] Hence his own endeavours to create and abide by an elaborate rhetoric in his own poetry, to provide a proper counter-balance to his poetical insight – his new definitions of rhyme, of poetic diction, and of sprung rhythm. And within each of these prosodic categories he approves a proper tension between the individuality of the poet and the authority of his medium. He stresses the compatibility of freedom with rhyme, of rhythmic freedom within controlled metrical laws, the instress of the poet expressing himself within the inscape of a poem.

Hopkins' understanding of poetry is here, as always, sensitive and informed. Like so many of his literary observations, these ideas illuminate not only what he was himself aiming at in his poetry, but the essential nature of all great art. But in many of his own poems, even, perhaps especially, in his greatest, the tension between the urgency of what he has to express and the rigour of his forms is extreme. His tense rhythms suggest, perhaps more than the inscape of self-expression, a sustained and violent repression of the self. In them we can read the failure of inscape to meet Hopkins' deepest needs. The theory of inscape, so brilliant and flawless, so complete, remained merely an intellectual solution.

3 Criticism: John Ruskin and Matthew Arnold

The two greatest critics of the high Victorian period, Ruskin and Arnold, unlike the modern critic with his narrowly-defined area of expertise, undertook as their field of intellectual enquiry no less than the whole of human culture. Less immediately concerned with theology than their clerical contemporaries, Keble, Newman, and Hopkins, and more prominently involved in the Victorian world of arts and letters, between them they considered and pronounced upon literature, architecture, painting, religions and societies – ancient and modern, English and European. Both men assume a relationship between religion and aesthetics at every turn, whether they are criticising a painting, a building, or a poem, making recommendations about education, or interpreting the Bible. Yet, in line with their religious positions, they are more concerned with the moral implications of art and aesthetics than with the strictly theological. Ruskin and Arnold also distinguish themselves from the Tractarian tradition by their interest in the moral relationship that exists between art and society. In the course of both of their careers, we see a movement away from an early purely aesthetic criticism of particular works of art towards a more general and socially committed diagnosis of culture in moral and political terms. As Raymond Williams points out:

An essential hypothesis in the development of the idea of culture is that the art of a period is closely and necessarily related to the generally prevalent 'way of life', and further that, in consequence, aesthetic, moral, and social judgements are closely interrelated. Such a hypothesis is now so generally accepted, as a matter of intellectual habit, that it is not always easy to remember that it is essentially a product of the intellectual history of the nineteenth century.[1]

Certainly both Ruskin and Arnold were unusually aware of the social and historical conditions which shaped the creation of works of art in both the past and the present. They were accordingly acutely conscious of the historical situation in which they themselves were writing, and clearly felt a moral responsibility to respond to contemporary issues. Yet as sensitive as they were to the inescapability of their cultural circumstances and the relativity of man's position in history, both writers concomitantly erected value systems which were absolute and a-historical, in an attempt to transcend their historical condition.

Despite their progressiveness in some respects, and their significance in the development of a modern critical tradition, both Ruskin and Arnold have been immortalised, more often than not by their direct heirs, as intrepid moralisers of the aesthetic experience. As Swinburne's fictitious Frenchman remarks of the English Victorian critic, as typified by Ruskin and Arnold:

ils ont la manie de vouloir réconcilier les choses irréconciliables. On voit cela partout, dans la politique, dans les beaux arts, dans la vie pratique, dans la vie idéale... Venons aux arts; que veut-on d'un peintre? de la peinture? fi donc! Il nous faut un peu de morale, un peu d'intention, le beau vrai, le vrai beau, l'idée actuelle, l'actualité idéale, mille autres choses très-recommandables dans ce genre-là. C'est ce malin esprit, très-peu spirituel, qui est venu souffler aux poëtes la belle idée de se poser en apôtres réconciliateurs entre le croyant et le libre penseur.[2]

This cry has been taken up by many a critic since. A real Frenchman, Proust, wrote of Ruskin, whom he actually admired enormously:

Les doctrines qu'il professait étaient des doctrines morales et non des doctrines esthétiques, et pourtant il les choisissait pour leur beauté. Et comme il ne voulait pas les présenter comme belles, mais comme vraies, il était obligé de se mentir à lui-même sur la nature des raisons qui les lui faissaient adopter.[3]

Less charitably, Roger Fry designated Ruskin 'that old fraud', complaining that 'He was too virtuous... Everything had to be squared – even those finicky palaces must be morally good.'[4] T. S. Eliot compounds the picture by describing how 'Ruskin, with a genuine sensibility for certain types of art and architecture, succeeded in satisfying his nature by translating everything immediately in terms of morals.'[5] Indeed, one does not have to look far into Ruskin to see that these critics have a point. The central doctrine of *The Stones of Venice* – the superiority of the Gothic style to Renaissance decadence – is argued from an avowedly ethical standpoint:

It is not the form of this [Renaissance] architecture against which I would plead... But it is the moral nature of it which is corrupt.[6]

Eliot is more hostile still in his account of Arnold's position. He not only doubts the soundness of Arnold's musical ear, but he suggests too that his criticism of poetry

is very much influenced by his religious attitude. His taste is not comprehensive. He seems to have chosen, when he could,...those subjects in
connexion with which he could best express his views about morals and
society.[7]

Eliot's views on Arnold as a religious thinker are notorious: 'In
philosophy and theology he was an undergraduate; in religion a
Philistine.'[8] Eliot was, of course, prejudiced by his own religious
attitudes, as an Anglo-Catholic convert careful of his dogma, and his
aesthetic position, in the vanguard of Modernist orthodoxy. Recent
critical opinion, by considering Ruskin as affirming more positive
aesthetic values for contemporary art than Modernism, or alternatively
as belonging to the very aesthetic tradition out of which Modernism
grew, and by defending Arnold as a significant religious thinker and
critic, offers a more measured appraisal.[9]

But if the virulence of the Modernists' views of Ruskin and Arnold
may be explained and questioned, the substance of their assessment
remains to be considered. The critical writing of both Ruskin and
Arnold is defined by their persistent merging of 'Hebrew' and 'Hellene',
of religious and aesthetic categories. As Eliot said, 'Literature, or
Culture, tended with Arnold to usurp the place of religion', and from
his work he found that only two possible conclusions could be drawn:
'(1) that Religion is Morals, (2) that Religion is Art'.[10] Equally one
might argue that often in Ruskin's early writings religion usurped the
place of art, and that his aesthetic appreciation sometimes collapsed
under the weight of the moral it had to bear.[11]

This may be explained partly in terms of the cultural conditions
within which they were writing. Their tendency to appropriate to art
and aesthetic experience values and functions which had traditionally
belonged to religion was no doubt related to the decline of Christianity
in the mid-Victorian period induced by the combined forces of scientific
discovery and German biblical criticism. The associated problems of
dissolution of faith in a stable system of absolute and immutable values
raised by evolution in the physical sciences and by the historicism of
nineteenth-century philosophical thought was compounded by a volatile
political situation. The 1860s, the period when Ruskin turned his hand
to political economy and Arnold wrote *Culture and Anarchy*, was a
decade in which concern over the Reform question and its social and
educational implications was paramount. Ever since the French
Revolution, democracy had been perceived as not only inevitable, but
inevitably accompanied by chaos and instability. However, not since
the beginning of the 1830s, in the period leading up to the first Reform

Beauty and Belief

Act, had the question of democracy and its social implications been so urgently debated in England.

The two periods, as George Eliot pre-eminently realised when she wrote *Middlemarch*, present interesting parallels, and the major literary works which emerged in response to the Reform issue in the 1830s and the 1860s may be fruitfully compared. Coleridge's *On the Constitution of the Church and State* has been mentioned already in this study in relation to its contribution to the debate over the proper relations between Church and State, but of course a further dimension to the political context of Coleridge's last great work was the increasing agitation for parliamentary reform which preceded the passage of the first Reform Bill. Coleridge's response to the impending extension of the suffrage was to assume that democracy would endanger traditional social, political, and cultural values, and to urge, in consequence, the necessity of a national clerisy, an intellectual and moral élite, whose role would be to maintain those values in the face of the ensuing moral vicissitudes and social upheaval.[12] He recognised and accepted the inevitability of social change yet feared what democracy might bring. Hence he reasserted the permanent, transcendent, a-historical and invulnerable values of religion, morality and art to counter the anarchic social consequences of democratisation. In pursuit of what Ben Knights has called an 'Idealist historicism', he perceived the clerisy as arbitrating between the historical and the transcendental, between the phenomenal world and the noumenal, between the forces of progression and the forces of reaction.[13] In practice, confronted by the threat of anarchy and disintegration, his real allegiance was to the transcendental and the moral, and to the preservation of the *status quo*.

Coleridge's idea of the clerisy and its function re-emerged in the works of a number of later writers. Arnold's ideas relating to an élitist 'remnant', and a State made up of the 'best self' of each class, are, as Ben Knights has shown, clearly in the Coleridgean tradition.[14] As in the case of Coleridge, they imply a belief in 'the unsoundness of the majority' and a certainty that 'the unsoundness of the majority, if it is not withstood and remedied, must be their ruin'.[15] Alarmed by the implications of social and political equality, and anxious to prevent cultural disintegration by imposing cultural discipline, Arnold, like Coleridge, attempted to mediate between the incompatible alternatives of historical relativism and immutable values, between democratic and aristocratic systems, between Liberalism and Conservatism. Ruskin likewise was anxious to reconcile apparently opposing epistemological and political principles. Acutely sensitive to the principle of flux in the

110

natural world, he constantly recalled the observer of nature to eternal, immutable, transcendental values. Politically 'by nature and instinct a Conservative', distrustful of 'liberty' and 'anarchy', and by his own confession 'a violent Tory of the old school', he nevertheless claimed also to be 'a Communist of the old school'.[16] He wrote to Sidney Cockerell in 1886, 'of course I am a Socialist – of the most stern sort – but I am also a Tory of the sternest sort'.[17] Coleridge was a Tory philosopher who, according to John Stuart Mill, was 'a better Liberal than Liberals themselves';[18] Arnold was an authoritarian and élitist Liberal; Ruskin was a 'radical Tory'.[19] Each sought to impose order on the chaos and instability of his temporal situation and to synthesise the fragmented details of the actual into a harmonious and unified ideal.

According to Ben Knights, 'the intellectual's attempt to make himself feel that he is not conditioned' historically is directly related to the fact that 'conditioning by the blind forces of society and history is identified with threatening pressures within the self, so that self-knowledge and the mastery that is believed to arise from it are seen as the road to freedom'.[20] The evasions which we find in Ruskin's and Arnold's social and political writings are symptomatic of deeper and more personal evasions. When T. S. Eliot describes Arnold's criticism as being characteristically 'tinged by his own uncertainty, by his own apprehensions, his own view of what it was best that his own time should believe',[21] he pinpoints an important reason behind Arnold's, and Ruskin's, concern to relate their aesthetic judgements to some religious structure. For both Arnold and Ruskin, their tendency to think about beauty and art in moral terms, and about religion in aesthetic terms, is directly related to other characteristic and shared attitudes and problems; most importantly, anxiety concerning the self, a profound fear of introspection, and a compensatory urging of objectivism.

The writings of both Ruskin and Arnold are informed by a sometimes obsessive concern with the question of the self in aesthetics and religion, yet they consistently evade the most central philosophical questions. The crucial aesthetic and epistemological problems raised by the German Idealists, which had exercised Coleridge, Newman, and Hopkins so profoundly, remain unanswered and unexplored in Ruskin's and Arnold's work. Lapsing all too often into imprecise terminology and emotive rhetoric, they rely upon dogmatic assertion to suggest a mastery of the intellectual issues which they did not in reality have. In a disastrous retreat from the real philosophical problems, they relentlessly advance the claims of objectivism and disinterestedness in every sphere – creative, critical, perceptive, epistemological, and political. It seems very likely that this curious and specific intellectual inadequacy in two writers who were otherwise so able derives from deeper personal insecurities. Both Ruskin and Arnold tried to sink their respective problems with the self, and their related difficulties with the conflicting claims of the emotional, moral, religious, aesthetic, and intellectual life, within a great vision of culture in which 'Hebrew' and 'Hellene', and subjective and objective, could unproblematically merge.

John Ruskin

I

It is not an unreasonable claim to say that Ruskin literally reshaped Victorian taste in art. While he did not, of course, single-handedly reinstate Turner, inspire and champion the Pre-Raphaelites in their early days, or promote a Gothic Revival in architecture, he was largely responsible for establishing what we now regard as the characteristic tenor of Victorian art and aesthetics. He affirmed the significance of the aesthetic dimension in life in an age when, under the pressure of modern industrial development and burgeoning capitalism, that dimension was becoming marginal to the real business of life and perilously close to being lost altogether. He encouraged artists and laymen alike to appreciate the beauty of nature, art, and architecture, and to deprecate the ugliness of all that deformed nature and human creativity.

The substance of his aesthetic is embodied in *Modern Painters*, the first volume of which appeared in 1843 and the last seventeen years later, and *The Stones of Venice*, published from 1851 to 1853. The early volumes of *Modern Painters* are about the divinely inspired 'Truths' of nature, and the inadequacies of landscape painting before Turner which failed to depict these truths. Here, and in *The Stones of Venice*, he insists upon the faithful representation of the truths of nature in art and architecture. But by the time he completed the final volume of *Modern Painters* in 1860, Ruskin was a changed man living in a changed world. Darwin had shattered the conventional understanding of the divinity of nature, and Ruskin, along with many other Victorians, had to re-appraise and adjust his earlier conviction of an uncomplicated relationship between the divinity of nature and the moral significance of art. Ruskin's ideas about God, nature, and art were always firmly and exclusively based upon his own profoundly felt experience. He was, unlike Hopkins or Newman, always contemptuous of abstraction, and scornfully dismissive of philosophical theorising in both aesthetics and religion. Hence when he could no longer feel with any certainty the divine meaning of nature, he had neither the inner resources nor the philosophical resources to sustain him, and was obliged to turn his main critical effort away from aesthetic concerns to social questions.[22]

But back in the 1840s Ruskin's faith in the divinity of the natural landscape was as yet unshaken. His aim in writing *Modern Painters* was 'to bring to light, as far as may be in my power, that faultless, ceaseless, inconceivable, inexhaustible loveliness, which God has stamped upon all things, if man will only receive them as He gives them'.[23] The beauty of nature is in God's image and aesthetic experience is divinely inspired: ' "He hath made everything beautiful, in his time", became for me thenceforward the interpretation of the bond between the human mind and all visible things.'[24] His description of the sun breaking through a storm-cloud and lighting up the surrounding mountain peaks as a revelation of God is eloquent of his youthful religio-aesthetic experience of nature:

And then I learned – what till then I had not known – the real meaning of the word Beautiful. With all that I had ever seen before – there had come mingled the associations of humanity – the exertion of human power – the action of human mind. The image of self had not been effaced in that of God. It was then only beneath those glorious hills that I learned how thought itself may become ignoble and energy itself become base – when compared with the absorption of soul and spirit – the prostration of all power – and the cessation of all will – before, and in the Presence of, the manifested Deity. It was then only that I understood that to become nothing might be to become more than Man; . . . It was then that I understood that all which is the type of God's attributes – which in any way or in any degree – can turn the human soul from gazing upon itself – can quench in it pride – and fear – and annihilate – be it in ever so small a degree, the thoughts and feelings which have to do with this present world, and fix the spirit – in all humility – on the types of that which is to be its food for eternity; – this and this only is in the pure and right sense of the word BEAUTIFUL.[25]

In volume one of *Modern Painters*, Ruskin describes nature as having 'a body and a soul like man; but her soul is the Deity'.[26] Ruskin moves from the physical to the sacramental landscape with an ease and naturalness which confirms his deep conviction of their relatedness, as in his evocation of divine immanence in an Alpine landscape:

the rose-light of [the white glaciers'] silent domes flushing that heaven about them and above them, piercing with purer light through its purple lines of lifted cloud, casting a new glory on every wreath as it passes by, until the whole heaven, one scarlet canopy, is interwoven with a roof of waving flame, and tossing, vault beyond vault, as with the drifted wings of many companies of angels: and then, when you can look no more for gladness, and when you are bowed down with fear and love of the Maker and Doer of this, tell me who has best delivered this His message unto men![27]

In volume two of *Modern Painters* Ruskin delineates four sources from which the sense of beauty is derived, all of which are divine: the record of conscience, written in things eternal; a symbolising of divine attributes in matter; the felicity of living things; the perfect fulfilment of their duties and functions.[28]

First of all he valued the sanctity of nature, reading it as a 'record of conscience'. From earliest youth, he tells us in *Modern Painters*, he had experienced a sense of the supernatural in nature:

although there was no definite religious sentiment mingled with it, there was a continual perception of Sanctity in the whole of nature, from the slightest thing to the vastest; – an instinctive awe, mixed with delight; an indefinable thrill, such as we sometimes imagine to indicate the presence of a disembodied spirit. I could only feel this perfectly when I was alone; and then it would often make me shiver from head to foot with the joy and fear of it, when after being some time away from the hills, I first got to the shore of a mountain river, where the brown water circled among the pebbles... I cannot in the least *describe* the feeling; but... I am afraid, no feeling *is* describable.[29]

Although he cannot hope to describe his intuition of God's presence in nature, he does attempt to define the exact nature of the divine characteristics of natural things. He concludes that natural beauty signifies two things: those external qualities which are typical of divine attributes – this he terms 'Typical Beauty'; and the appearance of 'felicitous fulfilment of functions' in living things – this he calls 'Vital Beauty'. His theory of Typical Beauty is classical, drawn from formal visual conceptions of the beautiful, while Vital Beauty owes much to Romantic theories of poetry, to notions of moral emotion and sympathy, and depends upon the idea of expression. At the centre of Ruskin's ideas about beauty lies a profound sense of the beauty of order; the natural order of Typical Beauty and the moral order of Vital Beauty. Typical Beauty is the beauty of forms and of certain qualities of forms which owe their aesthetic attractiveness to the fact that they embody different aspects of the divine nature and convey an idea of the immaterial. He discusses the aesthetic representation of infinity, of proportion, of unity as a type of divine comprehensiveness, of repose as a type of divine permanence, of symmetry as a type of divine justice, of purity as the type of divine energy, of moderation as the type of government by law. The theory of Typical Beauty is the natural extension of Ruskin's Evangelical belief into the realm of aesthetics.[30]

'Setting the characters of typical beauty aside', Ruskin says, 'the pleasure afforded by every organic form is in proportion to its appearance of healthy vital energy.'[31] In this category Ruskin places the 'moral purpose and achievement' of the Alpine flower sturdily surviving the snows:

> Throughout the whole of the organic creation every being in a perfect state exhibits certain appearances or evidences of happiness; and is in its nature, its desires, its modes of nourishment, habitation, and death, illustrative or expressive of certain moral dispositions or principles.[32]

Vital Beauty is a principle of sacramental energy which Ruskin read into the motion, change, and energy that he observed in all living things. He attributes Vital Beauty to the energies of the deity and in this way avoids the temptation subjectively to infer sensibility in an inanimate object.

In both Typical and Vital Beauty, the physical fact expresses and symbolises the supernatural. Vital Beauty expresses the spirit, the energy, the fulfilment of life informed by God, while Typical Beauty expresses the nature of God. By reconciling the ideas of symbolism and expression in these twin concepts of divine beauty, Ruskin reconciles the material and the immaterial, and shows that the beautiful thing is beautiful because of its spirituality. Aesthetic appreciation becomes, therefore, a moral, even a religious exercise.

Ruskin was anxious to rectify the popular misconception which vulgarised the concept of the capacity to respond to beauty as 'aesthetic'. He dismissed the purely aesthetic faculty as capable merely of superficial, sensual apprehension of things. The perception of the beautiful is a moral activity, and operates on the higher level of theoretic perception. Having made clear the hierarchy of perceptive modes, Ruskin suggests that nevertheless *theoria* is an extension of *aesthesis*, that they are not opposing faculties but complementary. The theoretic faculty gathers together and arranges the scattered pleasures of sight, and makes possible

> not only a feeling of strong affection towards the object in which they exist, but a perception of purpose and adaptation of it to our desires; a perception, therefore, of the immediate operation of the Intelligence which so formed us.[33]

Theoria is the development of *aesthesis* to include man's moral and religious consciousness. It is only by the operation of the Theoretic Faculty that we can get to the ideal form of a thing:

the perception is altogether moral, and instinctive love and clinging to the lines of light. Nothing but love can read the letters, nothing but sympathy catch the sound; there is no pure passion that can be understood or painted except by pureness of heart... the right Christian mind will... find its own image wherever it exists.[34]

Ruskin elaborates his ideas about the Theoretic Faculty and related theories of beauty as a means of emphasising the moral nature of the beautiful. The Theoretic Faculty is concerned with that area between the operation of the eye and of the mind which Ruskin defined as 'moral', and as such it includes elements of both sight and imagination, at that stage in the perceptive process when it is partially structured by the conceptual process but not yet a fully formulated concept. As George Landow points out, Ruskin is working within a tradition of 'emotionalist moral philosophers' in which the term 'moral' means simultaneously 'ethical' and 'referring to all mental processes'.[35] As such, the analysis of the Theoretic Faculty represents an appeal for the unity of human consciousness. In volume one of *Modern Painters*, Ruskin explains the perception of beauty thus: 'Ideas of beauty, then, be it remembered, are the subjects of moral, but not of intellectual perception.'[36] He defines perfect taste as the ability to derive the greatest possible pleasure from those material sources which are attractive to our moral nature in its purity and perfection. He indicates that, although our moral feelings are intricately involved in our intellectual processes – he speaks of 'the intellectual lens and moral retina, by which, and on which, our informing thoughts are concentrated and represented'[37] – there is no deliberate exertion of the intellect in the perception of beauty, that 'even the right after-action of the Intellect upon facts of beauty so apprehended, is dependent on the acuteness of the heart-feeling about them'.[38] Ruskin seems to be making two points: first that aesthetic perception is unconscious and automatic; secondly that aesthetic responses are made by the same faculty which makes moral evaluations. These two ideas are linked when he describes morality as '*an instinct in the hearts of all civilized men, as certain and unalterable as their outward bodily form*'.[39] Ruskin's theory relates aesthetic sensibility firmly to moral sensibility:

With this kind of bodily sensibility to colour and form is intimately connected that higher sensibility which we revere as one of the chief attributes of all noble minds, and as the chief spring of real poetry. I believe this kind of sensibility may be entirely resolved into the acuteness of bodily sense of which I have been speaking, associated with love, love I mean in its infinite and holy functions, as it embraces divine and human and brutal intelligences, and hallows the physical perception of external objects by association, gratitude, veneration, and other pure feelings of our moral nature...perception is so quickened by love, and judgement so tempered by veneration, that, practically, a man of deadened moral sensation is always dull in his perception of truth.[40]

His aim in writing *Modern Painters* is 'to summon the moral energies of the nation to a forgotten duty', to encourage men to enter upon an investigation of 'the value and meaning of mental impressions...with seriousness proportioned to the importance of rightly regarding those faculties over which we have moral power, and therefore in relation to which we assuredly incur a moral responsibility'.[41]

Ruskin draws an analogy between the very processes and functions of aesthetic and moral judgement. Since, in the matter of aesthetic taste, we may exercise choice, our taste becomes a subject of will, and therefore of moral duty or negligence, for wherever power is given there is responsibility attached. We have a moral duty to prefer certain sense impressions above others:

And this is precisely analogous to the law of the moral world, whereby men are supposed not only capable of governing their likes and dislikes, but the whole culpability or propriety of actions is dependent upon this capability; so that men are guilty or otherwise, not for what they do, but for what they desire, the command being not Thou shalt obey, but Thou shalt love, the Lord thy God; a vain command if men were not capable of governing and directing their affections.[42]

By means of this comparison with the working of the moral sense, Ruskin suggests that we have a power and a corresponding duty in matters of the senses. He later pointed to this passage relating perception to the moral world as 'the radical theorem, not only of this book, but of all my writings on art'.[43] He also perceives the moral feelings and the creative imagination in a mutually dependent relationship:

there is reciprocal action between the intensity of moral feeling and the power of imagination; for, on the one hand, those who have keenest sympathy are those who look closest and pierce deepest, and hold securest; and on the other, those who have so pierced and seen the melancholy deeps of things are filled with the most intense passion and gentleness of sympathy.[44]

The cultivation of the imagination is dependent upon moral awareness,[45] and so the perception of the beautiful becomes a moral act.[46] Art and morality act upon and react against each other:

And all delight in fine art, and all love of it, resolve themselves into simple love of that which deserves love. That deserving is the quality which we call 'loveliness'... and it is not an indifferent nor optional thing whether we love this or that; but it is just the vital function of all our being.[47]

As John Rosenberg remarks, 'it is impossible to abstract the moral tone from Ruskin's aesthetic criticism'[48] in his writings about art. An artist may be irreligious but he cannot be immoral, for his very artistic greatness is a sign of his moral powers. The interdependence of aesthetic and moral values was a central principle of Ruskin's thoughts on art. He tried to elucidate the moral significance even of the abstract qualities of painting. And so the types of beauty symbolising God are also formal qualities of art. Ruskin derived his concept of aesthetic order from moral laws which are themselves derived from the nature of God:

> orderly balance and arrangement are essential to the perfect operation of the more earnest and solemn qualities of the Beautiful, as being heavenly in their nature, and contrary to the violence and disorganisation of sin; so that the seeking of them, and submission to them, are characteristic of minds that have been subjected to high moral discipline.[49]

The principles of composition which he puts forward in *The Elements of Drawing* equally bear a moral significance and testify to his habit of perceiving things in moral terms. Indeed, he says, 'There is no moral vice, no moral virtue, which has not its *precise* prototype in the art of painting.'[50]

In volume two of *Modern Painters* Ruskin says, 'Man's use and function...are, to be the witness of the glory of God.'[51] If this is true of mankind in general, then how much more so of the artist. Hence the aphorism Ruskin placed at the beginning of *The Laws of Fésole* – 'All great art is praise.' Since Ruskin attributed all beauty to divine sources, and since art records, interprets, and expresses this beauty to mankind, then art of necessity carries moral and religious value. He believed that art was an instrument of morality, but rejected overt didacticism in painting or poetry.[52] Art can only be effective 'indirectly and occultly'.[53] Although art can be useful to orthodox religion, in, for example, the imaginative representation of biblical scenes, in general Ruskin held that in this very specific sense the religious function of art was questionable. The true religious influence in art is much more subtle. For example, it may stimulate the observer's imagination to enable him to participate sympathetically in an experience and thus refine his moral nature. The most important didactic function of art, though, is expressed by Ruskin in *The Queen of the Air*:

> as all lovely art is rooted in virtue, so it bears fruit of virtue, and is didactic in its own nature. It is often didactic also in actually expressed

thought, as Giotto's, Michael Angelo's, Dürer's, and hundreds more; but that is not its special function, – *it is didactic chiefly by being beautiful*; but beautiful with haunting thought, no less than with form.[54]

By this he means first of all that perception of certain modes of beauty stimulates moral sympathy and emulation, and secondly that, being beautiful itself, it is a symbol of God, and therefore to experience it is a religious act. Hopkins also explores this idea when he recognises Typical Beauty in an object's 'inscape', and Vital Beauty in its 'instress', both of which can be conveyed by a poem which has its own inscape and instress. Art is necessarily religious, because it represents Typical Beauty in its form, and Vital Beauty, that 'felicitous fulfilment of functions' which expresses the energies of the deity in its inspiration. In *Modern Painters* Ruskin wanted to prove that 'no supreme power of art can be attained by impious men; and that the neglect of art, as an interpreter of divine things, has been of evil consequence to the Christian world'.[55] He refers to art as 'sacred invention':

the name it bears being rightly given even to invention formal, not because it forms, but because it finds. For you cannot find a lie; you must make it for yourself. False things may be imagined, and false things composed; but only truth can be invented.[56]

Ruskin's belief in the interconnection of morality and art manifests itself practically in his own interpretations of art, and is most clearly seen in his discussion of the nature of Gothic. Convinced of the dependence of all creativity upon the moral character of the artist and, more broadly and significantly, of his society, Ruskin cannot examine art purely in aesthetic terms. The unity of Gothic culture in particular permits him to integrate his discussion of art, religion, morality and society. In *The Stones of Venice* he establishes an iconography of interpretation, whereby the details of Gothic architectural style may be read as reflecting the religious and moral nature of Gothic society. Thus

the arch line is the moral character of the arch, and the adverse forces are its temptations; . . . this, in arch morality and in man morality, is a very simple and easily to be understood principle, – that if either arch or man expose themselves to their special temptations or adverse forces, *outside* of their voussoirs or proper and appointed armour, both will fall.[57]

He suggests that by acknowledging naturalism rather than perfection as the end of art, Gothic proves itself to be a pre-eminently Christian style, in that it is manifestly the work of men whose individualism and freedom is bound up with an acknowledgement of imperfection. Ruskin finds a corollary between the Gothic school of architecture, which depends upon and celebrates the imperfect creativity of the individual craftsman, and Christianity which, without fear or pride, humbly confesses its imperfection and contemplates its sins, and bestows its highest dignity upon the acknowledgement of unworthiness. Transposing religious criteria to aesthetics, Ruskin sees the very essence of the Fortunate Fall embodied in Gothic, which is the most Christian, because the most imperfect, the most human, of architectural schools.

Curiously, though, what is perceived as a virtue in Gothic is criticised in Romantic art, again for religious reasons. Ruskin claims that Romantic particularity and detail in art (as opposed to neo-classical generality) derives from Original Sin. For the Fall, he claimed, the 'Adamite Curse',[58] caused an 'evil diversity'[59] among men, and made an ideal of human beauty impossible. This seems a far cry from his own delight in detail, but it is bound up with his reluctance to admit that subjectivity has any part of beauty. It is only by grounding the beautiful actually in divine nature that Ruskin can conceive of men whose moral sensibilities have been utterly perverted by the Fall properly finding religious and moral value in beauty.

The fact that he derives his theories of imagination and creative truth from religious sources implies his belief in the poet or artist as a prophet. He often adopts a sermonising tone and Scriptural language to imply the visionary authority of the artist:

...vision it is, of one kind or another, – the whole scene, character, or incident passing before them as in second sight, whether they will or no, and requiring them to paint it as they see it; they not daring...to alter one jot or tittle of it as they write it down or paint it down; it being to them in its own kind and degree always a true vision or Apocalypse, and invariably accompanied in their hearts by a feeling correspondent to the words, – 'Write the things *which thou hast seen*, and the things which *are*.'[60]

The artist is conceived of as a visionary high priest, a mediator between God and man, an interpreter of eternal truths to men:

Both [preachers and painters] are commentators on infinity, and the duty of both is to take for each discourse one essential truth, seeking particularly and insisting especially on those which are less palpable to ordinary observation, and more likely to escape an indolent research; and to impress that, and that alone, upon those whom they address, with every illustration which can be furnished by their knowledge, and every adornment attainable by their power.[61]

The artist's first function is to 'see', and 'to see clearly is poetry, prophecy, and religion, – all in one'.[62]

II

Ruskin's main purpose in writing *Modern Painters* was to teach people to see, and, as he said some forty years after writing the first volume:

natural phenomena...can only be seen with their properly belonging joy, and interpreted up to the measure of proper human intelligence, when they are accepted as the work, and the gift, of a Living Spirit greater than our own.[63]

His conviction of the correlation between the phenomenal and a moral or visionary landscape stimulated him to exert all his powers to understand and describe even the most insignificant of natural objects with unusual precision and commitment. But there is also another dimension to his religio-aesthetic philosophy. Ruskin's belief in the divinity of nature and the moral meaning of beauty validates his own intense emotional response to nature and art. His description of his famous 'unconversion' before a painting by Veronese in Turin in 1858 suggests among other things a deep-seated Evangelical belief, now being radically questioned, that it is wrong to be passionately moved by sensuous beauty:

I was struck by the Gorgeousness of life which the world seems to be constituted to develop...Can it be possible that all this power and beauty is adverse to the honour of the Maker of it? Has God made faces beautiful and limbs strong, and created these strange, fiery, fantastic energies, and created the splendour of substance and the love of it...only that all these things may lead His creatures away from Him?[64]

This explains his anxiety to distinguish between '*theoria*' and mere '*aesthesis*'. In *The Storm Cloud of the Nineteenth Century*, written many years later, in 1884, he confessed that without this sense of the divinity of nature *Modern Painters* could never have been written,[65] for unless it were in the service of God the dedication of one's life to the contemplation of beauty would be inexcusably self-indulgent.

In *Modern Painters* itself, Ruskin takes a firm stand against self-indulgence in both art and criticism. He believed that the Romantic imagination, dominated by the idea of the supremacy of the feelings, had drifted into greater and greater imprecision when recording the facts of nature. In reaction, he reasserts the value of factual representation, and claims the rendering of the 'objective fact' as a necessary prerequisite of the deepest aesthetic insight. His concern with the minute observation of nature derived from a fear of the subjective, and a corresponding need to objectify experience.

Ruskin struggled to re-establish the reality of the concrete sensory world as an objective moral entity. It was his insistence upon the independent integrity of nature, in reaction to a profound distrust of what he defined as a Romantic reliance upon the self, that led him to his characteristically laborious precision in looking at and recording the details of nature and stressing the autonomous being of phenomena. Ruskin defines his understanding of form in landscape as

that perfect and harmonious unity of outline with light and shade, by which all the parts and projections and proportions of a body are fully explained to the eye; being nevertheless perfectly independent of sight or power in other objects, the presence of light upon a body being a positive existence, whether we are aware of it or not, and in no degree dependent upon our senses.[66]

He advises all young artists to 'go to Nature in all singleness of heart, and walk with her laboriously and trustingly, having no other thoughts but how best to penetrate her meaning, and remember her instruction'.[67] In the chapter entitled 'The Lamp of Beauty' in the *Seven Lamps of Architecture* (1849), he states that 'man cannot advance in the invention of beauty, without directly imitating natural form', for 'all most lovely forms and thoughts are directly taken from natural objects'.[68] The alternative, an overbearing artistic presence, can only result in 'the violation of specific form, the utter abandonment of all organic and individual character of object'.[69] As Robert Hewison observes, Ruskin's concern to uphold the objective existence of beauty led him to develop an aesthetic which attempts to identify the abstract visual qualities both of nature and of the work of art. He tried to delineate those formal qualities of a work of art which are aesthetically pleasing regardless of the work's content.[70] In this, of course, he comes ironically close to Pater's formalism, the difference being that what Ruskin was concerned to exclude from the aesthetic experience was a too subjective mind, while Pater wished to exclude all that was not truly a part of pure aesthetic appreciation. In the same way as he believed that natural forms in landscape existed independently of human perceptive experience, Ruskin sought out an autonomous beauty in art. He tried to re-establish a real link between nature and man by showing his readers how to appreciate and respond to the visual forms objectively existing in nature and art. Above all, he appealed to the artist to escape the prison of his own subjectivity, to see nature as it was, and to represent the truth of form, free from all subjective association.

If there are apparent similarities between Ruskin and Pater in their common appreciation of form, though, their respective views on the question of the artistic personality are antithetical. Ruskin felt that, as a preliminary preparation for the creative act, the artist must submit to nature. He must be prepared to repress his own personality, in the manner of Keats' 'negative capability' and Wordsworth's 'wise passiveness'. Ruskin taught that the artist must free himself from introspection and become a mere 'mirror of truth...passive in sight, passive in utterance'.[71] He says of the artist:

As long as we remember him, we cannot respect him. We honour him most when we most forget him. He becomes great when he becomes invisible.[72]

The play and power of the imagination 'depend altogether on our being able to forget ourselves and enter, like possessing spirits, into the bodies of things about us'.[73] In the greatest art, the artist ceases to exist and the natural energy of landscape takes over. Of Turner, Ruskin wrote, 'it seemed to me that in these later subjects Nature herself was composing with him'.[74] Ruskin records this phenomenon of total harmony between artist and nature in his description in *Praeterita* (1886) of his own experience of drawing a tree at Fontainebleau in 1842: 'I saw that [the beautiful lines] "composed" themselves, by finer laws than any known of men.'[75]

One method by which Ruskin aimed to help the artist look at the world objectively was to establish 'laws' by which nature might be analysed and demand that art should be based upon firm scientific principles. He believed in the importance of a properly structural appreciation of nature. He describes how Turner not only saw the outward appearance of natural things but 'he learned their organization'.[76] The great draughtsman will, he says, delight 'to trace these laws of government'.[77] Ruskin's awareness of the structural organisation of natural objects is quite different from Coleridge's, as Patricia Ball points out.[78] For Coleridge, the consciousness of structural harmony was essentially a philosophical notion. For Ruskin, experience was empirical, founded on strict scientific principle. He discovers the structure of a fact by observation, Coleridge by creative mental speculation. Ruskin objectifies perception through scientific observation of natural law. Thus his description of the structural relationship inherent in a spray of leaves:

any group of four or five leaves, presenting itself in its natural position to the eye, consists of a series of forms connected by exquisite and complex symmetries...[79]

Once attention is truly directed away from the self and on to the object perceived, Ruskin proceeds, generality is no longer possible. For as soon as one looks clearly, it becomes evident that one can no more generalise about the appearance of trees or clouds than one can generalise about human appearance. Ruskin disapproved of generality and reaffirmed the individuality of detail:

the so-called general idea is important, not because it is common to all the individuals of that species, but because it separates that species from everything else. It is the distinctiveness, not the universality of the truth, which renders it important.

all truths...are valuable in proportion as they are particular, and valueless in proportion as they are general...every truth is valuable in proportion as it is characteristic of the thing of which it is affirmed.

Nothing is so great a sign of truth and beauty in mountain drawing, as the appearance of individuality.[80]

But within this world of individuality it is possible to comprehend ideal form, for nature gives us 'various, yet agreeing beauty':

And out of this mass of various, yet agreeing beauty, it is by long attention only that the conception of the constant character – the ideal form – hinted at by all, yet assumed by none, is fixed upon the imagination for its standard of truth.[81]

The observant eye may actively search out the design of the whole and seize the essential form, the Platonic 'perfect idea', from the midst of surface flux:

The perfect *idea* of the form and condition in which all the properties of the species are fully developed, is called the Ideal of the species...[82]

Ruskin was always careful to distinguish between individual and specific characteristics of beautiful forms:

The true ideal of landscape is precisely the same as that of the human form; it is the expression of the specific – not the individual, but the specific – characters of every object, in their perfection. There is an ideal form of every herb, flower, and tree, it is that form to which every individual of the species has a tendency to arrive, freed from the influence of accident or disease.[83]

Turner, being 'the master of the science of *Essence*',[84] was the champion of the specific, the Pre-Raphaelites merely of the individual. Hopkins made similar efforts to grasp the perfect form, the inscape of a thing of beauty. His description of primroses in a journal entry fulfils exactly Ruskin's desire for a knowledge of the 'specific' and 'distinctive' characters of things:

Take a *few* primroses in a glass and the instress of – brilliancy, sort of starriness: I have not the right word – so simple a flower gives is remarkable. It is, I think, due to the strong swell given by the deeper yellow middle.[85]

For Ruskin, as for Hopkins, the principles of form and energy were closely related. Following a close study of shells, Ruskin notes in his diary:

Form... may be considered as a function or exponent either of Growth or of Force, inherent or impressed;...and all forms are thus either indicative of lines of energy, or pressure, or motion, variously impressed or resisted, and are therefore exquisitely abstract and precise.[86]

His descriptions of mountains, skies, and water exemplify above all the 'exhaustless living energy with which the universe is filled'.[87] Energy is inherent not only in the obviously tumultuous movements of nature, but also in its strength in repose.

Although it is the details of the object's distinctive individuality, both as a species and as a unique being within that species, that preoccupy him most, Ruskin is also concerned with the spatial and temporal context of each natural object. He argues, for example, that the relation of the rock to the mountain, the cloud to the sky, is a part of the truth of their existence; that energy has a historical context, in that it inheres in change and development, and even the static present contains the memory of 'past commotion', the process of its becoming within its being. Throughout Ruskin's writings we find his attraction to the vital forms of things, to the 'lines of energy' which are so essential to an object's character, which make it the very thing itself.[88] In his descriptions of waves and plunging cataracts, of the outline of a mountain chain, of an aspen tree, of the 'energy and naturalism' of Gothic leaf designs, even in his descriptions of the most ephemeral of natural forms, cloud formations, the specific form is defined in terms of its energy.

III

Modern Painters was not primarily concerned with truth of landscape, however, but with the artist's representation of it. Ruskin construed the role of art as involving not simply the presentation of things as they are in themselves, but

as they appear to mankind. Science studies the relations of things to each other: but art studies only their relations to man: and it requires of everything...only this, – what that thing is to the human heart, what it has to say to men, and what it can become to them.[89]

The accurate study of fact was a preliminary to the artist's use of it. He recognised higher levels of truth, 'of impression as well as of form, – of thought as well as of matter'.[90] At the end of the first volume of *Modern Painters*, having advised all young artists to study nature with painstaking accuracy, Ruskin says:

Then, when their memories are stored, and their imaginations fed, and their hands firm, let them take up the scarlet and the gold, give the reins to their fancy, and show us what their heads are made of.[91]

Volume two deals with very different concerns to volume one in that it investigates not 'things outward, and sensibly demonstrable', but 'the value and meaning of mental impressions':[92]

The second great faculty is the Imaginative, which the mind exercises in a certain mode of regarding or combining the ideas it has received from external nature, and the operations of which become in their turn objects of the theoretic faculty to other minds.[93]

The perfect function of the imagination is the intuitive perception of truth – of a deeper truth, that is, than lies upon the surface of things. Poetry is 'the suggestion, by the imagination, of noble grounds for the noble emotions', and, he stresses, 'it is necessary to the existence of poetry that the grounds of these feelings should be *furnished by the imagination*'.[94] Observed beauty, then, is not falsified in any way, but is modified or coloured by the reflected image of the beholding mind. The artist must respect the integrity and autonomy of nature, but Ruskin acknowledges the need for selection, in order to accommodate higher truths to man's limited capacity for understanding.[95] The artist's task is to find within disparate and various nature an organic unity. His synthesising vision, his pursuit of integrated experience, is quite Coleridgean:

it is to be remembered that the great composers, not less deep in feeling, are in the fixed habit of regarding as much the relations and positions, as the separate nature, of things;...that nothing ever bears to them a separate or isolated aspect, but leads or links a chain of aspects – that to them is not merely the surface, nor the substance, of anything that is of import.[96]

For Ruskin, as for Wordsworth, the artist's mind vitalises all he sees:

Every incident of motion and of energy is seized upon with indescribable delight, and every line of the composition animated with a force and fury which are now no longer the mere expression of a contemplated external truth, but have origin in some inherent feeling in the painter's mind.[97]

In Ruskin's view, the artist must lose awareness of himself initially only in preparation for when he must cast 'a certain colouring of imagination' over his subject. The artistic imagination bridges the gap between perception and creativity, between the forms of nature and the forms of art. Ruskin's task was to achieve a satisfactory reconciliation of objective truth and artistic imagination, the artist's way of seeing. Having examined the nature of the object Ruskin shifts attention to the relationship between subject and object, moves from the realm of nature to the realm of art, and in this realm perceives the duty of the artist as twofold:

The whole function of the artist in the world is to be a seeing and feeling creature; to be an instrument of such tenderness and sensitiveness, that no shadow, no hue, no line, no instantaneous and evanescent impression of the visual things around him, nor any of the emotions which they are capable of conveying to the spirit which has been given him, shall either be left unrecorded, or fade from the book of record...The work of his life is to be two-fold only; to see, to feel.[98]

This is an admirable view of what art and the artist should aspire to, and it is an ideal which is realised with great accomplishment in Ruskin's own best work. But Ruskin's understanding and explanation of the relationship of seeing to feeling, of objective truth to subjective experience, in other words of the perceptive and imaginative processes, is less convincing. As we have seen, his dislike of what was in his view a characteristically Romantic inability to scrutinise the world other than with reference to the self, as reflecting and expressing a personal state of consciousness, provoked an extreme reaction – the facts of nature should no longer be thus debased, but should receive all man's attention. But when it came to discussing the role of the artistic imagination, selecting and arranging and creating as well as responding to nature, Ruskin was obliged to acknowledge that a significant degree of subjectivism was inevitably involved.

When he came to devise his theory of beauty Ruskin initially sought to protect it from subjectivism by denying the relevance of association,[99] self-contained explanations of the beautiful which remove it from its unchanging objective state to a dependence upon the changeable regions of the human mind. In the same way he initially denied the sublime the status of a separate aesthetic category in an attempt to avoid the dangers of emotional excess.

However, Ruskin's most direct confrontation of the problems of an aesthetic centred upon the feelings remains his discussion of the 'Pathetic Fallacy'. In a continuing struggle to protect his ideas of painting and poetry from the invasion of subjectivism, Ruskin argues that a great poet is not one who writes solely about his own emotions, nor is he one who imputes to external objects those emotions, but one who feels, yet is able to control those feelings enough to present the facts as they are, and leave room for the feelings of the reader. The inferior poet, dominated as he is by his own emotions, applies to natural forms terms which Ruskin felt should only be used to describe human emotion, and remains unable to acknowledge the integrity of the object's identity. The English Romantic poets, he felt, were concerned with the world merely as a set of symbols whose function was primarily to reveal the nature of the poet's psyche. The Pre-Raphaelites, the 'modern pathetic school' in painting,[100] were guilty of a similarly egotistical aesthetic:

The Pre-Raphaelites, taken as a body, have been culpably negligent in this respect, not in humble respect to Nature, but in morbid indulgence of their own impressions. They happen to find their fancies caught by a bit of an oak hedge, or the weeds at the side of a duck-pond, because, perhaps, they remind them of a stanza of Tennyson.[101]

Conversely, the greatest of modern artists, Turner, is 'a man of sympathy absolutely infinite'.[102] Ruskin suggests that the inability to distinguish between metaphor and fact, between reality and views of it, the confusion of the internal with the real landscape, far from indicating man's access to nature, implies his alienation from nature, and anthropomorphism only exacerbates this dualism.

This concern with the Pathetic Fallacy derives from Ruskin's characteristic mistrust of subjectivism and represents an effort to move the imaginative focus away from self-contemplation towards an autonomous object. Art, by its very nature, is about man's response to external phenomena, but in his view Romantic art had become oversubjective. In his chapter on the Pathetic Fallacy Ruskin tries to reverse the balance, and attempts to merge the subjective and objective urges, to demonstrate their vital connectedness:

The power, therefore, of thus fully *perceiving* any natural object depends on our being able to group and fasten all our fancies about it as a centre, making a garland of thoughts for it, in which each separate thought is subdued and shortened of its own strength, in order to fit it for harmony with others; the intensity of our enjoyment of the object depending, first, on its own beauty, and then on the richness of the garland.[103]

However, such a quest was to prove fraught with problems. First of all, if one accepts that the perception of the objective quiddity of things necessarily gives rise to an emotional effect within the perceiving mind, how does one distinguish between the emotion engendered by the object itself, and a human response which is merely subjective? Ruskin, like Hopkins,[104] was exercised by the problem of identifying the distinctive quality of the human response to natural beauty in a way which would adequately differentiate it from other human feelings:

Wordsworth's 'haunted me like a passion' is no description of it, for it is not *like*, but *is*, a passion; the point is to define how it *differs* from other passions, – what sort of human, pre-eminently human, feeling it is that loves a stone for a stone's sake, and a cloud for a cloud's.[105]

The difficulty of separating this valid passion for nature from the Pathetic Fallacy is testified to by the very frequency with which Ruskin offends against his own strictures and imposes his own eccentric interpretations upon nature.

Another problem was that, in every other respect than his attitude towards subjectivism, Ruskin was an artist and theorist very much within the Romantic tradition. He continually emphasised the need for intensity of emotion when responding to nature, and believed that the mind necessarily reflects back something of itself into the natural scene it observes:

Not only all vivid emotions, and all circumstances of exciting interest, leave their light and shadow on the senseless things and instruments among which, or through whose agency, they have been felt or learned, but I believe that the eye cannot rest on a material form, in a moment of depression or exultation, without communicating to that form a spirit and a life, – a life which will make it afterwards in some degree loved or feared, – a charm or a painfulness for which we shall be unable to account even to ourselves, which will not indeed be perceptible, except by its delicate influence on our judgement in cases of complicated beauty.[106]

Ruskin admitted that a genuine emotional response is a necessary corollary to the detailed observation of fact, that 'FINE ART is that in which the hand, the head, and the *heart* of man go together.'[107] But how could he guard against the emotional response taking over and making the work of art too subjective?

He sought a solution in the objectification of the emotions themselves. The ideal artist, he said, should have a capacity to distance himself sufficiently from his emotions:

the high creative poet might even be thought, to a great extent, impassive (as shallow people think Dante stern), receiving indeed all feelings to the full, but having a great centre of reflection and knowledge in which he stands serene, and watches the feeling, as it were, from afar off.[108]

The sense of beauty or of sublimity, in Ruskin's opinion, should find expression in disinterested emotion:

it is not the fear, observe, but the contemplation of death; not the instinctive shudder and struggle of self-preservation, but the deliberate measurement of the doom, which is really great or sublime in feeling... There is no sublimity in the agony of terror.[109]

Another way in which Ruskin attempts to demonstrate the objective existence of the beautiful is by admitting a strong emotional response, but suggesting also that everyone responds with identical emotions to specific visual qualities. By such a theory of uniform emotional reaction, Ruskin tries to uphold the concept of an eternal metaphysical order of beauty.

But this ran contrary to the kind of emotional response that Ruskin himself had to nature, which was unique and personal. Despite his recognition of the limitations of a subjectivist aesthetic, Ruskin was proposing what was, in substance, a Wordsworthian, emotionalist theory of painting and poetry. In his discussion of composition in volume five of *Modern Painters*, Ruskin points out that 'a great composition always has a leading emotional purpose, technically called its motive, to which all its lines and forms have some relation'.[110] The relationship between different art forms became fluid for Ruskin as he adopted the notion of art as a means of expression above and beyond a formal medium.[111] Not only does he transfer to the visual arts Wordsworthian ideas concerning the nature and function of poetry, and use metaphors from the other arts to elucidate principles of painting, but he also, in the very fact of turning art criticism into a creative genre, transmutes the visual mode of art into the literal mode. As Wilde remarks, Ruskin, like Pater, treated 'the work of art simply as a starting-point for a new creation'.[112]

Romantic theories of art tend to concentrate on the nature and function of the artist. It is significant that we are presented with the 'Truths' of nature through the medium of art in *Modern Painters* and that the artist is given the role of guiding our response, of interpreting nature, and making possible the revitalisation of a relationship between man and his world which has deteriorated. Ruskin revered the 'high and solitary minds' of the great artists,[113] so unique, so intensely original.[114] In short, there is much to counteract the scientific detailing of objective fact in *Modern Painters* – the exaltation of the artist, the mystical power of nature, the imagination, intense emotional response to fine detail.

Ruskin tried to reconcile the claims of subjectivism and objectivism in his own writing, and often he triumphed. But sometimes he seems to tread a precarious path between a subjective, lyrical style of criticism and a pedantic, painstaking, antiquarianism. He was himself a prey to acute subjectivism. Although he endeavoured to explore the identity, the individual expression, the selfhood of the physical objects he studied, he could not escape his own self. In his diaries, notebooks, and sketches Ruskin attempts to capture the autonomous power of objects through an ever more precise and intense notation of their innermost phases and structures. But as he labours to mark the distinctions between individual forms more and more minutely his task becomes frighteningly complex and he finds himself overwhelmed by a sea of detail to which it is impossible to respond normally:

abysses of life and pain, of diabolic ingenuity, merciless condemnation, irrevocable change, infinite scorn, endless advance, immeasurable scale of beings incomprehensible to each other, every one important in its own sight and a grain of dust in its Creator's – it makes me giddy and desolate beyond all speaking.[115]

Ruskin's confession in an Addendum to his 1853 Edinburgh Lecture on Pre-Raphaelitism that 'it is possible to love this truth of reality too intensely'[116] suggests that he sometimes felt swamped by the sense of chaotic fragmentation around him. Far from calling forth a truly objective response, the minute particularisation of detail causes him to retreat further into himself.

The effects of emotional subjectivism, arising out of the very attempt to be objective, are occasionally apparent in Ruskin's published writings on nature and art. In some of his works he seems to walk a knife-edge between a rather pedantic cataloguing of detail on the one hand and a purely interpretative, sometimes wildly imaginative flight of fancy on the other. At such times, his preoccupation with the distinctive, his mania for detail, his excessive concern to organise his response around objective precision, will suddenly culminate in a statement which removes the work, without warning, from objective description to highly subjective interpretation. For example, he concludes a sensitive and learned discussion of Gothic naturalism in architecture with the judgement that

Those cornices are the Venetian Ecclesiastical Gothic; the Christian element struggling with the Formalism of the Papacy, – the Papacy being entirely heathen in all its principles. That officialism of the leaves and their ribs means Apostolic Succession, and I don't know how much more, and is already preparing for the transition to old Heathenism again, and the Renaissance.

Now look to the last cornice (g). That is Protestantism, – a slight touch of Dissent, hardly amounting to schism, in those falling leaves, but true life in the whole of it. The forms all broken through, and sent heaven knows where, but the root held fast; and the strong sap in the branches; and, best of all, good fruit ripening and opening straight towards heaven, and in the face of it, even though some of the leaves lie in the dust.

Now, observe. The cornice *f* represents Heathenism and Papistry, animated by the mingling of Christianity and nature. The good in it, the life of it, the veracity and liberty of it, such as it has, are Protestantism in its heart: the rigidity and saplessness are the Romanism of it.[117]

This cannot be put down simply to typical Victorian Evangelical paranoia. Ruskin's vision of an objective, unchanging reality, far from preserving him from excessive self-consciousness, all too often broke down into profound subjectivism through the very extremity of his effort to maintain it.

IV

In March 1840, Ruskin decided 'to keep one part of diary for intellect and another for feeling'.[118] This rather peculiar decision suggests not only that Ruskin was in some very important ways quite unlike Words-worth and Coleridge, who would never have conceived of such a division, but also that he had profound misgivings about the nature of the relationship between self-scrutiny and other kinds of mental activity. What exactly was the connection between the self and external nature? His suspicion of all things German and his habitually scornful dismissal of abstraction join forces to make his evasion of what is surely the central question in perception seem like a triumphant refutation of Romantic metaphysical speculation. He disposes of what he calls privately 'the vile rubbish of the metaphysicians'[119] in one paragraph in his discussion of the 'Imaginative Faculty' in volume two of *Modern Painters*:

Unfortunately, the works of metaphysicians will afford us in this most interesting inquiry, no aid whatsoever. They who are constantly en-deavouring to fathom and explain the essence of the faculties of mind, are sure, in the end, to lose sight of all that cannot be explained (though it may be defined and felt); and because, as I shall presently show, the essence of the Imaginative faculty is utterly mysterious and inexplicable, and to be recognized in its results only, or in the negative results of its absence, the metaphysicians, as far as I am acquainted with their works, miss it altogether, and never reach higher than a definition of Fancy by a false name.[120]

He is more vituperative still in his Appendix to volume three on German philosophy. He rejects German metaphysics as 'pure, definite, and highly finished nonsense',[121] and expresses a loathing for the fashionable bandying of the words 'objective' and 'subjective', 'two of the most objectionable words that were ever coined by the troublesomeness of metaphysicians'.[122] As an Evangelical, his faith rested on feelings rather than systems, and on the Bible. He is therefore just as contemptuous of the other main German intellectual contribution to nineteenth-century thought, Scriptural criticism, which was gradually eroding the sacred authority of the Bible. But his failure to confront the crucial questions about the nature of perception and imagination, the relation of nature to the divine, and the implications of historical and geological developments, his abhorrence for all theories and his reliance on feelings, meant that he was ill-equipped to cope with the changes that he was forced to recognise as the 1850s drew to a close.[123]

His only resources were emotional, and under such pressure they proved inadequate. As early as 1851 he was writing that his faith was 'being beaten into mere gold leaf, and flutters in weak rags from the letter of its own forms...If only the geologists would let me alone, I could do very well, but those dreadful Hammers! I hear the clink of them at the end of every cadence of the Bible verses.'[124] In volume three of *Modern Painters* he complains that 'with us...the idea of the Divinity is apt to get separated from the life of nature'.[125] He begins to concentrate less on nature itself and more on its moral meaning for mankind whereby the 'conditions of mountain structure' have been 'calculated for the delight, the advantage, or the teaching of men; prepared, it seems, so as to contain...some beneficence of gift, or profoundness of counsel'.[126] By 1860, when he was finishing *Modern Painters*, his once divine landscape is invaded by images of evolution:

The autumn sun, low but clear, shines on the scarlet ash-berries and on the golden birch-leaves, which, fallen here and there, when the breeze has not caught them, rest quiet in the crannies of the purple rock. Beside the rock, in the hollow under the thicket, the carcase of a ewe, drowned in the last flood, lies nearly bare to the bone, its white ribs protruding through the skin, raven-torn; and the rags of its wool still flickering from the branches that first stayed it as the stream swept it down. A little lower, the current plunges, roaring, into a circular chasm like a well...down which the foam slips in detached snow-flakes. Round the edges of the pool beneath, the water circles slowly, like black oil; a little butterfly lies on its back, its wings glued to one of the eddies, its limbs feebly quivering; a fish rises, and it is gone.[127]

It is an image of redundancy, the raven feeding on the lamb. By the time he wrote *The Storm Cloud of the Nineteenth Century*, in 1884, his vision of nature had darkened over completely, taken over by plague-winds and storm-clouds:

...the sky is covered with grey cloud; – not rain-cloud, but a dry black veil, which no ray of sunshine can pierce; partly diffused in mist, feeble mist, enough to make distant objects unintelligible, yet without any substance or wreathing, or colour of its own. And everywhere the leaves of the trees are shaking fitfully, as they do before a thunderstorm; only not violently, but enough to show the passing to and fro of a strange, bitter, blighting wind...It looks partly as if it were made of poisonous smoke; very possibly it may be: there are at least two hundred furnace chimneys in a space of two miles on every side of me. But mere smoke would not blow to and fro in that wild way. It looks more to me as if it were made of dead men's souls...[128]

He speaks of past ages when God was an integrated part of nature:

In the entire system of the Firmament, thus seen and understood, there appeared to be, to all the thinkers of those ages, the incontrovertible and unmistakable evidence of a Divine Power in creation, which had fitted, as the air for human breath, so the clouds for human sight and nourishment; – the Father who was in heaven feeding day by day the souls of His children with marvels, and satisfying them with bread, and so filling their hearts with food and gladness.[129]

But those days are immeasurably far away from modern man, who has lost his instinctual sense of the divine in nature, and has drifted into 'hesitating sentiment, pathetic fallacy, and wandering fancy'.

Ruskin eventually regained something of his early feeling for nature, and some of the last things he wrote, such as his collection of essays on geology, entitled *Deucalion*, and especially the charming and whimsical 'Lecture on Snakes', suggest a new mythopoeic outlook. But even here, in his delightful 'spiritual version of the development of species', in which he argues that a serpent is not only 'as Professor Huxley showed you, a lizard that has dropped his legs off', but 'a duck that has dropped her wings off...a fish that has dropped his fins off...And...a honeysuckle, with a head put on',[130] it is clear that he has failed to resolve the difficulties and contradictions he had encountered some thirty years earlier. He writes:

All these living forms, and the laws that rule them, are parables, when once you can read; but you can only read them through love, and the sense of beauty; and some day I hope to plead with you a little, of the value of that sense, and the way you have been lately losing it.[131]

And we sympathise with his insistence on the irreducibility of aesthetic experience. But, for all his desire to be objective, he is still resisting Darwinism in favour of myth, on the grounds that 'both in science and literature...the feeblest myth is better than the strongest theory'.[132]

Ruskin's curious reluctance to engage in theory, whether philosophical or scientific, seems to have been bound up with his reluctance to confront something deep within himself. He wished to bury his head in the sand, and evade the implications of Darwinism and German Idealism, not only for Victorian religion and aesthetics, but also for his own identity. But as much as he might have wished to brush the metaphysicians away 'like spiders'[133] and to eliminate Darwinism by striking Darwin's works out of his list of books,[134] they could not so easily be dismissed. And, partly because of his failure fully and openly to acknowledge their theories, Ruskin's early religio-aesthetic philosophy, as he doubtless knew, was henceforth no longer tenable.

V

Ruskin's earlier writings imply a belief in the possibility of refining human sensibility through the study of art, and a faith in the interpretation of art, not only as a moral act, but as an instrument of aesthetic education, through the presentation of moral truths. But as time went on, there was a perceptible shift in his position, which is best expressed by his dictum, 'Good pictures do not teach a nation; they are the signs of its having been taught.'[135] This idea of the relationship between art and the society which produced it was always implicit even in his early writing on art, and it is developed most memorably in his chapter 'On the Nature of Gothic' in *The Stones of Venice* (1851) when he invites the reader to 'look around this room of yours', and find there in its ugly uniformity all the evidence of an enslaved condition. But as he lost his faith in the divinity of nature, and as he became confirmed in his role of a Victorian Prophet and Sage, he shifted ground, and although still very much an art historian, Slade Professor at Oxford from 1870, and a lecturer and writer on art throughout his life, instead of concentrating his efforts on the interpretation of art as a way of teaching the nation, he moved into a more directly social and political mode:

I utterly disdain to speak a word about art in the hearing of any English creature – at present.
Let us make our Religion true, and our Trade honest. *Then* and not till then will there be even so much as *ground* for casting seed of the Arts.[136]

In *Unto this Last* (1860), *Sesame and Lilies* (1865), and *Fors Clavigera* (1871–7), he sees the way to refine and improve the human condition in terms of the development of an improved social government and political economy, a proper attitude to work, and a more enlightened educational system. Ruskin's growing politicism aligns him firmly with the

Coleridgean and Carlylean tradition, and his unusual brand of socialism, based almost totally on his aesthetic sensibility, provides a baton for William Morris to take up as an earlier generation of Pre-Raphaelites had taken up his theories about painting. This is the intellectual ground, too, on which Ruskin and Arnold most significantly meet, in that both were motivated by a desire to give art the burden of saving society, then go on to develop a view of society which depends on a particular idea of culture. And it is also perhaps the personal ground on which they meet. Both men moved away from the aesthetic concerns of their youth, and plunged instead into the public *melange* of political and social debate. This means that the world has benefited from some inspired and original works on culture and society, works, which, for many modern readers, seem more relevant and important than their earlier writings. But it also meant that both Ruskin and Arnold avoided having to come to terms with the more deeply involving and disturbing questions about the self which they encountered in their youthful writings but left unresolved. As George Eliot wisely observes in *Middlemarch*, 'I know no speck so troublesome as self.'[137]

Matthew Arnold

I

When Arnold was once criticised for being as dogmatic as Ruskin, he claimed that there was an important difference: Ruskin was 'dogmatic and wrong'.[138] But the comparison was an acute one, especially given that their dogmatism derived from similar intellectual and, fundamentally, personal inadequacies. Arnold was considerably influenced by Ruskin, even if he was not always in agreement with him and felt he should never like him.[139] His only published critical discussion of Ruskin's work, in 'The Literary Influence of Academies', serves his argument for the establishment of a literary academy in England. To illustrate the general 'want of balance of mind and urbanity of style' in English literature, Arnold compares two passages of Ruskin's prose, the first a description of the Swiss lakes and mountains, the second a passage about the etymology of Shakespearean names, and pronounces the former the writing of genius, the latter absurd and provincial.[140] His attitude towards Ruskin was always equivocal. For example, we know from Arnold's reading lists that he planned to read volume three of *Modern Painters* in March 1856,[141] the year in which it was published, and some eighteen years later we find him jotting down a quotation in his notebook from the same work:

There is not a moment of any day of our lives when nature is not producing picture after picture and working still upon such exquisite and constant principles of such perfect beauty that it is quite certain it is all done for us, and intended for our perpetual pleasure.[142]

But he uses this quotation to illustrate a particular kind of religious statement which he is bent on criticising in *God and the Bible*.[143] It is Ruskin the art critic who most interests Arnold, not, as one would expect, the critic of society. In 1865, Arnold planned to write a review of Joseph Milsand's newly published *L'Esthétique anglaise, étude sur M. John Ruskin* for the *Pall Mall Gazette*.[144] Unfortunately his intention remained unrealised. It is interesting to speculate whether Arnold would have been alert to the philosophical shortcomings of Ruskin's theories of perception and aesthetics. For the same shortcomings are to be found in Arnold's writings, except that in his case his central concern is epistemological, and it is in this area that he fails to do justice to the Kantian tradition.

On the face of it, Arnold's attitude towards German Romantic philosophy seems not unlike Ruskin's. Like Ruskin, he frequently denounces German metaphysicians for the vagueness of their jargon and the bewildering abstraction and aridity of their systems:

What a series of philosophic systems has Germany seen since the birth of Goethe! and what sort of a stay is any one of them compared with the poetry of Germany's one great poet?[145]

And he similarly chose to oversimplify the vastly complicated questions of seeing and judgement by demanding, like Ruskin, that the object should be seen 'as in itself it really is'.[146]

But actually Arnold's relationship with Kant was far more complex than it might at first appear from his own disclaimers. First of all, encouraged by both his friend Clough and his reading of Carlyle, Arnold had read widely in philosophy during his years at Oxford. Kenneth Allott's publication of Arnold's reading lists in three early diaries from the years 1845–7[147] reveals his familiarity not only with Plato and Aristotle, but with Schelling, Kant, and Herder too. For example, he read, or planned to read, the first part of Kant's *Critique of Pure Reason*, in translation in 1845 and in German in 1846, and Herder's *Metakritik* on Kant's Critique in 1846.[148] Schelling's *The Philosophy of Art: An Oration on the Relation between the Plastic Arts and Nature* heads his reading list for 1847.[149] And A. W. Benn notes that Arnold generally passed for a disciple of Hegel, 'probably without ever having read him'.[150] But, as Allott points out:

Between 1845 and 1850 I think it is possible to trace Arnold's growing impatience with German idealism and with such writers as Schelling whom at first he found stimulating and to some extent sympathetic.[151]

Arnold found the metaphysics of German Idealism increasingly uncongenial to the writing of poetry, and came to favour Locke and Spinoza. In a letter written in 1850 to Clough, he explained:

I go to read Locke on the Conduct of the Understanding: my respect for the reason as the rock of refuge for this poor exaggerated surexcited humanity increases. Locke is a man who has cleared his mind of vain repetitions, though without the positive and vivifying atmosphere of Spinoza about him.[152]

Arnold's reading of Spinoza later inspired him to write 'The Bishop and the Philosopher' for *Macmillan's Magazine* in 1863, expanded into 'Spinoza and the Bible' for *Essays in Criticism, First Series*. In the latter he wrote:

To be great [the philosopher] must have something in him which can influence character, which is edifying; he must, in short, have a noble and lofty character himself, a character – to recur to that much-criticised expression of mine – *in the grand style*.[153]

Clearly, Kant, for Arnold, lacked the 'grand style'. Nevertheless, we can trace throughout his notebooks a continuing interest in the German Idealists, which distinguishes Arnold's antipathy from Ruskin's. In 1858, for example, he notes Kuno Fischer's descriptions of Kant's transcendental philosophy and Bacon's empirical philosophy,[154] while in 1874 he records the definition in the *Dictionnaire de la langue française* of 'Métaphysique – (selon Kant)', and Hegel's definition of 'substance'.[155] A note for 1877 reads:

'The primary question of metaphysics: *How is knowledge possible?*'
'"Kant set himself to ascertain what the relations are which are necessary to constitute any intelligent experience", or (which is the same) "any knowable world".'[156]

The implications of Kantian metaphysics invade Arnold's intellectual interests in every sphere: his ideas about the epistemological nature of poetry, about the suggestive rather than definitive power of language, and about a religion with an ethical basis yet a mystical transcendence. Nevertheless, his attitude towards Kant is highly equivocal, and the cause of his ambivalence may be traced to a reluctance to confront with due clarity the question of the self.

Critical attention has often quite naturally focused on Arnold's role as mediator between opposite extremes. His writing encourages us to think of him as a reconciler of Hebrew and Hellene, of Romanticism and classicism, of Newman and Huxley, of radical and conservative, and, in line with these other oppositions, of the subjective and the objective. But it has also been noticed that his critical position is frequently related to more personal concerns. This may simply represent a biographical factor. For example, it is arguable that Arnold's desire to reconcile traditional religion and contemporary thought, conservative and radical strains, is rooted in the dichotomous influences on him of Newman and Keble (his godfather) on the one hand and his father, Thomas Arnold, on the other. More significantly, the source of a theoretical idea may be located deep in his psyche: as Alba Warren suggests, Arnold's early formalistic poetic theory can only be accounted for, in a criticism which is predominantly Romantic, as a reflection of his need for form in *life*.[157] Arnold's critical reconciliations are perhaps less objectively determined than personally conceived.

This is nowhere more evident than in the case of Arnold's attitude towards the self. The very word is a constantly recurring motif in his writing – 'The Buried Self', 'Self-dependence', the 'best self'. In an endless struggle with his own sense of self, Arnold relentlessly searches for objective sanctions for his own feelings and convictions about art, literature, society, and religion. In itself, this is not unnatural; but as the objective authorities pile up, we become increasingly aware that his need for them is obsessive: classical form, touchstones, the 'culture' of Western Civilisation, verifiable 'natural truth' in the Bible, a common body of moral experience, and, ultimately and most revealingly, the 'Eternal not-ourselves'. Sadly, and perhaps inevitably, Arnold failed in his effort to achieve the complete transcendence of self that he desired. The objective sanctions he invoked so doggedly in his critical, social, and religious writings are usually subjectively determined by an all too recognisable Matthew Arnold.

II

We are told, 'by one who knew him well' (probably his brother Thomas), that Arnold

plunged very deeply in the years following his father's death in the vast sea of Goethe's art and Spinoza's mysticism...He had already in 1845 drifted far away from orthodox Christianity, so that the appearance of the translation of Strauss's *Leben Jesu* in that year – an epoch-making book for many – found him uncurious and uninterested.[158]

We know from his early diaries that Goethe and Spinoza were not the only thinkers to whom Arnold turned in those years of spiritual crisis. For he may have drifted far from orthodox Christianity, but he was still searching for an adequate substitute for it. Some may ascribe his entire literary history to this search, but certainly the immediacy and tension of that first period of religious doubt and philosophical enquiry is an important background to the poetry he wrote between the mid forties and the publication of the 1853 edition of the *Poems* with its important Preface.

He read widely during this period in the traditions of Locke and of Kant, of rationalism and of Romanticism, he explored both Western and Eastern religious philosophies, and the inconsistency of his own philosophical position, as reflected in the poetry and the unpublished prose of this period, is in part due to the pluralism of his interests. But the catholicity of his intellectual enterprise seems only to have confirmed his despair. T. S. Eliot locates Arnold's own spiritual crisis very specifically in the mood of his time, when he says of his 'Stanzas from the Grande Chartreuse' that they

voice a moment of historic doubt, recorded by its most representative mind, a moment which has passed, which most of us have gone beyond in one direction or another; but it represents that moment for ever.[159]

The melancholy tone of the poem and its Romantic view of the 'ghost-like' cloistered monks with their 'cowled forms' and their 'white uplifted faces' suggests an ascetic ideal of Christianity which, as we know from the famous description of Oxford with which he introduces his lecture on Emerson, Arnold always associated with Newman.[160] As William Madden suggests, 'Stanzas from the Grande Chartreuse' indicates the deep and important connection between Romanticism and Christianity in Arnold's experience,[161] which offset the robust liberalism of his father's religious position and the rationalism of his intellectual milieu as an undergraduate. But the thrust of the poem shows just how far Arnold had moved from traditional Christianity, and how alienated he felt in the modern world. The poet realises that he cannot succumb to nostalgia as a way of evading his disenchantment with the modern world, and he recognises that the cloistered life of the monks is symbolic of a more significant dislocation from the needs of modern life.[162]

Arnold's attitude at this time towards the position of historical Christianity in the modern world is clear: it is 'But a dead time's exploded dream'. Yet the painfulness of his own purgatorial dilemma, strung between the discredited values of the old world and the unsympathetic coldness of the new, is equally clear. Newman had conjoined Christian faith with Wordsworthian feeling. Loss of faith, therefore, had a terrible corollary for Arnold – a loss of the ability to feel:

I cannot conceal from myself the objection which really wounds and perplexes me from the religious side is that the service of reason is freezing to feeling, chilling to the religious moods and feeling and the religious moods are eternally the deepest being of man, the ground of all joy and greatness for him.[163]

Arnold felt, then, not only spiritually and morally, but emotionally and aesthetically deprived. As he wrote to Clough:

These are damned times – everything is against one – the height to which knowledge is come, the spread of luxury, our physical enervation, the absence of great *natures*, the unavoidable contact with small ones, newspapers, cities, light profligate friends, moral desperadoes like Carlyle, our own selves, and the sickening consciousness of our difficulties.[164]

The juxtaposition of the 'damned times' and 'our own selves' is an important motif of the correspondence between Arnold and Clough, and an essential element in the success of Arnold's poetry. For many readers, it is the representative quality of Arnold's poems, the sense they give of conveying a universally painful mid-Victorian experience, rather than Arnold's facility with poetic language and form, which makes him a great poet. Arnold wrote to his mother in 1869:

My poems represent, on the whole, the main movement of mind of the last quarter of a century, and thus they will probably have their day as people become conscious to themselves of what that movement of mind is and interested in the literary productions which reflect it.[165]

If the success of his poetry is to some extent dependent on the fact that it perfectly expresses the anxieties of his age, it was nevertheless for Arnold an age which thwarted the imaginative life, in that it was inherently 'unpoetical', 'Not unprofound, not ungrand, not unmoving: – but *unpoetical*.'[166] The paradox of Arnold's poetry is that it seeks to present and analyse 'the modern situation in its true *blankness* and *barrenness*, and *unpoetrylessness*'.[167]

In line with his attribution of his own difficulties in writing poetry to the uncongenial mood of the times, he tends, in his poetry, to locate the source of the problems with which he is confronted in the human condition, and the *Zeitgeist*. In 'Dover Beach', for example, his loss of faith is presented less as a personal than a historical crisis:

The Sea of Faith
Was once, too, at the full, and round earth's shore
Lay like the folds of a bright girdle furled.
But now I only hear
Its melancholy, long, withdrawing roar,
Retreating, to the breath
Of the night-wind, down the vast edges drear
And naked shingles of the world.

Ah, love, let us be true
To one another! for the world, which seems
To lie before us like a land of dreams,
So various, so beautiful, so new,
Hath really neither joy, nor love, nor light,
Nor certitude, nor peace, nor help for pain;
And we are here as on a darkling plain
Swept with confused alarms of struggle and flight,
Where ignorant armies clash by night.[168]

It is, of course, convincing to account for his own loss of faith in this way: this was an age which witnessed the 'disappearance of God'. But this is also a love poem, and here, as in other poems in the series addressed to the mysterious Marguerite, we might suspect the persona's self-justifications of being an elaborate device to shift the focus away from his own emotional difficulties to some larger cultural crisis. Elsewhere, he assigns his romantic failure to an objective cause, which he describes variously as 'Necessity', a 'God', 'Ye guiding Powers'[169] – a conscious imaginative device, but one which suggests the nature of his own dilemma.

Arnold's poems hang in perfect tragic tension, between a flawed individual and his inevitable destiny. Both his own weaknesses and a hostile or indifferent universe contribute in the sealing of his fate. Arnold's love poems are in many ways his greatest, in that they show most poignantly of all the isolation of the human being and the impossibility of communication in the modern world. But, at the same time, they also show most clearly Arnold's propensity to construct objective explanations for his own deepest problems.

To say this is not, of course, to deny the very real intellectual and spiritual problems which faced Arnold as a Victorian. Both his early poetry and his correspondence with Clough are haunted by a sense of the degradation of modern civilisation, and of the insufficiency of modern intellectual traditions. Against a background of the ever diminishing hold of Christianity and the ever increasing grip of scientific materialism, what, for example, was the relationship between man and nature?

This, perhaps the most central and traditional concern of poetry, was no easy matter for an agnostic to determine in the middle of the nineteenth century. Tennyson's 'Nature, red in tooth and claw' was not the only matter for concern.[170] Wordsworth's sacramentalism was impossible for a non-believer to recapture. But was the only alternative the possibility offered by Kant, Fichte, and Schelling: that nature depended entirely on human perception, on the 'world-creating self'?[171] Coleridge's much-quoted 'Dejection' states the Kantian position:

> O Lady! we receive but what we give,
> And in our life alone does Nature live.[172]

Arnold confronts the philosophical question of whether the reality of nature is internal or external, subjectively or objectively defined in the poems he wrote on Wordsworth's death, 'The Youth of Nature' and its sequel 'The Youth of Man'. Arnold's position is made clear in the early lines of both poems:

> We, O Nature, depart
> Thou survivest us![173]

> Rydal and Fairfield are there;
> In the shadow Wordsworth lies dead.
> So it is, so it will be for aye.
> Nature is fresh as of old,
> Is lovely: a mortal is dead.[174]

Nevertheless, Wordsworth 'lent a new life to these hills', and on his death 'darkness returns to our eyes'.[175] Was he responsible for creating what he saw, or was it really there? The poet puts the question directly to nature:

> For, oh! is it you, is it you,
> Moonlight, and shadow, and lake,
> And mountains, that fill us with joy,
> Or the poet who sings you so well?

Nature's reply makes it clear that 'More than the singer are these':

> 'Loveliness, magic, and grace,
> They are here! they are set in the world,
> They abide;...
> The poet who sings them may die,
> But they are immortal and live...'[176]

Arnold's repudiation of the Kantian–Coleridgean position is made even clearer in 'The Youth of Man', where his speakers are an old married couple musing on the folly of their youth, when they arrogantly believed that

> Nature is nothing; her charm
> Lives in our eyes which can paint,
> Lives in our hearts which can feel.[177]

But now it is 'They, not Nature are changed', while the 'Soul of the world' rules on. The exhortation in the closing lines of the poem is:

> Sink, O youth, in thy soul!
> Yearn to the greatness of Nature;
> Rally the good in the depths of thyself![178]

In 'The Youth of Nature' Arnold similarly suggests that the root of the problem of the relationship between man and nature lies in his failure to know 'the unlit gulph of himself':

> Ye know not yourselves; and your bards –
> The clearest, the best, who have read
> Most in themselves – have beheld
> Less than they left unrevealed.
> Ye express not yourselves...[179]

In the same way, Empedocles tries

> To see if we will now at last be true
> To our own only true, deep-buried selves,
> Being one with which we are one with the whole world.[180]

'Resolve to be thyself' is a clarion call that resounds through his poetry and his letters to Clough:

> 'Resolve to be thyself; and know that he
> Who finds himself, loses his misery!'[181]

But the reality all too often involves either a lapsing into an extreme and 'unhealthy' form of subjectivism – witness Arnold's recognition of just this failing in Clough; 'you poor subjective, you'[182] – or, in an attempt to avoid this state, a complete withdrawal from the self. In his essay 'On the Modern Element in Literature', Arnold translates Lucretius' description of *ennui* as a state in which 'everyone flies from himself'.[183] Indeed, as Lionel Trilling points out,[184] in a post-Kantian universe, the self became an intolerable burden for many intellectuals in the nineteenth century. Empedocles mourns the fact that 'we feel, day and night,/The burden of ourselves'.[185] For the aesthetic, ethical, and metaphysical self-determination that underpinned Kantian philosophy carried with it implications that many found difficult to bear. Self-dependence had its responsibilities. It also had its painful corollaries, for it was but a short step from personal responsibility to isolation and alienation.

In 'The Buried Life' Arnold suggests that, in order to protect man's 'genuine self', his 'identity', from being squandered away, Fate

> Bade through the deep recesses of our breast
> The unregarded river of our life
> Pursue with indiscernible flow its way.[186]

But the self could not be so suppressed without incurring pain, for often, in the middle of everything,

> There rises an unspeakable desire
> After the knowledge of our buried life.[187]

Yet, try as we might to pierce through to the mystery of 'Our hidden self', it will remain an 'elusive shadow', relieved only by momentary glimpses of self-knowledge.

Arnold's painful sense of the desirability yet impossibility of real self-knowledge, and his fear of the self either being swallowed up by or taking over the objective world, were questions which impinged significantly on his ideas about the role of the poet. Long before he made his public critical proclamations about poetry, Arnold had begun formulating his thoughts, in his letters to Clough and in his poetry itself, on the proper stance of the poet, the proper subject-matter for poetry, and the function of poetry in the modern world. His speculations about poetry are as wide-ranging and inconsistent as his philosophical speculations and his thoughts about the self, but his concern is usually with the question of whether the poet should engage himself in the world or remain aloof and detached.

In 'Stanzas in Memory of the Author of Obermann', in which he compares himself with Goethe, Wordsworth, and Senancour, and identifies with the latter's clear head, 'feeling chill', and 'icy' despair rather than with 'Wordsworth's sweet calm, or Goethe's wide/And luminous view', Arnold voices the dilemma of the nineteenth-century poet:

> Ah! two desires toss about
> The poet's feverish blood.
> One drives him to the world without,
> And one to solitude.[188]

The vocation of the poet is a solitary one, and Empedocles, in his anguished cry to Apollo, explores the poetic and personal costs of his isolation:

> Thou keepest aloof the profane,
> But the solitude oppresses thy votary!
> The jars of men reach him not in thy valley –
> But can life reach him?
> Thou fencest him from the multitude –
> Who will fence him from himself?[189]

At the height of his despair, Empedocles understands that the poet is essentially alienated, caught between two worlds, the peak and the plain, solitude and the multitude, contemplation and action, aspiration and resignation, and that there is no escape:

> ... only death
> Can cut his oscillations short, and so
> Bring him to poise. There is no other way.[190]

This conflict is one that Arnold voices at many points in his early poetry and in his letters to Clough, and it is perhaps metaphorically true to say that Empedocles' solution was the only way of resolving the problem of the poet's self for Arnold too. Only death, the poetic suicide represented by the literary manifesto of the 1853 Preface, could bring Arnold to that classical poise he was always in search of. There was, for him too, 'no other way'.[191]

The theme of the poet's true stance is taken up again in 'The Strayed Reveller', which opens with an abandonment to sensation which is more characteristic of Keats or Maurice de Guérin than of Arnold. Immediately the vexed question of the poet's self is apparent. In one sense the Youth's engagement with reality is highly subjective. Yet in another, in that he 'aspires to be a sort of Aeolian harp',[192] he is receptive rather than creative, passively giving up his selfhood to the objective world rather than imposing his subjective interpretation of that world. But is it possible for the poet to see the world entirely objectively, 'as in itself it really is', without surrendering his identity?

> such a price
> The Gods exact for song:
> To become what we sing.[193]

The price is that the poet shall experience the pain of which he writes. But this is only the corollary of a more important cost: the sacrifice of the self, Keats' 'Negative Capability'. The poet cannot retain a godlike detachment from the reality of which he writes. He must subsume himself in that reality. In one sense, the Youth is asserting his discovery of his inner self through an act of perception whereby subject and object become as one. But in another sense irony is at work, and the Youth's synthesis seems highly equivocal. At best it might be seen to depend on youthful innocence and undeveloped intellect, at worst as the effect of a mythical vintage of wine, unavailable in the average Victorian cellar, on an adolescent who can hold neither his drink nor his philosophy.

'The Scholar Gipsy' presents the other side of the dialogue. Here the hero has opted out of the world before he has been polluted by it:

For early didst thou leave the world, with powers
Fresh, undiverted to the world without,
Firm to their mark, not spent on other things.[194]

'Fly our paths, our feverish contact fly', the poet urges, for in the world
'each half-lives a hundred different lives'.[195] The only way to protect
one's self from the world is to withdraw from it.

But, finally, Arnold himself chose neither of these positions. His path
was to be that of the poet of 'Resignation':

> The poet, to whose mighty heart
> Heaven doth a quicker pulse impart,
> Subdues that energy to scan
> Not his own course, but that of man.[196]

When he writes in this non-personal way about man, he does so from a
position of detachment – 'uncravingly'; 'From some high station he
looks down.' He does not write of his own deepest sense of isolation
and alienation, 'And does not say: *I am alone*', but rather celebrates the
general life:

> Before him he sees life unroll,
> A placid and continuous whole –
> That general life, which does not cease,
> Whose secret is not joy, but peace.[197]

How different this is from the Wordsworthian sense of the spiritual life
of nature, and of its organic wholeness. For the poet of 'Resignation',
the things of nature 'Seem to bear rather than rejoice'. The poem is
dramatic, and Arnold is adopting a position here on poetry as he does
in quite different ways in other poems. Nevertheless it seems to be the
position which identifies most closely with his own.

It seems likely that Arnold's preference for the poet's adoption of a
classical detachment from the world is closely related to a fear of
becoming consumed by the world, to a reluctance to 'negative' the self.
At an ironic distance, he might endeavour to understand without having
to submit to empathic vision. But paradoxically, the very decision
to retain his vulnerable identity by courting disinterestedness rather
than involvement meant that Arnold was forced into a position where
he had to surrender his true self. As Trilling explains it, 'He stood
ready to sacrifice poetic talent, formed in the solitude of the self, to the
creation of a character, formed in the crowding objectivity of the
world.'[198] Arnold abandoned his self and his highly-prized integrity
when he opted to write about the 'general life' rather than plumbing the
depths of his own soul. According to the view presented in 'Resignation',
'*Not deep the poet sees, but wide.*' Arnold was oddly prophetic when he

wrote in 'Stanzas in Memory of the Author of Obermann', 'He only lives with the world's life,/Who hath renounced his own' and completes the statement with the spare words, 'I in the world must live.'[199] Arnold's own decision to live in the world, to enter the public fray of literary criticism, of religious and political debate, meant that he had to renounce his own deepest self.

The critical explanations for Arnold's move from poetry to prose, from the near-aestheticism of his early poetry and poetics to an increasingly moral view of the function of poetry, and from a broadly subjective to a more objective mode of discourse, have been many and various. Fulweiler, for example, believes that Arnold lost faith in the creative power of language, and that the shift from imaginative literature to critical writing reflects that failure of confidence.[200] For Madden, on the other hand, Arnold, though inhibited by the ethical and intellectual currents of his generation, never lost his faith in the aestheticism of his youth, and he continued to defend the creative poetic imagination in his critical works. His movement from poetry into prose was due to a loss of faith in his own power as a poet to realise the union of imagination and reason which he was formulating in his criticism.[201] My own conclusion is that Arnold's abandonment of poetry as the central medium of expression was probably due to his realisation of his personal failure to resolve the problem of the poet's engagement with his subject, to his recognition that his own need for detachment and the necessary empathy of the poet were irreconcilable. In a letter to Clough, Arnold wrote 'Shairp urges me to speak more from myself: which I less and less have the inclination to do: or even the power.' Shairp explained his own views of Arnold's poetic problems to Clough: 'Mat, as I told him, disowns man's natural feelings, and they will disown his poetry: If there's nothing else in the world but blank dejections, it's not worth while setting them to music.'[202]

To whatever reason we attribute the shift in Arnold's endeavours, it is hard to refute Trilling's conclusion that in so doing Arnold betrays his real self in favour of an objectively determined idea of how the individual should relate to his world. Lurking beneath even the most sustained poetic illustration of his critical creed of 1853, 'Sohrab and Rustum', are strong suggestions of the buried self which Arnold has suppressed – the battle to the death between his own youthful aestheticism and his father's vigorous moralism – and for many the poem is chiefly successful as a metaphorical account of Arnold's defeat as a poet.[203] It is interesting, and a little ironic, that this was one of the poems referred to by an appreciative critic whose words Arnold copied out in his notebook:

Sohrab and Rustum, or *The Sick King in Bokhara*, does more for culture than a world of essays and reviews, and disquisitions on the hideous middle class. The pamphlet reprint of 'Selected Poems', bought at an American railway station by some man who perhaps purchases at adventure, may do more to cultivate the love of beauty and the love of nature, to educate and console, than many great volumes of theology.[204]

It is rather sad to imagine Arnold in 1882 ruefully copying out these comments (and we don't, incidentally, find many references in his notebooks to reviews and criticism of his own work), for while the critic praises Arnold's poetry it is at the expense of consigning the last twenty years of a sustained literary effort in prose to oblivion.

III

Arnold's poetry is unusually self-referential in its metacritical concerns. But it is to his prose that we must turn for a more theoretically defined pronouncement on his critical position. Arnold's first important published critical statement was the Preface to the 1853 edition of his *Poems*. But his journey towards that statement is interestingly charted in his letters to Clough during the period 1847 to 1853.

Hillis Miller observes that although Arnold's statements about poetry sometimes seem contradictory, the basis of his criticism is always the ideal of a poetry which will be a reconciliation of opposites.[205] The concept of poetry as uniquely providing a ground for the reconciliation of ethical, philosophical, and religious concerns would be considered by many to be a Romantic one. Arnold's relationship with the Romantic tradition is complex. In many respects, he admired the Romantic poets. The influence of Wordsworth on Arnold was profound, and extended throughout his life. As Trilling describes, 'His boyhood had been spent in the Lake Country and under Wordsworth's affectionate eye. He had roamed Loughrigg, skated on Rydal Water and boated on Windermere.'[206] The references to Wordsworth, both overt and oblique, in his poetry are many, and suggest how deep was his debt to him. Vincent Buckley has observed that Arnold was drawn to Wordsworth partly because his intimacy with nature seemed to allow him to avoid the complexity of the modern world.[207] But when we look at the quotations from Wordsworth that he wrote down in his later notebooks, it is clear that it was his ideal of poetry as a moral power that appealed to him. In 1867, Arnold notes the following, from a letter from Wordsworth to Lady Beaumont concerning his poems:

They will cooperate with the benign tendencies in human nature and society, and will, in their degree, be efficacious in making men wiser, better, and happier.[208]

In 1879, after an interval of twelve years, he records the following passage from the same letter:

Trouble not yourself upon their present reception; of what moment is that, compared with what is, I trust, their destiny! – To console the afflicted; to add sunshine to daylight by making the happy happier; to teach the young and gracious of every age to see, to think, to feel, and therefore to become more actively and securely virtuous; – this is their office, which I trust they will faithfully perform long after we (that is all that is mortal of us) are mouldering in our graves.[209]

And two years later he notes, again from the same letter, 'To be incapable of a feeling of poetry, in my sense of the word, is to be without love of human nature and reverence for God.'

In the 1840s Arnold was introduced to the writings of Schiller, through his reading of Carlyle and Bulwer Lytton. He later recalled this period as

the happiest time in my life – *The Student, The Life of Schiller*, came into my hands just at the moment I wanted something of the kind. I shall never forget what they then gave to me – the sense of a wider horizon, the anticipation of Germany, the opening into the great world.[210]

Carlyle represents Schiller as the ultimate reconciler, identifying his Christianity as a true 'aesthetic religion' and explaining his views on poetry as containing within itself 'the essence of philosophy, religion, art'.[211]

Arnold clearly found this view of poetry as incorporating within itself and harmonising all aspects of human experience very appealing. Yet he did not consistently acknowledge Romantic poets and theorists as his teachers in this respect. For example, in a famous letter to Clough, written in 1852, he recommends the inclusiveness of the classical authors as the only appropriate model for the modern poet:

Modern poetry can only subsist by its *contents*: by becoming a complete *magister vitae* as the poetry of the ancients did; by including, as theirs did, religion with poetry, instead of existing as poetry only, and leaving religious wants to be supplied by the Christian religion.[212]

This is the kind of statement which, although apparently un-ambiguous, has been the source of a great deal of confusion in the evaluation of Arnold's views on poetry, a confusion which seems to derive from Arnold himself. Arnold's volte-face from the near-aestheticism of the late 1840s to the moral poetics of the 1853 Preface is notorious,[213] and it is complicated by both his reluctance to acknowledge the profound influence upon him of Romantic writers and thinkers and his persistent distortion of Romanticism as a superficial and maudlin exercise in self-indulgence.[214] In his touchy repudiations of Romanticism, as defined by himself and conflated with subjectivism, and in his pronouncements on the related questions of the relative importance of form and content, the nature of poetry, and the role of the poet, we might justifiably seek further grounds for his eventual elevation of poetry to a moral and finally a quasi-religious function.

The much-discussed shift from Arnold's critical position in the late 1840s to his stance in the 1853 Preface is generally acknowledged to be problematical. Alba Warren expresses the essence of the problem: 'The trouble is to account for what looks like a classical theory of poetry in a criticism dominantly romantic.'[215] David Delaura takes the problem one stage further when he explains:

The difficulty we still experience in defining the shifts in Arnold's poetics up to 1853 derives in part from the simplicity of our categories. The alleged aestheticism and formalism of the forties was from the first carefully 'moralized', and was compatible with a rejection of Keats and Tennyson. The supposed moralism of 1852–53 must somehow be squared with the endorsement of 'perfection of form' in the letter to Mrs Forster of September 1858.[216]

The general point here is unquestionable, but is the source of the difficulty to be located in the simplicity of our categories, or in the confusion of Arnold's own?

Critical discussion has focused on the dramatic shift between his statement of 1849 that 'form [is] the sole *necessary* of Poetry'[217] and his antithetical claim of 1852 that 'Modern poetry can only subsist by its *contents*'.[218] Yet how does that relate to his presumed movement also from an essentially Romantic position to a stridently classical one? Surely we associate formal perfection rather with classicism, and that art in which what is being expressed seems to transcend the confines of pure form with Romanticism.

This central confusion gives way to others in Arnold's letters. There are a number of points, for example, where he seems to regard form and content as being at war – a very unclassical attitude to adopt. For example, in 1849 he writes:

I often think that even a slight gift of poetical expression which in a common person might have developed itself easily and naturally, is overlaid and crushed in a profound thinker so as to be of no use to him to help him to express himself.[219]

And later, in 1853, he complains:

I have written out my Sohrab and Rustum, and like it less. – Composition, in the painter's sense – that is the devil. And, when one thinks of it, our painters cannot *compose* though they can show great genius – so too in poetry is it not to be expected that in this same article of *composition* the awkward incorrect Northern nature should shew itself? though we may have feeling – fire – eloquence – as much as our betters.[220]

An uneasy peace is achieved by a sleight of hand whereby form is triumphantly assimilated to content:

Nay in Sophocles what is valuable is not so much his contribution to psychology and the anatomy of sentiment, as the grand moral effects produced by *style*. For the style is the expression of the nobility of the poet's character as the matter is the expression of the richness of his mind.[221]

But the cracks are simply papered over in this resolution. 'The style is the man' theory is one which we associate with the most Romantic aspects of Ruskin's and Pater's and Newman's aesthetics. Arnold's subsequent development of his theory of the 'grand style' in his critical prose actually makes style a kind of moral agent, an instrument of restraint. Arnold's compromise seems a far cry from that perfect unification of content and form which Hegel identified as the most significant characteristic of classical art.[222] Rather, it is an example of the blurring of distinctions, the fudging of concepts, to which Eliot referred when he complained of Arnold's 'loose jargon' and 'conjuring tricks', whereby one name is silently substituted for something quite different.[223]

In any attempt to explain Arnold's inconsistencies and contradictions, his letters to Clough, more than his published writings, afford a unique opportunity to consider the psychological context in which he developed his critical ideas. Arnold's uneasy friendship with Clough is intimately bound up with his personal struggle to define his own moral, intellectual, and aesthetic standpoint. Many of his most striking statements about form and content in poetry, about Romantic and classical modes, and about other writers, are clarified when considered in relation to their personal context.

It is thought by some that Clough was the major influence in determining Arnold's movement away from the aestheticism and formalism of the 1840s to the moralism of his poetics in 1853, by others that Arnold's position in the 1853 Preface is 'emphatically anti-Cloughian'.[224] Without wishing to indulge in Arnoldian compromise, one can hold both statements to be true if one interprets 'anti-Cloughian' as 'anti-subjective'. Certainly the nature of their friendship is an important background to an understanding of Arnold's aesthetic attitudes during this period. As Robin Biswas observes, these years saw also a shift in their friendship from a relationship in which Clough was Arnold's teacher and guide to one in which the positions were reversed and Arnold was offering advice to his unsuccessful friend:

the tension and unease in the friendship involved two radically opposed standpoints on the question of how to live, fundamental standpoints from which both men derived their critical bearings regarding the nature and function of literature.[225]

The emphasis of Arnold's early letters upon the primacy of form and composition is almost certainly to do with his view that Clough's main defects as a poet were formal. Many of his statements are directly aimed at Clough, and those that are not often seem to have Clough in mind:

More and more I feel bent against the modern English habit (too much encouraged by Wordsworth) of using poetry as a channel for thinking aloud, instead of making anything.[226]

Yet theirs was a very close and difficult friendship. Arnold seems to have thought of Clough as his *alter ego*, his Mr Hyde. He clearly felt vulnerable to the very weaknesses that he saw all too well in Clough, and began to resent him as an influence which he felt to be antagonistic to his life as a poet:

You certainly do not seem to me sufficiently to desire and earnestly strive towards – assured knowledge – activity – happiness. You are too content to *fluctuate* – to be ever learning, never coming to the knowledge of the truth. This is why, with you, I feel it necessary to stiffen myself – and hold fast my rudder.[227]

He virtually accuses Clough of deliberate subversion, when he has evidently been persuaded by him to read Keats' letters:

What a brute you were to tell me to read Keats' Letters. However it is over now: and reflexion resumes her power over agitation.

What harm he has done in English Poetry. As Browning is a man with a moderate gift passionately desiring movement and fulness, and obtaining but a confused multitudinousness, so Keats with a very high gift, is yet also consumed by this desire: and cannot produce the truly living and moving, as his conscience keeps telling him. They will not be patient neither understand that they must begin with an Idea of the world in order not to be prevailed over by the world's multitudinousness.[228]

His judgement of Keats is bound up very closely with his own insecurities. His sense of self is always precarious. In one letter he can quote to Clough, as a kind of clarion call, Wordsworth's 'By our own spirits [are we deified]', yet in another he perceives his self as rebellious, requiring mastery:

> What I must tell you is that I have never yet succeeded in any one great occasion in consciously mastering myself. I can go thro: the imaginary process of mastering myself and see the whole affair as it would then stand, but at the critical point I am too apt to hoist up the mainsail to the wind and let her drive.[229]

Arnold's untiring concern with Clough's waywardness, and his constant effort to define and identify his friend's weaknesses had, then, a very personal basis. He was in some sense analysing himself and voicing his fears about the dangerousness of some of the attitudes to which he was himself temperamentally prone. Arnold's tribute to Clough on his death, in his last Oxford lecture on Homer, is expressed in the vocabulary of his own established critical doctrine:

> in so eminent a degree, he possessed these two invaluable literary qualities – a true sense for his object of study, and a single-hearted care for it...In the study of art, poetry, or philosophy, he had the most undivided and disinterested love for his object in itself, the greatest aversion to mixing up with it anything accidental or personal. His interest was in literature itself.[230]

In praising Clough for his 'undivided and disinterested love for the object in itself', he seems to be actually celebrating the mature Arnold, who, by 1853, had triumphed over the subjectivism of his youth.

Vincent Buckley describes the 1853 Preface as 'marginal to his work, and a piece of specious self-defence',[231] but its very speciousness and defensiveness indicate its significance. The editors of Arnold's letters to Clough consider the Preface to be 'in some respects his most important critical utterance'.[232] Certainly it is the pivotal point between his early poetry and his later critical effort.

The central purpose of the Preface, Arnold says, is to explain his exclusion of 'Empedocles on Etna' from the first edition of his *Poems*. He does not, he says, exclude it because it treats of a past time, but rather because of his conviction that no poetical enjoyment can be derived from situations

> in which the suffering finds no vent in action; in which a continuous state of mental distress is prolonged, unrelieved by incident, hope, or resistance; in which there is everything to be endured, nothing to be done. In such situations there is inevitably something morbid, in the description of them something monotonous.[233]

The modern poet is told, he complains, quoting the critic J. M. Ludlow, that 'A true allegory of the state of one's own mind in a representative history...is perhaps the highest thing that one can attempt in the way of poetry':

An allegory of the state of one's own mind, the highest problem of an art which imitates action! No assuredly, it is not, it never can be so: no great poetical work has ever been produced with such an aim...Faust itself... is defective.[234]

He identifies all such introspection and self-obsession with Romanticism, and urges instead the central characteristics of classical poetry:

I fearlessly assert that *Hermann and Dorothea, Childe Harold, Jocelyn, The Excursion,* leave the reader cold in comparison with the effect produced upon him by the latter books of the *Iliad,* by the *Oresteia,* or by the episode of Dido. And why is this? Simply because in the three last-named cases the action is greater, the personages nobler, the situations more intense: and this is the true basis of the interest in a poetical work, and this alone.[235]

He rejects not only so-called Romantic subjectivism in the subject-matter of poetry, but also Romantic detail and individualism in expression:

what distinguishes the artist from the mere amateur, says Goethe, is Architectonicè in the highest sense; that power of execution, which creates, forms, and constitutes; not the profoundness of single thoughts, not the richness of imagery, not the abundance of illustration.[236]

The detailed example he gives of the flaws inherent in the latter is Keats' 'Isabella, or the Pot of Basil'.

Some critics have interpreted the 1853 Preface at face value, as a simple rejection of Romanticism.[237] It has been pointed out that Arnold's criticism of the Romantic poets for weak-mindedness, subjectivity, and formlessness was shared and anticipated by a significant minority of contemporary reviewers.[238] Others, however, have judged his rejection of Romanticism and his erection of a classical ideal for art as symptomatic of deeper unacknowledged and unresolved personal and aesthetic problems.[239] I myself am inclined to agree with Kenneth Allott that the real issue of the 1853 Preface is the rejection of subjectivity.[240] In the Preface Arnold refers to a statement by Goethe, and his own response is very revealing:

Two kinds of *dilettanti,* says Goethe, there are in poetry: he who neglects the indispensable mechanical part, and thinks he has done enough if he shows spirituality and feeling: and he who seeks to arrive at poetry merely by mechanism, in which he can acquire an artisan's readiness, and is without soul and matter. And he adds that the first does most harm to art, and the last to himself. If we must be *dilettanti*: if it is impossible for us, under the circumstances amidst which we live, to think clearly, to feel nobly, and to delineate firmly: if we cannot attain to the mastery of the great artists: – *let us, at least, have so much respect for our art as to prefer it to ourselves*.[241]

The self must be suppressed, in terms of the subject-matter, the style of expression, and finally in the poet's whole enterprise. It seems that this was the only way that Arnold could escape what were clearly for him the self-destructive tendencies of introspection in both his art and his life. Five years after the publication of the Preface, he acknowledged, in a letter to his sister, that his tragedy *Merope*, written in the classical mode he had recommended in the Preface, belonged to a less ambitious kind of poetry than did 'Empedocles on Etna'. But he explains his reasons for preferring to write in the classical style:

People do not understand what a temptation there is, if you cannot bear anything not *very good*, to transfer your operations to a region where form is everything... but to attain or approach perfection in the region of thought and feeling, and to unite this with perfection of form, demands not merely an effort and a labour, but an actual tearing of oneself to pieces, which one does not readily consent to (although one is sometimes forced to it) unless one can devote one's whole life to poetry.[242]

Kenneth Allott suggests that 'a region where form is everything' should be translated as 'a region where the artist's struggle is exclusively with form and expression because the subject does not involve the perplexities of his own development'. He concludes that 'the pseudo-classicism of the Preface must therefore be seen as a direct evasion of the strains and anxieties of genuine poetic creation'.[243]

It is fascinating to speculate upon the psychological processes of which the 1853 Preface was the culmination. The tangible outcome was a critical statement which rejected the idea of poetry as self-expression and instead urged an ideal of poetry which would be morally ennobling. In line with this, Arnold also pursued and promoted a new critical ideal, a similarly objective appraisal of literature, in which the aesthetic appreciation of literature became inextricably bound up with more general cultural, moral and religious issues.

As a critic, Arnold provided some essential terms for modern critical discussions concerning taste and judgement, for he was really the first to establish literary criticism as an intellectual discipline in England and the United States. Even if one does not actually agree with his literary judgements, or with the critical criteria by which he makes them, he is almost indispensable as a reference point. Hopkins, for example, responded to a derogatory comment on Arnold by Robert

Bridges, 'I have more reason than you for disagreeing with him and thinking him very wrong, but nevertheless I am sure he is a rare genius and a great critic.'[244] Twentieth-century critics as diverse as T. S. Eliot, F. R. Leavis, Lionel Trilling, and Raymond Williams, even when in radical disagreement with Arnold, owe their intellectual lineage to him to some extent.[245]

In 1857, Arnold was elected to the Professorship of Poetry at Oxford, an office which he held for two terms until 1867. He was the first layman to occupy the Chair and he made great innovations. He was the first to lecture in English; hitherto the Professor of Poetry had always addressed his audiences in Latin. More important were the innovations he made in the way he spoke about poetry. Continuing some important themes of the 1853 Preface, he argued that art should not be conceived as something isolated from life, as a rarified activity, but as interacting with the society that produced it and for which it was produced. Throughout his critical career, Arnold directs his theories less towards the aesthetics of poetry than towards the complex conditions of modern life and to how poetry, by helping to cultivate the moral and intellectual and aesthetic awareness of the reader, might enable society to comprehend and evaluate the times. His inaugural lecture was entitled 'On the Modern Element in Literature', and it is on this modern element, if not always on modern literature as such, that his criticism henceforth concentrates. The lecture is typical of the method of literary evaluation that Arnold was to develop in his subsequent critical writings, in that it shows the social and political determination of literature, and makes social and political judgements an integral part of the discussion of literature.

The fact that his critical concern is clearly with general issues and definitions rather than with the close sensitive reading of poetry itself means that he sometimes makes rather puzzling statements and imbalanced judgements about individual writers. This is particularly noticeable in his essays on the younger generation of Romantic poets, where he explains their weaknesses as poets in terms of their character defects, their lack of moral fibre or their vulgarity:

Some of Byron's most crying faults as a man, – his vulgarity, his affectation, – are really akin to the faults of commonness, of want of art, in his workmanship as a poet.[246]

It is interesting to compare Ruskin's attitude to Byron. He admires the essential nobility of Byron, in particular his 'accurate and powerful' observation, and the force and precision of his style. He warns, though, that Byron should only be read when taste is formed.[247]

In his essay on Shelley, which is largely a response to Dowden's newly published biography, Arnold comes, after twenty pages of horrified reportage of the details of his life, to pronounce in the final paragraph upon his poetry:

It is his poetry, above everything else, which for many people establishes that he is an angel... In poetry, no less than in life, he is a beautiful *and ineffectual* angel, beating in the void his luminous wings in vain.[248]

There is not much suggestion of the 'unacknowledged legislator' here, nor is there any hint of Shelley's commitment to revolutionary agitation in anything else that Arnold ever said about him:

> What boots it, Shelley! that the breeze
> Carried thy lovely wail away,
> Musical through Italian trees
> Which fringe thy soft blue Spezzian bay?
> Inheritors of thy distress
> Have restless hearts one throb the less?[249]

Few people would assume that Shelley was trying to make his readers' hearts *less* restless. While it is only fair to point out that the lyrical qualities of Shelley's poetry are still commonly emphasised at the expense of the political, Ruskin strikes us as being a much more sensitive reader when he isolates instead Shelley's intense love of nature, his indignation at pain and injustice, and his honest unbelief.[250]

Arnold's tendency to weight his readings of particular poets in order to make some general critical statement about the function of poetry or the proper nature of the poet has been widely criticised by some modern readers. Eliot, for example, complains that 'he was so conscious of what, for him, poetry was *for*, that he could not altogether see it for what it is', and even then, he argues,

the *use* to which he put poetry was limited; he wrote about poets when they provided a pretext for his sermon to the British public; and he was apt to think of the greatness of poetry rather than of its genuineness.[251]

Although Eliot claims that it is unclear how Arnold finds morals in poetry, find them he will, and Eliot identifies in this 'the same weakness, the same necessity for something to depend upon, which makes him an academic poet' making him also an academic critic. Vincent Buckley believes likewise that Arnold's critical position on the question of the intrinsic value of poetry is 'debatable', but that 'he has a most exaggerated view of the value of poetry as (so to speak) a social agent'.[252] Helen Gardner captures the essence of Arnold's critical style when she writes:

He was interested in trying to sum up writers by some expressive formula which would epitomize what he found most valuable in them, and was interested not in the elucidation of a work as in some sense independent of all its writer's other works, an aesthetic whole, or in analysing the idiosyncracies of a writer's modes of thought and expression in the context of the thought of his age.[253]

In his literary criticism alone there is a formidable number of memorable expressive formulae: Arnold bestowed his terms 'high seriousness' and 'the grand style', invoked his 'touchstones', treated literature as a 'criticism of life', and saw 'the object as in itself it really is' like a tireless schoolmaster. A glance at his notebooks reveals a liking for aphoristic maxims in others too. Phrases beginning 'le but de l'art', 'le but essenticl de l'art', 'faith is', 'La religion est', 'the Greek ideal is this', 'True wisdom is', 'the most deeply impressive works of art are...' ring through the notebooks, some of them repeated again and again.[254] Once again this suggests Arnold's tendency to avoid both the individual aesthetic talents of particular poets and artists and the dangers of exercising a too subjective judgement. The formulaic structure of his critical statements, 'poetry is...', 'art is...', 'religion is...', allows him to take refuge behind a supposed objectivity in the critical as in the creative sphere.

The criticism of literature is also removed from the personal if it can be viewed as the useful interpretation of an art form which itself has a moral function within the organic whole of civilisation. Developing his idea of literature as a *'magister vitae'*, Arnold maintains, 'Whoever seriously occupies himself with literature will soon perceive its vital connection with other agencies', for 'Literature is a part of civilisation; it is not the whole.'[255] For Arnold, the moral function of poetry is twofold. On the one hand, its role is to interpret the moral world 'by expressing with inspired conviction, the ideas and laws of the inward world of man's moral and spiritual nature'.[256] On the other, its function is perceived as the offering of a Wordsworthian 'healing power'. Poetry is, or should be, 'a stay to us'.[257] 'The right function of poetry', we are told, 'is to animate, to console, to rejoice – in one word, to *strengthen*'.[258] Conjoining the two functions, Arnold says 'we have to turn to poetry to interpret life for us, to console us, to sustain us'.[259]

In a very interesting discussion of Arnold's criticism, Vincent Buckley considers how his moralism distorts and limits his critical insights, and locates the source of the weaknesses of his critical position in its unintentional subjectivism. Arnold accounts for poetry

too much in terms of elevated sentiment, of truth turned too easily into feeling, of style. Because of the limitations of his actual vision of poetry, he tends to estimate it too much in terms of its presumed effects; and he can know those effects only as they occur in himself. However he may try to reach a point of complete disinterestedness, his demands are basically subjective, as well as personal.[260]

Arnold recognised the impossibility of arbitrating between his personal responses to art and his duty as a critic to appeal to a universally accepted system of aesthetic values. Indeed, it was no doubt his awareness of the real difficulty of evading the self and subjectivity in all aesthetic experience, critical as well as creative, that encouraged him to move further and further away from talking directly about the aesthetics of literature in the direction of the social and political implications of criticism and culture.

IV

As 'Literature' tends to drift into 'Criticism' in Arnold's critical vocabulary, so 'Criticism' overlaps into 'Culture'. He had never really separated the idea of literature from criticism, nor had he separated either from actual practical life, as his most famous definition makes clear: Literature is a 'criticism of life'.[261] His own experiences as a poet had early convinced him that society was a condition of literature, but as he developed his ideas about the relationship between art and society became more complex, until in one of his last essays we find him praising the acuteness of Amiel for characterising high society as itself 'a form of poetry'. He enthusiastically quotes Amiel's description of high society:

These select gatherings produce without intending it a sort of concert for eye and ear, an improvised work of art. By the instinctive collaboration of everybody concerned, wit and taste hold festival, and the associations of reality are exchanged for the associations of imagination.[262]

But on the whole he is more concerned, in his writings about criticism and culture, to suggest how the individual might equip himself to interpret the modern world and to act responsibly with the new power that democracy had given him. In this context, literature, criticism, and culture were perceived as means of moral and intellectual deliverance, as the saviours of the modern world, rather than as merely ornamental.

Arnold's most important statement of his critical principles is to be found in his essay entitled 'The Function of Criticism at the Present Time', published in *Essays in Criticism* in 1864. He opens this essay with a quotation from his earlier essay 'On Translating Homer':

Of the literature of France and Germany, as of the intellect of Europe in general, the main effort, for now many years, has been a critical effort; the endeavour, in all branches of knowledge, theology, philosophy, history, art, science, to see the object as in itself it really is.[263]

Certainly this is a fair representation of Arnold's main endeavour, even if we might question his attribution of it to the world at large. He continues:

life and the world being in modern times very complex things, the creation of a modern poet, to be worth much, implies a great critical effort behind it; else it must be a comparatively poor, barren, and short-lived affair.[264]

He defines criticism as '*a disinterested endeavour to learn and propagate the best that is known and thought in the world*'.[265] He urges here a Hellenistic disinterestedness and objectivity which seems to have grown out of the personal needs of the 1853 Preface and to be preparing the ground for the thoroughgoing movement into political and social theory in *Culture and Anarchy*, which was published in 1869.

The writing of *Culture and Anarchy* was, as has been suggested, directly occasioned by the social and political unrest in England during the period leading up to the second Reform Act of 1867. Arnold's purpose in writing it was to allay the fears of the upper classes now that a very large proportion of the working classes had been given the vote, and also to suggest how a huge uneducated class was to be taught how to participate in the running of the nation. The gist of its argument is that England exists in a state of Anarchy, not only in the open signs of working-class unrest but also in the more insidious creeds of middle-class *laissez-faire* Liberalism, 'doing as one likes', and he warns that this Anarchy will only get worse if 'Culture' is not heeded, and if a strong State is not formed to transcend class interest. Arnold was writing in the line of men like Coleridge, Newman, Carlyle, Kingsley, F. D. Maurice, and his own father in recommending cultural education for the masses on higher grounds than simple expediency – Macaulay's 'We must educate our masters' – when he wrote:

The whole scope of the essay is to recommend culture as the great help out of our present difficulties; culture being a pursuit of our total perfection by means of getting to know, on all the matters which most concern us, the best which has been thought and said in the world; and through this knowledge, turning a stream of fresh and free thought upon our stock notions and habits, which we now follow staunchly but mechanically, vainly imagining that there is a virtue in following them staunchly which makes up for the mischief of following them mechanically. This, and this alone is the scope of the following essay. And the culture we recommend is, above all, an inward operation.[266]

It is primarily an inward operation, but Culture ultimately leads Arnold to conceive of true human perfection as 'a *harmonious* perfection, developing all sides of our humanity; and as a *general* perfection, developing all parts of our society'.[267] Social Anarchy, he seems to imply, is only a manifestation of spiritual Anarchy.

The Culture and Anarchy polarity is not the only one Arnold puts forward in this work. The other is 'Hebraism and Hellenism – between these two points of influence moves our world.' He defines these two terms as he will use them thus:

The uppermost idea with Hellenism is to see things as they really are; the uppermost idea with Hebraism is conduct and obedience...The governing idea of Hellenism is *spontaneity of consciousness*; that of Hebraism, *strictness of conscience.*[268]

The present age, he warns, is in the grip of Hebraism at the very time that it really needs to be able to 'see the object as in itself it really is' in the new age of democracy. He urges Victorian England to take ancient Greece as its model and guide. Only by cultivating the Hellenic qualities of 'Culture', 'imaginative reason' and 'sweetness and light', the Greek ideal of comprehensiveness, harmony, and totality, could modern society be saved from its divisiveness.

Arnold himself was very pleased with his chapters on Hebraism and Hellenism, and said in a letter to his mother that they were 'so true that they will form a kind of centre for English thought and speculation on the matters treated in them'.[269] To the extent that several books have been published on Victorian Hellenism and that Arnold's version figures prominently, he was right.[270] But they have not all been entirely complimentary about Arnold's depiction of Hellenism. David Delaura, for example, remarks that 'His Hellenic ideal of comprehensiveness... easily becomes something like a diplomatic strategy in the ideal of "facing in every direction" and the hatred of "all over-preponderance of single elements".'[271] Richard Jenkyns describes Arnold's account of Hellenism as being 'riddled with faults'. In the first place, he argues, 'he was wrong about the Greeks: neither in their literature nor in their lives did they attain to the harmony, the radiancy, the "balance and regulation of mind" that he himself valued so highly'.[272] He then goes on to point out a confusion in Arnold's use of the terms 'Hellenism' and 'Hebraism' which arises out of the fact that they are sometimes to be understood symbolically, to denote two types of human impulse, and sometimes historically, in which sense 'the Jews were not always Hebraic or the Greeks Hellenic'.[273] A further weakness in Arnold's account of Hellenism is identified as the fact that it seems to represent such different and unrelated qualities. As Jenkyns says, sweetness and light 'represent the aesthetic qualities that he most admired, but they also represent the power of unprejudiced reason; these are two very different things'.[274]

A similar problem, one which lies at the heart of his discussion of Hebraism and Hellenism, is that Arnold swings between presenting us with an extreme polarisation on the one hand and a confused identification on the other. The concluding words, quoted from Jowett, of Arnold's Preface to *Last Essays* have a special significance to his own work:

The moral and intellectual are always dividing, yet they must be re-united, and in the highest conception of them are inseparable.[275]

This is exactly what Arnold seems to do with his Hebraism and Hellenism: he distinguishes and polarises them only to urge that they should be united:

Elsewhere we have drawn out a distinction between Hebraism and Hellenism, – between the tendency and powers that carry us towards doing, and the tendency and powers that carry us towards perceiving and knowing...Hebraism strikes too exclusively upon one string in us; Hellenism does not address itself with serious energy enough to morals and righteousness. For our totality, for our general perfection, we need to unite the two...Hebraism at its best is beauty and charm; Hellenism at its best is beauty and charm. As such they can unite; as anything short of this, each of them, they are at discord, and their separation must continue.[276]

Many may feel, however, that such a severance of Hebraism and Hellenism, of moral and aesthetic qualities, of righteousness and intelligence, is misleading in the extreme. Might not Arnold's essentially Hellenic qualities of 'sweetness and light' equally be argued as Hebraic characteristics? Or might not the 'strength and energy' that he recognises as a necessary complement to 'sweetness and light' equally be seen as aesthetic rather than moral qualities?[277]

Arnold's polarisation of Hebraism and Hellenism is the more puzzling when we take into account the fact that he himself quite naturally brought the two together, as we see from both unpublished and published writings. For example, in his notebooks he often juxtaposes a 'Hebraic' with a 'Hellenic' text, and expresses admiration for those men who marry in themselves Hebraic and Hellenic qualities, men like Goethe, Spinoza, and Heinrich Heine. It is significant that what really intrigues Arnold about these writers is their very mixed racial and cultural identity. Spinoza, for example, was born a Jew, later repudiated Judaism and changed his name, but was never baptised, and wrote with all the virtues of Hellenism.[278] Heine was born in Hamburg, amidst all the culture of Germany, and was also a Jew by race, and this in part explains for Arnold his 'intense modernism, his absolute freedom, his utter rejection of stock classicism and stock romanticism, his bringing all things under the point of view of the nineteenth century':

By his perfection of literary form, by his love of clearness, by his love of beauty, Heine is Greek; by his untameableness, by his 'longing which cannot be uttered', he is Hebrew.[279]

Arnold's description of Heine recalls certain Victorian fictional characters who also unite within themselves all the virtues of the Judaic and the Hellenic traditions: George Eliot's Daniel Deronda and Disraeli's Sidonia in *Coningsby*, for example.

In *Literature and Dogma* Arnold says that 'our being is aesthetic and intellective, as well as...moral',[280] and certainly we find in his own judgements the complementary influence of Hebraism and Hellenism. His aesthetic judgements are always balanced out by moral considerations and his ethical judgements by his sense of beauty. So much so, that he often finds it impossible to stay behind the barriers that he himself has erected. Thus, for the Greeks, we are told that 'the aim of tragedy was *profound moral impression*';[281] Homer's grand style was essentially moral;[282] and at the end of an essay designed to contrast pagan and medieval religious sentiment, the former 'treating the world according to the demand of the senses' and the latter 'treating the world according to the demand of the heart and imagination', he refers to a century of Greek life when Simonides, Pindar, Aeschylus, and Sophocles were writing poetry which combined the outward and sensible with the inward and symbolical: 'No other poets, who have so well satisfied the thinking power, have so well satisfied the religious sense.'[283] After quoting from the *Oedipus Tyrannus* he triumphantly challenges St Francis or Luther to 'beat that!'.

But while the Hebraic and the Hellenic do seem to coexist in Arnold's own make-up, theirs is not an entirely easy coexistence. Arnold's history is one of trying to reconcile tendencies within his own self which he seemed to fear were liable to pull him in different directions. He felt his own psychological vulnerability to Anarchy only too sharply. In his prose writings he often seems to be projecting his own personal anxieties on to the social order. The only practical solution to spiritual Anarchy in modern society, he argues, is a strong State. He postulates the State as the 'centre of light and authority', the organ of the 'best self',[284] and in this way attempts to reconcile the demands of individualism, the self, and a controlling objective authority. He imagines this 'best self' of every class as a minority group of 'aliens', 'who are mainly led, not by their class spirit, but by a general *humane* spirit, by the love of human perfection'.[285] Such an ideal of disinterested government which transcends class difference is one that few would argue with, even if it is founded on an impossibility: the divorce of class from interest. But the significant point is that Arnold is here turning alienation, the theme which he treats so centrally and so poignantly in his early poetry, into a triumphant capacity for disinterestedness. Alienation, far from debarring him from any useful role in modern society, far from being the province of the isolated poet, far from implying a melancholy Empedoclean Romanticism, is transformed into the saviour of society, the instrument of a properly Hellenic government. Alienation itself has been objectified.

A. Dwight Culler explains Arnold's writings on Culture, indeed his humanistic vision in general, as an attempt to erect an objective value system to counteract the subjectivism of the times:

the whole effort of Arnold's critical essays was to give to the body of world literature the character of an objective standard of excellence. The diseases of his countrymen were all diseases of self – on the one hand, the eccentricities of Romantic individualism, and on the other, the partisan zeal of political and religious conflict – and the cure for these diseases was a system of value which was larger than the self and perfectly distinct from it. Such a system Arnold found in culture, 'the best that is known and thought in the world'.[286]

And he explains Arnold's failure to realise that ideal by the fact that when he sought those objective standards, 'whether in an English Academy, or in the idea of the State or in his celebrated "touchstones" for poetry, he ended by reintroducing the self in another guise'.[287] Seeing the object 'as in itself it really is' proved to be no easy matter, even for its most ardent champion.[288]

V

Yet Arnold persisted in his quest for objectivity more doggedly than ever in his writings on religion and the Bible. His aim is to reveal to his readers the biblical text 'as it really is'. He endeavours 'to see what the Bible really is' in order to show 'that the Bible is really based upon propositions which all can verify' once it has been demythologised.[289] But once again, his presumed objectivity is misleading, and the 'objective' criteria he erects are really subjectively determined. His sense of the need for objectivity is legitimate, and his endeavour to attain it is a noble one, but both his assumptions and his conclusions are naïve.

Arnold's ideas about Religion in the 1870s developed naturally out of his ideas about Culture of the 1860s; in fact, for a period the two areas of experience seem to be virtually indistinguishable conceptually, until he turns to write specifically about the Bible and historical Christianity. In *Culture and Anarchy*, Arnold declares himself 'above all, a believer in culture' and his argument is for 'a faith in culture'.[290] He presents us with a version of Culture that bears a marked resemblance to Christianity. Culture is 'a study of perfection':

It moves us by the force, not merely or primarily of the scientific passion for pure knowledge, but also of the moral and social passion for doing good.

Its motto, borrowing the authority of a Bishop of the Church of England, is 'To make reason and the will of God prevail'.[291] Religion and Culture seem to be identical, not only in their nature, but also in their conclusions:

Religion says: *The Kingdom of God is within you*; and culture, in like manner, places human perfection in an *internal* condition, in the growth and predominance of our humanity proper, as distinguished from our animality.[292]

Culture, then, is not only of like spirit with poetry; it is also of like spirit with religion, just as religion will subsequently be seen to be of like spirit with poetry, in a characteristically Arnoldian circularity of argument. If anything, in that it is more comprehensive and inclusive in character, 'culture goes beyond religion, as religion is generally conceived by us';[293] a significant qualification.

Secular Culture is conceived in more and more religious terms, until it is finally called upon in the service of religion: 'Culture, then, and science and literature are requisite, in the interest of religion itself':[294]

when religion is called in question because of the extravagances of theology being passed off as religion, one disengages and helps religion by showing their utter delusiveness. They arose out of the talents of able men for reasoning, and their want...of literary experience. By a sad mishap for them the sphere where they show their talents is one for literary experience rather than for reasoning.[295]

His avowed objective in writing *Literature and Dogma* is closely connected with the aim of '*culture*, the acquainting ourselves with the best that has been known and said in the world', and thus with the history of the human spirit:

One cannot go far in the attempt to bring in, for the Bible, a right construction, without seeing how necessary is something of culture to its being admitted and used.[296]

In 1861, Benjamin Jowett wrote a letter to a friend informing him that Convocation were going to consider and possibly censure the radical and controversial *Essays and Reviews*, to which he had been a major contributor. His comments on the temper of the times have an obvious significance for Arnold's effort:

At present the book is a sort of bugbear among the Bishops and Clergy, showing, I venture to think, that some inquiries of the sort were needed, if the evidences of religion are to have anything but a conventional value. In a few years there will be no religion in Oxford among intellectual young men, unless religion is shown to be consistent with criticism.[297]

Just as Arnold's investigations into Culture were in response to the *Zeitgeist*, so his reassessment of Christianity and the grounds of faith stemmed from his awareness of the fact that the new intellectual context demanded a revision of traditional religious ideas and beliefs.

Although he was alive to the fact that his was a scientific age, one which demanded empirical proof for all its speculations, Arnold was less concerned about the implications of Darwinism for Christianity than he was about the impact of modern developments in philosophy and the growth of historical Scriptural studies on the orthodox cosmology. As we have seen, Arnold had become acquainted with the main principles of German transcendentalism as an undergraduate, and although he subsequently lost sympathy with Idealism as a philosophical system, he maintained an intellectual interest, so that in 1877 we find him noting down from an article by T. H. Green on Herbert Spencer and G. H. Lewes the primary question of metaphysics:

'Kant set himself to ascertain what the relations are which are necessary to constitute an intelligent experience' or (which is the same) 'any knowable world.'[298]

Kant's emphasis on the centrality of the self in experience and knowledge had been extended into the sphere of religious discourse by Fichte, Schelling and Schleiermacher. German philosophers, and in particular Hegel, who had evolved a philosophical system which emphasised the idea of development in the dialectical process of thesis, antithesis, and synthesis, had provided a solid metaphysical basis for nineteenth-century German theology, which could easily assimilate the evolutionary discoveries of Darwin.[299] But the acceptance of modern German philosophical thought in England was slow and limited, and the publication of George Eliot's translation of Strauss's *Das Leben Jesu* in 1846 had a devastating effect on Victorian faith. In this first piece of German historical criticism to be read on any scale in England, Strauss reconciles Hegel's intellectual system with Christian theology, and denies the supernatural and miraculous elements of Christianity.

We know that Arnold was left 'uncurious and uninterested' by Strauss's *Das Leben Jesu*.[300] His brother Tom explains this by the fact that he had 'already in 1845 drifted far away from orthodox Christianity', but it is perhaps more to the point that his familiarity with the Idealist philosophers who had prepared the way for Strauss and the German historical critics had also prepared the way for his own unamazed acceptance of Strauss. Although familiarity had bred contempt in the case of the abstract metaphysical systems of Strauss's philosophical antecedents, Arnold's own religious and biblical criticism follows closely in the line of Strauss's more practical critical approach to historical Christianity. Strauss had argued that it was necessary to appreciate that the narrators of ancient Israel

> testify sometimes, not to outward facts, but to ideas... [and] constructions which even eye-witnesses had unconsciously put upon the facts, imagination concerning them, reflections upon them, reflections such as were natural to them and at the same time of the author's level of culture... [A New Testament narrative] is a plastic, naive, and, at the same time, often most profound expression of truth, within the area of religious feeling and poetic insight. It results in a narrative, legendary, mythical in nature, illustrative, often of spiritual truth in a manner more perfect than any hard, prosaic statement could achieve.[301]

If Arnold was directly anticipated by Strauss, he was also greatly influenced by Spinoza, from whom he learned to apply the methods of historical criticism to Scripture in a literary way. In the *Tractatus Theologico-Politicus*, Spinoza undertakes an objective examination of the Bible in order to consider the meaning of prophecy and God's reasons for choosing the prophets. He concludes that, since the prophets were clearly chosen for their piety, their authority 'has weight only in matters of morality...their speculative doctrines affect us little'.[302] And how literally, he asks, can we interpret their words? Arnold explains Spinoza's position in his essay 'Spinoza and the Bible':

> The prophets clearly declare themselves to have received the revelation of God through the means of words and images; – not, as Christ, through immediate communication of the mind with the mind of God... Whence,

then, could the prophets be certain of the truth of a revelation which they received through the imagination, and not by a mental process?[303]

We must view the prophets, Spinoza argues, in a way that Arnold clearly endorses, historically, and take into account the cultural assumptions of the time and the richly metaphorical nature of the Hebrew language. The keynotes of Arnold's Scriptural criticism are struck here by a philosopher praised by Arnold as having 'a noble and lofty character himself, a character...*in the grand style*' and a 'positive and vivifying atmosphere'.[304]

Arnold would doubtless have developed the historical interests that he did had he not had a father who was both Regius Professor of Modern History at Oxford from 1841 until his death in 1842 and himself interested in the historical interpretation of Scripture, but as it was he saw his own liberal critical principles as the natural continuation and extension of Dr Arnold's. Like his son, Thomas Arnold has been seen as influenced by those German biblical critics who, in the manner of Spinoza, 'attempted to synchronize, along Kantian lines, the "barren learning" of the rationalist critics...and the fervour of the less-informed Pietists'.[305] Certainly Arnold would have found in his father an openness to German ideas which was unusual for the times, and an enlightened attitude towards Scriptural interpretation which specifically paved the way for his own critical effort. In his 'Essay on the Right Interpretation of the Scriptures', published in 1832, Dr Arnold argued that 'questions of criticism' were to be distinguished from 'questions of religion', that criticism was not dangerous or subversive, and that it must be engaged in if the modern educated man was to continue to derive benefit from reading the Bible.

Arnold was aware, like his father, of the backwardness of the English in facing up to the necessity for changing the way they viewed their religion. He wrote in a letter of 1882:

The central fact of the situation always remains for me this: that whereas the basis of things amidst all chance and change has even in Europe generally been for ever so long supernatural Christianity, and far more so in England than in Europe generally, this basis is certainly going – amidst the full consciousness of the continentals that it is going, and amidst the provincial unconsciousness of the English that it is going.[306]

Even in the heart of Oxford Arnold had been forced to recognise this 'provincial unconsciousness' at work when he heard the Chancellor of the University, Lord Salisbury, blandly announce 'There shall be no more within these walls the idea of severing religion and dogma than there is the idea of severing daylight from sun.'[307]

But that was exactly what Arnold wanted to do. He was convinced of the utter futility of theological argumentation and metaphysical abstraction as effective bulwarks against the encroachment of unbelief. He thoroughly endorsed Spinoza's thesis:

The religion of all the great churches of Christendom is a religion which is not that of the Bible; it is a huge gloss put upon the Bible by generations of metaphysical theologians; the Bible, honestly and intelligently read, gives us a religion quite different and far simpler.[308]

Arnold devotes a whole chapter of *God and the Bible* to exposing 'The God of Metaphysics' as fallacious and confusing: 'even when we talk of the *being* of things, we use a fluid and literary expression, not a rigid and scientific one'.[309] Scathing about the imprecisions of logicians and metaphysicians, and contemptuous of the mechanical criticism of German biblical critics,[310] he finds fault with popular Christianity because of its intellectual inadequacies and its dependence upon a different kind of mystification:

The objections to popular Christianity are not moral objections, but intellectual revolt against its demonstrations by miracle and metaphysics.[311]

As his long campaign against Nonconformity would lead us to expect, Arnold was no more in favour of too rigid an adherence to the letter of the Bible than he was of High Church dependence on dogma. In his notebook he recorded a quotation from an essay published in the *Revue des Deux Mondes* in 1868 which reads, 'La lettre n'est pas l'esprit et la Bible n'est pas la religion. Le Christianisme existait avant que les évangélistes et les apôtres eussent écrit.'[312] He believed that traditional Christianity, in all its forms, had been shown to be obsolete, yet that there was a core of 'natural truth' of moral law and spiritual consolation which had to be re-established in its rightful place lest it be lost along with the forms and systems of Christianity which were being so readily demolished by modern criticism.[313] This standpoint was the basis for all his religious writings of the 1870s.

In 1870, Arnold published an essay on 'St Paul and Protestantism' which established the tone of his subsequent work on the way the Scriptures should be approached in the nineteenth century. St Paul, he argues, uses language in a literary way:

Paul, like the other Bible-writers, and like the Semitic race in general, has a much juster sense of the true scope and limits of diction in religious deliverances than we have. He uses within the sphere of religious emotion expressions which, in this sphere, have an eloquence and a propriety, but which are not to be taken out of it and made into formal scientific propositions.[314]

It is as absurd, he says, to try to draw out a scientific theology from a Scriptural quotation

as if we took from a chorus of Aeschylus one of his grand passages about guilt and destiny, just put the words straight into the formal and exact cast of a sentence of Aristotle, and said that here was the scientific teaching of Greek philosophy on these matters.[315]

He explains the source of the problem as the fact that both modern English and ancient Greek distinguish quite clearly between scientific and poetic language, whereas Hebrew is exclusively a poetic language: 'The Bible utterances have often the character of a chorus of Aeschylus, but never that of a treatise of Aristotle.' Yet the modern reader has generally made the mistake of taking them as scientifically true. He describes instead St Paul's vivid, figurative, emotionally-charged mode of expression as essentially oriental. Paul 'orientalises' when he speaks in the imaginative, metaphorical language of the Bible, and it is as poetry that we should interpret that language. Arnold makes his point even more clearly in the Preface to his *A Bible-Reading for Schools*, published in 1872. Here he argues that the reading of Isaiah as a school text will serve the cause of '*Letters*' rather than of religion as such. Maintaining that 'the Bible's application and edification' should be distinguished from its 'literary and historical substance', he observes that 'through the Bible only have the people much chance of getting at poetry, philosophy, and eloquence'.[316]

In his Preface to *God and the Bible*, Arnold wrote:

At the present moment two things about the Christian religion must surely be clear to anybody with eyes in his head. One is, that men cannot do without it: the other they cannot do with it as it is.[317]

Arnold set himself the task of renovating traditional Christianity for its own good. His aim in *Literature and Dogma* and *God and the Bible* was to protect religion from the destructive intellectual currents of a hostile *Zeitgeist* by demythologising it: stripping it of its theological, metaphysical and supernatural basis, and retaining only the spiritual experience and the moral truth which were empirically verifiable. The immediate object of *Literature and Dogma*, he explained, was

to reassure those who feel attachment to Christianity, to the Bible, but who recognise the growing discredit befalling miracles and the supernatural. Such persons are to be reassured, not by disguising or extenuating the discredit which has befallen miracles and the supernatural, but by insisting on the natural truth of Christianity...by the sanction of miracles Christianity can no longer stand; it can stand only by its natural truth.[318]

His aim is to take the emphasis away from the intellectual aspects of Christianity which are inaccessible and of no real interest to the modern man, the metaphysics and the dogma of orthodoxy, and to pay more attention to giving a satisfactory intellectual explanation of those elements of Christianity which seemed to be most at odds with the new intellectual currents of the age. In this way, Arnold hoped to save at least the imaginative, emotional, and moral experience of Christianity for the masses, even though he felt bound to deny the dogmatic foundations upon which they were traditionally based. He wished to show that

when we come to put the right construction on the Bible, we give to the Bible a real experimental basis, and keep on this basis throughout; instead of any basis of unverifiable assumption to start with, followed by a string of other unverifiable assumptions of the like kind, and as the received theology necessitates.[319]

In *Literature and Dogma* Arnold continues to pursue the argument he began in 'St Paul and Protestantism' that 'the language of the Bible is fluid, passing, and literary, not rigid, fixed, and scientific'.[320] He takes as an example the word 'God', which, he says,

is used in most cases as by no means a term of science of exact knowledge, but a term of poetry and eloquence, a term *thrown out*, so to speak, at a not fully grasped object of the speaker's consciousness, a *literary* term, in short; and mankind mean different things by it as their consciousness differs.[321]

He had said much the same about the language of the Prayer Book too in his essay 'A Psychological Parallel'.[322] It is certainly true that the theologian must be alive to the literary qualities of the biblical text if he is to engage in the act of textual interpretation at all. There is, after all, a rich tradition of literary exegesis in Scriptural scholarship which, as we have seen, was still very much alive in nineteenth-century theology. But outside the Church a rather different emphasis began to develop when Coleridge suggested that the Bible should be read like any other work of literature.[323] In 1859, Jowett contributed an essay to *Essays and Reviews* on 'The Interpretation of Scripture' in which he urged that the 'true meaning' of the biblical text should be restored: both its historical meaning, and its meaning for the nineteenth century. In 1869, Arnold wrote in a letter to his mother that the major work of Coleridge's and Dr Arnold's time had been 'the exploding of the old notions of literal inspiration in Scripture, and the introducing of a truer method of interpretation'.[324]

Arnold clearly saw himself as working within the same tradition as his father and Coleridge, and indeed Newman, but in his argument that the Bible should be read as literature the shift made by Coleridge and Dr Arnold from orthodoxy is taken a stage further. Arnold implies that the Scriptures are historically contingent, and that they depend upon interpretation for their validity. He also uses the word 'literature' in a rather different sense than his predecessors. In 'The Bishop and the Philosopher', his essay on Colenso and Spinoza, he conveniently asks himself the question, 'But what, it may be asked, has literary criticism to do with books on religious matters?' His answer is that 'Religious books come within the jurisdiction of literary criticism so far as they affect general culture.'[325] We notice the same limitation that we observed in his actual literary criticism: that it is remarkably *un*-literary. Arnold was not really interested in textual criticism or elucidation. His literary sense thrilled rather to the moral and emotional fervour of the religious language of the Bible. Speaking of the Prayer Book, he says that for those of us

who can no longer put the literal meaning on them which others do, and which we ourselves once did, they retain a power, and something in us vibrates to them. And not unjustly. For these old forms of expression were men's sincere attempt to set forth with due honour what we honour also; and the sense of the attempt gives a beauty and an emotion to the words, and makes them poetry.[326]

But, as Stephen Prickett argues, Arnold does not use the word 'poetry' in his biblical criticism in the traditional literary sense of the word. Although his descriptions of poetry as a language of 'emotion', 'thrown out' after 'great objects', recall the poetic tradition of Wordsworth and Coleridge and the theological tradition of Butler, Keble and Newman, the whole tenor of his work is to 'deny the very concept on which the idea of the "poetic" interpretation of Scripture rested, that is, that poetry is the expression in words of something that can be put in no other way'.[327] Arnold's literary criticism is at its weakest exactly where he tries to deal with the vexed question of the relation of form to content, and the problem reveals itself in his search for a simplified paraphrase of the Bible's poetry, its myths and symbols, a process which neither the Romantic poets nor the 'poetic' theologians could have contemplated.

When we try to identify the source of this very fundamental difference between Arnold's 'literary' approach to the Bible and those of his apparent antecedents, we find it in his sense that the object of the exercise is the verification of Scriptural truth. Unlike his predecessors, Arnold is anxious to show 'that the Bible is really based upon propositions which all can verify',[328] for he believes that the modern scientific world is one that demands empirical verification. The Bible, he argues, can be demythologised to reveal its 'natural truth', for it embodies timeless moral values to which every human being may testify from his own experience.

Arnold's appeal to a God of experience, rather than to a God of miracles or metaphysics,[329] may be traced back ten years, for in his essay on 'Marcus Aurelius' we find the terms of the religious experience he was later to extol in *Literature and Dogma*:

The paramount virtue of religion is, that it has *lighted up* morality; that it has supplied the emotion and inspiration needful for carrying the sage along the narrow way perfectly, for carrying the ordinary man along it at all.[330]

In this essay, not only is Christianity linked with morality and emotion, it also seems indistinguishable from the beliefs of a Roman Stoic moralist: 'the morality of Marcus Aurelius...reminds one of Christian morality' because of 'its accent of emotion'.[331] In Arnold's poetry of the same period, there is often a similar emphasis on the moral rather than the spiritual and supernatural elements of Christianity. 'The Better Part' opens with the lines:

> Long fed on boundless hopes, O race of man,
> How angrily thou spurn'st all simpler fare!

and ends with the exhortation to be 'such men as' Christ.[332] In 'The Divinity' he recalls St Bernard's words and the fact that they are no longer recognised in modern theology:

> *God's wisdom and God's goodness!* – Ay, but fools
> Mis-define these till God knows them no more.
> *Wisdom and goodness, they are God!* – what schools

> Have yet so much as heard this simpler lore?
> This no saint preaches, and this no Church rules;
> 'Tis in the desert, now and heretofore.[333]

A similar moral emphasis pervades 'Rugby Chapel' too, where Arnold endeavours to show that his father 'was not only a good man saving his soul by righteousness, but that he carried so many others along with him in his hand, and saved them...along with himself'.[334] Elsewhere, he calls the Church of England '*a great national society for the promotion of goodness*'.[335]

The central purpose of *Literature and Dogma* was to show that behind the figurative, imaginative language of the Bible lived a body of human and moral insights which was eternally valid for mankind. Conduct, he claims, is 'three-fourths of life';[336] given that, it is crucial that we should be concerned about it. To this end, religion can help us, for, as he argues, the object of religion is conduct. He continues: 'the antithesis between *ethical* and *religious* is...quite a false one', for although he admits that there is a difference between religion and morality, it is only a difference of degree. For Arnold, the degree seems to be entirely emotionally determined, for, as he infamously expressed it, 'the true meaning of religion is...*morality touched by emotion*',[337] 'ethics heightened, enkindled, lit up by feeling'.[338]

It has been remarked that the emphasis in *Literature and Dogma* radically contradicts his discouragement of Hebraism and promotion of Hellenism in *Culture and Anarchy*. However, the kind of religion he recommends in *Literature and Dogma* was always an important part of his idea of Culture, so although the terminology may seem to be contradictory, the sense is not. The perception of Christianity as morality does not necessarily represent a betrayal of his earlier position.

A more serious objection is sustained by those who are unconvinced by Arnold's view that, as T. S. Eliot put it, 'Religion is morals.'[339] F. H. Bradley was the first to point out that Arnold's definition of religion was tautological, and many critics since have agreed. Although this might sometimes be explained as the outraged response of orthodoxy,[340] such is by no means always the case. Lionel Trilling, for example, like Bradley himself, has no religious axe to grind when he objects:

clearly it is not *any* emotion that touches morality and translates it into religion but specifically an emotion about an outside and transcendent force, or help, or criterion, referred to as 'who' or 'God' or 'eternal life' or 'the kingdom of heaven'.[341]

And it is interestingly a Catholic critic, A. O. J. Cockshut, who offers the most convincing defence of Arnold's faith. Referring to the much-criticised phrase 'morality touched with emotion', he argues that the emotion to which Arnold referred was very deep, and very religious, even if not in an acceptable historical sense Christian, and that

despite his rejection of miracles, he believed with all his being in the death and resurrection of the self, the need for each soul to be baptised into Christ's death.[342]

He sees Arnold as a lonely figure, separated from Newman by his distrust of the supernatural dimension of Christianity, and from Huxley and Herbert Spencer by his profound awareness of the spiritual meaning of the central miracle of the Resurrection for man's soul.[343] Arnold *was* a lonely figure in the Victorian religious scene, and the isolation of his position presumably only strengthened his desire to authenticate his beliefs by reference to a general human experience, the moral experience, which could validate his own perception of the claims of Christianity. But was his premise that the spheres of science and morality were methodologically identical a valid one? Can we accept the empirical verification he offers as an adequate substitute for all that he sweeps away? Can religious truth, especially a religious truth that is not only moral but avowedly emotional, poetic, and humanistic, be verified in a scientific way?

Arnold's insistence upon the need for verification stems, of course, from his awareness that subjective moral and religious instincts must be endorsed by some objective factor, and he calls first of all simply upon the universal moral experience of mankind to supply such an endorsement. But he also feels the need for some higher objective moral sanction to which the inner moral sense of each human being responds. Although he dispenses with the God of historical Christianity, who has traditionally filled that role, he erects in His place, as the almighty guarantor of human morality, 'the Eternal Not-ourselves which makes for Righteousness'. He claims Israel's consciousness of 'the not ourselves which makes for righteousness' as the real germ of religious consciousness out of which sprang the 'mighty growth of poetry and tradition' which is Christianity.[344] In his search for authority Arnold tries to give permanent validity to the moral authority of subjective experience by relating it, in a way that could be empirically verified, to an eternal moral principle, higher than the self, the reality of 'the not ourselves which makes for righteousness'. Man's moral knowledge is a 'central clue in our moral being which unites us to the universal order'.[345] But the logical contradiction is immediately apparent. Arnold is calling upon subjective experience as empirical proof by which to verify subjective experience objectively. However elaborately it is conceived and named, Arnold's objective moral authority is really still dependent upon emotional intuition and subjective assertion.

It has been remarked that Arnold's subordination of religion to morality and his denial of metaphysical knowledge belongs to the tradition of Kant's ethical Idealism.[346] Another central assumption of Arnold's religious writings, that God's truth cannot be articulated in human language, also implies an idea of God's transcendence which is very Kantian. This assumption is implicit in his refusal to limit religious truths to dogmatic formulations and in his insistence that the language of the Bible is 'language *thrown out* at an object of consciousness not fully grasped, which inspired emotion'.[347] It is also apparent in his respect for the very tentativeness of what Spinoza is 'driving at'[348] and in the imprecision and fluidity of his own terms for a God who remains transcendent: the eternal 'not ourselves', 'a stream of tendency'.[349]

But however Kantian he may be in some respects, Arnold is emphatically *un*-Kantian in his faith in empiricism. Lionel Trilling identifies the root of all Arnold's difficulties as the fact that

he is basically confused about the nature of fact and verification. He wants apodictic certainty of God but he wants it according to an empirical notion of science, a science which is experience purely, nothing more than organized common-sense, in which the content of any scientific law is only the account of the order of our sensations. For rigor, exactness, universality and system he has no respect...But if one is committed to a method of science purely empirical – and not very strict – one can have no apodictic proofs.[350]

Once again, Arnold falls uncomfortably between two stools. On the one hand his whole effort in his religious writings amounts to a contradiction of Newman's opposition of faith and reason,[351] for his very purpose has been to make religion reasonable. Yet on the other hand his commitment to empirical methods makes it impossible for him to aspire to the attainment of an absolute truth, established on incontrovertible evidence. Of Kant's three kinds of judgements, problematical, assertorial, and apodictical, Arnold was forced by his own self-imposed limitations to rest in the assertorial. After he has borrowed what he wanted from both Newman and Kant and rejected what did not suit him, the so-called synthesis of faith and reason with which he is left, in that it is a watered-down version of both, is in the final analysis rather lame.[352]

Just as there is a central ambiguity in Arnold's concept of reason which proves to be a fatal flaw in his argument, there is a similar ambiguity in his ideas about the nature and function of poetry, and in particular the nature of its relationship with religion. On the one hand, in his religious writings he tries to convince us that mere poetry must be displaced in order that the natural truth of religion may be made more accessible. Yet on the other we are told that it is only in its poetry that the future of the Church lies, that it is poetry alone which will guarantee the survival of Christianity. Here we seem to have another volte-face, which has its source in contradictions at the very heart of Arnold's ideas about poetry.

Although the title of *Literature and Dogma* might lead us to believe that we can expect a Coleridgean discussion of the Bible as literature, in fact Arnold's purpose is to persuade us that much of Christian religion and dogma may be discounted as merely literary, or what he calls by the German name of *Aberglaube*, 'Extra-belief', 'that which we hope, augur, imagine'.[353] Such were the 'Messianic ideas, which were the poetry of life to Israel in the age when Jesus Christ came'. Arnold traces the evolution of this Messianic *Aberglaube* through the course of Christian history, and argues that ultimately, as the personal influence of Jesus faded,

the *Aberglaube* was perpetuated, placed out of reach of all practical tests, and made stronger than ever. With the multitude, this *Aberglaube*, or extra-belief, inevitably came soon to surpass the original conviction itself in attractiveness and seeming certitude. The future and the miraculous engaged the chief attention of Christians; and, in accordance with this strain of thought, they more and more rested the proof of Christianity, not on its internal evidence, but on prophecy and miracle.[354]

While, he repeats, there is nothing at all wrong with being attracted by the *Aberglaube* of Christianity, while it is only natural that men should 'take short cuts to what they ardently desire,...should tell themselves fairy-tales about it, should make these fairy-tales the basis for what is far more sure and solid than the fairy-tales, the desire itself', they finally have to pay for it when they discover that the *Aberglaube* is *not* certain, 'and then the whole certainty of religion seems discredited'.[355] As he says in *God and the Bible*, 'it is ideas, not imaginations, which endure',[356] and it is necessary, in the modern age of ideas, to penetrate the *Aberglaube* of miraculous myth and fairy-tale if we are to recover the original meaning of Christianity, the moral teachings of Jesus Christ.[357] 'As our literary sense widens', he argues, 'the notion of a secret sense in the Bible, and of the Fathers' disengagement of it' proves to be 'a mere dream'.[358] It is curious that Arnold should see this as the result of the widening of the literary sense. What is so very striking about Arnold's conclusions is their tendency to reduce the extraordinary literary richness of the Bible to 'mere' poetry which can and should be tossed aside. Although he may at first seem to be in the tradition of literary interpreters of the Scriptures, he is actually, as he did with the ideas of Newman, and Kant, and the Romantic poets, turning their approach to the literary riches of the Bible on its head.

However, perversely, as Hoxie Neale Fairchild points out, 'When we are trying to think about religion, Arnold bids us renounce all the poetry; when we are reading poetry, he bids us observe how truly religious it is.'[359] Although Arnold believes that the truth of Christianity must be distinguished from its poetry, he also holds that poetry can and often does express the most profound truths. This idea, which was to form the substance of his later writings, had been anticipated in his earliest critical work. In the brief advertisement to the second edition of *Poems* (1854) he had asserted that the virtues of great poetry could cure England's problems, not only in literature and art, but in religion and morals as well.[360] In the 1853 Preface itself he had called attention to the religious character and function of poetry. And since then he had continually stressed that the noblest and most serious forms of art 'possess religiousness'.[361]

Although he had never been won over by the dogmas of the Catholic Church, he had always felt the attraction of its poetry and traditions which recalled 'all the pell mell of the men and women of Shakespeare's plays'.[362] Arnold's statements on the poetic aspects of Christianity became more and more explicit as his career went on. Rightly understood, he suggested in *Literature and Dogma*, the cures worked by Jesus were no miracles but 'eminently natural', 'like the grace of Raphael, or the grand style of Phidias'.[363] And we can learn how to read the Bible 'as it really is' by simple analogy with the way in which we read and interpret Homer, for 'Homer's poetry was the Bible of the Greeks.'[364] But it was in *God and the Bible* that he first advanced the idea that he was to articulate at greater length in his last critical essays:

As the Catholic architecture, so the Catholic worship is likely to survive and prevail, long after the intellectual childishness of Catholic dogma and the political and social mischiefs of the Roman system have tired out men's patience with them. Catholic worship is likely, however modified, to survive as the general worship of Christians, because it is the worship which, in a sphere where poetry is permissible and natural, unites the most of the elements of poetry.[365]

In a letter of 1874, Arnold wrote:

My ideal would be, for Catholic countries, the development of something like old Catholicism, retaining as much as possible of old religious services and usages, but becoming more and more liberal in spirit.[366]

The substance of his late writings on religion is that although 'Ultramontanism, sacerdotalism, and superstition' must be dispensed with, the Church may still retain 'the beauty, the richness, the poetry, the infinite charm for the imagination, of its own age-long growth'.[367] Arnold's view of the religion of the future as an aestheticised version of the historical Catholic Church is stated most fully in his essay 'Irish Catholicism and British Liberalism' in 1878:

I persist in thinking that the prevailing form for the Christianity of the future will be the form of Catholicism; but a Catholicism purged, opening itself to the light and air, having the consciousness of its own poetry, freed from its sacerdotal despotism and freed from its pseudo-scientific apparatus of superannuated dogma. Its forms will be retained, as symbolizing with the force and charm of poetry a few cardinal facts and ideas, simple indeed, but indispensable and inexhaustible, and on which our race could lay hold only by materializing them.[368]

It seems that Arnold is saying that the rich symbolism of the Church may be retained as long as it is recognised as being untrue, as being *merely* poetry. Gone is Newman's sense of the organic relationship between the forms of Christianity and its profoundest truths. The true strength of the Church depends upon 'its powers of attractiveness'.[369] Nonconformity is discounted, therefore, for its ugliness, and Catholicism, divested of its theological grounds, is embraced for its beautiful forms.

Arnold's resumption of his literary critical interests in the last ten years of his life did not stop him pursuing the implications of the ideas about the relationship between religion and poetry he had begun to develop in his religious period. In his much-quoted predictions in 'On Poetry' and 'The Study of Poetry', he speculates that, once orthodox Christianity has been finally discredited, poetry itself will take over its function:

The future of poetry is immense, because in poetry, where it is worthy of its high destinies, our race, as time goes on, will find an ever surer and surer stay. There is not a creed which is not shaken, not an accredited dogma which is not shown to be questionable, not a received tradition which does not threaten to dissolve...Our religion has materialised itself in the fact, in the supposed fact; it has attached its emotion to the fact, and now the fact is failing it. But for poetry the idea is everything; the rest is a world of illusion, of divine illusion. Poetry attaches its emotion to the idea; the idea *is* the fact. The strongest part of our religion today is its unconscious poetry.[370]

That being the case, he concludes that 'most of what now passes with us for religion and philosophy will be replaced by poetry'.[371]

VI

In turning to write once again about poetry in his final years, then, Arnold did not feel that he was abandoning the religious cause. Certainly in these last essays, his conviction of the religious function of poetry is evident in everything he says about the writers he chooses to discuss. Poetry is, by now, an 'interpretation of the world', and the success or failure of a poet depends upon how well he fulfils this function. In his important essay on Wordsworth, he defined poetry as 'nothing less than the most perfect speech of man, that in which he comes nearest to being able to utter the truth'.[372] By the end of his career, all religious, moral, and aesthetic qualities seem to have converged in the idea of poetry, which is perceived as performing a religious function of a higher and more far-reaching kind than the more narrowly defined religious function of the poetry of the Christian Church. The basis of this coalescence seems to be that poetry too, like his 'religion of righteousness', is conceived by Arnold as 'morality touched with emotion', as moral sentiment. He actually defines his sense of the term 'moral' as 'having "the character of poetic truth"'.[373]

By depriving religion of its dogmatic foundations, Arnold had effectively reduced it to a state of mind, 'a sentiment of the numinous', which 'has its active effect in moral sentiment', as Vincent Buckley describes it.[374] And as Arnold himself says, this religious sentiment is 'best not regarded alone, but considered in conjunction with the grandeur of the world, love of kindred, love, gratitude, etc.'[375] He considers it most often of all, though, in conjunction with poetry, his claims for which are similarly moral and sentimental. We turn to poetry 'to interpret life for us, to console us, to sustain us'.[376] Poetry has a moral effect upon us, it deals with moral subjects, and it has a moral value because it is in some way true. But given that he has been at great pains to distinguish the poetry of the Bible from its 'natural truth' as well as from scientific truth, what can he mean when he talks of 'poetic truth'? His identification of poetry and truth is possible only at the expense of whittling away the essential meanings of both.

It has been a common criticism of Arnold that, by giving a quasi-religious status to the best poetry, he has in fact devalued the traditional concepts of both poetry and religion.[377] T. S. Eliot isolated Arnold's central weakness when he drew attention to his 'vagueness of definition', and his evasion of the central issues by consistent conceptual and linguistic imprecision. We are indeed constantly struck by how often Arnold asks us to redefine our vocabulary, words, even, which he makes into linchpins of his arguments: 'moral', 'criticism', 'culture', 'form', 'subject', 'truth', 'reason', 'poetry', and most significantly of all, 'religion'. 'Literature, or Culture', Eliot argued, 'tended with Arnold to usurp the place of Religion',[378] but, he objects,

nothing in this world or the next is a substitute for anything else; and if you find that you must do without something, such as religious faith or philosophic belief, then you must just do without it.[379]

In which case, 'to ask of poetry that it give religious and philosophic satisfaction, while deprecating philosophy and dogmatic religion, is of course to embrace the shadow of a shade'.[380]

Arnold attempts to mediate between two quite different positions – a faith in morality and a faith in art – in a way that recalls Ruskin rather than Newman or Keble or Hopkins. The thought of both Arnold and Ruskin is fraught with contradictions. Both, although in some respects quite radical (politically, and, in Arnold's case, intellectually and theologically), are essentially very conservative in their desire to shore up traditional religious, moral and philosophical beliefs and attitudes against the threatening *Zeitgeist*. And neither resolves the question of how to transcend the limitations of subjectivism satisfactorily even though both tried to do so by relating aesthetic experience to morality. For all their efforts their 'objective' conclusions may be reduced to subjective assertion in the final analysis, and their desperate attempts to escape the self leave them all the more firmly immersed. 'The total effect of Arnold's philosophy', as Eliot says, leaves 'Religion to be laid waste by the anarchy of feeling.'[381] The total effect of Ruskin's, one might add, was to drive him mad.

But in many ways Arnold's position was an even more complicated one than Ruskin's, for he was not only saying with the early Ruskin, 'Religion is Morals' and 'Art is Morals', but saying with Pater and Wilde that 'Religion is Art', and that Hebraism should be making way for Hellenism. Eliot remarks that because Arnold himself was morally such a puritan, he did not realise that statements like ' "The power of Christianity has been in the immense emotion which it has excited" ' is a counsel to get all the emotional kick out of Christianity one can, without the bother of believing it', and prepared the way for the complete aestheticisation of Christianity by Pater and Wilde. Certainly, by the time we reach the works of Pater and Wilde, the tendency to merge religious and aesthetic categories which began within the theological formulations of orthodox Christianity has a quite different character. An awareness of the aesthetic aspects of theology and faith and of the place of poetry in a structure of belief has evolved into a thoroughly aestheticised religion, religion for art's sake, and the worship of a religion of art. Mediating between Newman and Pater in his religious writings, and between Ruskin and Wilde in his writings on literature and art, Arnold played an important role in determining that development in Victorian religio-aesthetic theory.

4 Aestheticism: Walter Pater and Oscar Wilde

Arnold died in 1888, the year in which his niece, Mrs Humphry Ward, published *Robert Elsmere*. This enormously popular novel tells the story of an Anglican priest, married to a very devout woman, who comes to have doubts about historical Christianity and gives up his orders. He becomes a Unitarian, does mission work in the East End of London, and abandons dogma to concentrate on faith, ethics and good works. His decision causes serious strains in his marriage, but he and his wife are finally reconciled before his untimely death ends the novel. Arnold read and enjoyed the first volume of the novel before he died, although his niece doubted whether the second and third volumes would have appealed to him, as he had 'little sympathy with people who "went out"'.[1] Arnold himself unfortunately left no critical comment on the novel, but others have found significant similarities between Robert Elsmere's religious conclusions and Arnold's own. Oscar Wilde's Cyril, in 'The Decay of Lying', describes *Robert Elsmere* as 'simply Arnold's *Literature and Dogma* with the literature left out'.[2] Lionel Trilling's more measured estimation is that

the intellectual world in which Elsmere lived was Arnold's world, the religious ferment which so stirred England moved Arnold too and was increased by him. Above all, Elsmere's intention was Arnold's – to preserve faith through the demolition of dogma, to the end that ethics might emerge and fraternity prevail.[3]

Neither Pater nor Wilde wrote much formally about Matthew Arnold, but both commented critically on *Robert Elsmere*, and from what they wrote about the religious history of the hero of that novel we can postulate their views on Arnold's religious position.

Pater reviewed *Robert Elsmere* for the *Guardian* and approved of it aesthetically: 'it has charmed the literary sense'.[4] Even his judgement of the moral characters of the hero and his wife is made on aesthetic grounds:

both alike...have a genuine sense of the eternal moral charm of 're-nunciation', something even of the thirst for martyrdom, for those

183

wonderful, inaccessible, cold heights of the *Imitation,* eternal also in their aesthetic charm.[5]

However, he cannot approve Elsmere's theological position, and this not because he regrets, as Mrs Ward supposed Arnold would, his leaving the Church. Elsmere's duty as a priest was 'to achieve as much faith as possible in an age of negation',[6] and he was right in ceasing to be a clergyman when he lost faith in historical Christianity. But, Pater objects,

it strikes us as a blot on his philosophical pretensions that he should have been both so late in perceiving the difficulty, and then so sudden and trenchant in dealing with so great and complex a question. Had he possessed a perfectly philosophic or scientific temper he would have hesitated...one by one, Elsmere's objections may be met by considerations of the same *genus,* and not less equal weight, relatively to a world so obscure, in its origin and issues, as that in which we live.[7]

Pater's own attitude towards historical Christianity at this time is clearly indicated in a letter he wrote to Mrs Humphry Ward:

To my mind, the beliefs and the function in the world, of the historic Church, form just one of those obscure but all-important possibilities, which the human mind is powerless effectively to dismiss from itself, and might wisely accept, in the first place, as a workable hypothesis.[8]

His discussion of the hero of her novel in his review confirms this position, for he sets against those who cannot be sure that the sacred story is true, and struggle with their honest intellectual doubts, 'a large class of minds which cannot be sure it is false', who 'make allowance in their scheme of life for a great possibility'.[9] The question of the day, he argues, is not so much a doctrinal one, whether one is 'High' or 'Low', Ritualistic or Methodist, but one of the opposition between, in Mrs Ward's words,

Two estimates of life – the estimate which is the offspring of the scientific spirit, and which is for ever making the visible world fairer and more desirable in mortal eyes; and the estimate of Saint Augustine.[10]

Pater argues for a Christianity which is actually 'broader' and more tolerant than Arnold's Liberal Christianity, and which rests upon a conception of the 'infinite nature' of Christ, rather than Arnold's more narrowly conceived human nature.[11]

Wilde writes about *Robert Elsmere* only in the dialogue between Cyril and Vivian in 'The Decay of Lying'. Cyril claims to be 'quite devoted to it':

Not that I can look upon it as a serious work. As a statement of the problems that confront the earnest Christian it is ridiculous and antiquated...

It is as much behind the age as Paley's *Evidences* or Colenso's method of Biblical exegesis. Nor could anything be less impressive than the unfortunate hero gravely heralding a dawn that rose long ago, and so completely missing its true significance that he proposes to carry on the business of the old firm under the new name.[12]

Vivian is less charitable still when he refers to it as 'deliberately tedious':

Robert Elsmere is of course a masterpiece – a masterpiece of the *genre ennuyeux*, the one form of literature that the English people seems thoroughly to enjoy. A thoughtful young friend of ours once told us that it reminded him of the sort of conversation that goes on at a meat tea in the house of a serious Nonconformist family, and we can quite believe it. Indeed it is only in England that such a book could be produced. England is the home of lost ideas.[13]

For Wilde, *Robert Elsmere* is above all a bad novel, aesthetically. But elsewhere there is evidence to suggest that he considered Elsmere's, and, by extension, Arnold's dilemma and spiritual struggle to be not only *passé* but essentially misguided. Elsmere was seduced by a scientific view of life, as Pater points out, and the very basis of Arnold's religious endeavour was his sense of the need to establish the truth of religion on a sure scientific footing. Wilde believed, on the contrary, that 'Religions die when they are proved to be true. Science is the record of dead religions.'[14] He makes Gilbert argue, in 'The Critic as Artist', that 'the theologians of the Broad Church Party...seem to me to spend their time in trying to explain their divinity away',[15] while Vivian in 'The Decay of Lying' regrets 'the growth of common sense in the English Church' as 'a degrading concession to a low form of realism'.[16]

Moreover, Arnold rested his case for the empirical proof of Christianity upon moral grounds. Since religion was 'morality touched by emotion',[17] it was possible for Arnold to regard the Emperor Marcus Aurelius, the Stoical philosopher, as in essence a Christian.[18] Yet for Marius, the hero of Pater's religious novel *Marius the Epicurean*, published three years before *Robert Elsmere*, Marcus Aurelius' Stoical morality, and in particular his joylessness and his intolerance of the life of the senses, suffer by contrast with Cornelius' simple goodness and joy, and with the beauty and grandeur of Christianity.[19] Wilde moves even further away from the characteristically Arnoldian emphasis on morality. The hero of *The Picture of Dorian Gray*, published in 1890, five years after *Marius the Epicurean*, is judged by Pater to fail as an experiment in true Epicureanism, in that he loses the moral sense entirely.[20] *The Picture of Dorian Gray* certainly has a moral, as Wilde himself was anxious to point out and Pater was the first to comment on, namely, 'that vice and crime make people coarse and ugly'.[21] But it is hardly likely that we would find a defender of the traditional moral scheme in the author of the following maxims:

Aesthetics are higher than ethics;
Truth is entirely and absolutely a matter of style;
To morals belong the lower and less intellectual spheres;
Wickedness is a myth invented by good people to account for the curious attractiveness of others;
In its rejection of the current notions about morality, [sin] is one with the higher ethics.[22]

It is certainly true that both Pater and Wilde developed highly aestheticised forms of Christianity in their writings, and that they may be seen as taking their place in a lineage extending from Newman through Arnold to the nineties.[23] But it is also true that they arrived at their respective conclusions about the relationship between religious and aesthetic experience from very different positions. Caution must be exercised in the attribution of influence, for Pater and Wilde both reacted against the traditions which nurtured them and the writers whom they most respected. Wilde's haunting line, 'each man kills the thing he loves',[24] is highly pertinent to his own and to Pater's intellectual development.

This is as apparent in their critical as it is in their religious writings. If we compare Pater and Wilde to Ruskin and Arnold it is clear that they shared a number of important critical attitudes. Pater read Ruskin shortly before he left school.[25] While he apparently remained unconvinced by Ruskin's insistence upon '*theoria*', he was taught by him not only how to study, appreciate, and elucidate works of art, but also the art of creative criticism in imaginative prose. Pater learned from Ruskin that the true significance of the visual arts lay in their capacity to convey feeling through the imaginative recreation of visual data. Like Ruskin, he believed that art should be not the simple imitation of objective reality, but the expression of the artist's emotional and spiritual response to what he saw. Pater's doctrine of the transformation of the life of sensations into art, his idea of art as a combination of emotion, intellect and imagination, as the expression of the noblest human spirit, does not significantly depart from Ruskin's own theories of art.[26]

Perhaps more important for both of them, in practice at least, than their verbal recreation of the work of art itself, was their articulation of what they considered to be the appropriate sensibility of the aesthetic critic. Both perceived the historical past in a highly personal way, making it accessible by filtering it through their own imaginative appreciation of individual works of art and artists. They were attracted by significantly different periods of history, of course – Pater opting for fifteenth-century Italy, Ruskin for the purity of Gothic – but they were guided by the same principle of unity of culture which these eras seemed to them severally to represent.

Both men were humanists, both believed unflaggingly in the unity of the human spirit, but this basic belief led them in two very different directions. Their shared belief that art was the expression of man's totality and must be justified in terms of his whole nature resulted in Ruskin's fears lest the concentration on visual sensibility that art demanded should make him abandon his moral nature, on the one hand, and Pater's reluctance to forgo any area of human experience through the necessary limitations incurred under an absolute moral system, on the other. Thus, although they share a firm conviction of the necessary relation of art to the rest of human experience, and see this as a moral relation, they veer off from this to the two extremes where history has placed them, and while Ruskin's whole effort is directed towards the Christianisation of Romantic aesthetic theory, Pater elaborates a secular version of the same.

Wilde himself brackets Ruskin and Pater together as types of the 'creative' impressionistic critic. Gilbert, in 'The Critic as Artist', observes that they both treat 'the work of art simply as a starting-point for a new creation':

Who cares whether Mr. Ruskin's views on Turner are sound or not? What does it matter? That mighty and majestic prose of his, so fervid and so fiery-coloured in its noble eloquence, so rich in its elaborate symphonic music, so sure and certain, at its best, in subtle choice of word and epithet, is at least as great a work of art as any of those wonderful sunsets that bleach or rot on their corrupted canvases in England's Gallery... Who, again, cares whether Mr. Pater has put into the portrait of Mona Lisa something that Leonardo never dreamed of? The painter may have been merely the slave of an archaic smile, as some have fancied, but whenever I pass into the cool galleries of the Palace of the Louvre, and stand before that strange figure 'set in its marble chair in that cirque of fantastic rocks, as in some strange light under sea', I murmur to myself, 'She is older than the rocks among which she sits...'[27]

Wilde became acquainted with both Ruskin and Pater when he went to Oxford in 1874. As Pater, he fell under Ruskin's spell as a young and impressionable student. In his first term he attended Ruskin's lectures on Florentine art, and became involved in his bizarre project to build a road across a swamp in nearby Ferry Hincksey. This was the beginning of a long discipleship and friendship. Years later, in 1888, Wilde wrote to Ruskin:

The dearest memories of my Oxford days are my walks and talks with you, and from you I learned nothing but what was good. How else could it be? There is in you something of prophet, of priest, and of poet, and to you the gods gave eloquence such as they have given to none other, so that your message might come to us with the fire of passion, and the marvel of music, making the deaf to hear, and the blind to see.[28]

At the very same time as he came under the influence of Ruskin he first read Pater's *Studies in the History of the Renaissance*, 'that book which has had such a strange influence over my life' as he was later to write in *De Profundis*. But then, in his carefree years at Oxford, it was his 'golden book',[29] and the 'prophetic' teachings of Ruskin were counterbalanced by the 'aesthetic' teachings of Pater. In some ways their respective influences on the young Wilde were complementary, but in others they were antithetical. Ruskin and Pater both wrote aesthetic criticism in the Romantic tradition, but Pater was also a Hellenist. He saw in the Renaissance a brilliant fusion of the Christian and classical traditions, not, as Ruskin, a catastrophic and decadent corruption of the pure Christianity of the Middle Ages by pagan culture. Their perceptions of Ancient Greece were by no means the same, but Wilde and Pater were more in the Arnoldian tradition in their espousal of Hellenism.[30] They were also very Arnoldian in their elevation of criticism into a creative act. 'Mr. Wilde', wrote Pater, in his review of *The Picture of Dorian Gray*, 'carries on, more perhaps than any other writer, the brilliant critical work of Matthew Arnold.'[31]

The critical doctrines of Arnold and Ruskin, Pater and Wilde often seem to coexist quite happily because of their common consensus about the significance of art, culture, and criticism in life, and we frequently find echoes of the earlier writers in the works of the later. However, their doctrines sometimes conflict. Richard Ellmann has shown how in Wilde's work, from the early poem 'Hélas!', through *The Picture of Dorian Gray*, the critical writings, *Salome* and *De Profundis*, Pater and Ruskin 'came to stand heraldically, burning unicorn and uninflamed satyr, in front of two portals of his mental theatre. He sometimes allowed them to battle, at other times tried to reconcile them.'[32] Ellmann explores the way in which Wilde identifies these two 'tutelary voices from the university' with forces within his own psyche, forces which, more often than not, are at war. This conflict suggests that perhaps more important than the commonality of their religious, moral and aesthetic concerns are their differences.

Aestheticism

According to Yeats, Pater's 'revolutionary' prose-poem, by which he meant the passage on the Mona Lisa from the essay on Da Vinci in *The Renaissance*, signalled the 'revolt against Victorianism', against 'irrelevant' natural description, against 'scientific and moral discursiveness'[33] – in other words, against all that Ruskin and Arnold had come to represent. It is certainly common to view Ruskin and Arnold on the one hand and Pater and Wilde on the other as representing polarities of nineteenth-century views on art and aesthetics, the former standing for art for morality's sake, the latter for art for art's sake. Ruskin's strictures are frequently overturned by his disciples. In *The Renaissance* Pater completely contradicts everything Ruskin claimed about that period in *The Stones of Venice*. Wilde likewise parodies Ruskin's most fervent beliefs about the relationship between nature and art when he says that 'Life imitates Art' and that 'A really well-made buttonhole is the only link between Art and Nature.' Both Wilde and Pater similarly parody Ruskin's and Arnold's obsession for objectivity. Wilde's Vivian says:

If we take Nature to mean natural simple instinct as opposed to self-conscious culture, the work produced under this influence is always old-fashioned, antiquated, and out of date. One touch of Nature will make the whole world kin, but two touches of Nature will destroy any work of Art. If, on the other hand, we regard Nature as the collection of phenomena external to man, people only discover in her what they bring to her. She has no suggestions of her own. Wordsworth went to the lakes, but he was never a lake poet. He found in stones the sermons he had already hidden there. He went moralising about the district, but his good work was produced when he returned, not to Nature, but to poetry.[34]

Here he manages to discredit not only Ruskin's idea of Nature as an objective criterion for aesthetic worth but his earnest discussion of Pathetic Fallacy too. Arnold is similarly parodied. Pater inverts Arnold's famous definition of criticism in the Preface to *The Renaissance* even while apparently invoking it:

'To see the object as in itself it really is', has been justly said to be the aim of all true criticism whatever; and in aesthetic criticism the first step towards seeing one's object as it really is, is to know one's own impression as it really is...[35]

Perhaps Pater is being more realistic about the business of perception, but here he flagrantly turns Arnold's famous objective manifesto into a statement of the subjectivism of the critical act. Wilde is less subtle still in his flouting of Arnold, when he makes Gilbert argue that 'the primary aim of the critic is to see the object as in itself it really is not'.[36]

We are clearly wrong to see a simple line of development from Ruskin and Arnold to Pater and Wilde. But we are also wrong if we simply polarise them. The connections and distinctions are more subtle and interesting than their own and others' rhetoric might suggest. In particular, when considering the relationship between religious and aesthetic ideas in the writings of Pater and Wilde, it is important to discriminate the precise nature of their beliefs in the moral value of art, for their creation of a religion of art is more substantial than is usually assumed and their aestheticised versions of Christianity are seriously related to their doctrines about art.

I

In the 1860s, when Ruskin and Arnold were at the height of their careers, Pater was only just beginning to publish his first essays and Wilde was still a boy. In 1888, when Arnold died and Ruskin was slipping into his final decade of insanity, Pater's influence was at its height and Wilde was himself beginning to publish seriously. By 1891, the momentous year in which he met Lord Alfred Douglas, he had already published *The Soul of Man Under Socialism, The Picture of Dorian Gray*, his book of critical essays collected under the title *Intentions*, and two collections of short fiction. Twenty-five years after the publication of *Culture and Anarchy*, the social and political climate was very different. As Raymond Williams has observed, 'The temper which the adjective Victorian is useful to describe is virtually finished in the 1880s', although Victoria still had twenty years to reign, and 'the new men who appear in that decade, and who have left their mark, are recognizably different in tone'.[37]

The context within which Wilde set about deflating the complacent bourgeois morality of the high Victorian period was one in which the electorate had been extended and State-imposed reforms had begun to erode the *laissez-faire* individualism of middle-class mid-Victorian England. The 1880s and 1890s saw the emergence of the first British Socialist organisation of any note, the Social Democratic Federation, and the formation of the Fabian Society.[38] Although no Fabian himself, Wilde reputedly wrote his only social pamphlet, *The Soul of Man Under Socialism*, after hearing Shaw lecture on Fabian Socialism. In it, he proclaims that 'Human slavery is wrong, insecure, and demoralising', and urges the establishment of Socialism, which 'would relieve us from the sordid necessity of living for others which, in the present condition of things, presses so hardly upon almost everybody'. The poor, he says, are 'ungrateful, discontented, disobedient, and rebellious', and, more-over, 'They are quite right to be so.'[39] Although there are certain aspects of Wilde's position which recall Arnold's – most notably, his insistence upon self-culture as the only basis for the proper development of society, and his demand for clear-sighted intellectualism – Wilde's social assumptions are clearly quite different from Arnold's in the 1860s. Democracy is no longer a looming threat. It is acknowledged as having arrived, and the social reforms which should in consequence have been instituted are perceived to be long overdue. Although Wilde wishes indeed to see the Government replaced by a 'State', its chief function would be to organise labour, and to be 'a voluntary manufacturer and distributor of necessary commodities',[40] not to prevent Anarchy.

As we have seen, Arnold's and Ruskin's resistance to political change was related to their instinctive resistance to the principles of evolution and historicism. Here too, Wilde and Pater inhabited a different intellectual environment. In fact, many of Pater's and Wilde's aesthetic, religious, and moral ideas originated in response to Darwin's discoveries in the physical sciences. Despite Ruskin's reluctance to accept the implications of Darwinian science, the intellectual character of the Victorian age was largely determined by the fact that it was forced to come to terms with the theory of evolution. In the sphere of religious thought, Darwinism challenged the biblical fundamentalists, but more profound and far-reaching, as we have seen, was the threat it posed to the Paleyan Argument from Design. The central tenet of evolution, the mechanism of random variation and natural selection, ran counter to the very essence and ideal of Design. As Darwin himself observed, 'We can no longer argue that, for instance, the beautiful hinge of a bivalve shell must have been made by an intelligent being, like the hinge of a door by a man. There seems to be no more design in the variability of organic beings, and in the action of natural selection, than in the course which the wind blows.'[41] Less threatening, but equally radical, were the applications of the evolutionary method to other areas of human experience. Herbert Spencer, for example, extended the arguments of the biologists and paleontologists when he claimed that language, the fine arts, society, beliefs, and customs must also have evolved from simpler to more complex forms:

...this law of organic evolution is the law of all evolution. Whether it be in the development of the Earth, in the development of Life upon its surface, in the development of Society, of Government, of Manufactures, of Commerce, of Language, Literature, Science, Art, this same advance from the simple to the complex, through successive differentiation, holds uniformly.[42]

This exhaustive application of the principle of evolution across the whole field of human culture suggests that for Spencer, as for other Victorians, once the guiding concepts of *stasis* and *telos* had been called into question, there were no areas of human experience which were not a legitimate focus of evolutionary rather than teleological explanation. Thus it became not only possible but logical to ask whether man's sense of the beautiful was a naturally evolving one, and whether man's moral judgement could be said to have evolved through a process of natural selection analogous to that in the physical world. In this way, and striking as it did at the very foundations of religious, moral and aesthetic assumptions, Darwinism provided the impulse for new explorations into the philosophy of human experience – an impulse which both Pater and Wilde exploited with energy and imagination.

Indeed, historicism, relativism, change, development, are central themes in all their aesthetic and ethical thinking. Wilde's witty analogy in 'The Critic as Artist' reminds us how closely his sense of the evolutionary physical world was bound up with his own moral and aesthetic consciousness:

Aesthetics, in fact, are to Ethics in the sphere of conscious civilisation, what, in the sphere of the external world, sexual is to natural selection. Ethics, like natural selection, makes existence possible. Aesthetics, like sexual selection, make life lovely and wonderful, fill it with new forms, and give it progress, and variety, and change.[43]

Pater's citation in the first chapter of *Plato and Platonism* of 'The bold paradox of Heraclitus' which has re-emerged in the theories of Darwin and Hegel is more sedate:

the idea of development (that, too, a thing of growth, developed in the process of reflexion) is at last invading one by one, as the secret of their explanation, all the products of the mind, the very mind itself, the abstract reason; our certainty, for instance, that two and two make four.[44]

Here, at the end of his career, Pater is holding as tenaciously as ever to the belief in relativism which characterised his earliest writings. His notorious Conclusion to his *Studies in the History of the Renaissance* opened with the words, 'To regard all things and principles of things as inconstant modes or fashions has more and more become the tendency of modern thought.'[45] At first he illustrates this in terms of scientific thought and the nature of physical reality: 'That clear perpetual outline of face and limb is but an image of ours...a design in a web, the actual threads of which pass out beyond it.'[46] He then turns to 'the inward world of thought and feeling', where he finds 'the whirlpool is still more rapid, the flame more eager and devouring'. Perceptions of external objects are 'loosed into a group of impressions', until ultimately 'the whole scope of observation is dwarfed into the narrow chamber of the individual mind', 'the individual in his isolation'.[47] This disturbing reduction of consciousness to a random collection of momentary impressions lacking all continuity undermines the substantiality of the human mind itself. It is significant that, even though experience is perceived by Pater to be necessarily solipsistic, the self is a prison from which the spirit may only perhaps be set free 'for a moment':

Experience, already reduced to a group of impressions, is ringed round for each one of us by that thick wall of personality through which no real voice has ever pierced on its way to us, or from us to that which we can only conjecture to be without. Every one of those impressions is the impression of the individual in his isolation, each mind keeping as a solitary prisoner in its own dream of a world.[48]

Pater questioned the fixed character of human identity, and perceived the subjectivity of experience as imprisoning, but given that it is all we have left to us in a world without objective absolutes, we must learn to savour it and profit as best we can from it:

Not the fruit of experience, but experience itself, is the end. A counted number of pulses only is given to us of a variegated, dramatic life. How may we see in them all that is to be seen in them by the finest senses? How may we pass most swiftly from point to point, and be present always at the focus where the greatest number of vital forces unite in their purest energy? To burn always with this hard, gemlike flame, to maintain this ecstasy, is success in life...we have an interval, and then our place knows us no more...For our one chance lies in expanding that interval, in getting as many pulsations as possible into the given time.[49]

These were the words that seduced Pater's decadent disciples into the hedonism of the nineties. They also heralded a move away from Ruskin's and Arnold's emphasis on objectivism in aesthetics. Although Pater's most admired artist, Leonardo da Vinci, and his model of an aesthetic critic and art historian, Winckelmann, were both men of science, and he himself frequently used the techniques and terminology of scientific investigation, his own criticism remained unshakeably impressionistic: 'as in the study of light, of morals, of number, one must realise such primary data for one's self, or not at all'.[50] A properly scientific approach for Pater involved the recognition and acceptance of the principle of flux, and for this reason his aesthetic was essentially and necessarily subjective. Similarly, and again in direct contradiction to Ruskin, Pater believed that the individuality of the artist's vision is more important than 'truth to nature'. In a review of the *Correspondance de Gustave Flaubert*, he writes:

Impersonality in art, the literary ideal of Gustave Flaubert, is perhaps no more possible than realism. The artist *will* be felt; his subjectivity must and will colour the incidents, as his very bodily eye *selects* the aspects of things.[51]

He traces the creative process in his essay on Wordsworth and describes the way in which 'the outward object appears to take colour and expression, a new nature almost, from the prompting of the observant mind'; how the actual world dissolves, and is recreated by the artist.[52] In his essay on 'Style', Pater talks of the fine line between fact and the writer's representation of it, which is 'an expression no longer of fact but of his sense of it, his peculiar intuition of a world, prospective, or discerned below the faulty conditions of the present, in either case changed somewhat from the actual world'.[53] And, for Pater, the greater the subjectivism, the greater the work of art:

For just in proportion as the writer's aim, consciously or unconsciously, comes to be the transcribing, not of the world, not of mere fact, but of his sense of it, he becomes an artist, his work *fine* art.[54]

Throughout his critical essays on literature and art Pater is pre-occupied primarily with finding 'what is unique in the individual genius which contrived after all, by force of will, to have its own masterful way with that environment'.[55] His subject is always the mysterious individuality of the artistic personality, for he believed the work of art to be above all the expression of the personality of its creator. Thus of the works of Luca della Robbia, he says:

They bear the impress of a personal quality, a profound expressiveness, what the French call *intimité*, by which is meant some subtler sense of originality – the seal on a man's work of what is most inward and peculiar in his moods, and manner of apprehension: it is what we call *expression*, carried to its highest intensity of degree.[56]

In his essay on Wordsworth, Pater asks, 'What are the qualities in things and persons which he values, the impression and sense of which he can convey to others, in an extraordinary way?',[57] while of Botticelli he asks, 'What is the peculiar sensation, what is the peculiar quality of pleasure, which his work has the property of exciting in us, and which we cannot get elsewhere?'[58]

In this way, Ruskin's emphasis on 'truth to nature' is largely replaced by a stress on truth to the individuality of the artist:

Literary art...like all art which is in any way imitative or reproductive of fact – form, or colour, or incident – is the representation of such fact as connected with soul, of a specific personality, in its preferences, its volition and power.[59]

Pater's attitude towards the relation of art to personality is a Romantic one:

'The style is the man', complex or simple, in his individuality, his plenary sense of what he really has to say, his sense of the world.[60]

He rejoices in the subjectivism which he associates with Romanticism, 'a consciousness brooding with delight over itself',[61] and finds it entirely appropriate to the relativism of the Victorian age. As Harold Bloom argues, where Wordsworth, Keats, Arnold, Mill (and he might have added Ruskin) fought imaginatively against excessive self-consciousness, Pater welcomes it, and in so doing inaugurates the decadent phase of Romanticism.[62]

That arch-decadent Wilde espoused Pater's subjectivist cause and made it the linch-pin of his aesthetic. 'Art', he says, in *The Soul of Man Under Socialism*, 'is the most intense mode of individualism that the world has known.'[63] It is autonomous – 'Art never expresses anything but itself' – for 'the artist...builds...a world more real than reality itself'.[64] In fact, to seek objectivism in art is an impossible ideal:

The difference between objective and subjective work is one of external form merely. It is accidental, not essential. All artistic creation is absolutely subjective. The very landscape that Corot looked at was, as he said himself, but a mood of his own mind...For out of ourselves we can never pass, nor can there be in creation what in the creator was not. Nay, I would say that the more objective a creation appears to be, the more subjective it really is.[65]

Ruskin's contempt for the Pathetic Fallacy is flouted. Similarly, his championing of the 'truth' of great art is dismissed. Instead, it is the aesthetic critic who dictates the meaning, and indeed the greatness, of the work of art. In his critical essays, Wilde develops what he once said in defence of *The Picture of Dorian Gray*: 'It is the spectator, and not life, that art really mirrors.'[66] In 'The Critic as Artist' he posits that it is the beholder, rather than the creator, who 'lends to the beautiful thing its myriad meanings'.[67] Truth is merely 'one's last mood', for, as he argues in 'The Truth of Masks', 'in aesthetic criticism attitude is everything. For in art there is no such thing as a universal truth.'[68] Criticism is avowedly subjective and impressionistic. 'Certainly the first step in aesthetic criticism is to realise one's own impressions', he declares in 'Pen, Pencil, and Poison: A Study in Green', and in 'The Critic as Artist' he cites Aristotle as the first aesthetic critic for doing just that. As the title of the last-named work suggests, Wilde's aim was to elevate the role of the critic to that of artist. Just as the artist lays bare his soul in his art, so the aesthetic critic is really exploring his own sensations and psyche rather than the work of art before him. Criticism's most perfect form is 'in its essence purely subjective. For the highest Criticism deals with art not as expressive but as impressive purely.' Such criticism is 'the record of one's own soul', 'the only civilized form of autobiography, as it deals not with the events, but with the thoughts of one's life'. The critic's 'sole aim is to chronicle his own impressions'.[69] And of course Wilde's profile of the aesthetic critic was itself a self-portrait. He saw himself as the supreme aesthetic critic, and as such as an artist; an artist, moreover, 'the quality of whose work depends on the intensification of personality'.[70]

Pater's and Wilde's 'decadent' Romanticism represents the exact converse of Ruskin's and Arnold's 'moralised' Romanticism. Both developments are variants on Coleridge's idea of the creative imagination as a divine faculty, 'the living power and prime agent of all human perception, and as a repetition in the finite mind of the eternal act of creation in the infinite I AM'.[71] But whereas Ruskin and Arnold, and indeed Newman and Keble, found in Coleridge's alignment of the imagination and the transcendent the authority for a moralised aesthetic, Pater and Wilde made the creative I AM the basis for a thoroughgoing aestheticism grounded in the divine authority of the self.

II

Although he was himself increasingly embarrassed by his monstrous progeny, Pater was certainly perceived by many of his contemporaries as a pure aesthete. He was satirised as such in the figure of Mr Rose in W. H. Mallock's *New Republic*, and pastiched in Wilde's aesthetic Lord Henry Wotton in *The Picture of Dorian Gray*. In his review of Wilde's novel Pater is obliged to distinguish his own early Epicurean doctrines from the views expressed by the main characters in Wilde's novel, all of which, most blatantly those of Lord Henry Wotton, are in varying degrees crude renderings of the Conclusion to *The Renaissance*. He submits that Lord Henry may have been intended as a 'satiric sketch', and adds:

Mr. Wilde can hardly have intended him, with his cynic amity of mind and temper, any more than the miserable end of Dorian himself, to figure the motive and tendency of a true Cyrenaic or Epicurean doctrine of life... Lord Henry, and even more the, from the first, suicidal hero, loses too much of life to be a true Epicurean – loses so much in the way of impressions, of pleasant memories, and subsequent hopes, which Hallward, by a really Epicurean economy, manages to secure.[72]

But for all his reluctance to accept the honour they conferred upon him, Pater was hailed by the men of the nineties as the pioneering champion in England of 'art for art's sake'. His early work, most notably his essays on Leonardo da Vinci, Botticelli, and Winckelmann, expounded the 'art for art's sake' doctrine, and he consistently emphasised the aesthetic perfection of any given work of art rather than invoking moral values. From his defence of *The Picture of Dorian Gray* to his defence of his own innocence on the witness stand, Wilde likewise maintained that art and ethics were essentially unrelated. In a letter to the editor of the *St James's Gazette* in response to a condemnation of *The Picture of Dorian Gray* on moral grounds, Wilde claims:

I am quite incapable of understanding how any work of art can be criticised from a moral standpoint. The sphere of art and the sphere of ethics are absolutely distinct and separate.[73]

In line with this, in a letter to the editor of the *Daily Chronicle* he recalls the difficulty he experienced in keeping the moral of the story in 'its proper secondary place', and regrets that it is only too apparent.[74] To the editor of the *Scots Observer* he proclaims, 'an Artist, sir, has no ethical sympathies at all. Virtue and wickedness are to him simply what the colours on his palette are to the painter.'[75] When he *is* interested in the relation of art to morality, it is in a characteristically perverse way, as when in his essay on the artist–criminal Thomas Griffiths Wainwright he considers how

his crimes seem to have had an important effect upon his art. They gave a strong personality to his style, a quality that his early work certainly lacked...One can fancy an intense personality being created out of sin.[76]

As for more orthodox theories on the ethical effects of art, all this 'had been done once for all by Plato'.[77] In modern criticism, to seek moral grounds for one's aesthetic preferences is 'always the last refuge of people who have no sense of beauty'.[78] For the true aesthete, he repeated,

the first condition of criticism is that the critic should be able to recognize that the sphere of Art and the sphere of Ethics are absolutely distinct and separate. When they are confused, Chaos has come again. They are too often confused in England now...[79]

As a result of this conviction, throughout Wilde's writings convention is flouted and normal moral categories are outrageously reversed:

all the arts are immoral, except those baser forms of sensual or didactic art that seek to excite to action of evil or of good. For action of every kind belongs to the sphere of ethics.[80]

But despite their antagonism towards Ruskinian aesthetics and conventional morality, both Wilde and Pater betray a moral sensitivity in their work and are interested in exploring the possibilities for a redefinition of the moral implications of aesthetic experience. Richard Ellmann has argued that in Wilde's work an ethical view of art coexists with its own cancellation.[81] Wilde's frequently expressed conviction of the disengagement of art from life is counterbalanced by his manifest fascination with their profound and mysterious connectedness. As we have seen, Wilde believed there to be a 'terrible moral' in *The Picture of Dorian Gray*, albeit 'a moral which the prurient will not be able to find in it':[82]

The real moral of the story is that all excess, as well as all renunciation, brings its punishment, and this moral is so far artistically and deliberately expressed that it does not enunciate its law as a general principle, but realises itself purely in the lives of individuals, and so becomes simply a dramatic element in a work of art, and not the object of the work of art itself.[83]

Sin, guilt, and punishment are similarly the central themes of his play *Salome*. In *The Soul of Man Under Socialism*, Socialism is defined in moral rather than political terms. And again, 'The Ballad of Reading Gaol' and *De Profundis* are all about sin and moral regeneration. It is in the latter work, when attempting to describe Christ's peculiar manner of moral enlightenment, that Wilde articulates most clearly the special moral character of art:

he is just like a work of art. He does not really teach one anything, but by being brought into his presence one becomes something.[84]

Wilde was of course one of the very young men who Pater rightly feared might be misled by the apparent endorsement of hedonism embodied in the Conclusion to *Studies in the History of the Renaissance*.[85] He decided to omit the Conclusion from the second edition of the book, and restored the suspect chapter in the third edition in 1888 only because it had been explained and modified in the mean time by *Marius the Epicurean*, a novel which he apparently regarded as a religio-aesthetic apologia.[86] The decision shows a moral awareness which one would have not perhaps suspected from a reading of the earlier works, but it is a dimension which makes itself increasingly apparent in Pater's mature work. Some critics have drawn attention to the fact that as Pater's work developed he became more and more concerned with the ethical responsibilities of art and criticism, and that even in *The Renaissance* he is more conscious of the deeper ethical values of art than is sometimes supposed.[87] This is not quite Eliot's position, though, when he argues that Pater was 'always primarily the moralist', as is clear from the qualification 'certainly, a writer may be none the less classified as a moralist, if his moralizing is suspect or perverse'.[88] He goes on:

His famous dictum: 'Of this wisdom, the poetic passion, the desire of beauty, the love of art for art's sake has most; for art comes to you professing frankly to give nothing but the highest quality to your moments as they pass, and simply for those moments' sake', is itself a theory of ethics; it is concerned not with art but with life. The second half of the sentence is of course demonstrably untrue, or else being true of everything else besides art is meaningless; but it is a serious statement of morals.[89]

Eliot regards Pater as a moralist in that he is as concerned with the moral and emotional overtones of sensuous experience as with the aesthetic experience itself, but he clearly views his morality as subversive. Whether or not we agree, there is an important distinction to be made between Pater's and Wilde's celebration of the unique morality of aesthetic experience and the proponents of the received morality with whom we have so far been concerned.

Pater's special moral aesthetic derives from his belief in a natural correlation between the beautiful and the good, and in the fundamental asceticism of human nature. He expresses his theory of the integration of purity and beauty in 'Diaphaneitè', an essay which expounds the chastening of the senses, 'a mind of taste lighted up by some spiritual ray within':[90]

The beauty of the Greek statues was a sexless beauty; the statues of the gods had the least traces of sex. Here there is a moral sexlessness, a kind of impotence, an ineffectual wholeness of nature, yet with a divine beauty and significance of its own.[91]

The artist must have this 'clear crystal nature'[92] and be, in his moral transparency, an image of divine perfection. Jan Gordon has observed that there are problems attendant upon the extension of these kinds of aesthetic principles to ethical conduct:

If the self is projected throughout the universe, then the loss of moral differentiation is a feature concomitant to a life transformed to art. The loss of the human implied in Paterian de-individuation, when carried over into ethics, implies a loss of human values which is often translated by his *fin de siècle* successors as either amorality or immorality.[93]

Pater's moral aesthetic could be all too easily coarsened or misinterpreted by his decadent successors, but he was seriously concerned to understand the relationship between aesthetic experience and a moral system. As Pater's student at Oxford, Hopkins wrote an essay for him on 'The Origin of Our Moral Ideas' in which he attempted to formulate a cognitive process which would be valid for both aesthetic perception and ethical understanding.[94] It is interesting to see the different conclusions to which their respective speculations on the relationship between aesthetics, morality, and religion led them, but it is reasonable to assume that the essay arose out of tutorial discussion with Pater.

Pater cites Plato as his historical model and as the philosophical authority for his own synthesis of ethics and aesthetics:

Platonic aesthetics, remember! as such, are ever in close connexion with Plato's ethics. It is life itself, action and character, he proposes to colour; to get something out of that irrepressible conscience of art, that spirit of control, into the general course of life, above all into its energetic or impassioned acts.[95]

He conveniently forgets the expelling of the poets for moral irresponsibility in Book x of *The Republic*, and chooses to ignore the fact that in Plato's hierarchy of values aesthetics are subordinated to a moral system. For Pater, art remains the only way of life, sensibility supersedes morality. Plato's, and indeed Ruskin's concern is to include aesthetics in an ethical system. Pater's is the assimilation of ethics to aesthetics. Moral virtue is but one beauty among many. A similar distinction should be recognised between Pater's position and Arnold's. Whereas Arnold believed that the strongest part of our religion is its unconscious poetry, Pater sees a personal dedication to art as itself a kind of religious act:

The basis of the reconciliation of the religions of the world would thus be the inexplicable activity and creativity of the human mind itself, in which all religions alike have their root, and in which all alike are reconciled.[96]

Pater's moral and religious aesthetic hence has a quite different emphasis from Ruskin's and Arnold's theories of perception. As Frank Kermode explains it, for Pater, aprioristic morality is replaced by 'sensibility':

art is what is significant in life, and so sensibility or insight, corruptible as it is, is the organ of moral knowledge, and art, for all its refusal to worship the *idola* of vulgar morality, is the only true morality; indeed, it is nothing less than life itself.[97]

Even in his most 'moral' works, every ethical attitude, every religious discovery, is grounded in an aesthetic preference. He establishes his 'religion of art' as a curious rival religion to Ruskin's Evangelicalism, Arnold's Liberalism, and indeed the Oxford Movement's dogmatic orthodoxy alike.

These important distinctions must be borne in mind, but it is still true to say that Pater did perceive an ethical dimension in art. Although he denied that art bore any moral responsibility or didactic function, he nevertheless conceded that it could have a profound moral effect. In his essays on Wordsworth and *Measure for Measure*, he concentrates upon the educative power of the great artist:

> The office of the poet is not that of the moralist, and the first aim of Wordsworth's poetry is to give the reader a peculiar kind of pleasure. But through his poetry, and through this pleasure in it, he does actually convey to the reader an extraordinary wisdom in the things of practice.[98]

His moral statements always subvert the received Victorian ethic, as in his inversion of Carlyle's famous espousal of action in *Sartor Resartus*:

> That the end of life is not action but contemplation – *being* as distinct from *doing* – a certain disposition of the mind: is, in some shape or other, the principle of all the higher morality. In poetry, in art, if you enter into their true spirit at all, you touch this principle, in a measure: these, by their very sterility, are a type of beholding for the mere joy of beholding. To treat life in the spirit of art, is to make life a thing in which means and ends are identified: to encourage such treatment, the true moral significance of art and poetry... Their work is, not to teach lessons, or enforce rules, or even to stimulate us to noble ends; but to withdraw the thoughts for a little while from the mere machinery of life, to fix them, with appropriate emotions, on the spectacle of those great facts in man's existence which no machinery affects...[99]

Pater certainly makes moral claims for poetry here, but in a characteristically un-Victorian way. Similarly, at the end of his essay on *Measure for Measure*, Pater says that the essence of true justice is 'a finer knowledge through love' and goes on to add:

> It is not always that poetry can be the exponent of morality; but it is this aspect of morals which it represents most naturally, for this true justice is dependent on just those finer appreciations which poetry cultivates in us the power of making, those peculiar valuations of action and its effect which poetry actually requires.[100]

Even in *The Renaissance* Pater cherishes many of the deeper ethical values which art should hold for humanity. While he denies that art has any overt moral or religious purpose, he recognises that it accomplishes an important ethical result in enlarging and orientating the soul. His reasons for studying the Italian Renaissance are 'not merely for its positive results in the things of the intellect and the imagination, its concrete works of art, its special and prominent personalities, with their profound aesthetic charm, but for its general spirit and character, for the ethical qualities of which it is a consummate type'.[101]

Pater closes his essay on 'Style' by making the distinction between good art and great art depend upon not the form but the matter which is embodied. But it is in fact the identity of form and matter which is the whole basis of Pater's definition of 'style'. Form and content must be completely fused in the artist's mind quite apart from their material embodiment, and then the artist is able to give perfect external shape to his mental conception. In his stress on the relationship between form and content in art, Pater comes very close to Newman's personalist doctrine of style, and indeed often echoes his dictum, 'Thought and speech are inseparable from each other. Matter and expression are parts of one: style is a thinking out into language.'[102] Pater too viewed expression as the clarification of thought itself and hence believed in the importance of precise correspondence between thought and word.

Far from urging the irrelevance of subject-matter, Pater is concerned to demonstrate that the formal aim is achieved only if the mind is in control of its subject. He looks for the quality of 'mind' in style. When the artist has come to terms with his own personal sense of fact, his work will naturally shape itself into the formal unity of a work of art, informed by his conception of its meaning as a whole. 'In literary art as in all other art, structure is all-important', but 'all depends upon the original unity, the vital wholeness and identity, of the initiatory apprehension or view.'[103] The formal shape of literary art is more than a complex verbal structure: aesthetic form is the physical expression of a mode of perception which determines both the creation and the criticism of art.

Pater was concerned elsewhere with the organic fusion of content and form in the work of art itself, and here he was evidently influenced by his reading of Hegel's aesthetics.[104] In his *Lectures on Fine Art*, Hegel classifies all art into symbolic, classical, and Romantic kinds. In symbolic art, he argues, the material form predominates over the spiritual meaning. In Romantic art, on the other hand, the spiritual meaning cannot be contained in or expressed by the sensuous form. Classical art represents aesthetic perfection precisely because in it we experience a perfect conjunction of content and form:

the perfection of art reached its peak here precisely because the spiritual was completely drawn through its external appearance; in this beautiful unification it idealised the natural and made it into an adequate embodiment of spirit's own substantial individuality.[105]

In Greek art, material reality and spirit, being and meaning, are perfectly fused. The work of art is identical with that which it signifies:

The supreme works of beautiful sculpture are sightless, and their inner being does not look out of them as self-knowing inwardness in this spiritual concentration which the eye discloses. This light of the soul falls outside them and belongs to the spectator alone; when he looks at these shapes, soul cannot meet soul nor eye eye.[106]

Pater's discussion and classification of the arts in terms of the degree to which form realises content is very Hegelian. In his essay on Winckelmann, for example, he writes:

But take a work of Greek art, – the Venus of Melos. That is in no sense a symbol, a suggestion, of anything beyond its own victorious fairness. The mind begins and ends with the finite image, yet loses no part of the spiritual motive. That motive is not lightly and loosely attached to the sensuous form, as its meaning to an allegory, but saturates and is identical with it.[107]

It is an ideal art, 'in which the thought does not outstrip or lie beyond the proper range of its sensible embodiment'.[108] The doctrine of the 'perfect identification of matter and form' is the basis of his argument in the essay entitled 'The School of Giorgione'. Here he claims music as the highest art form, for it represents the most perfect synthesis of content and form:

For while in all other kinds of art it is possible to distinguish the matter from the form, and the understanding can always make this distinction, yet it is the constant effort of art to obliterate it.[109]

Thus, in this specific sense, *All art constantly aspires towards the condition of music*, although Pater is careful to insist upon a proper distinction between the different modes of expression of different art forms.

If Wilde's judgement is to be accepted, both Pater and Newman realised their ideal of the perfect reconciliation of content and form in their own prose styles: 'in Mr Pater, as in Cardinal Newman, we find the union of personality with perfection'.[110] As so often, Wilde's aesthetic enunciations on the relation between form and content in art are really a reworking of Pater's own. We frequently hear echoes, for example, of Pater's 'All art constantly aspires towards the condition of music.' In 'The Critic as Artist' Wilde cites music as 'the perfect type of art', and in *De Profundis* we are told:

What the artist is always looking for is the mode of existence in which soul and body are one and indivisible: in which the outward is expressive of the inward: in which form reveals...Music, in which all subject is absorbed in expression and cannot be separated from it, is a complex example, and a flower or a child a simple example, of what I mean...[111]

But elsewhere he proclaims literature as the ideal art form, in this case, though, not so much because of the unity of content and form, as because its medium, the written word, provides more scope for emotional, spiritual, and intellectual expression. In an unsigned article written in 1887, he declares:

For the domain of the painter is widely different from the domain of the poet. To the latter belongs Life in its full and absolute entirety; not only the world that men look at, but the world that men listen to also; not merely the momentary grace of form, or the transient gladness of colour, but the whole sphere of feeling, the perfect cycle of thought, the growth and progress of passion, the spiritual development of the soul. The painter is so far limited, that it is only through the mask of the body that he can show us the mystery of the soul; only through images that he can handle ideas; only through its physical equivalents that he can deal with psychology.[112]

And in 'The Critic as Artist' he makes it clear that literature is a superior art form because it offers more than just formal perfection:

For the material that painter or sculptor uses is meagre in comparison with that of words. Words have not merely music as sweet as that of viol and lute, colour as rich and vivid as any that makes lovely for us the canvas of the Venetian or the Spaniard, and plastic form no less sure and certain than that which reveals itself in marble or in bronze, but thought and passion and spirituality are theirs also, are theirs indeed alone.[113]

Again, as with Pater, it is clear that the emotional and spiritual substance of a given work of art is as significant as its formal perfection. In his not very complimentary review of 'Mr Swinburne's Last Volume', although Wilde commends Swinburne's work 'for song's sake', 'so marvellous a music-maker is he', he bewails its lack of substance: 'But what of the soul? For the soul we must go elsewhere.'[114] Wilde seems to be making more than a purely aesthetic judgement when he says of beauty that it is 'the symbol of symbols. Beauty reveals everything because it expresses nothing. When it shows us itself, it shows us the whole fiery-coloured world.' Beauty is not equated with form, rather it 'fills with wonder a form which the artist may have left void, or not understood, or understood incompletely'.[115]

While they were delighted by the formal perfection of Hellenic art, both Wilde and Pater yearned after the soul of Romanticism. Like Arnold and Newman, they sought to reconcile the claims of Hellenism and Romanticism. In his essay 'The English Renaissance of Art', Wilde wrote 'It is really from the union of Hellenism, in its breadth..., its calm possession of beauty, with the passionate colour of the romantic spirit, that springs the art of the nineteenth century in England.' Pater's vision of the reconciliation of the Greek and Romantic spirits is at the heart of his essay on Winckelmann. It is also central to his Arnoldian perception of Goethe as one of those exceptional souls who was able to transcend the subjectivist dilemma of modern art by fusing the Romantic spirit with the Hellenic:

Goethe illustrates a union of the Romantic spirit, in its adventure, its variety, its profound subjectivity of soul, with Hellenism, in its transparency, its rationality, its desire of beauty.[116]

For Wilde, Christ himself is the supreme example of such a union of Romantic and Hellenic. In *De Profundis* he tells of his plan to write on 'Christ as the precursor of the romantic movement in life'.[117] But Christ was also, for Wilde, first and foremost an individual and the proponent of individualism, and 'the new Individualism is the new Hellenism', as he concludes in *The Soul of Man Under Socialism*.[118]

Part of Pater's and Wilde's fascination with the Renaissance derives from their appreciation of the convergence of Hellenism and Christianity in that period. As Pater wrote, in his essay 'Pico della Mirandola':

No account of the Renaissance can be complete without some notice of the attempt made by certain Italian scholars of the fifteenth century to reconcile Christianity with the religion of ancient Greece.[119]

Wilde finds in early Italian religious painting an appealing allegory of the Renaissance:

It was the fashion of early Italian painters to represent in mediaeval costume the soldiers who watched over the tomb of Christ, and this, which was the result of the frank anachronism of all true art, may serve to us as an allegory. For it was in vain that the middle ages strove to guard the buried spirit of progress. When the dawn of the Greek spirit arose, the sepulchre was empty, the grave-clothes laid aside. Humanity had risen from the dead.[120]

They delight in every example of the meeting of Greek and Christian. 'It is always a source of pleasure and awe to me', Wilde writes, 'to remember that the ultimate survival of the Greek chorus, lost elsewhere to art, is to be found in the servitor answering the priest at Mass.'[121] In *Plato and Platonism*, on the other hand, Pater attempts to unite Hellenism with Christianity through the mediation of Plato by emphasising Plato's belief in moral education through aesthetic experience.[122] Indeed, Pater's and Wilde's shared conviction of the desirability of a perfect fusion of content and form, and, in a related way, of Romanticism and classicism, of Christianity and Hellenism, is not confined to their writings on art. We may in fact find a direct analogue to these concerns in their religious writings. As Wilde says in 'The Critic as Artist',

It is not merely in art that the body is the soul. In every sphere of life Form is the beginning of things...Forms are the food of faith, cried Newman in one of those great moments of sincerity that made us admire and know the man.[123]

This is the real clue to a proper understanding of the aesthetic import of their religious works. For their emphasis on the fusion of form and content in art is, like Newman's, the aesthetic analogue of their concern to cancel the opposition between religious and moral experience on the one hand, and intellectual and aesthetic perception on the other.

III

Pater's and Wilde's respective attitudes towards Christianity have always eluded confident definition. Was their evident attraction to Catholicism mere affectation, or was it genuine? The question is further complicated in Wilde's case by his witty and ironic tongue, by his delight in outraging the prurient, and by the rich profanity of his imagination. The difficulty of determining their sincerity may also be explained by the fact that their wish to unite the claims of Christianity and Hellenism derived from their own tendency to oscillate between a desire for religious faith and a love of art and beauty. Wilde's adult life was a prolonged flirtation with the Roman Catholic Church, and it is amusing to read of the way in which he was, on successive occasions, lured away by the Hellenic spirit just as he was on the point of committing himself to the Christian. In his early letters, written as an undergraduate, after a whole series of rather self-consciously pious missives to his friends on the subject of conversion to Rome, this or that theological point or holy service, and fine religious feelings, we begin to suspect his sincerity. Despite the frequent earnest expressions of his longing to see Rome, and his exhortations to the privileged friend who does manage to visit the papal city, '*Do* be touched by it, *feel* the awful fascination of the Church, its extreme beauty and sentiment, and let every part of your nature have play and room', Wilde forgoes the opportunity of a first visit because he has to pay his subscription to a club:

I am sorry to say that I will not see the Holy City this Easter at any rate: I have been elected for the St. Stephen's Club and £42 is a lot to pay down on the nail...[124]

When he does finally find the funds to set off for Rome, he allows himself *en route* to be spirited away by his tutor to Greece. His two letters to Reginald Harding on the subject, one written just prior to his departure, the other from Corfu, can be amusingly juxtaposed:

I start for Rome on Sunday; Mahaffy comes as far as Genoa with me: and I hope to see the golden dome of St. Peter's and the Eternal City by Tuesday night.
This is an era in my life, a crisis. I wish I could look into the seeds of time and see what is coming.
I shall not forget you in Rome, and will burn a candle for you at the Shrine of Our Lady.

I never went to Rome at all! What a changeable fellow you must think me, but Mahaffy my old tutor carried me off to Greece with him to see Mykenae and Athens. I am awfully ashamed of myself but I could not help it and will take Rome on my way back.[125]

Neither were such Hebraic–Hellenic dilemmas confined to his student days. After leaving prison he again went to Italy and was again overcome by his desire to see Rome and the Pope. He wrote to Robert Ross, 'It will be delightful to be together again, and this time I really must become a Catholic.'[126] But he was also overcome by desire for a fifteen-year-old seminarist:

I gave him a little book of devotion, very pretty, and with far more pictures than prayers in it; so of great service to Giuseppe, whose eyes are beautiful. I also gave him many *lire*, and prophesied for him a Cardinal's hat, if he remained very good and never forgot me. He said he never would: and indeed I don't think he will, for every day I kissed him behind the high altar.[127]

This curious juxtaposition of Popes, Cardinals and pretty young boys continues into the art gallery:

I have been three times to see the great Velasquez of the Pamfili Pope: it is quite the grandest portrait in the world. The entire man is there. I also go to look at that voluptuous marble boy I went to worship with you at the Museo Nazionale. What a lovely thing it is![128]

Torn between popery and pederasty, Wilde spoke the truth when he complained, 'The Cloister or the Café – there is my future. I tried the Hearth, but it was a failure.'[129]

From evidence such as this we might be forgiven for concluding that his attachment to Catholicism was no more significant or enduring than his attachment to Giuseppe. When he was an undergraduate, his Catholicism was probably no more than a pose. Conversions to Rome were very fashionable among his fellow students – at least six of his friends at Oxford were converted while he was there, and several of his subsequent friends, including Robert Ross and Bosie, were either Catholics or converted at some point in their lives.[130] Wilde seemed rather to like the idea of living in a hotbed of Catholicism and himself 'on the brink', his head full of romantic nonsense about Rome and his room full of pictures of the Pope and Cardinal Manning.[131] But by 1878 he seems to have moved out of his Catholic phase and into a new infatuation with a Swinburnian style of Hellenism, and it is hard to reconcile his subsequent lifestyle with the idea that he was serious about his religious beliefs. His habit of lighthearted irreverence, while often witty and amusing, also makes it hard to take him seriously as a thoroughgoing Christian. As a student, he frequently described himself as being 'caught with the wiles of the Scarlet Woman'.[132] Later he used to enjoy shocking Gide with his blasphemous parables. He delighted in bringing together the sacred and profane, as in a letter to Ross, in which he describes a friend's *ménage à trois*: 'none of the members sleep: the girl – a rose-like thing I hope – lies in the middle, and knows the pleasure and insecurity of the *Via Media*'.[133]

But the question remains whether his wit really conceals a soul which wanted fervently to believe. Wilde always maintained that parental pressure was responsible for his failure to become a Roman Catholic. Near the end of his life, he said:

Much of my moral obliquity is due to the fact that my father would not allow me to become a Catholic... The artistic side of the Church would have cured my degeneracies.[134]

But although at least the first part of this claim was undoubtedly true, and indeed Wilde had been cut out of his cousin's will for his 'Romish leanings' as a student,[135] it is significant that Wilde still had not been received into the Catholic Church even then. It seems far more likely that it was something within Wilde's own self which prevented his becoming a Catholic. The tragedy of the man who cannot believe is writ deep in the pages of *De Profundis*:

I would like to found an order for those who *cannot* believe: the Confraternity of the Faithless one might call it, where on an altar, on which no taper burned, a priest, in whose heart peace had no dwelling, might celebrate with unblessed bread and a chalice empty of wine. Everything to be true must become a religion. And agnosticism should have its ritual no less than faith. It has sown its martyrs, it should reap its saints, and praise God daily for having hidden Himself from man.[136]

His sorrow at his inability to believe seems very genuine here, and he is not short of friends who have been prepared to testify to the authenticity of his religious aspirations, from fellow undergraduates to fellow prisoners. Often he was knocked back by those who were unsympathetic to his style and did not take him seriously. He reputedly sobbed bitterly when his request to go into a retreat after his release from prison was politely refused by the Jesuit House in Farm Street, and although he treated Ross's doubts that he was in earnest lightly, Ross's later regrets that he did not help his friend more positively were perhaps justified.[137] Even Wilde's deathbed conversion was ambiguous as there is some doubt whether he was really conscious.[138]

In short, it is extremely difficult to tie down Wilde's religious attitudes with any certainty. For every acquaintance or critic who dismisses him as an impostor, there is one who, taking Wilde at his own word, compares him with Christ.[139] It is more balanced and realistic to accept that his dual sympathies for Catholicism and what we may loosely call Hellenism pulled him in two different directions throughout much of his life. His Christian sympathies compete most obviously of all with his Hellenistic bent in his early poetry. Alongside those composed at the height of his Catholic ardour, such as 'San Miniato' and 'Rome Unvisited', are a number of poems which testify to a growing inclination in another direction. The final lines of 'Sonnet, written in Holy Week at Genoa' sigh:

> Ah, God! Ah, God! those dear Hellenic hours
> Had drowned all memory of Thy bitter pain,
> The Cross, the Crown, the Soldiers and the Spear.[140]

In 'Ave Maria Gratia Plena' he compares the splendid classical vision of the coming of God to the somewhat limp Christian version as depicted by Rossetti in his 'Ecce Ancilla Domini':

> A kneeling girl with passionless pale face,
> An angel with a lily in his hand,
> And over both with outstretched wings the Dove.[141]

Charming, but rather insipid after

> ...some great God who in a rain of gold
> Broke open bars and fell on Danae:
> Or a dread vision as when Semele
> Sickening for love and unappeased desire
> Prayed to see God's clear body, and the fire
> Caught her white limbs and slew her utterly.

In 'Humanitad' Wilde laments the passing of ancient Greece, 'When soul and body seemed to blend in mystic symphonies', and the advent of 'the new Calvary'

> Where we behold, as one who in a glass
> Sees his own face, self-slain Humanity.[142]

Humanity is identified with the crucified Christ:

> O smitten mouth! O forehead crowned with thorn!
> O chalice of all common miseries!
> Thou for our sakes that loved thee not hast borne
> An agony of endless centuries,
> And we were vain and ignorant nor knew
> That when we stabbed thy heart it was our own real hearts we slew.
>
> Being ourselves the sowers and the seeds
> The night that covers and the lights that fade,
> The spear that pierces and the side that bleeds,
> The lips betraying and the life betrayed...

But man may, like Christ, be resurrected, and be made whole, and the final vision is of a divinity which is an ambiguous reconciliation of the pagan and the Christian Gods: 'That which is purely human, that is Godlike, that is God.'

This coming together of the Christian and the Hellenic, either in conflict or in reconciliation, is a feature of many of Wilde's subsequent writings. In *The Soul of Man Under Socialism* a Ruskinian kind of Christian socialism is merged with a Paterian expansion of the personality. The forces of Hebrew and Hellene are tragically opposed in *The Picture of Dorian Gray* in the hero's antithetical mentors, Basil Hallward and Lord Henry Wotton. And Christian morality and pagan sensuality are again brought face to face as Jokanaan and Salome in *Salome*.[143]

Hesketh Pearson writes that Wilde 'often spoke in parables' and 'thought and taught in stories'.[144] In many of his published stories he introduces problems of a sensuous or aesthetic nature into what is otherwise a fairly traditional parable structure. In 'The Young King', a prince refuses to bedeck himself in splendid vestments and jewellery at his coronation to spare the labour of others, but in prayer to Christ his beggar's rags are transformed into robes and jewels more splendid than earthly finery. In 'The Fisherman and his Soul' the hero sells his soul for the love of a mermaid, and the soul tries thereafter to tempt him into sin with promises of great riches. The hero of 'The Star-Child' is deprived of his great beauty in punishment for his pride and arrogance, but he regains his good looks and fortune when he takes pity on a poor, ugly, diseased beggar. Wilde's later *Poems in Prose*, especially 'The Artist', 'The Master', 'The House of Judgement', and 'The Doer of Good', are even more striking for the economy with which they cast the Christian story and Christian morality into a new and often very poignant light. Yeats recalls the 'terrible beauty' of one of these parables, 'The Doer of Good', as it was first told him by Wilde:

Christ came from a white plain to a purple city, and as He passed through the first street He heard voices overhead, and saw a young man lying drunk upon a window-sill. 'Why do you waste your soul in drunkenness?' He said. 'Lord, I was a leper and You healed me, what else can I do?' A little further through the town He saw a young man following a harlot, and said, 'Why do you dissolve your soul in debauchery?' and the young man answered, 'Lord, I was blind, and You healed me, what else can I do?' At last in the middle of the city He saw an old man crouching, weeping upon the ground, and when He asked why he wept, the old man answered, 'Lord, I was dead and You raised me into life, what else can I do but weep?'[145]

Yeats was greatly moved by this story, and indeed many of Wilde's parables seem obliquely to express the tragic and unresolved dilemmas within Wilde's own life. But some readers there were who resented Wilde's distortions of the Christian story, Christ's morality, and even Christ himself. The focus of their dissatisfaction was perhaps inevitably Wilde's most important religious statement, his letter composed in prison and addressed to Lord Alfred Douglas, which was later published under the title De Profundis. Wilde's credibility as a believer stands or falls for most readers according to their attitude to this work, which was denounced by the Rev. H. C. Beeching in Westminster Abbey as 'a doctrine of devils' (it will become clear why in my later discussion of De Profundis), yet went into five editions within a year of being published.

Pater's religious career was similarly chequered, and his attitude towards Christianity is similarly inconsistent and ambiguous. We encounter the same kinds of problems in determining his religious position as with Wilde but in a more acute form, for his life is more sparsely documented and his writing less directly autobiographical. There are glimpses of a Wildean aptitude for irreverence. One anecdote concerning the youthful Pater tells how he scandalised a pious friend named McQueen by saying that it would be fun to seek ordination without believing a word of it.[146] We shall never know whether Pater was reckless enough to carry the joke through because McQueen scotched the plan, if it ever really was a plan, by writing a letter of objection to the Bishop of London. There are shades of Wilde's vision of the Church as a seductive 'scarlet woman' in Pater's essay 'Poems by William Morris':

Quite in the way of one who handles the older sorceries, the Church has a thousand charms to make the absent near. Like the woman in the idyll of Theocritus – 'draw to my house the man I love,' is the cry of all her bizarre rites.[147]

In his early writings, Pater indulged his preference for a thoroughly aestheticised version of Christianity. His most explicit argument for a purely aesthetic religion, divorced from orthodox Christianity, is to be found in his essay on Coleridge's writings. Here Pate rimplies the cultivation of modes of religious consciousness utterly for their own sake, freed from the obligation of theological or ethical rationale. It is a paradoxically objectless faith, shorn of metaphysical and transcendental dimensions, the substance of which seems to reside in the rather meagre remnant of Christian inwardness:

There are aspects of the religious character which have an artistic worth distinct from their religious import. Longing, a chastened temper, spiritual joy, are precious states of mind, not because they are part of man's duty or because God has commanded them, still less because they are means of obtaining a reward, but because like culture itself they are remote, refined, intense, existing only by the triumph of a few over a dead world of routine in which there is no lifting of the soul at all. If there is no other world, art in its own interest must cherish such characteristics as beautiful spectacles...Religious belief, the craving for objects of belief, may be refined out of our hearts, but they must leave their sacred perfume, their spiritual sweetness, behind.[148]

Although the younger Pater was in some of his early writings and behaviour definitely Wildean, unlike his disciple he was not deliberately outrageous in public once he had matured. He was also more inclined than Wilde to be careful in matters of religion and the evidence suggests that he tended more towards faith than doubt. But the documentation is scanty, to say the least, and his religious life is as shadowy as the rest of his personal life.

The facts of his personal religious practice are so sparsely and unreliably documented, and so ambiguous, that it is necessary to turn to his mature published work for further enlightenment. Indeed William Sharp went so far as to assert that

he is one of those authors of whom there can never be any biography away from his writings...the inner life of Walter Pater is written throughout each of his books, woven 'like gold thread' through almost every page, though perhaps most closely and revealingly in *Marius the Epicurean*.[149]

Unfortunately, this insight does not easily resolve the question of Pater's commitment to Christianity, for *Marius the Epicurean* is not, like *De Profundis*, directly autobiographical, and the question remains how much of it is personal. And moreover the same critical problem arises as with *De Profundis*, for *Marius the Epicurean* is itself the subject of a series of contradictory responses and interpretations. Two distinct and opposed critical positions may, however, be discerned within this literature. On one side of the critical divide we find Eliot arguing that in *Marius the Epicurean* Pater 'Hellenized purely',[150] apparently endorsing Thomas Wright's view that Pater came to regard religion as 'merely a department of art'.[151] This perception is challenged by later critics of the work, such as Graham Hough and David Delaura, who see in Marius' attraction to Christianity a definite moral and mystical quality which they believe brings Pater's religious thought closer to a normative conception of Christianity.[152] The inevitable result of this critical opposition has been the creation of an artificial division between the aesthetic and religious aspects of Christianity in *Marius the Epicurean*. But a closer examination of that work suggests that we need not be faced with a rigid choice between Pater the aesthete and Pater the Christian ethicist. And a reconsideration of *De Profundis* suggests a similar modification of the traditional interpretations of Wilde as alternatively decadent impostor or Christ-figure. For the aesthetic and the spiritual appeal of Christianity for both Pater and Wilde fused in one undeniably authentic source – their shared sense of the beauty of Christ incarnate.[153]

IV

In his earlier writings, Pater had openly declared himself against that Ruskinian style of art criticism which confused religious and moral principle with aesthetic judgement. Yet he himself was not always able to keep these two areas conceptually distinct, for the belief in relativism which underlay his own aesthetic philosophy trespassed into his thoughts on religion and morality. Seduced as he was by the doctrine of flux, Pater experienced difficulties in subscribing to a religion based upon belief in absolutes, and committed to his faith in sensibility and experience, he had little sympathy with transcendentalism. His verdict on Coleridge's struggle to defend moral and religious absolutism in the face of relativism is sympathetic but unambiguous:

We see him trying to apprehend the absolute, to stereotype one form of faith, to attain, as he says, 'fixed principles' in politics, morals, and religion, to fix one mode of life as the essence of life, refusing to see the parts as parts only; and all the time his own pathetic history pleads for a more elastic moral philosophy than his, and cries out against every formula less living and flexible than life itself.[154]

Though it was the moral and religious implications of Pater's aesthetic which brought him notoriety, Pater was by no means dismissive of religion altogether; indeed, consistently with his concept of a unified human culture, he viewed religion as a necessary aspect of man's experience, and believed that

all religions may be regarded as natural products, that, at least in their origin, their growth, and decay, they have common laws, and are not to be isolated from the other movements of the human mind in the periods in which they respectively prevailed; that they arise spontaneously out of the human mind, as expressions of the varying phases of its sentiment concerning the unseen world.[155]

For Pater, though, it was important to distinguish between the rigid, dogmatic forms of religion, and the flexible, developing, imaginative aspect. Only the latter could fit in with the preoccupation with relativism which is so characteristic of both his essay on 'Coleridge's Writings' and his most quoted work, *The Renaissance*. In the development of any religion, he claimed,

While the ritual remains unchanged, the aesthetic element, only accidentally connected with it, expands with the freedom and mobility of the things of the intellect. Always, the fixed element is the religious observance; the fluid, unfixed element is the myth, the religious conception.[156]

Moreover, in the essay on 'Coleridge's Writings', Pater specifically applies his relativistic conclusions to the intellectual and moral life:

The relative spirit, by its constant dwelling on the more fugitive conditions or circumstances of things, breaking through a thousand rough and brutal classifications, and giving elasticity to inflexible principles, begets an intellectual *finesse* of which the ethical result is a delicate and tender justice in the criticism of human life.[157]

Here we find the religio-ethical analogue to Pater's aesthetic impressionism in this vision of developing religious conceptions and the flux of contending moral beliefs and attitudes. Nonetheless this refusal to countenance religious and ethical finalities need not imply a total rejection of Christianity.

In his conviction that the impact of relativism upon nineteenth-century thought demanded some adjustment in religious thinking and some movement towards a historical approach to dogma, Pater was, of course, not alone. His search for some alternative to the foundation of that dogma – the venerable Argument from Design – was one shared by Newman. We have seen how Newman found no reassurance of the existence of a benevolent Creator in the physical world.[158] His solution was to turn inwards, to find his proof of the existence of God in his sense of conscience, and to utilise the theory of evolution in the service of Christianity in his exposition of the theory of development in Christian doctrine.

There are suggestions of both of these aspects of Newman's thought in Pater's mature work *Marius the Epicurean*:

[Marius] hardly knew how strong that old religious sense of responsibility, the conscience, as we call it, still was within him – a body of inward impressions, as real as those so highly valued outward ones – to offend against which, brought with it a strange feeling of disloyalty as to a person.[159]

Belief in development is just as firmly held by Pater's young hero: 'Ritual, like all other elements of religion, must grow and cannot be made – grow by the same law of development which prevails everywhere else, in the moral as in the physical world.'[160] Such a statement, albeit one that refers not specifically to Christianity, might seem to imply that Pater, in *Marius the Epicurean*, has succeeded in reconciling his religious beliefs with his relativist convictions very much as Newman did. Yet a closer reading of *Marius the Epicurean* suggests that such a reconciliation, while a preoccupation of his earlier writings, is not in fact Pater's major concern in that work. Rather, at this point in his intellectual development Pater had adopted an entirely new aesthetic approach to Christianity – one which concerned itself less with questions of dogma, and more with his developing awareness of the figure of Christ.

No doubt this shift is easily mistaken for a lack of religious seriousness in *Marius the Epicurean*. In his biography of Pater, A. C. Benson, for example, criticises this presentation of Christianity:

But the weakness of the case is, that instead of emphasising the power of sympathy, the Christian conception of Love, which differentiates Christianity from all other religious systems, Marius is after all converted, or brought near to the threshold of the faith, more by its sensuous appeal, its liturgical solemnities; the element, that is to say, which Christianity has in common with all religions, and which is essentially human in character.[161]

While it is true that Marius undergoes an aesthetic conversion of sorts, it focuses not upon the ceremony but upon the substance of Christianity – that which may be said indeed to differentiate it from other religious systems – Christ, made man; Christ perceived, however, less in moral terms than in terms of the beauty of His character, His poetry. Hence perhaps Benson's confusion: for Marius' response is not to an objectively realised religious system; it is rather a highly personal, subjective response to the spiritual, to the mystical presence of Christ.

The whole tenor of Pater's writing seems to confirm a sympathy with his hero's approach to Christianity. In his art criticism, Pater, in reaction to Ruskinian religio-moral aesthetics, adopted an aesthetic relativism, which itself demanded, as a corollary, a vital assertion of the subjective self. For just as his relativism translated itself to religious and moral worlds, so too did his subjectivism. Far from exhibiting a hankering after objectivity – at least in the sense in which Ruskin sought it – his intuition of moral truths was analogous to physical sensation: 'How reassuring', Marius sighs, 'after so long a debate about the rival *criteria* of truth, to fall back upon direct sensation, to limit one's aspirations after knowledge to that!',[162] sentiments which perhaps betray Pater's weariness with the religious battles being waged in his own time. But, once again, it must be stressed that Pater's reliance upon sensuous apprehension, upon a highly subjective response to the spiritual, was only a more extreme manifestation of a phenomenon which had altered the character of the Church in England in the nineteenth century. Newman himself, the most rigorously intellectual theologian of his age, had compared the perception of God to the experience of sense-perception.[163] And Hopkins, Pater's former student, articulated an elaborate philosophy delineating the sensuous apprehension of God: 'Over again I feel thy finger and find thee.'[164] Like Newman, Hopkins derives his most convincing proof of the existence of God from his 'selfbeing', his 'consciousness and feeling' of himself, his 'taste' of himself.[165] So far from confirming him in his reputation for religious heterodoxy, Pater's profound subjectivism and its significance for his religious ideology as expressed in *Marius the Epicurean* mark him as sharing the distinctive spiritual style of his age.

Pater's fascination with the workings of his own consciousness led him to seek an answering selfhood in the world around him. He was fascinated by personalities. Indeed, when we turn to *Marius the Epicurean* we find that its hero's philosophical development is charac-terised not so much by a mastery of abstractions as by his intimacy with a series of personalities who embody those abstractions. First of all, he encounters pure paganism in the figure of Flavian, in whom 'Marius saw the spirit of unbelief, achieved as if at one step.'[166] Flavian remained, for his friend, 'an epitome of the whole pagan world, the depth of its corruption, and its perfection of form'.[167] In Flavian, Marius found 'his own Cyrenaic philosophy, presented thus, for the first time, in an image or person, with much attractiveness... a concrete image, the abstract equivalent of which he could recognise afterwards, when the agitating personal influence had settled down for him, clearly enough, into a theory of practice'.[168] In Flavian, Pater found a living proponent of the doctrine of the Conclusion to *The Renaissance*.

However, by the time of writing *Marius the Epicurean* Pater had become aware of an inherent contradiction at the heart of this aesthetic. The very attempt to record minute impressions of distinctive forms composing a world in flux, even though the purpose is to celebrate one's subjective response to that flux, inevitably gives to the forms described an absolute definition. Through Marius, Pater acknowledges the paradox inherent in the urge to trap the transience of things in one who had taken for his philosophical ideal the pleasure of the ideal present, the mystic NOW:

there would come, together with that precipitate sinking of things into the past, a desire, after all, to retain 'what was so transitive'. Could he but arrest, for others also, certain clauses of experience, as the imaginative memory presented them to himself! In those grand, hot summers, he would have imprisoned the very perfume of the flowers. To create, to live, perhaps, a little while beyond the allotted hours, if it were but in a fragment of perfect expression: – it was thus his longing defined itself for something to hold by amid the 'perpetual flux'.[169]

Marius' aesthetic desire to hold on to beautiful experiences within the flux translates itself into the human sphere with greater urgency. With Flavian's death, the painful implications of the philosophy of flux for humanity become tangible:

To Marius...the earthly end of Flavian came like a final revelation of nothing less than the soul's extinction. Flavian had gone out as utterly as the fire among those still beloved ashes.[170]

Heraclitean flux became for Marius 'but an authority for a philosophy of the despair of knowledge'.[171]

Marius' despair at man's extinction along with the things of nature in a world defined by flux recalls Tennyson's, when the loss of a dear friend makes tangible the implications for humanity of evolution:

> And he, shall he,
> Man, her last work, who seemed so fair,
> Such splendid purpose in his eyes,
> Who rolled the psalm to wintry skies,
> Who built him fanes of fruitless prayer,
>
> Who trusted God was love indeed,
> And love Creation's final law –
> Though Nature, red in tooth and claw
> With ravine, shrieked against his creed –

> Who loved, who suffered countless ills,
>   Who battled for the True, the Just,
>   Be blown about the desert dust,
> Or sealed within the iron hills?
>
> No more?[172]

A similar sense of outrage at man's wastage along with the rest of nature in the 'Heraclitean Fire' of the evolutionary process is voiced by Hopkins:

> Million-fuelèd, ˡ nature's bonfire burns on.
> But quench her bonniest, dearest ˡ to her, her clearest-selvèd
>   spark
> Man, how fast his firedint, ˡ his mark on mind is gone!
> Both are in an unfathomable, all is in an enormous dark
> Drowned. O pity and indig ˡ nation! Manshape, that shone
> Sheer off, disseveral, a star, ˡ death blots black out; nor mark
>   Is any of him at all so stark
> But vastness blurs and time ˡ beats level.[173]

Hopkins, though, derives 'comfort' from his faith in the Resurrection. Christ, for him, called a halt to the randomness and waste: 'Enough! the Resurrection, / A heart's clarion! Away grief's gasping, joyless days, dejection', and gave man the jewel of everlasting life, 'immortal diamond'. It comes as no surprise when at the beginning of volume two of his novel Pater explicitly invites comparison between Rome in early Christian times and Victorian England:

That age and our own have much in common – many difficulties and hopes. Let the reader pardon me if here and there I seem to be passing from Marius to his modern representative – from Rome, to Paris or London[174]

and that, moreover, confronted by mortality, Marius' source of comfort is the very same as Hopkins'.

Just as he had been brought into an intensely personal relationship with paganism through the personality of Flavian, so Marius comes to Christianity through the characters of Cornelius and Cecilia. He asks, in the early days of his friendship with Cornelius, 'of what possible intellectual formula could this mystic Cornelius be the sensible exponent?'. Different as his relationships with Flavian and Cornelius were, they were alike in representing for Marius 'reconciliations to the world of sense, the visible world':

And it was still to the eye, through visible movement and aspect, that the character, or genius of Cornelius made itself felt by Marius...For,

consistently with his really poetic temper, all influence reached Marius...
through the medium of sense.[175]

However, Christianity goes one step further than any other religion
in this respect: its very deity manifests itself in a human form, a human
character, in the figure of Christ. And it was this aspect of Christianity
which came to hold such attractions for Pater. Again, this stress on the
humanity and physicality of Christ was a characteristically nineteenth-
century one. We have seen how the leaders of the Oxford Movement,
for example, and Hopkins, habitually spoke of Christ as a close and
intimate friend, as a personal companion who was always by their side.
While it is not Pater's style to identify the characters in his drama, he
indicates, in a dreamlike mystical sequence, that the ultimate 'companion' for whom Marius and, by extension perhaps, he himself was
groping, was Christ. Marius questions

whether there had not been – besides Flavian, besides Cornelius even,
and amid the solitude which in spite of ardent friendship he had perhaps
loved best of all things – some other companion, an unfailing companion,
even at his side throughout;...
...he passed from that mere fantasy of a self not himself, beside him in
his coming and going, to those divinations of a living and companionable
spirit at work in all things, of which he had become aware from time to
time in his old philosophic readings – in Plato and others...
...That divine companion figured no longer as but an occasional way-
farer beside him; but rather as the unfailing 'assistant', without whose
inspiration and concurrence he could not breathe or see, instrumenting
his bodily senses, rounding, supporting his imperfect thoughts.[176]

These are the terms not only of Newman's 'conscience' but of Hopkins'
vision of Christian grace:

it is Christ in his member on the one side, his member in Christ on the
other. It is as if a man said: That is Christ playing at me and me playing
at Christ, only that it is no play but truth; that is Christ *being me* and me
being Christ.[177]

Earlier in *Marius the Epicurean*, Pater had asked, 'Humanity, a universal
order, the polity, its aristocracy of elect spirits, the mastery of their
example over their successors...But where might Marius search for
all this, as more than an intellectual abstraction?'[178] Before he died, he
found his answer – in Christ, the human embodiment of a divinity and
a religious and moral system.

Pater's attraction to Christianity was indeed aesthetic in nature. He
had explored the aesthetic elements of religious worship in his 'Imaginary
Portrait', 'The Child in the House'. Florian Deleal is attracted to a
Christianity which,

translating so much of its spiritual verity into things that may be seen, condescends in part to sanction this infirmity, if so it be, of our human existence, wherein the world of sense is so much with us.[179]

In his essay on Dante Gabriel Rossetti, Pater regards Christian sacramentalism or 'aesthetic worship' as cancelling the distinction between spirit and matter.[180] And in *Marius the Epicurean* he admires 'the aesthetic charm of the Catholic Church, her evocative power over all that is eloquent and expressive in the better mind of man, her outward comeliness'.[181] But it is important to distinguish his attitude towards Christianity in *Marius the Epicurean* from the self-indulgent aesthetic effusion that is frequently and mistakenly attributed to him. Pater certainly transferred the terminology and methodology of his aesthetic to religion, but his aesthetic attraction to the Church related decisively to the figure of Christ himself.

Like Arnold, Pater felt that it was necessary to redress the balance in Christianity away from the Hebraic, moralistic emphasis towards the Hellenic ideals of beauty, order, clarity.[182] He deliberately relates these Hebraic and Hellenic aspects back to the two sides of Christ's character:

In the history of the church, as throughout the moral history of mankind, there are two distinct ideals, either of which it is possible to maintain – two conceptions, under one or the other of which we may represent to ourselves men's efforts towards a better life – corresponding to those two contrasted aspects...as discernible in the picture afforded by the New Testament itself of the character of Christ. The ideal of asceticism represents moral effort as essentially a sacrifice, the sacrifice of one part of human nature to another, that it may live the more completely in what survives of it; while the ideal of culture represents it as a harmonious development of all the parts of human nature, in just proportion to each other. It was to the latter order of ideas that the church, and especially the church of Rome, in the age of the Antonines, freely lent herself.[183]

Like Newman, Pater took the authority for his own position from the primitive Christian Church. In Marius' Rome, he found incontrovertible justification for the reinstatement of beauty as a Christian ideal. For Pater, even asceticism had its beauty, the beauty of self-sacrifice, but his real argument was for a cultural humanism that was essentially Greek, for the 'sweetness and light' which Arnold had urged:

It was Christianity in its humanity, or even its humanism, in its generous hopes for man, its common sense and alacrity of cheerful services, its sympathy with all creatures, its appreciation of beauty and daylight.[184]

She was for reason, for common sense, for fairness to human nature, and generally for what may be called the naturalness of Christianity. – As also for its comely order:[185]

worship – 'the beauty of holiness', nay! the elegance of sanctity – was developed with a bold and confident gladness.[186]

It is appropriate, then, that Pater describes Marius' awakening faith in terms that suggest the organised aesthetic response demanded by a work of art:

It was not in an image, or series of images, yet still in a sort of dramatic action, and with the unity of a single appeal to eye and ear, that Marius about this time found all his new impressions set forth, regarding what he had already recognised, intellectually, as for him at least the most beautiful thing in the world.[187]

The image of Cecilia 'was already become for him like some matter of poetry',[188] while his faith structured his refracted spiritual intuitions – again, like a work of art, functioning as 'some ampler vision, which should take up into itself and explain this world's delightful shows, as the scattered fragments of a poetry, till then but half understood, might be taken up into the text of a lost epic, discovered at last'.[189]

And, as one would expect, since Pater's response to Christianity is aesthetic, we may find many characteristics in his writing about religion that recall the preoccupations which dominate his art criticism: his insistence upon the concrete sensuous experience, for example, and its presentation in an exclusively subjective, impressionistic style. But the most significant connection of all between his writings on religion and art is to be found in the stylistic doctrine of the perfect merger of content and form. As we have seen, the theory of the 'perfect identification of matter and form' forms the substance of his argument in the essay entitled 'The School of Giorgione', and is the basis of his ideal of Hellenic perfection in art. The synthesis that had for so long represented his aesthetic ideal was realised in the person of Christ incarnate. And it is here that we find the real point of fusion between Pater's aestheticism and his faith – a fusion too readily dismissed by Eliot as an imperfect synthesis of art, philosophy, religion, ethics, and literature.[190] For while it is true that Pater's synthesis, like those of most of his contemporaries, was flawed, a proper appreciation of the real nature and focus of that synthesis in *Marius the Epicurean* shows that it was not as imperfect as has generally been assumed. Rather, given the Victorian preoccupation with the interrelation of religious and aesthetic ideas, Pater's location of that synthesis in the figure of Christ represents a serious and original attempt to confront the crucial religious issues of the nineteenth century.

Eliot was right, though, to see *Marius the Epicurean* as 'a document of one moment in the history of thought and sensibility in the nineteenth century'. Yeats once said that to his generation, *Marius the Epicurean* was the only sacred book,[191] and indeed the novel does seem to offer the *fin de siècle* agnostic a fictional exploration of possible kinds of religious assent, just as *Robert Elsmere* had offered the Victorian agnostic alternative forms of faith than historical Christianity. It is significant that Elsmere made his decision to leave the Church of England ministry on moral and intellectual grounds, and worked himself into an early grave, whereas Marius, anticipating the deathbed conversions of numerous decadent would-be Catholics,[192] concludes his pilgrimage in search of Christian faith with his death, so that we are never asked to endorse him as a practising Christian.

V

We never have the opportunity of seeing how Wilde conducted himself as a Roman Catholic either, as his was, of course, the supreme example of a life of profligacy mended by a deathbed conversion. Wilde refers somewhat critically to Marius' spiritual escapades in his own religious apology, *De Profundis*:

> In *Marius the Epicurean* Pater seeks to reconcile the artistic life with the life of religion in the deep, sweet and austere sense of the word. But Marius is little more than a spectator: an ideal spectator indeed, and one to whom it is given 'to contemplate the spectacle of life with appropriate emotions', which Wordsworth defines as the poet's true aim: yet a spectator merely, and perhaps a little too much occupied with the comeliness of the vessels of the Sanctuary to notice that it is the Sanctuary of Sorrow that he is gazing at.[193]

De Profundis differs from *Marius the Epicurean* in that it is directly autobiographical and not distanced at a fictional remove. But it is not only in formal terms that Wilde is more deeply implicated in his work. Wilde felt, with some justification, that his own experiences of defamation and imprisonment qualified him to identify with Christ in a much more personal way than Marius, or indeed Pater, could do. For Wilde, Christ is above all the type of profound suffering. Wilde's sense of identification with Christ informs *De Profundis* and does indeed make it a grander and more moving work than *Marius the Epicurean*. This mocking exposer of Victorian 'earnestness' wrote at the end of his life a profoundly serious work which was not, in the seemly Victorian sense, 'earnest', but truly 'in earnest'.[194] In it, he comes to terms with the problem of the relationship between religious and aesthetic experience and identity which eluded so many of his contemporaries by literally identifying the 'infinite I AM' of God with the creative 'I AM' of the artist.

Wilde saw himself, and others[195] perceived him similarly, as society's scapegoat, and he clearly implies a comparison between Christ's betrayal and his own tragic history:

The little supper with his companions, one of whom had already sold him for a price: the anguish in the quiet moonlit olive-garden: the false friend coming close to him so as to betray him with a kiss: the friend who still believed in him, and on whom as on a rock he had hoped to build a House of Refuge for Man, denying him as the bird cried to the dawn: his own utter loneliness, his submission, his acceptance of everything: and along with it all such scenes as the high priest of Orthodoxy rending his raiment in wrath, and the Magistrate of Civil Justice calling for water in the vain hope of cleansing himself of that stain of innocent blood that makes him the scarlet figure of History: the coronation-ceremony of Sorrow, one of the most wonderful things in the whole of recorded time: the crucifixion of the Innocent One before the eyes of his mother and of the disciple whom he loved; the soldiers gambling and throwing dice for his clothes...[196]

The language of 'little suppers' and 'false friends' is that of Wilde's own milieu; his own judges were the 'high priests of orthodoxy'. To aid the identification, Christ is throughout described as an artist, as Wilde had so often described himself:

Nor is it merely that we can discern in Christ that close union of personality with perfection which forms the real distinction between classical and romantic Art and makes Christ the true precursor of the romantic movement in life, but the very basis of his nature was the same as that of the nature of the artist, an intense and flamelike imagination. He realized in the entire sphere of human relations that imaginative sympathy which in the sphere of Art is the sole secret of creation... Christ's place indeed is with the poets. His whole conception of Humanity sprang right out of the imagination and can only be realized by it.[197]

Wilde develops each of these aspects of Christ's personality, all of which bear a strong resemblance to his own. Christ has 'an intense and flamelike imagination', He burns with 'a hard gem-like flame', in fact, and sanctifies the aesthetic imagination. 'Christ is the most supreme of individualists', moreover, He was 'the first individualist in history':

he gave to man an extended, a Titan personality. Since his coming the history of each separate individual is, or can be made, the history of the world.[198]

And, again after the fashion of Wilde, Christ is a romantic, with all the charming waywardness of romanticism:

I see in Christ not merely the essentials of the supreme romantic type, but all the accidents, the wilfulnesses even, of the romantic temperament also.[199]

He is the 'palpitating centre of romance'.[200] And in case we should still fail to remark the resemblance to Wilde himself, Christ is also 'the leader of all the lovers'.[201]

As a scapegoat, a poet, an individual, a lover, Wilde is Christlike; as a sinner he is loved and forgiven. In a poignantly personal passage, in which we recognise a distant echo of Ruskin's idea of Gothic as the most Christian because the most imperfect of art forms, Wilde writes wistfully:

But it is when he deals with the Sinner that he is most romantic, in the sense of most real. The world had always loved the Saint as being the nearest possible approach to the perfection of God. Christ, through some divine instinct in him, seems to have always loved the sinner as being the nearest possible approach to the perfection of man. His primary desire was not to reform people, any more than his primary desire was to relieve suffering. To turn an interesting thief into a tedious honest man was not his aim. He would have thought little of the Prisoners' Aid Society and other modern movements of the kind. The conversion of a Publican into a Pharisee would not have seemed to him a great achievement by any means. But in a manner not yet understood of the world he regarded sin and suffering as being in themselves beautiful, holy things, and modes of perfection.[202]

These are the sentiments of 'Pen, Pencil, and Poison', only this time applied to himself.

Just as Christ is both sufferer and redeemer of sins, He is both artist and work of art:

his entire life also is the most wonderful of poems. For 'pity and terror' there is nothing in the entire cycle of Greek Tragedy to touch it.[203]

Nothing in Aeschylus, or Dante, or Shakespeare 'can be said to equal or even approach the last act of Christ's passion':

when one contemplates all this from the point of view of Art alone one cannot but be grateful that the supreme office of the Church should be the playing of the tragedy without the shedding of blood, the mystical presentation by means of dialogue and costume and gesture even of the Passion of her Lord.[204]

Or Christ's life may be described as an idyll, 'so entirely may sorrow and beauty be made one in their meaning and manifestation'.[205] In this respect, too, Wilde finds analogies with his own life, which he now sees as itself a work of art:

as though my life, whatever it had seemed to myself and others, had all the while been a real Symphony of Sorrow, passing through its rhythmically-linked movements to its certain resolution, with that inevitableness that in Art characterises the treatment of every great theme.[206]

Wilde's realisation of Christ as a man of sorrow is more personal and persuasive than Marius' detached contemplation, but in some significant respects he is derivative. For example, he leans heavily on Pater's idea in *Marius the Epicurean* of Christ as a work of art. In particular, he enlarges upon Pater's suggestion of Christ Himself as representative of a perfect identification of form and content. Sorrow, he argues, as the most extreme of human emotions, 'is at once the type and test of all great art':

Truth in Art is the unity of a thing with itself: the outward rendered expressive of the inward: the soul made incarnate: the body instinct with spirit. For this reason, there is no truth comparable to Sorrow.[207]

Christ is like the Greek gods in the sense that He is the physical incarnation of a spiritual idea:

And feeling, with the artistic nature of one to whom Sorrow and Suffering were modes through which he could realise his conception of the Beautiful, that an idea is of no value till it becomes incarnate and is made an image, he makes of himself the image of the Man of Sorrows, and as such has fascinated and dominated Art as no Greek god ever succeeded in doing.[208]

And the reason? Wilde explains the fact that Christ transcends the ancient pagan deities in purely aesthetic terms. Christ is the more perfectly classical work of art:

For the Greek gods, in spite of the white and red of their fair fleet limbs, were not really what they appeared to be.[209]

As such, the incarnate Christ became the type of truth in art:

The song of Isaiah, '*He is despised and rejected of men, a man of sorrows and acquainted with grief: and we hid as it were our faces from him*', had seemed to him to be a prefiguring of himself, and in him the prophecy was fulfilled. We must not be afraid of such a phrase. Every single work of art is the fulfilment of a prophecy. For every work of art is the conversion of an idea into an image. Every single human being should be the fulfilment of a prophecy. For every human being should be the realisation of some ideal, either in the mind of God or in the mind of man. Christ found the type, and fixed it, and the dream of a Virgilian poet, either at Jerusalem or at Babylon, became in the long progress of the centuries incarnate in him for whom the world was waiting. '*His visage was marred more than any man's, and his form more than the sons of men*', are among the signs noted by Isaiah as distinguishing the new ideal, and as soon as Art understood what was meant it opened like a flower at the presence of one in whom truth in Art was set forth as it had never been before. For is not truth in Art, as I have said, 'that in which the outward is expressive of the inward; in which the soul is made flesh, and the body instinct with spirit: in which Form reveals'?[210]

Wilde has here created a myth which, surprisingly, has important features in common with Hopkins' inscape myth. For, although written with Wilde's customary extravagance, it manages to express a reconciliation of aesthetics and Christianity which, like Hopkins', centres on the Incarnation of Christ, whose inscape encompasses perfect beauty and supreme suffering, and has a direct bearing on the question of aesthetic form. But one would not wish to make great claims for the theological credibility of either Wilde's or Pater's idea of Christ as a work of art. Their versions of Christ have little to do with historical Christianity and are decidedly heterodox. In fact, it would have been inconsistent of them had it been otherwise, for religion, like art, is subjectively defined, and essentially relativistic. Moreover, their theories did not have to *work*, as Hopkins' or Newman's or even Arnold's had to for them. Wilde and Pater were not as deeply committed to establishing a religious position according to which they could live their lives. For all Wilde's conviction of the personal implications of the Christian story for himself, one still feels that historical Christianity at least remains on the periphery of his life.

And this is even more the case with Pater. Even more than for writers like Newman and Hopkins, Pater's was a highly refined intellectual resolution of the question of the relation between religion and aesthetics. For all his desire to be instinctual and spontaneous, Pater's conclusions seem remarkably detached. They have little to do with self-expression. And with perhaps some surprise we realise how this may be said even of his art criticism. As Wilde observes, he catches 'the colour and accident and tone of whatever artist or work of art he deals with'.[211] Harold Bloom points out that 'Paterian *askesis* is less a sublimation (as it seems when first used in the "Preface") than it is an aesthetic self-curtailment, a giving up of certain powers so as to help achieve more originality in one's self-mastery.'[212] It is frequently remarked that Pater's whole life was an exercise in self-repression. It might also be argued that even in his intellectual pursuits the self is repressed. It is perhaps significant that Pater and Wilde, like Ruskin and Arnold before them, turned from writing lyrical poetry in their youth to criticism. Bloom observes that Pater turned to writing his *Imaginary Portraits* in order to escape the confession that wells up in the essay on Leonardo da Vinci and in the Conclusion by creating a fictive self.[213] In one of those 'Imaginary Portraits', 'Sebastian van Storck', the hero concludes:

one's wisdom, therefore, consists in hastening, so far as may be, the action of those forces which tend to the restoration of equilibrium, the calm surface of the absolute, untroubled mind, to *tabula rasa* by the extinction in one's self of all that is but correlative to the finite illusion – by the suppression of ourselves.[214]

He anticipates peace as 'Detachment', and yearns 'to hasten hence: to fold up one's whole self, as a vesture put aside...To restore *tabula rasa*, then, by a continual effort at self-effacement'.[215] Was this the only way the author could find peace of mind too? Rarely does Pater write in the first person in his portraits: he prefers to speak through his character, adopting a fictional mask.[216]

Wilde also approved of the 'truth of masks': 'Man is least himself when he talks in his own person. Give him a mask, and he will tell you the truth.'[217] In 'The Critic as Artist', Gilbert suggests that not only the artist but the critic too has impersonal and objective forms at his disposal. He then demonstrates to Ernest that the aesthetic critic is not by any means limited to a subjective form of expression:

The method of the drama is his, as well as the method of the epos. He may use dialogue...or adopt narration, as Mr. Pater is fond of doing, each of whose Imaginary Portraits...presents to us, under the fanciful guise of fiction, some fine and exquisite piece of criticism...And you see now, Ernest, that the critic has at his disposal as many objective forms of expression as the artist has. Ruskin put his criticism into imaginative prose, and is superb in his changes and contradictions; and Browning put his into blank verse, and made painter and poet yield up their secret; and M. Renan uses dialogue, and Mr. Pater fiction, and Rossetti translated into sonnet-music the colour of Giorgione and the design of Ingres...[218]

Wilde's dicta here are realised in the form he chooses for his own work. 'The Critic as Artist', like 'The Decay of Lying', is of course itself a dialogue, and in general his preference is for dramatic or fictional forms, for parables, and for aphorisms. Despite Gilbert's assurances that there is no essential difference between objective and subjective work because all artistic creation is absolutely subjective,[219] his evident preference for indirect modes of expression seems perverse in one who so vigorously promotes subjectivism. For all his espousal of the cult of personality, is it perhaps the case that Wilde is as mystified by his own self as Arnold ever was by his? In *De Profundis* alone does he confront his true self, and there he proclaims, with a terrible honesty, 'The soul of man is unknowable', 'the final mystery is one's self', and cries 'Who can calculate the orbit of his own soul?'[220]

Does this mean that Wilde and Pater too failed to resolve their anxieties about the self, that for all their rhetoric of liberation they were caught in the same Victorian toils as Ruskin and Arnold? I would suggest, rather, that their convictions about the relativistic nature of their post-Darwinian world made it impossible for them not only to sink their self-consciousness into an objectively defined orthodox religious structure, but also to believe in a self that was fixed, solid and definable. Given Pater's extraordinary description of identity in flux at the beginning of the Conclusion, and Wilde's wholehearted endorsement of it, it would have been inconsistent of them to aspire to seek, fix, and proclaim as some objective entity their own selves in the conventional Victorian autobiographical mode without subverting the fluctuating truth of their identity. The self, like the physical world, is a thing in flux, not a substantial entity to be once and for all comprehended and mastered. But as our selfhood, experience succeeding experience, is all we can be sure of, then we are bound to explore it, not in an Arnoldian way, but by monitoring our shifting impressions of things outside ourselves which are themselves in flux. Hence Pater's and Wilde's shared belief in art criticism as a mode of self-discovery or, as Gerald Monsman describes it, 'criticism as a form of creative self-portraiture'.[221]

For both Pater and Wilde, the appreciation of art enabled them not only to plumb the depths of their fluid and unknowable selves, but to reach out to the absolute realities of 'things in themselves' which lie beyond human experience. As Monsman points out,

Pater spoke of 'the great central prayer of this generation, to put ourselves in the way of light we so greatly desire – in the "way of hope" – the point where things may look less confused than they do'. Only some such visionary work, like the lifting of 'a cunningly contrived panel' as at the shrine of Aesculapius or the image of Cecilia herself, can approach, if not completely attain to, that 'open passage' leading from the 'sleepy' dreamworld of the solitary cell 'to things as they are in themselves, to absolute realities'.[222]

Both Pater and Wilde firmly believed that our response to art was necessarily subjective and that interpretation was all. The same is true of our response to absolute realities. Christ is perceived by Pater and Wilde as a work of art, and as such is created by each in his own image. Religious and aesthetic experience is profoundly related in their philosophies and criticism, but in their philosophy art is always the clue. The pattern of thought has thus turned full-circle. The movement which began in the 1830s with the Oxford Tractarians' exploration of the aesthetic dimensions of historical Christianity concludes in the 1890s with a religion of art.

Conclusion

'We were the last romantics', wrote Yeats in 'Coole Park and Ballylee, 1931', and indeed all the writers I have discussed were the direct heirs to ideas about art, religion, and identity initiated by the Romantics.[1] That Romantic inheritance took many different forms, and in this study I have concentrated on the legacies of Wordsworth and Coleridge to a group of central Victorian writers. I have tried to draw attention to the fact that certain tensions incipient in the thought of Wordsworth and Coleridge, tensions between poetry and religion, rebellion and reaction, individualism and authority, continued to manifest themselves throughout the Victorian period. As the century proceeded, that is, and society became increasingly democratic, religion in turn became increasingly personal and secular. The 'revolution' conventionally associated with Romanticism was indeed not really achieved until the end of the nineteenth century.

The Oxford Tractarians, writing at the beginning of the period, were, as a matter of principle, committed to opposing any threat to the sacred authority of the Church. As a result they were inclined either to underplay or to Christianise the secularising tendencies of Wordsworth's mythopoeic vision, and to distrust Coleridge's speculative conclusions. Nevertheless, Christian orthodoxy did not by any means disqualify serious exploration of certain crucial aspects of Romantic theory. On the contrary, Coleridge's theories about the symbolic properties of language, and Kantian problems relating to epistemology and perception, were arguably confronted more honestly and pursued with more resourcefulness and intellectual rigour by Newman and Hopkins than by any of the non-Catholic writers considered in this study. Conversely, Ruskin and Arnold, whilst accepting the precariousness of the Church's position, sustained the Coleridgean tradition of safeguarding Christian and aristocratic values by endowing Art and Culture with moral and religious qualities. They did so, however, at the expense of over-simplifying and evading fundamental epistemological questions concerning subjectivism and the nature of perception. And it is only in the writings of Pater and Wilde in the 1880s and 1890s that the full implications of Romantic tendencies to secularise *and* personalise Christianity are realised in so far as religion is embraced as a work of art and the figure of Christ Himself is appropriated into a personal myth.

We have seen how Coleridge's central belief in the divine nature of the creative imagination developed into two traditions in the Victorian period, the one emphasising the interrelation of aesthetic and moral experience, the other lending to art itself a religious status. At the end of the nineteenth century, the latter, aestheticised version of the Romantic tradition evolved naturally into Symbolism. In 1899, the year before Wilde died, Arthur Symons celebrated the dawning of a new era in art:

It is all an attempt to spiritualise literature, to evade the old bondage of rhetoric, the old bondage of exteriority...Mystery is no longer feared, as the great mystery in whose midst we are islanded was feared by those to whom that unknown sea was only a great void. We are coming closer to nature, as we seem to shrink from it with something of horror, disdaining to catalogue the trees of the forest. And as we brush aside the accidents of daily life, in which men and women imagine that they are alone touching reality, we come closer to humanity, to everything in humanity that may have begun before the world and may outlast it.

Here, then, in this revolt against exteriority, against rhetoric, against a materialistic tradition; in this endeavour to disengage the ultimate essence, the soul, of whatever exists and can be realised by the consciousness; in this dutiful waiting upon every symbol by which the soul of things can be made visible; literature, bowed down by so many burdens, may at last attain liberty, and its authentic speech. In attaining this liberty, it accepts a heavier burden; for in speaking to us so intimately, so solemnly, as only religion had hitherto spoken to us, it becomes itself a kind of religion, with all the duties and responsibilities of the sacred ritual.[2]

Symons' Symbolist manifesto indicates the direction which Pater's and Wilde's aestheticism took in the years to follow. Yeats, the culmination of this 'aesthetic Romantic' tradition, regarded Pater as the first Modern,[3] and in his poetry he explores the question of identity and creativity, as does Wilde, through his philosophy of the mask:

> I call to the mysterious one who yet
> Shall walk the wet sands by the edge of the stream
> And look most like me, being indeed my double,
> And prove of all imaginable things
> The most unlike, being my anti-self,
> And, standing by these characters, disclose
> All that I seek.[4]

He opens his soul to the mysterious creative force in life, and forges from it his own humanist mythology:

> I mock Plotinus' thought
> And cry in Plato's teeth,
> Death and life were not
> Till man made up the whole,
> Made lock, stock and barrel
> Out of his bitter soul,
> Aye, sun and moon and star, all.
> And further add to that
> That, being dead, we rise,
> Dream and so create
> Translunar Paradise.[5]

Yeats resolves the Coleridgean problem of the nature of the relationship between identity, creativity and transcendental awareness through imaginative synthesis within a framework of phenomenal experience.

But alongside Yeats and the Symbolists, a different tradition feeds into Modernism, a tradition epitomised in the work of Conrad, which may be said to have grown out of a sense of the failure or obsolescence of Ruskinian moralised aesthetics. Conrad shared Ruskin's sense of the moral purpose of art, and his belief that the artist's task is 'above all to make you *see*'.[6] But what he sees bears little resemblance to Ruskin's vision in *Modern Painters* of the divinity of nature and humanity. *Heart of Darkness* was published in 1899, the same year as Symons' *The Symbolist Movement in Literature*, but it has none of that work's optimism. By 1899, the clink of the geologists' hammers which had pursued Ruskin so relentlessly had developed into a thundering certainty that the material universe no longer had a moral or a meaning. Marlow's nostalgia for 'something natural, that had its reason, that had a meaning', for 'a world of straight-forward facts', is exposed as a mere dream:[7] 'We live in the flicker.' Thrown back on to his existential resources, Conrad's hero journeys in search of his identity. But the human identity he is forced to recognise, the heart of darkness at the centre of human consciousness, is too horribly depraved to contemplate. The cosmological pessimism of the novel is profound. The modern individual, bereft of God, stands alone. It is a devastating vision of cosmic isolation, and one which provides a striking counterpoint to the religious intensity of Yeats' mythological synthesis.

This study began with Eliot's dismissive account of the 'various chimerical attempts to effect imperfect syntheses' of art, philosophy, religion, ethics, and literature which constitute the main intellectual endeavour of the Victorian period. Yet it was out of these attempts at philosophical synthesis, out of their successes as well as their failures, that the contradictions of Modernism itself sprang. The chilling line 'Mistah Kurtz – he dead' had signified the end of a particular kind of humanism for Eliot himself, and his 'unreal city', peopled by 'hollow men', rivals Conrad's own as a vision of the spiritual void at the heart of modernity. Yet Eliot did not stray for ever in the wasteland. He repudiated Conrad's ethic of desperation and his later writings testify to a profound belief in redemption through art:

> Words move, music moves
> Only in time; but that which is only living
> Can only die. Words, after speech, reach
> Into the silence. Only by the form, the pattern,
> Can words or music reach
> The stillness, as a Chinese jar still
> Moves perpetually in its stillness.[8]

Despite his earlier criticism of Victorianism, Eliot – no one better – understood the meaning of tradition:

> Whatever we inherit from the fortunate
> We have taken from the defeated
> What they had to leave us – a symbol:
> A symbol perfected in death.[9]

And, like the Victorians whose works have formed the basis of this study, he recognised that in all great art the timeless and the temporal coincide:

> We shall not cease from exploration
> And the end of all our exploring
> Will be to arrive where we started
> And know the place for the first time.[10]

In his later literary criticism, Eliot explores the relationship between the creation and criticism of literature and the Christian ethic. He proclaims, in his essay on 'Religion and Literature', that 'Literary criticism should be completed by criticism from a definite ethical and theological standpoint',[11] and in *After Strange Gods* the 'tradition' within which the poet writes is perceived as being properly complemented by 'orthodoxy', by, in effect, the moral and spiritual truths of Christianity.[12] Eliot, the Anglo-Catholic critic in whom Newman's commitment to Catholicism and Arnold's commitment to criticism come together, brought the Victorian religio-aesthetic tradition into the twentieth century.[13]

After Strange Gods is, however, subtitled *A Primer of Modern Heresy*, and the opening words of the Preface are 'Le monde moderne avilit', 'The modern world debases'. Later in the lectures we are told that 'amongst writers the rejection of Christianity...is the rule rather than the exception', and that blasphemy is obsolescent in the age of unbelief in which we live.[14] The lectures are, as Vincent Buckley points out, a profession of faith to a secular world.[15] We have seen how in the nineteenth century the diminishing power of Christianity left a gap which culture came steadily to fill as art began to take over the properties and functions of religion. Today, when the hold of Christianity is even more tenuous, the tendency to worship at the altar of aestheticism is even more pronounced. As Tom Wolfe recently observed in the 1983 T. S. Eliot Lectures *The Social Psychology of the Arts*, 'today, art...is the religion of the educated classes'.[16] The wealthy now donate their money to the Arts, not the Church, their names go on plaques in opera houses, not on pews, and dealers, curators, and artists have become the modern 'art clerisy'. Art indeed is the new 'élitist religion'. The immense distance we have travelled from the world of Newman's Christian aesthetic may be gauged from Wolfe's description of the opening of the Vatican art show at the Metropolitan Museum of Art in New York in 1983, where a number of Roman Catholic dignitaries were to be seen mingling rather uncomfortably with the sophisticated Manhattan art clerisy: 'Who', asked one bewildered New York art dealer of another, 'Who are these unbelievable people?'

Notes

Full publication details are given here only for items not included in the Select bibliography.

INTRODUCTION

1 T. S. Eliot, 'Arnold and Pater' (1930), in *Selected Essays* (1972 (1932)), p. 442.

2 Eliot, 'The Metaphysical Poets' (1921), in *Selected Essays*, p. 287.

3 Although Plato condemns art as mere imitation in the tenth book of the *Republic*, in the earlier books and in the *Phaedrus* he approves the educational value of beauty, arguing that formal beauty has a beneficent effect upon conduct and character. Cf. *The Republic of Plato*, trans. F. M. Cornford (Clarendon Press, 1941), pp. 78–90, and *The Dialogues of Plato*, trans. B. Jowett (5 vols., Clarendon Press, 1892 (4 vols., 1871)), Vol. I, pp. 391–489. In his *Critique of Judgement* Kant argues that sensitiveness to the sublime and to natural beauty implies a susceptibility to moral ideas, and that the creation and appreciation of beauty are symptomatic of a highly developed moral sense. Cf. Immanuel Kant, *The Critique of Judgement*, trans. James Creed Meredith (1952), Vol. II, # 29, 'Modality of the judgement on the sublime in nature', pp. 115–17, and # 59, 'Beauty as the symbol of morality', pp. 221–5.

4 Cf., for example, Dante, 'La Vita Nuova', Spenser, 'An Hymne of Heavenly Beautie', Wordsworth, *The Prelude*, ii, 396–418, iii, 127–39, xii, 151–73, *The Excursion*, iv, 1207–29.

5 Cf. Margaret Maison, *Search Your Soul, Eustace: A Survey of the Religious Novel in the Victorian Age* (Sheed & Ward, 1961), and Hoxie Neale Fairchild, *Religious Trends in English Poetry*, Vol. IV, *Christianity and Romanticism in the Victorian Era, 1830–1880* (1957) for full critical surveys of the religious novels and poetry of the period.

6 Cf. Coleridge, *Confessions of an Inquiring Spirit: Letters on the Inspiration of the Scriptures* (1840); Benjamin Jowett, 'The Interpretation of Scripture', in *Essays and Reviews* (1859); Matthew Arnold, *Literature and Dogma* (1873); Charles Gore, 'The Holy Spirit and Inspiration', in *Lux Mundi* (1889).

7 Eliot, 'The Metaphysical Poets', in *Selected Essays*, p. 287.

8 Coleridge, *Biographia Literaria, or Biographical Sketches of My Literary Life and Opinions*, ed. James Engell and W. Jackson Bate (1983), Vol. II, pp. 15–16.
9 Cf. M. H. Abrams, *The Mirror and the Lamp: Romantic Theory and the Critical Tradition* (1953), p. 329.
10 *Hegel's Aesthetics: Lectures on Fine Art*, trans. T. M. Knox (1975), Vol. I, p. 518.
11 *Ibid.*, p. 529.
12 Cf. E. D. Hirsch Jr., *Wordsworth and Schelling: A Typological Study of Romanticism* (1960); A. C. Bradley, *English Poetry and German Philosophy in the Age of Wordsworth* (Manchester University Press, 1909); A. C. Bradley, *Oxford Lectures on Poetry* (Macmillan, 1909), p. 129.
13 Cf. *Biographia Literaria*, Vol. I, chapters 7–13 for references to Kant and Schelling. For further reading on Coleridge's indebtedness to German philosophy see the introduction and notes by Engell and Bate cited in n. 8 above, and René Wellek, *Immanuel Kant in England: 1793–1838* (Princeton University Press, 1931); G. N. G. Orsini, *Coleridge and German Idealism* (Southern Illinois University Press, 1969); Thomas McFarland, *Coleridge and the Pantheist Tradition* (Clarendon Press, 1969); Norman Fruman, *Coleridge: The Damaged Archangel* (George Allen & Unwin, 1972).
14 *Biographia Literaria*, Vol. I, pp. 268 and 271.
15 *Ibid.*, Vol. I, pp. 272–3.
16 *Ibid.*, Vol. I, p. 283.
17 Kant, *Critique of Pure Reason*, trans. Norman Kemp Smith (1929), pp. 82 and 257–75.
18 Wordsworth, *The Prelude, or Growth of a Poet's Mind*, ed. Ernest de Selincourt (1926), II, lines 401–5.
19 Ruskin, *Works*, V, p. 201.
20 Charles Darwin, *The Origin of Species by Means of Natural Selection* (1859, 1872), p. 414.
21 Robert Bridges, *The Testament of Beauty* (1929), III, line 774.
22 Ruskin, *Works*, XXV, p. 219.
23 Cf. Newman, *Essays Critical and Historical* (1872), Vol. II, p. 442.

1 THEOLOGY: KEBLE, NEWMAN, AND THE OXFORD MOVEMENT

1 Newman, *Lectures on Certain Difficulties felt by Anglicans in Submitting to the Catholic Church* (1850), p. 8.
2 Newman, *Lectures on the Prophetical Office of the Church, viewed relatively to Romanism and Popular Protestantism* (1837), p. 20.
3 Newman, *Apologia Pro Vita Sua* (1864), pp. 150–1.
4 Bishop Stanley of Norwich, *Hansard*, 3rd Series, LIV, p. 557 (22 May 1840).

5 For the fullest account of the context in which the Oxford Movement came into being see Owen Chadwick, *An Ecclesiastical History of England: The Victorian Church* (1966), Vol. I, pp. 7–168.

6 Cf. Richard D. Altick, *Victorian People and Ideas* (Norton, 1973), p. 204.

7 James Anthony Froude, 'The Oxford Counter-Reformation', in *Short Studies on Great Subjects* (1899 (1867)), Vol. IV, pp. 239–40.

8 William Palmer, *A Narrative of Events connected with the Publication of the Tracts for the Times* (Rivingtons, 1843), pp. 99–100.

9 Newman, 'The State of Religious Parties', *British Critic and Quarterly Theological Review*, Vol. XXV (1839), 400–2. The essay was later reprinted as 'Prospects of the Anglican Church'. Other significant figures in this High Church tradition were John Jebb, Bishop of Limerick, and Joshua Watson, owner of the *British Critic*.

10 R. I. Wilberforce, *A Charge to the Clergy of the East Riding, delivered at the Ordinary Visitation a.d. 1851* (1851), pp. 10–11, quoted in David Newsome, *The Parting of Friends: A Study of the Wilberforces and Henry Manning* (1966), p. 14.

11 *Ibid.*, p. 14. Cf. also Newsome, 'The Evangelical Sources of Newman's Power', in *The Rediscovery of Newman: An Oxford Symposium*, ed. John Coulson and A. M. Allchin (1967).

12 Owen Chadwick, *The Mind of the Oxford Movement* (Stanford University Press, 1960), p. 27; W. E. Gladstone, *Gleanings of the Past Years* (7 vols., John Murray, 1879), Vol. VII, pp. 209–12, quoted in Newsome, *The Parting of Friends*, p. 8.

13 Keble, *Lectures on Poetry, 1832–1841*, trans. E. K. Francis (1912), Vol. II, p. 272.

14 *Dublin Review*, Vol. XX, No. XL (June 1846), 452–3.

15 Newman, *Essays Critical and Historical* (1872), Vol. II, pp. 443–4.

16 *Ibid.*, Vol. II, p. 442.

17 J. T. Coleridge, *A Memoir of the Rev. John Keble, M.A., Late Vicar of Hursley* (1870), p. 398.

18 Cf. Newman's description of his first meeting with Keble, *Apologia Pro Vita Sua*, pp. 75–7, and Arnold's lyrical description of Newman's Oxford, with which he introduces his lecture on Emerson, Super, X, p. 165.

19 Marilyn Butler, *Romantics, Rebels and Reactionaries: English Literature and its Background 1760–1830* (1981), p. 6. Cf. also A. O. Lovejoy, 'On the Discrimination of Romanticisms', *PMLA*, Vol. XXXIX (1924), 229–53, and Hugh Honour, *Romanticism* (Allen Lane, 1979; Penguin, 1981), for similar views on the diversity of Romanticism.

20 *Letters II*, p. 99.

21 Cf. Basil Willey, *Nineteenth Century Studies* (Chatto & Windus, 1949); David Newsome, *Two Classes of Men: Platonism and English Romantic Thought* (1974); John Coulson, *Newman and the Common*

Tradition: A Study in the Language of Church and Society (1970); Coulson, *Religion and Imagination* (1981); Stephen Prickett, *Romanticism and Religion: The Tradition of Coleridge and Wordsworth in the Victorian Church* (1976).

22 Butler, *Romantics, Rebels and Reactionaries*, pp. 1–10.

23 Cf. G. B. Tennyson, *Victorian Devotional Poetry: The Tractarian Mode* (1981), p. 17: 'Sir Walter Scott may enjoy pride of place among those cited by Newman as disposing the mind of the age toward what was to become Tractarianism, but the two most influential figures in the formation of Tractarian poetics were surely Wordsworth and Coleridge.' See Prickett, *Romanticism and Religion*, pp. 190–1, on the complex question of Coleridge's 'influence' on Newman.

24 See, in particular, Wordsworth's Preface to the *Lyrical Ballads*, and Coleridge's 1795 *Lectures on Revealed Religion*, his *Lay Sermons*, *Biographia Literaria*, *Aids to Reflection*, and *On the Constitution of the Church and State*.

25 Newman, 'The State of Religious Parties', 402.

26 Keble, *Lectures on Poetry*, Vol. I, p. 317.

27 *Ibid.*, Vol. I, p. 8.

28 *Ibid.*, Vol. II, p. 260.

29 Butler, *Romantics, Rebels, and Reactionaries*, p. 8.

30 John Jones, *The Egotistical Sublime* (Chatto & Windus, 1964), p. 157. Cf. his chapter 'The Baptised Imagination' and also E. C. Batho, *Later Wordsworth* (Cambridge University Press, 1933) for accounts of Wordsworth's later Christian poetry.

31 Cf. M. H. Abrams, *Natural Supernaturalism: Tradition and Revolution in Romantic Literature* (1971), p. 91.

32 Cf. H. G. Schenk, *The Mind of the European Romantics: An Essay in Cultural History* (1969), p. 172.

33 *Letters, Conversations, and Recollections of S. T. Coleridge*, ed. Thomas Allsop (1836), Vol. I, p. 107. Cf. the discussion of the confusion of Platonist and Naturalist positions in Wordsworth's poetry in Stephen Prickett's *Romanticism and Religion*, Chapter 3.

34 Coleridge, *Lectures 1795 On Politics and Religion*, ed. Lewis Patton and Peter Mann (1971), pp. 94 and 339; 'Religious Musings', lines 9–10; 'Frost at Midnight', lines 59–61; 'The Destiny of Nations', lines 18–20; *Lay Sermons*, ed. R. J. White (1972), pp. 28–31.

35 'The Eolian Harp', lines 44–57.

36 Newman, *Essays and Sketches*, ed. Charles Frederick Harrold (1948), 'Prospects of the Anglican Church', Vol. I, p. 338 (reprinted from 'The State of Religious Parties').

37 Coulson, *Religion and Imagination*, pp. 6–15.

38 Coulson, *Newman and the Common Tradition*, p. 40.

39 See John Colmer's Introduction to his edition of *On the Constitution of the Church and State* (1976) for a full discussion of the religious and political context in which the work was written.

40 *Ibid.*, p. xxxiv.
41 *Ibid.*, pp. lix–lxi.
42 Cf. Newsome, *Two Classes of Men*, p. 60.
43 Keble, *Lectures on Poetry*, Vol. II, p. 270.
44 For a comprehensive discussion of Tractarian poetics see Tennyson, *Victorian Devotional Poetry*, pp. 12–71. For discussions of Romantic poetics see Abrams, *The Mirror and the Lamp*, and Paul Hamilton's recent stimulating study *Coleridge's Poetics* (1983). For an examination of Tractarian poetics in relation to the Victorian critical tradition, see Alba H. Warren, *English Poetic Theory, 1825–1865* (1950).
45 Keble, *Occasional Papers and Reviews* (1877), 'Life of Sir Walter Scott', p. 12.
46 *Ibid.*, p. 16.
47 *Ibid.*, p. 12.
48 *Ibid.*, p. 6.
49 Keble, *Lectures on Poetry*, Vol. I, p. 53; Vol. II, pp. 37, 96.
50 Cf. David Newsome's provocative study of Newman in the light of Coleridge's remark in *Table Talk*, 2 July 1830: 'Every man is born an Aristotelian, or a Platonist. I do not think it possible that any one born an Aristotelian can become a Platonist; and I am sure no born Platonist can change into an Aristotelian.' Newsome concludes that Newman was, in fact, born a Platonist yet became an Aristotelian through his Oxford education, an education which Keble, of course, shared. Newsome, *Two Classes of Men*, in particular pp. 1–7, 57–72.
51 Keble, *Occasional Papers and Reviews*, 'Life of Sir Walter Scott', p. 17.
52 *Ibid.*, p. 17.
53 *Ibid.*, p. 18. Cf. Abrams, *The Mirror and the Lamp*, p. 147.
54 In this he departs from the general tendency of the Romantics to dislike allegory. Cf. for example Hazlitt's advice to those readers of Spenser who fear his allegorical complexities: 'If they do not meddle with the allegory, the allegory will not meddle with them. Without minding it at all, the whole is as plain as a pike-staff' (*The Complete Works of William Hazlitt*, ed. P. P. Howe (21 vols., Dent, 1930–4), Vol. V, p. 38).
55 Cf. Keble, *Lectures on Poetry*, Vol. I, pp. 257–60.
56 Keble, *Occasional Papers and Reviews*, 'Copleston', p. 151.
57 *O.E.D.* definition 3(d) of 'Poetry', 'Extended (with reference to the etymology) to creative or imaginative art in general', cites as first usage D. Stewart, *Encyclopaedia Britannica* (1815), also Ruskin, *Modern Painters*, III.iv.i.15 (1856).
58 Keble, *Lectures on Poetry*, Vol. I, p. 42.
59 *Ibid.*, p. 47.
60 Cf. Prickett, *Romanticism and Religion*, p. 111.
61 A theory which, as G. B. Tennyson points out, 'roughly parallels Coleridge's distinction between the Imagination and the Fancy, but

Keble also harmonizes it with his larger theory of poetry as religious expression', *Victorian Devotional Poetry*, p. 64. Cf. also Prickett, *Romanticism and Religion*, p. 116.

62 Keble, *Lectures on Poetry*, Vol. I, p. 53.
63 Keble, *Occasional Papers and Reviews*, 'Sacred Poetry', p. 86.
64 Keble, *Lectures on Poetry*, Vol. I, p. 54.
65 Keble, *Occasional Papers and Reviews*, 'Sacred Poetry', p. 86.
66 *Ibid.*, p. 90.
67 Keble, *Occasional Papers and Reviews*, 'Life of Sir Walter Scott', p. 24.
68 Cf. Abrams, *The Mirror and the Lamp*, p. 146.
69 Cf. Prickett, *Romanticism and Religion*, p. 113.
70 Cf. David Delaura, *Hebrew and Hellene in Victorian England: Newman, Arnold, and Pater* (1969), p. 24, and Geoffrey Tillotson, 'Newman's Essay on Poetry', in *John Henry Newman: Centenary Essays* (Burns, Oates and Washbourne, 1945), pp. 184–5. See also n. 50 above.
71 Newman, *Essays and Sketches*, 'Poetry, with reference to Aristotle's Poetics', Vol. I, p. 62.
72 *Ibid.*, p. 58.
73 *Ibid.*, p. 65.
74 *Ibid.*, p. 64.
75 *Ibid.*, p. 60.
76 Newman, *The Idea of a University defined and illustrated* (1873), pp. 273–4.
77 *Ibid.*, p. 276. Newman cites Aristotle's 'magnanimous man' in this context: 'the elocution of a great intellect is great. His language expresses, not only his great thoughts, but his great self', *ibid.*, p. 280.
78 *Ibid.*, p. 228.
79 Newman, *An Essay in Aid of a Grammar of Assent* (1870), p. 107.
80 Newman, *Essays and Sketches*, 'Poetry, with reference to Aristotle's Poetics', Vol. I, p. 74.
81 Cf. Harold L. Weatherby, *Cardinal Newman in his Age: His Place in English Theology and Literature* (1973), pp. 114–15.
82 Newman, *The Idea of a University*, p. 276.
83 Newman, *Historical Sketches* (1899 (1872–3)), Vol. II, p. 227.
84 Cf. Walter E. Houghton, *The Art of Newman's 'Apologia'* (1945), p. 18.
85 *The Letters and Diaries of John Henry Newman*, ed. Charles Stephen Dessain *et al.* (Nelson, 1971), Vol. XXI, p. 461.
86 Newman, *The Idea of a University*, pp. 74–5.
87 Newman, *Sermons, Chiefly on the Theory of Religious Belief, preached before the University of Oxford* (1843), p. 110.
88 Newman, *The Idea of a University*, p. xix.
89 Newman, *Essays Critical and Historical*, Vol. I, p. 41.
90 *The Prose Works of William Wordsworth*, ed. W. J. B. Owen and

Jane Worthington Smyser (1974), Vol. I, p. 120, from Preface to *Lyrical Ballads* (1800).

91 *Ibid.*, Vol. III, p. 65, from Essay, supplementary to the Preface.

92 *Ibid.*, Vol. III, p. 65.

93 Basil Willey explains how Coleridge's theory of the Imagination was 'inseparable from the defence of religion' in *Nineteenth Century Studies*, pp. 31–44, and claims that religion, for Coleridge, was 'the *raison d'être* of everything else' in *Samuel Taylor Coleridge* (1972), p. 69. For a more rigorous discussion of the relation of Coleridge's religious discourse to his poetics, see Hamilton, *Coleridge's Poetics*, pp. 121–32, 186–92. Stephen Prickett devotes a whole chapter to Coleridge's philosophical concern with religious language: *Romanticism and Religion*, Chapter 1. Cf. also Coulson, *Newman and the Common Tradition*.

94 Coleridge, *Lay Sermons*, pp. 28–9.

95 *Ibid.*, p. 30.

96 *Ibid.*, p. 62.

97 Newman, *Essays and Sketches*, 'Prospects of the Anglican Church', Vol. I, p. 358. NB: this essay was written in 1839, before Newman's conversion.

98 J. T. Coleridge, *A Memoir of the Rev. John Keble*, p. 199.

99 Keble, *Lectures on Poetry*, Vol. II, p. 478.

100 This recalls St Augustine of Hippo's argument, based on personal experience, that the Platonists had prepared the ground for Christianity. Cf. *The Confessions of St Augustine*, trans. E. B. Pusey (Random House, 1949 (1838)), p. 140.

101 Keble, *Lectures on Poetry*, Vol. II, p. 479.

102 Newman, *Apologia Pro Vita Sua*, pp. 184–5.

103 *John Henry Newman: Autobiographical Writings*, ed. Henry Tristram (Sheed & Ward, 1956), p. 82.

104 Newman, *The Idea of a University*, pp. 249–67.

105 *Ibid.*, p. 265.

106 Cf. Delaura, *Hebrew and Hellene in Victorian England*, pp. xi, xvi, 47; and A. Dwight Culler, *The Imperial Intellect: A Study of Newman's Educational Ideal* (1955), p. 235.

107 Keble, *Lectures on Poetry*, Vol. II, pp. 479–80.

108 *Ibid.*, p. 481.

109 NB: Coleridge is himself careful to suggest that religion and poetry cannot be equated. Religion uses poetic symbolism to express 'its great object' (*Lay Sermons*, p. 90). Cf. Hamilton, *Coleridge's Poetics*, p. 130.

110 Newman, *The Idea of a University*, p. 80.

111 *Ibid.*, p. 230. Cf. also *Sermons, Chiefly on the Theory of Religious Belief, preached before the University of Oxford*, p. 349.

112 Newman, *The Idea of a University*, pp. 78–9.

113 *Ibid.*, pp. 80–1.

114 Wilfred Ward, *The Life of John Henry Cardinal Newman* (1912), Vol. II, pp. 354–6.
115 Newman, *The Idea of a University*, p. 122. Cf. also *Letters II*, p. 95.
116 Ruskin, 'The Laws of Fésole', in *Works*, XV, pp. 351–5. Cf. also *Works*, XIX, p. 394.
117 Cf. Coleridge, *Biographia Literaria*, Vol. II, p. 12. Cf. also *Lay Sermons*, p. 90, 'Religion finitely express[es] the *unity* of the infinite Spirit by being a total act of the soul.'
118 Prickett, *Romanticism and Religion*, pp. 99–100.
119 Cf. Stephen Prickett's chapter 'Newman: Imagination and Assent' in *Romanticism and Religion*, pp. 174–210, for a full discussion of similarities and distinctions between Coleridge and Newman.
120 Newman, *An Essay in Aid of a Grammar of Assent*, p. 343.
121 *Ibid.*, p. 106.
122 *Ibid.*, p. 107.
123 *Ibid.*, p. 101.
124 *Ibid.*, p. 104.
125 Newman, *An Essay on the Development of Christian Doctrine* (1845), pp. 55–6.
126 Newman, *An Essay in Aid of a Grammar of Assent*, p. 281.
127 *Ibid.*, p. 303.
128 *Ibid.*, p. 309.
129 *Ibid.*, p. 337.
130 *Ibid.*, p. 115.
131 *The Letters and Diaries of John Henry Newman*, ed. Dessain *et al.*, Vol. XXVI, p. 95.
132 Newman, *An Essay in Aid of a Grammar of Assent*, p. 251. Cf. Prickett, *Romanticism and Religion*, p. 202.
133 Newman, *Parochial and Plain Sermons* (1868), Vol. V, p. 44. NB: Newman was in fact using this phrase particularly of the Roman Catholic Church, but it is an appropriate expression of the way both men viewed the Church of England as Tractarians also.
134 J. T. Coleridge, *A Memoir of the Rev. John Keble*, p. 302.
135 Letter to Heinrich Voss, 1805, quoted in Schenk, *The Mind of the European Romantics*, p. 94.
136 Keble, *Occasional Papers and Reviews*, 'Life of Sir Walter Scott', pp. 7–8.
137 *The Prose Works of William Wordsworth*, Vol. I, p. 140, from Preface to *Lyrical Ballads*.
138 Wordsworth, *The Prelude* (1850), XIII, lines 366–78.
139 Coleridge, *Lectures 1795 On Politics and Religion*, p. 94.
140 *Ibid.*, pp. 338–9.
141 'Religious Musings', lines 9–10.
142 'Frost at Midnight', lines 59–61; 'The Destiny of Nations', lines 18–20.
143 Coleridge, *Lay Sermons*, p. 30.

144 Cf. Coleridge, *Lectures 1795 On Politics and Religion*, p. 95 n.
145 *The Works of that Learned and Judicious Divine Mr. Richard Hooker*, ed. Keble (1836), Vol. I, p. lxxxix.
146 Joseph Butler, *The Analogy of Religion, Natural and Revealed, to the Constitution and Course of Nature* (1736).
147 The analogical argument is of course apparent from the Athanasian Creed.
148 Keble, *The Christian Year: Thoughts in Verse for the Sundays and Holydays Throughout the Year* (1895 (1827)), 'Trinity Sunday', p. 131.
149 Keble, *Tracts for the Times*, Vol. VI, No. 89 (1839), p. 29.
150 Cf. *Confessions of an Inquiring Spirit: Letters on the Inspiration of the Scriptures*, ed. Henry Nelson Coleridge (1840). See Prickett, *Romanticism and Religion*, pp. 44-7.
151 Keble, *Tracts for the Times*, Vol. VI, No. 89, pp. 54-5. Cf. W. J. A. M. Beek, *John Keble's Literary and Religious Contribution to the Oxford Movement* (1959), p. 112.
152 Keble, *Tracts for the Times*, Vol. VI, No. 89, p. 165.
153 Keble, *Occasional Papers and Reviews*, 'Sacred Poetry', pp. 99-100.
154 Keble, *Sermons for the Christian Year* (1875-80), Vol. II, S. VI, p. 64.
155 *Ibid.*, Vol. IX, S. XLIV, p. 530.
156 *Ibid.*, Vol. I, S. VI, p. 65.
157 Keble, *The Christian Year*, 'Fourth Sunday after Trinity'.
158 Keble, *Tracts for the Times*, Vol. VI, No. 89, p. 141.
159 *Ibid.*, p. 144.
160 Keble, *On Eucharistical Adoration* (1857), p. 56.
161 *Ibid.*, p. 57.
162 *Ibid.*, p. 58.
163 Keble, *Letters of Spiritual Counsel and Guidance*, ed. R. F. Wilson (1870), p. 206.
164 Keble, *Tracts for the Times*, Vol. VI, No. 89, p. 29.
165 Prickett, *Romanticism and Religion*, p. 104.
166 Keble, *Lectures on Poetry*, Vol. I, p. 35.
167 Cf. Walter Lock, *John Keble: A Biography* (1893), p. 64, and Prickett, *Romanticism and Religion*, pp. 105-7.
168 Tennyson, *Victorian Devotional Poetry*, pp. 97-100. Cf. also pp. 223-4 for an interesting discussion of the relationship between Keble's *The Christian Year* and Wordsworth's *Ecclesiastical Sonnets*.
169 Georgina Battiscombe, *John Keble: A Study in Limitations* (1963), p. 104.
170 From 'Devotional Incitements'. The poem is discussed in detail by Tennyson, *Victorian Devotional Poetry*, pp. 94-5.
171 Keble, *Occasional Papers and Reviews*, 'Sacred Poetry', p. 92.
172 From 'Fourth Sunday after Advent', *The Christian Year*, cited in Tennyson, *Victorian Devotional Poets*, p. 96.

173 Cf. Newman, *An Essay on the Development of Christian Doctrine*, p. 113.
174 Newman, *Essays and Sketches*, 'Poetry, with reference to Aristotle's Poetics', Vol. I, p. 67.
175 Newman, *Apologia Pro Vita Sua*, p. 90.
176 *Ibid.*, pp. 77–8.
177 *Ibid.*, p. 67.
178 *Ibid.*, pp. 88–9.
179 Newman, *Essays Critical and Historical*, Vol. II, pp. 191–3.
180 *Letters and Correspondence of John Henry Newman during his Life in the English Church*, ed. Anne Mozley (1898 (1891)), Vol. I, p. 161.
181 Newman, *Sermons, Chiefly on the Theory of Religious Belief, preached before the University of Oxford*, p. 70.
182 Newman, *Essays Critical and Historical*, Vol. I, p. 42. Newman's Ockhamism may help to explain why his reception in Roman Catholic circles was so cool, for nineteenth-century Roman Catholic theology was predominantly neo-Thomist in its emphasis on system.
183 Newman, *The Arians of the Fourth Century* (1833), pp. 63–4.
184 Newman, *An Essay in Aid of a Grammar of Assent*, p. 260.
185 Newman, *An Essay on the Development of Christian Doctrine*, p. 51.
186 Newman, *An Essay in Aid of a Grammar of Assent*, p. 482.
187 Newman, *Apologia Pro Vita Sua*, p. 377.
188 Newman, *An Essay in Aid of a Grammar of Assent*, p. 391.
189 *Ibid.*, pp. 391–2.
190 Newman, *The Idea of a University*, pp. 225–6.
191 *Ibid.*, pp. 453–4.
192 Newman, *An Essay in Aid of a Grammar of Assent*, p. 479.
193 Newman, *Sermons, Chiefly on the Theory of Religious Belief, preached before the University of Oxford*, p. 33.
194 *The Letters and Diaries of John Henry Newman*, ed. Dessain *et al.*, Vol. XXV, p. 97.
195 Newman, *Parochial Sermons*, 6 vols. (1834–42), Vol. II, p. 235.
196 *The Philosophical Notebooks of John Henry Newman*, ed. Edward Sillem (1969–70), Vol. II, pp. 49–51.
197 Newman, *An Essay on the Development of Christian Doctrine*, p. 51.
198 Newman, *An Essay in Aid of a Grammar of Assent*, pp. 87–8.
199 *Ibid.*, pp. 89–90.
200 *Ibid.*, p. 91.
201 Newman, *Discussions and Arguments on Various Subjects* (1872), 'The Tamworth Reading Room', p. 294.
202 Newman, *Discourses Addressed to Mixed Congregations* (1849), p. 199.
203 *The Letters and Diaries of John Henry Newman*, ed. Dessain *et al.*, Vol. XI, p. 12, from a letter to T. W. Allies (9 October 1845).
204 Newman, *Apologia Pro Vita Sua*, p. 401.

205 Newman, *Sermons, Chiefly on the Theory of Religious Belief, preached before the University of Oxford*, p. 171.
206 *Ibid.*, p. 179.
207 *Ibid.*, p. 199.
208 Newman, *An Essay on the Development of Christian Doctrine*, pp. 132–3. This, in contrast to the ideas discussed earlier (cf. n. 182), *is* Thomist.
209 Newman, *An Essay in Aid of a Grammar of Assent*, p. 95.
210 *Ibid.*, p. 99.
211 *Ibid.*, p. 101.
212 *Ibid.*, p. 115.
213 *Ibid.*, p. 135.
214 *Ibid.*, p. 75.
215 *Ibid.*, p. 116.
216 *Ibid.*, p. 117.
217 Newman, *The Idea of a University*, p. 192.
218 Newman, *An Essay on the Development of Christian Doctrine*, p. 118.
219 Newman, *Apologia Pro Vita Sua*, p. 391.
220 *Ibid.*, p. 205.
221 *Ibid.*, p. 282, quoted from a letter published on the occasion of Tract No. 90.
222 Newman, *Lectures on Certain Difficulties felt by Anglicans in Submitting to the Catholic Church*, p. 80.
223 Newman, *An Essay in Aid of a Grammar of Assent*, p. 130.
224 *Ibid.*, pp. 135–6.
225 Coleridge, *Biographia Literaria*, Vol. II, p. 11.
226 Cf. Coulson, *Newman and the Common Tradition*, p. 11.
227 Newman, *Sermons, Chiefly on the Theory of Religious Belief, preached before the University of Oxford*, p. 285.
228 Newman, *An Essay on the Development of Christian Doctrine*, p. 94.
229 Newman, *The Idea of a University*, p. 134.
230 *The Philosophical Notebooks of John Henry Newman*, Vol. II, p. 71.
231 *The Letters and Diaries of John Henry Newman*, ed. Dessain *et al.*, Vol. XXV, p. 280, from a letter to Henry James Coleridge (5 February 1871).
232 Pater, *Marius the Epicurean* (1910), Vol. II, p. 9.
233 Newman, *The Idea of a University*, p. 45.
234 *Ibid.*, p. 50.
235 *Ibid.*, p. 67.
236 Newman, *Discussions and Arguments*, 'The Tamworth Reading Room', pp. 270–1.
237 Newman, *The Idea of a University*, p. 252.
238 Newman, *An Essay in Aid of a Grammar of Assent*, p. 75.
239 Newman, *The Idea of a University*, p. 310.
240 Newman, *Apologia Pro Vita Sua*, p. 285.
241 Newman, *An Essay on the Development of Christian Doctrine*, p. 95.

242 *Ibid.*, p. 337.
243 *The Letters and Diaries of John Henry Newman*, ed. Dessain *et al.*, Vol. XX, p. 224 (8 July 1862).
244 Newman, *An Essay on the Development of Christian Doctrine*, pp. 35–6.
245 *Ibid.*, pp. 36–7.
246 *Ibid.*, p. 55.
247 Newman, *Apologia Pro Vita Sua*, p. 322.
248 Newman, *Sermons, Chiefly on the Theory of Religious Belief, preached before the University of Oxford*, p. 29.
249 *Ibid.*, p. 31.
250 Hopkins, *Poems*, 28.
251 Newman, *Apologia Pro Vita Sua*, p. 192.
252 *Ibid.*, pp. 144–5.
253 Newman, *Lectures on Certain Difficulties felt by Anglicans in Submitting to the Catholic Church*, pp. 6–7.
254 *Ibid.*, p. 7.
255 E. S. Purcell, *The Life of Cardinal Manning* (2 vols., 1896 (1895)), Vol. I, p. 233.
256 Newman, *An Essay on the Development of Christian Doctrine*, p. 125.
257 *Ibid.*, p. 35.
258 *Ibid.*, p. 154.
259 *Ibid.*, p. 154.
260 Newman, *An Essay in Aid of a Grammar of Assent*, p. 458.
261 Newman, *Apologia Pro Vita Sua*, p. 386.
262 Newman, *Loss and Gain: The Story of a Convert* (1848), pp. 291–2.
263 Newman, *An Essay on the Development of Christian Doctrine*, p. 27.
264 Cf. Coulson, *Newman and the Common Tradition*, p. 146.
265 Newman, *The Via Media of the Anglican Church* (1877), Vol. I, p. xl.
266 Newman, *Lectures on Certain Difficulties felt by Anglicans in Submitting to the Catholic Church*, p. 181.
267 Newman, *Discourses Addressed to Mixed Congregations*, pp. 185–6.
268 *Ibid.*, p. 219.
269 Newman, *Apologia Pro Vita Sua*, Appendix 3, p. 31.
270 *Ibid.*, Appendix 3, p. 31.
271 Newman, *An Essay on the Development of Christian Doctrine*, pp. 52–3, from Guizot's *Lecture on European Civilization*.
272 Newman, *Lectures on Certain Difficulties felt by Anglicans in Submitting to the Catholic Church*, p. 188.
273 Newman, *Essays and Sketches*, 'Poetry, with reference to Aristotle's Poetics', Vol. I, p. 76.
274 Newman, *The Idea of a University*, p. 122.
275 Newman, *Essays Critical and Historical*, Vol. II, pp. 442–3.
276 *The Letters and Diaries of John Henry Newman*, ed. Dessain *et al.*, Vol. XII, pp. 219–22.
277 Ward, *The Life of John Henry Cardinal Newman*, Vol. I, p. 139.

278 *Ibid.*, p. 140.
279 *Ibid.*, p. 204 n.
280 *Faber: Poet and Priest, Selected Letters by Frederick William Faber, 1833–63*, ed. Raleigh Addington (1974), p. 98.
281 *Letters of John Henry Newman*, ed. Derek Stanford and Muriel Spark (1957), p. 124, from a letter to F. W. Faber (1 December 1844).
282 Newman, *Apologia Pro Vita Sua*, p. 80.

2 EPISTEMOLOGY AND PERCEPTION: GERARD MANLEY HOPKINS

1 *Letters II*, pp. 93–6. Cf. also pp. 15, 27–31, and *Letters I*, pp. 65–6.
2 *Poems*, 66.
3 *Poems*, 22.
4 *Letters III*, p. 20.
5 *Ibid.*, p. 93.
6 *Letters I*, pp. 95–6.
7 *Sermons*, pp. 35–6.
8 *Poems*, 62.
9 *Journals*, p. 252.
10 *Journals*, p. 139.
11 Henry Vaughan, 'Cock-Crowing', lines 19–22.
12 Henry Vaughan, 'Religion', lines 21–4.
13 Wordsworth, *The Prelude* (1850), XIV, lines 66–77.
14 Newman found Natural Theology inadequate for similar reasons. Cf. Newman, *The Idea of a University*, pp. 225–6, 453–4.
15 *Letters III*, p. 202.
16 Ruskin, *Works*, XV, p. 27 n. Cf. Alan Heuser, *The Shaping Vision of Gerard Manley Hopkins* (1958), pp. 9, 103 n.
17 *Journals*, p. 77.
18 *Ibid.*, p. 80.
19 *Letters III*, p. 204.
20 *Letters II*, p. 131.
21 *Letters III*, pp. 313–14.
22 *Ibid.*, p. 231.
23 *Ibid.*, p. 203.
24 *Ibid.*, p. 202.
25 Cf. Ruskin, *Works*, XI, p. 49; V, p. 124. The parallel is drawn by Alan Heuser in *The Shaping Vision of Gerard Manley Hopkins*, pp. 14–15.
26 *Sermons*, p. 41.
27 *Poems*, 72.
28 T. S. Eliot, 'Ash Wednesday'.
29 *Letters I*, p. 55.
30 Alfred H. Miles, ed., *The Poets and Poetry of the Nineteenth Century* (1906), p. 179.
31 *Journals*, p. 80.

32 *Ibid.*, p. 133.
33 *Ibid.*, p. 138.
34 *Ibid.*, p. 167.
35 *Ibid.*, p. 38.
36 *Ibid.*, p. 246.
37 *Letters I*, p. 48.
38 *Letters III*, p. 151.
39 Pater, *The Renaissance*, pp. 236–9.
40 Pater, *Appreciations*, p. 66.
41 *Ibid.*, p. 67.
42 *Journals*, p. 120.
43 *Journals*, p. 154.
44 *Ibid.*, p. 225.
45 Cf. Ruskin, *Works*, IV, pp. 87–8, 106, and VI, 321. See also Heuser, *The Shaping Vision of Gerard Manley Hopkins*, p. 26.
46 *Journals*, p. 46.
47 *Ibid.*, p. 152.
48 *Ibid.*, p. 178.
49 *Ibid.*, p. 178.
50 *Ibid.*, p. 144.
51 *Ibid.*, p. 146.
52 *Ibid.*, p. 27.
53 *Ibid.*, p. 155.
54 *Ibid.*, p. 139.
55 *Ibid.*, p. 195.
56 *Ibid.*, p. 195.
57 *Ibid.*, p. 230.
58 *Ibid.*, p. 204.
59 *Ibid.*, p. 72.
60 *Ibid.*, p. 38.
61 *Ibid.*, p. 138.
62 *Ibid.*, p. 138.
63 *Ibid.*, p. 178.
64 *Ibid.*, p. 181.
65 *Poems*, 58.
66 *Ibid.*, 38.
67 Cf. for example, Plato, *Theaetetus*, trans. John McDowell (Clarendon Press, 1973), 153e–154a; *Plato's Cosmology*, trans. Francis MacDonald Cornford (Kegan Paul, Trench, Trübner & Co., 1937), 45b–46a, 67c; Aristotle, *De Anima*, trans. J. A. Smith, in *The Works of Aristotle Translated into English*, ed. W. D. Ross (12 vols., Oxford University Press, 1908–52), Vol. III, 417a–424b. The best critical accounts of Hopkins' theory of perception are those of Heuser, *The Shaping Vision of Gerard Manley Hopkins*, and Patricia M. Ball, *The Science of Aspects: The Changing Role of Fact in the Work of Coleridge, Ruskin and Hopkins* (1971).

68 *Poems*, 12. This poem is cited by Alan Heuser in *The Shaping Vision of Gerard Manley Hopkins*, p. 15.
69 Cf. *Journals*, pp. 13, 14, 49, 59, 140, 145, 146, 248, 254–5.
70 *Letters I*, pp. 30–1.
71 See the section on Hegel in Anthony Ward, *Walter Pater: The Idea in Nature* (1966), pp. 43–77.
72 Cf. *Letters III*, p. 249, and *Journals*, pp. 115, 343.
73 *The Works of Thomas Hill Green*, ed. R. L. Nettleship (3 vols., 1885–8), Vol. III, p. 119, cited in *The Encyclopedia of Philosophy*, ed. Paul Edwards (8 vols., Collier–Macmillan, 1967), Vol. III, pp. 387–9.
74 *Letters II*, pp. 147–8.
75 Coleridge, *Biographia Literaria*, especially Chapters 7 and 9.
76 *Ibid.*, ed. James Engell and W. Jackson Bate (1983), Vol. I, p. 285.
77 *Ibid.*, Vol. I, p. 304.
78 Humphry House, *Coleridge*, Clark Lectures, 1951–2 (1953).
79 Kant, *Critique of Pure Reason*, p. 22.
80 *Ibid.*, p. 41.
81 *Ibid.*, p. 23.
82 *Ibid.*, p. 144.
83 Cf. Mary Warnock, *Imagination* (1976), pp. 28–33.
84 Kant, *Critique of Pure Reason*, pp. 144 n, 146.
85 *Poems*, 91.
86 Cf. Christopher Devlin, 'The Image and the Word', *The Month*, N.S. Vol. III (March 1950), 191.
87 Cf. *Poems*, 28. Throughout 'The Wreck of the Deutschland' response to God is sensuous and intuitive. In the image of the carrier-pigeon (st. 3) Hopkins alludes to the Scotist concept of the soul's instinctive memory of its divine origins.
88 Kant, *Critique of Pure Reason*, p. 82.
89 *Ibid.*, pp. 82, 257–75.
90 Wordsworth, *The Prelude* (1850), II, 401–5.
91 Kant, *The Critique of Judgement*, p. 51.
92 *Journals*, p. 95.
93 *Ibid.*, p. 74.
94 *Ibid.*, p. 196.
95 *Ibid.*, p. 80.
96 *Ibid.*, p. 76.
97 *Ibid.*, p. 95.
98 Cf. especially *Modern Painters*, Vol. I, Section II, Chapter 2, 'Of Truth of Colour', and Chapter 3, 'Of Truth of Chiaroscuro', and Section VI, Chapter 1, 'Of Truth of Vegetation', in Ruskin, *Works*, III, pp. 574–604.
99 *Journals*, p. 129.
100 *Poems*, 57.
101 *Ibid.*, 37.

102 *Journals*, p. 127.
103 *Ibid.*, p. 129.
104 *Ibid.*, p. 174.
105 *Ibid.*, p. 176.
106 *Ibid.*, p. 189.
107 *Ibid.*, p. 209.
108 *Ibid.*, p. 207.
109 *Ibid.*, p. 188.
110 *Ibid.*, p. 238.
111 *Sermons*, p. 137.
112 *Journals*, p. 231.
113 *Ibid.*, p. 221.
114 Devlin, 'The Image and the Word'. I am greatly indebted to this essay. I can do no better than attempt to paraphrase it in my own discussion of Scotus.
115 *Journals*, p. 125.
116 *Duns Scotus: Philosophical Writings, a Selection*, ed. and trans. Allan Wolter (1962), pp. 74, 121. NB: Devlin has, however, noted that Scotus' '*confuse-cognoscere*' and Hopkins' 'inchoate word' are not identical ('The Image and the Word', 115–16).
117 *Duns Scotus: Philosophical Writings*, pp. 105, 128–9. The importance of sensation in Hopkins' writings and in his developed theory of inscape is of course very great, although strictly within the context of these early essays Devlin notes a distinction between Hopkins' 'image (of sight or sound or *scapes* of the other senses)' and Scotus' '*species specialissima*', in that Hopkins specifically excludes sensation 'which presents itself unbidden', saying that he means the image that comes 'when deliberately formed or when a thought is recalled' (*Journals*, p. 125). See 'The Image and the Word', 117.
118 'The Image and the Word', 119–20.
119 *Duns Scotus: Philosophical Writings*, pp. 57, 177 n.
120 'The Image and the Word', 120.
121 Cf. that area between the operation of the senses and thought which Ruskin defined as 'moral' – resting at a definite stage in the perceptive process, where it is partially structured by the conceptual process, but not yet a fully formulated concept. Ruskin, *Works*, III, p. 111.
122 There are seven different meanings of the word 'buckle' listed in the *O.E.D.*, and all have been made use of in the many and various critical interpretations of this poem. There is conflict over whether the word is indicative or imperative, whether it means snapping together, fusing, or bending, breaking, collapsing; whether it implies buckling to, buckling under, buckling with. And for many, their entire reading of the poem, whether they see it as a poem of renunciation, stoic sacrifice and defeat (I. A. Richards, F. R. Leavis, William Empson, W. H. Gardner), or as one of joyful assertion of faith (Herbert Marshall McLuhan), hinges upon their interpretation

of that one word. I have chosen to interpret the word as I do on the grounds that it suggests the moment of yielding of general to particular, and expresses the Scotist perception of the inscape of a thing poised between universal being and the attainment of individuality. Such an interpretation seems to accord most satisfactorily with Hopkins' philosophy of inscape as I have discussed it.

123 *Journals*, p. 130.
124 'The Image and the Word', 201. Cf. also J. Hillis Miller, *The Disappearance of God: Five Nineteenth-Century Writers* (1975), p. 281.
125 *Metaphysics*, 5, 11, cited in Frederick Copleston, *A History of Philosophy* (9 vols., 1946–75), Vol. II, p. 512.
126 *Ibid.*, p. 517.
127 *Sermons*, p. 146.
128 *Ibid*, p. 151.
129 *Poems*, 28.
130 'The Image and the Word', 193.
131 Heuser, *The Shaping Vision of Gerard Manley Hopkins*, p. 25.
132 *Letters III*, pp. 21–2.
133 *Ibid.*, p. 226.
134 Cf. Louis Martz, *The Poetry of Meditation: A Study in English Religious Literature of the Seventeenth Century* (1954), pp. 25–39. See also the Conclusion, in which Hopkins is discussed.
135 *Sermons*, p. 263.
136 *Ibid.*, pp. 6, 109.
137 *Philippians*, 2:5–11.
138 *Letters I*, p. 175.
139 *Sermons*, p. 14.
140 'Man comes from God and must return to God. There are two movements in man: from his divinely-created being towards existence, and from his existing being towards God. These two movements were given to man by God; and by these two movements, man, if he so wishes, will infallibly return to God. I say if he so wishes, because man can change the direction of this movement...

Today, every man receives, as in the beginning, the first movement, which throws him into life; but the second movement, which throws the living man back towards God, is no longer given to him with the first movement. The second movement throws him living into death; but I am here to rescue man by baptism and set him back on the road which leads to God. So everything is put right: man is regenerated; he will walk, if he so wishes, towards God or he will return to Satan from whom I have delivered him; he will walk in the way of truth or of lies.' J. H. Gruninger, *A propos des cahiers de Marie Lataste*, Lyon (1952), 1.5.19–21, quoted in *Sermons*, Appendix I.
141 *Sermons*, pp. 137–8.
142 *Ibid.*, p. 197.

143 *Ibid.*, p. 194.
144 Cf. Heuser, *The Shaping Vision of Gerard Manley Hopkins*, pp. 36–8.
145 *Poems*, 28.
146 *Ibid.*, st. 30.
147 *Poems*, 31.
148 *Ibid.*, 72.
149 *Journals*, p. 261.
150 Miller, *The Disappearance of God*, p. 313.
151 *Sermons*, p. 129.
152 *Journals*, p. 254.
153 *Ibid.*, p. 199.
154 *Poems*, 38, 28.
155 *Ibid.*, 38.
156 *Journals*, p. 201.
157 *Ibid.*, p. 195.
158 *Poems*, 36.
159 Ruskin, *Works*, IV, pp. 146–7.
160 *Poems*, 31.
161 *Ibid.*, 58.
162 *Sermons*, p. 239.
163 *Ibid.*, p. 154.
164 *Ibid.*, p. 142.
165 *Ibid.*, p. 147.
166 *Poems*, 57.
167 *Sermons*, p. 122.
168 *Ibid.*, pp. 138–9.
169 *Ibid.*, pp. 171–2.
170 *Ibid.*, p. 156.
171 Kant, *Critique of Pure Reason*, pp. 135–61.
172 *Ibid.*, B430–B431.
173 See W. A. M. Peters, S.J., *Gerard Manley Hopkins: A Critical Essay towards the Understanding of his Poetry* (1948) for a stimulating discussion of the relation of Hopkins' poetic language and style to inscape.
174 *Letters I*, p. 66.
175 Cf. Miller, *The Disappearance of God*, p. 281.
176 *Journals*, p. 289.
177 *Ibid.*, p. 283.
178 *Ibid.*, pp. 84–5.
179 *Ibid.*, p. 126.
180 *Ibid.*, p. 125.
181 See Miller's chapter on Hopkins in *The Disappearance of God* for an interesting discussion of his ideas about and use of words.
182 *Journals*, p. 129.
183 *Poems*, 28, st. 30.
184 *Sermons*, p. 129.

185 *Ibid.*, p. 84.
186 *Poems*, 45.
187 Cf. also *Letters I*, p. 83.
188 *Letters III*, p. 370.
189 *Journals*, p. 236.
190 *Poems*, 33.
191 *Ibid.*, 62.
192 *Sermons*, p. 263.
193 *Poems*, 67.
194 *Letters I*, p. 137.
195 *Letters I*, pp. 50–1; *Letters III*, pp. 203–4, 216–19, 221–2.
196 For example, *Letters I*, pp. 38, 44–5, 78 n. i, 120.
197 *Letters I*, p. 141.

3 CRITICISM: JOHN RUSKIN AND MATTHEW ARNOLD

1 Raymond Williams, *Culture and Society, 1780–1950* (1961 (1958)), p. 137.
2 'They have a mania for wanting to reconcile irreconcilable things. It can be seen everywhere, in politics, in the arts, in practical life, in ideal life...Let us take the arts; what do we want from a painter? painting? Well now! we need a little morality, a little purpose, beautiful truth, truthful beauty, the real idea, ideal reality, a thousand other very commendable things of this kind. It is this evil spirit, hardly spiritual at all, which has inspired poets with the lovely idea of setting themselves up as apostles of peace reconciling the believer and the free thinker' (A. C. Swinburne, 'Matthew Arnold's New Poems' (1875 (1867)), in *Swinburne as Critic*, ed. Clyde K. Hyder (1972), p. 57).
3 'The doctrines which he taught were moral doctrines, not aesthetic doctrines, and yet he chose them on account of their beauty. And since he didn't want to present them as aesthetic but as true, he was obliged to lie to himself about the nature of the reasons which made him adopt them' (Marcel Proust, *Pastiches et Mélanges* (1947 (1919)), p. 167).
4 Virginia Woolf, *Roger Fry: A Biography* (1940), p. 280.
5 Eliot, 'Arnold and Pater' (1930), in *Selected Essays* (1972 (1932)), p. 438.
6 Ruskin, *Works*, XI, p. 46.
7 T. S. Eliot, 'Matthew Arnold' (1933), in *The Use of Poetry and the Use of Criticism: Studies in the Relation of Criticism to Poetry in England* (1948 (1933)), p. 110.
8 *Ibid.*, p. 105.
9 In a recent review of *John Ruskin's Labour: A Study of Ruskin's Social Theory* by P. D. Anthony (1984), Peter Fuller refers to the recent revival of Ruskin studies, and approves of the fact that 'Ruskin

emerges from P. D. Anthony's study as strikingly *modern*. His appeal is to a new wave of ecological, educational, ethical and aesthetic thinking...', Peter Fuller, 'Radical Toryism', *New Society*, Vol. LXVII (1 March 1984). See also Graham Hough, *The Last Romantics* (1949); Delaura, *Hebrew and Hellene in Victorian England*; William Robbins, *The Ethical Idealism of Matthew Arnold: A Study of the Nature and Sources of his Moral and Religious Ideas* (1959).

10 Eliot, 'Arnold and Pater', in *Selected Essays*, p. 434.

11 Sometimes, but not always. For example, morality does not outweigh beauty in his assessment of Holman Hunt's *Scapegoat*, of which he says in his 1856 Academy Notes, 'this may be very faithful and very wonderful painting – but it is not *good* painting; and much as I esteem feeling and thought in all works of art, still I repeat, again and again, a painter's business is first to *paint*' (*Works*, XIV, p. 65).

12 Coleridge, *On the Constitution of the Church and State*, pp. 53–4, 69. See Ben Knights, *The Idea of the Clerisy in the Nineteenth Century* (1978), Chapters 1 and 2 for an excellent account of the background to and development of Coleridge's idea of the clerisy.

13 Knights, *The Idea of the Clerisy in the Nineteenth Century*, pp. 25, 31, 35–6.

14 Matthew Arnold, *Culture and Anarchy*, Super, V, pp. 134–5 and 'Numbers; or The Majority and the Remnant', Super, X, pp. 143 ff. Cf. Knights, *The Idea of the Clerisy in the Nineteenth Century*, Chapter 4.

15 Super, X, p. 159.

16 E. T. Cook, *The Life of Ruskin* (George Allen, 1911), Vol. I, p. 473; Ruskin, *Works*, XVIII, p. 495; XXVII, pp. 167, 116–17. Cited in Alan Lee, 'Ruskin and Political Economy', in *New Approaches to Ruskin: Thirteen Essays*, ed. Robert Hewison (1981), pp. 75–6.

17 Quoted in P. Meier, *William Morris, Marxist Dreamer* (1978), p. 155.

18 *Mill on Bentham and Coleridge*, ed. F. R. Leavis (Cambridge University Press, 1980 (Chatto & Windus, 1950)), p. 167.

19 Cf. Fuller, 'Radical Toryism', and José Harris, 'Rebels against Capitalism', *The Times Literary Supplement* (31 August 1984), both reviewing Anthony, *John Ruskin's Labour*.

20 Knights, *The Idea of the Clerisy in the Nineteenth Century*, p. 3.

21 Eliot, 'Matthew Arnold', in *The Use of Poetry and the Use of Criticism*, p. 110.

22 It must be stressed, though, as John Rosenberg, Robert Hewison, Peter Fuller, and P. D. Anthony have all convincingly demonstrated, that there is only a shift of emphasis from his early aesthetic concerns to his later social writings, not a radical change of direction. His early writings on art certainly embraced social and political questions, and he remained enthusiastically committed to the arts throughout his life.

23 Ruskin, *Works*, III, p. 48; also V, p. 386 and XXIX, pp. 55–6.

24 *Ibid.*, XXXV, p. 315; also V, p. 384.
25 *Ibid.*, IV, pp. 364–5, from a posthumously published manuscript.
26 *Ibid.*, III, p. 148.
27 *Ibid.*, III, pp. 418–19.
28 *Ibid.*, IV, p. 210.
29 *Ibid.*, V, pp. 367–8.
30 Cf. Robert Hewison, *John Ruskin: The Argument of the Eye* (1976), pp. 58–62.
31 Ruskin, *Works*, IV, p. 151.
32 *Ibid.*, IV, p. 147.
33 *Ibid.*, IV, pp. 46–7.
34 *Ibid.*, IV, p. 191.
35 George Landow, *The Aesthetic and Critical Theories of John Ruskin* (1971), p. 157.
36 Ruskin, *Works*, III, p. 111.
37 *Ibid.*, IV, p. 36.
38 *Ibid.*, IV, p. 49.
39 *Ibid.*, XX, p. 49.
40 *Ibid.*, III, pp. 142–3.
41 *Ibid.*, IV, pp. 25–6, 28.
42 *Ibid.*, IV, p. 53 n.
43 *Ibid.*, IV, p. 287.
44 *Ibid.*, IV, p. 54.
45 *Ibid.*, IV, p. 257.
46 *Ibid.*, V, p. 376.
47 *Ibid.*, XVIII, p. 436.
48 John D. Rosenberg, *The Darkening Glass: A Portrait of Ruskin's Genius* (1963 (1961)), p. 12.
49 Ruskin, *Works*, XV, p. 118.
50 *Ibid.*, XIX, p. 307.
51 *Ibid.*, IV, pp. 126–7.
52 *Ibid.*, IV, p. 28.
53 *Ibid.*, XIX, p. 308.
54 *Ibid.*, XIX, p. 394 (my italics).
55 *Ibid.*, IV, p. 211.
56 *Ibid.*, VII, p. 250.
57 *Ibid.*, IX, p. 157; also IX, p. 371. Cf. Richard L. Stein, *The Ritual of Interpretation: The Fine Arts as Literature in Ruskin, Rossetti and Pater* (1975), pp. 78–9.
58 Ruskin, *Works*, IV, p. 184.
59 *Ibid.*, IV, p. 176.
60 *Ibid.*, V, p. 114.
61 *Ibid.*, III, p. 157.
62 *Ibid.*, V, p. 333.
63 *Ibid.*, XXVI, p. 334.
64 *Ibid.*, VII, p. xli.

65 *Ibid.*, XXXIV, p. 78.
66 *Ibid.*, III, p. 161.
67 *Ibid.*, III, p. 624.
68 *Ibid.*, VIII, pp. 139, 141.
69 *Ibid.*, III, p. 25.
70 Hewison, *John Ruskin: The Argument of the Eye*, p. 62.
71 Ruskin, *Works*, V, p. 125.
72 *Ibid.*, III, p. 470.
73 *Ibid.*, IV, p. 287; V, p. 125; and VI, p. 44.
74 *Ibid.*, XXXV, p. 310.
75 *Ibid.*, XXXV, p. 314. NB: this description, written forty-four years after the event, is not reliable evidence of an experience which is nowhere else documented. See Van Akin Burd, 'Another Light on the Writing of *Modern Painters*', *PMLA*, LXVIII (1953), 755–63.
76 *Ibid.*, III, p. 252.
77 *Ibid.*, XV, p. 116.
78 Cf. Ball, *The Science of Aspects*, p. 67.
79 Ruskin, *Works*, VII, p. 51.
80 *Ibid.*, III, pp. 152, 154, 469.
81 *Ibid.*, III, p. 146.
82 *Ibid.*, IV, p. 164.
83 *Ibid.*, III, p. 27.
84 *Ibid.*, V, p. 387.
85 *Journals*, p. 206.
86 *The Diaries of John Ruskin*, ed. Joan Evans and J. H. Whitehouse (1956–9), II, pp. 370–1.
87 Ruskin, *Works*, III, p. 383.
88 Cf. Ball, *The Science of Aspects*, pp. 94–6.
89 Ruskin, *Works*, XI, p. 48.
90 *Ibid.*, III, p. 104. Cf. Hewison, *John Ruskin: The Argument of the Eye*, p. 65.
91 Ruskin, *Works*, III, p. 624.
92 *Ibid.*, IV, p. 25.
93 *Ibid.*, IV, p. 36.
94 *Ibid.*, V, pp. 28–9.
95 Cf. *ibid.*, VI, p. 39 n.
96 *Ibid.*, VII, p. 234.
97 *Ibid.*, XII, p. 375.
98 *Ibid.*, VI, p. 49; also V, p. 124.
99 Cf. Hewison, *John Ruskin: The Argument of the Eye*, p. 57.
100 Ruskin, *Works*, VII, p. 233.
101 *Ibid.*, VI, p. 30.
102 *Ibid.*, XII, p. 37. For Pater also 'sympathy' was a significant virtue for the artist. By 'sympathy' he meant the growing of insight through feeling. He praises Lamb for having 'reached an enduring moral effect also, in a sort of boundless sympathy' (*Appreciations*, pp. 109–

10) and of Botticelli he says, 'His morality is all sympathy; and it is this sympathy, conveying into his work somewhat more than is usual of the true complexion of humanity, which makes him, visionary as he is, so forcible a realist' (*The Renaissance*, p. 56).

103 *Ibid.*, v, p. 359.
104 *Journals*, pp. 204, 215.
105 Ruskin, *Works*, xxxv, p. 219.
106 *Ibid.*, iv, p. 72.
107 *Ibid.*, xvi, p. 294.
108 *Ibid.*, v, p. 210.
109 *Ibid.*, iii, p. 129.
110 *Ibid.*, vii, p. 217.
111 For example, *ibid.*, v, p. 31.
112 Wilde, *Works*, p. 1029.
113 Ruskin, *Works*, iii, p. 136.
114 *Ibid.*, iv, p. 253.
115 *Ibid.*, xxxvi, p. 380, letter to Charles Eliot Norton, August 1861.
116 *Ibid.*, xii, p. 162.
117 *Ibid.*, ix, pp. 370-1.
118 *The Diaries of John Ruskin*, Vol. i, p. 74, 31 March 1840.
119 *Ibid.*, Vol. iii, p. 965, July 1877.
120 *Works*, iv, p. 224.
121 *Ibid.*, v, p. 425.
122 *Ibid.*, v, p. 201.
123 Just as he said that metaphysicians and philosophers should be brushed away like spiders (*Works*, v, p. 344), so he habitually denounced and ridiculed and tried to brush aside Darwinism. Cf. John D. Rosenberg, *The Darkening Glass: A Portrait of Ruskin's Genius* (1963 (1961)), pp. 22–45, and Hewison, *John Ruskin: The Argument of the Eye*, pp. 121–8 for the most interesting discussions of this period in Ruskin's life.
124 *Works*, xxxvi, p. 115.
125 *Ibid.*, v, p. 231.
126 *Ibid.*, vi, p. 385.
127 *Ibid.*, vii, pp. 268–9. Cf. Rosenberg's discussion of this and similar passages in *The Darkening Glass*, pp. 23–7.
128 Ruskin, *Works*, xxxiv, pp. 32–3.
129 *Ibid.*, xxxiv, pp. 10–11.
130 *Ibid.*, xxvi, p. 306.
131 *Ibid.*, xxvi, p. 305.
132 *Ibid.*, xxvi, p. 99.
133 *Ibid.*, v, p. 334.
134 *Ibid.*, xxxiv, p. 586.
135 *Ibid.*, xix, p. 57.
136 *Ibid.*, xxxvi, p. 543.

137 George Eliot, *Middlemarch: A Study of Provincial Life*, ed. Bert G. Hornback (Norton, 1977), p. 289.

138 *The Letters of Matthew Arnold, 1848–1888*, ed. G. W. E. Russell (1895), Vol. I, p. 200 (13 October 1863, to his mother).

139 *Ibid.*, Vol. I, p. 196 (16 June 1863, to his mother).

140 Super, III, pp. 250–2.

141 *The Notebooks of Matthew Arnold*, ed. Howard Foster Lowry, Karl Young, and Waldo Hilary Dunn (1952), p. 559.

142 *Ibid.*, p. 210 (from *Modern Painters*, III.i.i).

143 Super, VII, p. 385.

144 Roger L. Brooks, 'Some Unaccomplished Projects of Matthew Arnold', *Studies in Bibliography*, XVI (1963), 213–16.

145 From 'On Poetry' in Super, IX, p. 63. See also the chapter on 'The God of Metaphysics' in *God and the Bible*, Super, VII.

146 Super, III, p. 258.

147 Kenneth Allott, 'Matthew Arnold's Reading Lists in Three Early Diaries', *Victorian Studies* (March 1959). NB: Alan Harris, in 'Matthew Arnold: the Unknown Years', in *The Nineteenth Century and After*, Vol. CXIII (1933), 503, had previously drawn attention to the surprisingly wide-ranging philosophical content of these early diaries.

148 Allott, 'Matthew Arnold's Reading Lists', 258, 262, 263.

149 *Ibid.*, 263–4.

150 A. W. Benn, *The History of English Rationalism in the Nineteenth Century* (1906), Vol. II, p. 55.

151 Allott, 'Matthew Arnold's Reading Lists', 261 n.

152 *The Letters of Matthew Arnold to Arthur Hugh Clough*, ed. Howard Foster Lowry (1932), pp. 116–17 (23 October 1850).

153 Super, III, p. 181.

154 *The Notebooks of Matthew Arnold*, p. 7 (from Kuno Fischer, *Francis Bacon*, pp. 498–9).

155 *Ibid.*, pp. 214, 215.

156 *Ibid.*, p. 284 (from T. H. Green, 'Mr Herbert Spencer and Mr G. H. Lewes', the *Contemporary Review* (December 1877), Vol. XXXI, 26–34).

157 Warren, *English Poetic Theory, 1825–1865*, p. 155.

158 'Matthew Arnold, by one who knew him well', *Manchester Guardian* (18 May 1888).

159 *A Choice of Kipling's Verse*, ed. T. S. Eliot (1941), p. 7.

160 Super, X, p. 165.

161 William A. Madden, *Matthew Arnold: A Study of the Aesthetic Temperament in Victorian England* (1967), p. 70.

162 Arnold, *Poems*, 75, lines 67–90.

163 *Ibid.*, p. 519.

164 *The Letters of Matthew Arnold to Arthur Hugh Clough*, p. 111 (23 September 1849).

165 *The Letters of Matthew Arnold, 1848–1888*, Vol. II, p. 9 (5 June 1869).
166 *The Letters of Matthew Arnold to Arthur Hugh Clough*, p. 99 (Friday [early part of February] 1849).
167 *Ibid.*, p. 126 (14 December 1852).
168 Arnold, *Poems*, 59, lines 21–37.
169 *Ibid.*, 34, lines 9–16; 35, lines 59–66; 37, lines 19–24.
170 Although Arnold was concerned with the implications of evolution. Cf. *Poems*, p. 56 n, for the final stanza of 'In Utrumque Paratus' in the 1869 edition, and *Poems*, 47.I.ii, lines 177–81.
171 Lionel Trilling, *Matthew Arnold* (1949 (1939)), p. 92. Trilling considers this question of the challenge posed by Kant to his Victorian successors in his characteristically stimulating way. Cf. Chapters 3 and 4. Howard W. Fulweiler in *Letters from the Darkling Plain: Language and the Grounds of Knowledge* (1972), pp. 19–23, suggests that the conflicts and doubts experienced by both Arnold and Hopkins concerning the role of poetry in the modern world stemmed from the philosophical dilemma over whether reality should be defined in a Lockean way, as external, or in a Kantian way, as internal.
172 S. T. Coleridge, 'Dejection: An Ode', st. IV.
173 Arnold, *Poems*, 62, lines 1–2.
174 *Ibid.*, 61, lines 8–12.
175 *Ibid.*, 61, lines 14 and 58.
176 *Ibid.*, 61, lines 59–74 and 75–90.
177 *Ibid.*, 62, lines 27–37.
178 *Ibid.*, 62, lines 116–18.
179 *Ibid.*, 61, lines 103–7.
180 *Ibid.*, 47, II, lines 370–2.
181 *Ibid.*, 43, lines 31–2. Cf. also *The Letters of Matthew Arnold to Arthur Hugh Clough*, p. 130.
182 *The Letters of Matthew Arnold to Arthur Hugh Clough*, p. 89 (12 August 1848).
183 Super, I, p. 33.
184 Trilling, *Matthew Arnold*, pp. 112–30.
185 Arnold, *Poems*, 47, I, ii, lines 127–8.
186 *Ibid.*, 68, lines 38–44.
187 *Ibid.*, 68, lines 47–8.
188 *Ibid.*, 39, lines 93–6.
189 *Ibid.*, 47, II, lines 198–219.
190 *Ibid.*, 47, II, lines 220–34.
191 Cf. William Madden's view also, that Arnold makes it clear in the poem that the true function of the mind in the modern world is that assigned to it by Pausanias. He argues that henceforth Arnold's aesthetic consciousness would express itself in Pausanian poems of morality and in criticism. *Matthew Arnold: A Study of the Aesthetic Temperament in Victorian England*, p. 97.

192 Like Maurice de Guérin. Cf. Super, III, p. 30.
193 Arnold, *Poems*, 20, lines 232–4.
194 *Ibid.*, 78, lines 161–3.
195 *Ibid.*, 78, lines 221 and 169.
196 *Ibid.*, 22, lines 144–7.
197 *Ibid.*, 22, lines 189–92.
198 Trilling, *Matthew Arnold*, p. 135.
199 Arnold, *Poems*, 39, lines 103–4 and 137.
200 Fulweiler, *Letters from the Darkling Plain*, p. 82.
201 Madden, *Matthew Arnold: A Study of the Aesthetic Temperament in Victorian England*, pp. 129–30.
202 *The Letters of Matthew Arnold to Arthur Hugh Clough*, p. 104 (March 1849).
203 Cf. Trilling, *Matthew Arnold*, pp. 134–5, and Madden, *Matthew Arnold: A Study of the Aesthetic Temperament in Victorian England*, pp. 27–33.
204 Andrew Lang, 'Matthew Arnold', *The Century Magazine* (April 1882), Vol. XXIII, 863.
205 Miller, *The Disappearance of God*, p. 222.
206 Trilling, *Matthew Arnold*, p. 18.
207 Vincent Buckley, *Poetry and Morality: Studies on the Criticism of Matthew Arnold, T. S. Eliot and F. R. Leavis* (1959), p. 44.
208 *The Notebooks of Matthew Arnold*, p. 63 (from Wordsworth, letter to Lady Beaumont (21 May 1807), *Memoirs*, i.339).
209 *Ibid.*, p. 329 (from Wordsworth, letter to Lady Beaumont (21 May 1807), *Prose Works*, ii.176).
210 *The Life of Edward Bulwer, first Lord Lytton, by his Grandson* (1913), Vol. II, p. 446. Quoted in Madden, *Matthew Arnold: A Study of the Aesthetic Temperament in Victorian England*, pp. 12–13. The Introduction to this book is extremely useful for an understanding of the aesthetic influences on Arnold during this period.
211 Quoted in Madden, *Matthew Arnold: A Study of the Aesthetic Temperament in Victorian England*, pp. 12 and 11, from *Works of Thomas Carlyle* (1898), Vol. XXVII, p. 213, and XXV, p. 200.
212 *The Letters of Matthew Arnold to Arthur Hugh Clough*, p. 124 (28 October 1852).
213 See for example A. Dwight Culler, *Imaginative Reason: The Poetry of Matthew Arnold* (1966), R. K. Biswas, *Arthur Hugh Clough: Towards a Reconsideration* (1972), and Warren, *English Poetic Theory, 1825–1865*.
214 There are a number of interesting studies of Arnold's relationship with Romanticism, for example, W. A. Jamison, *Arnold and the Romantics* (1958), David G. James, *Matthew Arnold and the Decline of English Romanticism* (1961), and Leon Gottfried, *Matthew Arnold and the Romantics* (Routledge & Kegan Paul, 1963).
215 Warren, *English Poetic Theory, 1825–1865*, p. 152.

216 David J. Delaura, *Victorian Prose: A Guide to Research* (1973), p. 295.
217 *The Letters of Matthew Arnold to Arthur Hugh Clough*, pp. 98–9 (February 1849).
218 *Ibid.*, p. 124 (28 October 1852).
219 *Ibid.*, pp. 98–9 (Friday [early part of February] 1849).
220 *Ibid.*, p. 139 (3 August 1853).
221 *Ibid.*, p. 100 (1 March 1849).
222 *Hegel's Aesthetics: Lectures on Fine Art*, Vol. I, p. 517.
223 Eliot, 'Arnold and Pater', in *Selected Essays*, p. 436, and 'Matthew Arnold', in *The Use of Poetry and the Use of Criticism*, p. 113.
224 See Michael Timco, 'Corydon Had a Rival', in *Victorian Newsletter* (1961), for an example of the first view, and Biswas, *Arthur Hugh Clough: Towards a Reconsideration*, p. 213, for the second.
225 Biswas, *Arthur Hugh Clough: Towards a Reconsideration*, p. 214.
226 *Unpublished Letters of Matthew Arnold*, ed. Arnold Whitridge (1923), p. 17 (to his sister). Cf. also *The Letters of Matthew Arnold to Arthur Hugh Clough*, p. 66 (24 February 1848); p. 81 (24 May 1848); p. 89 (12 August 1848).
227 *The Letters of Matthew Arnold to Arthur Hugh Clough*, p. 146 (30 November 1853).
228 *Ibid.*, pp. 96–7 (Monday [after September, 1848–9]).
229 *Ibid.*, p. 88 (12 August 1848), from 'Resolution and Independence'; p. 110 (23 September 1849).
230 Super, I, p. 215.
231 Buckley, *Poetry and Morality*, p. 69.
232 *The Letters of Matthew Arnold to Arthur Hugh Clough*, p. 144 (10 October 1853).
233 Super, I, p. 2.
234 *Ibid.*, I, p. 8.
235 *Ibid.*, I, pp. 4–5.
236 *Ibid.*, I, p. 9.
237 For example, Sidney M. B. Coulling, 'Matthew Arnold's 1853 Preface: Its Origin and Aftermath', *Victorian Studies* (1964).
238 Cf. R. G. Fox, 'Victorian Criticism of Poetry: The Minority Tradition', *Scrutiny* (1951), cited in Delaura, *Victorian Prose: A Guide to Research*, p. 295.
239 See, for example, Warren, *English Poetic Theory, 1825–1865* and James, *Matthew Arnold and the Decline of English Romanticism*.
240 *Essays and Studies by Members of the English Association* (John Murray, 1968), cited in Delaura, *Victorian Prose: A Guide to Research*, p. 295.
241 Super, I, p. 15 (my italics).
242 *The Letters of Matthew Arnold, 1848–1888*, I, p. 73 (to Mrs Forster, 6 September 1858).

243 Kenneth Allott, 'A Background for "Empedocles on Etna"', *Essays and Studies* (1968), 99.

244 *Letters I*, p. 172.

245 Cf. Trilling, *Matthew Arnold*, p. 190, where he cites Eliot as saying that the academic literary opinions of our time were formed by Arnold, and considers some examples of nineteenth- and twentieth-century critics who were influenced by Arnold.

246 Super, IX, p. 224.

247 Cf. Ruskin, *Works*, XIII, p. 144; XXXIV, p. 44; XXXV, p. 144; V, pp. 25–6; XV, p. 227.

248 Super, XI, p. 327.

249 Arnold, *Poems*, 75, lines 139–44.

250 Cf. Ruskin, *Works*, XII, p. 121; V, p. 374; XXXIV, p. 343; XII, p. 121.

251 Eliot, 'Matthew Arnold', in *The Use of Poetry and the Use of Criticism*, p. 110.

252 Buckley, *Poetry and Morality*, p. 46.

253 Helen Gardner, 'The Drunkenness of Noah', in *The Business of Criticism* (1959), pp. 85–6.

254 *The Notebooks of Matthew Arnold*, pp. 18, 29, 40, 117, 341.

255 Super, VIII, p. 370.

256 *Ibid.*, III, p. 33.

257 *Ibid.*, IX, p. 62.

258 *Ibid.*, VIII, p. 1.

259 *Ibid.*, IX, p. 161.

260 Buckley, *Poetry and Morality*, p. 86.

261 Super, III, p. 209. See also *ibid.*, IX, 'Wordsworth' and 'The Study of Poetry' for Arnold's later use of this phrase with reference to poetry.

262 Super, XI, p. 279.

263 *Ibid.*, III, p. 258.

264 *Ibid.*, III, p. 261

265 *Ibid.*, III, p. 283.

266 *Ibid.*, V, pp. 233–4. Cf. Williams, *Culture and Society, 1780–1950*, pp. 121–3.

267 Super, V, p. 235.

268 *Ibid.*, V, pp. 163–5.

269 *The Letters of Matthew Arnold, 1848–1888*, Vol. II, p. 13.

270 See, for example, Delaura, *Hebrew and Hellene in Victorian England*; Richard Jenkyns, *The Victorians and Ancient Greece* (1980); Frank M. Turner, *The Greek Heritage in Victorian Britain* (1981).

271 Delaura, *Hebrew and Hellene in Victorian England*, p. 172. Quotations from *The Letters of Matthew Arnold, 1848–1888*, Vol. I, p. 360 (November 1865) and Vol. I, p. 287 (January 1865).

272 Jenkyns, *The Victorians and Ancient Greece*, p. 266.

273 *Ibid.*, p. 271.

274 *Ibid.*, p. 273.

275 Super, VIII, p. 162.
276 *Ibid.*, VI, pp. 124–5.
277 *Ibid.*, V, p. 178.
278 *Ibid.*, III, p. 56.
279 *Ibid.*, III, pp. 122 and 127–8.
280 *Ibid.*, VII, p. 388.
281 *Ibid.*, I, p. 60.
282 *Ibid.*, I, pp. 197–216.
283 *Ibid.*, III, pp. 225 and 230.
284 *Ibid.*, V, pp. 134–5.
285 *Ibid.*, V, p. 146.
286 Culler, *The Imperial Intellect: A Study of Newman's Educational Ideal*, p. 234.
287 Newman, *Apologia Pro Vita Sua*, ed. A. Dwight Culler (Riverside, 1956), pp. xvii–xviii.
288 But notice Lionel Trilling's very wise reminder: 'The beginning student of politics, the beginning student of philosophy, will explain at once the impossibility of ever seeing the object as it really is; nor was Arnold so naive as to think that in practical life, let alone in the metaphysics he hated, it could easily, or always, or completely be seen. But the limitations of men exist in varying degrees; surely it is not the limitation itself but the worship of limitation which is degrading' (*Matthew Arnold*, Introductory Note).
289 Super, VII, p. 144.
290 *Ibid.*, V, pp. 88–9.
291 *Ibid.*, V, p. 91.
292 *Ibid.*, V, p. 93.
293 *Ibid.*, V, p. 94.
294 *Ibid.*, VI, p. 409.
295 *Ibid.*, VI, p. 201.
296 *Ibid.*, VI, p. 151.
297 E. Abbott and L. Campbell, *The Life and Letters of Benjamin Jowett, M.A.* (1897), Vol. I, p. 345.
298 *The Notebooks of Matthew Arnold*, p. 284 (quoted from T. H. Green, 'Mr. Herbert Spencer and Mr. G. H. Lewes', the *Contemporary Review* (December 1877), Vol. XXXI, 34).
299 See Anthony Ward, *Walter Pater: The Idea in Nature*, pp. 43–52 for an interesting discussion of Darwin and Hegel.
300 Cf. n. 158 above.
301 Quoted in Park Honan, *Matthew Arnold: A Life* (1981), p. 364.
302 Trilling, *Matthew Arnold*, p. 324. Notice a similar distinction made between the speculative and the moral in 'Dr. Stanley's Lectures on the Jewish Church', Super, III.
303 Super, III, p. 162.
304 *Ibid.*, III, p. 181, and *The Letters of Matthew Arnold to Arthur Hugh Clough*, p. 117 (23 October 1850). Cf. Robbins, *The Ethical Idealism*

of Matthew Arnold, pp. 63–9, for a full account of the critical ideas common to Arnold and Spinoza.

305 See Merton A. Christensen, 'Thomas Arnold's Debt to German Theologians: A Prelude to Matthew Arnold's *Literature and Dogma*', *Modern Philology* (1957). Cf. also R. A. Forsyth, *The Lost Pattern: Essays on the Emergent City Sensibility in Victorian England* (1976), Chapter 9, for a detailed account of Dr Arnold's historicism.

306 *The Letters of Matthew Arnold, 1848–1888*, Vol. II, p. 201 (to Sir Mountstuart Grant Duff, 29 July 1882).

307 The *Guardian* (29 June 1870), quoted in Honan, *Matthew Arnold: A Life*, p. 365.

308 Super, III, p. 57.

309 *Ibid.*, VII, p. 193.

310 *Ibid.*, VII, p. 203.

311 *Ibid.*, VIII, p. 146.

312 *The Notebooks of Matthew Arnold*, p. 75 (from Victor Cherbuliez, 'Lessing', *Revue des Deux Mondes* (15 February 1868), Vol. LXXIII, 2nd period, 995).

313 See his essay on Colenso, 'The Bishop and the Philosopher', in Super, III. His alarm at the potential cost of truth is very apparent here where he fears loss of faith for the masses.

314 Super, VI, p. 20.

315 *Ibid.*, VI, p. 21.

316 *Ibid.*, VII, pp. 510 and 503. NB: Newman objected to Arnold's suggestion here that the Bible should be presented primarily as literature, although he admitted that religion was presented to young minds in the garb of poetry. See *The Letters and Diaries of John Henry Newman*, ed. Dessain *et al.*, Vol. XXVI, p. 95 (24 May 1872).

317 Super, VII, p. 378.

318 *Ibid.*, VI, pp. 142–3.

319 *Ibid.*, VI, p. 151.

320 *Ibid.*, VI, p. 152.

321 *Ibid.*, VI, p. 171.

322 *Ibid.*, VIII, p. 135.

323 Cf. for example Coleridge, *Confessions of an Inquiring Spirit: Letters on the Inspiration of the Scriptures*, ed. Henry Nelson Coleridge (1840).

324 *The Letters of Matthew Arnold, 1848–1888*, Vol. II, p. 23 (13 November 1869).

325 Super, III, pp. 40–1.

326 *Ibid.*, VIII, p. 135.

327 Prickett, *Romanticism and Religion*, p. 219.

328 Super, VI, p. 144.

329 Cf. Robbins, *The Ethical Idealism of Matthew Arnold*, p. 39.

330 Super, III, p. 134.

331 *Ibid.*, III, pp. 136 and 149.

332 Arnold, *Poems*, 101, lines 1–2 and 14.
333 *Ibid.*, 104, lines 9–14.
334 *The Letters of Matthew Arnold, 1848–1888*, Vol. I, p. 42 (to his mother, 27 February 1855).
335 Super, VIII, p. 67.
336 *Ibid.*, VI, p. 173. Cf. also VIII, p. 153.
337 *Ibid.*, VI, p. 176. Cf. also I, p. 63.
338 *Ibid.*, VI, p. 176.
339 Eliot, 'Arnold and Pater', in *Selected Essays*, p. 434.
340 In the case of T. S. Eliot and Hoxie Neale Fairchild, for example.
341 Trilling, *Matthew Arnold*, p. 340.
342 A. O. J. Cockshut, *The Unbelievers: English Agnostic Thought, 1840–1890* (1964), p. 63.
343 *Ibid.*, p. 172.
344 Super, VI, p. 196.
345 *Ibid.*, VI, p. 31.
346 Cf. Clement C. J. Webb, *A Century of Anglican Theology* (Basil Blackwell, 1923) and Robbins, *The Ethical Idealism of Matthew Arnold*, p. 173.
347 Super, VI, p. 189.
348 *Ibid.*, III, p. 364.
349 *Ibid.*, VI, pp. 181–91, 189.
350 Trilling, *Matthew Arnold*, pp. 358–9. Cf. also Delaura, *Hebrew and Hellene in Victorian England*, p. 78.
351 Cf. for example Newman, *Discourses Addressed to Mixed Congregations*, x, 'Faith and Private Judgement', and *Discussions and Arguments*, 'The Tamworth Reading Room'.
352 See Delaura, *Hebrew and Hellene in Victorian England*, for an extensive account of how Arnold used and abused Newman.
353 Super, VI, pp. 212–13.
354 *Ibid.*, VI, p. 231.
355 *Ibid.*, VI, p. 232.
356 *Ibid.*, VII, p. 397.
357 *Ibid.*, VII, p. 397.
358 *Ibid.*, VI, p. 378.
359 Hoxie Neale Fairchild, *Religious Trends in English Poetry*, Vol. IV, *Christianity and Romanticism in the Victorian Era, 1830–1880* (1957), p. 503.
360 Super, I, p. 17.
361 Cf. for example *ibid.*, V, p. 100; *The Notebooks of Matthew Arnold*, p. 27.
362 Super, III, p. 214.
363 *Ibid.*, VI, p. 144.
364 *Ibid.*, VI, p. 304.
365 *Ibid.*, VII, p. 396.

366 *The Letters of Matthew Arnold, 1848–1888*, Vol. II, p. 132.
367 Super, VIII, p. 333.
368 *Ibid.*, VIII, p. 334; also p. 162.
369 *Ibid.*, VIII, p. 86.
370 *Ibid.*, IX, p. 63.
371 *Ibid.*, IX, p. 161.
372 *Ibid.*, IX, p. 39.
373 *Ibid.*, IX, pp. 45–9.
374 Buckley, *Poetry and Morality*, pp. 27–8.
375 *The Letters of Matthew Arnold to Arthur Hugh Clough*, p. 115 (Tuesday, May 1850).
376 Super, IX, p. 161.
377 Cf. for example Buckley, *Poetry and Morality*, p. 48.
378 Eliot, 'Arnold and Pater', in *Selected Essays*, p. 434.
379 Eliot, 'Matthew Arnold', in *The Use of Poetry and the Use of Criticism*, p. 113.
380 *Ibid.*, p. 118.
381 Eliot, 'Arnold and Pater', in *Selected Essays*, p. 436.

4 AESTHETICISM: WALTER PATER AND OSCAR WILDE

1 Trilling, *Matthew Arnold* (1949 (1939)), p. 315.
2 Wilde, *Works*, p. 975.
3 Trilling, *Matthew Arnold*, p. 316.
4 *Essays from the Guardian*, p. 70.
5 *Ibid.*, p. 62.
6 *Ibid.*, p. 66.
7 *Ibid.*, p. 67.
8 *Letters of Walter Pater*, ed. Lawrence Evans (1970), p. 64.
9 *Essays from the Guardian*, pp. 67–8.
10 Quoted *ibid.*, p. 69.
11 *Ibid.*, p. 69.
12 Wilde, *Works*, p. 975.
13 *Ibid.*, p. 974.
14 *Ibid.*, p. 1205.
15 *Ibid.*, p. 1012.
16 *Ibid.*, p. 990.
17 Super, VI, p. 176; also IX, p. 63.
18 *Ibid.*, III, pp. 136, 149.
19 *Marius*, II, Chapter 18.
20 *Walter Pater: Essays on Literature and Art*, ed. Jennifer Uglow (1973), p. 143.
21 *Ibid.*, p. 144.
22 Wilde, *Works*, pp. 1058, 981, 1048, 1205, 1021–2.
23 See, for example, Eliot, 'Arnold and Pater' in *Selected Essays*, and Delaura, *Hebrew and Hellene in Victorian England*.

24 'The Ballad of Reading Gaol', Wilde, *Works*, pp. 843–60.
25 Edmund Gosse, *Critical Kit-Kats* (1896), p. 247.
26 Solomon Fishman, *The Interpretation of Art: Essays on the Art Criticism of John Ruskin, Walter Pater, Clive Bell, Roger Fry, and Herbert Read* (1963), pp. 59–60.
27 Wilde, *Works*, pp. 1028–9.
28 *The Letters of Oscar Wilde*, ed. Rupert Hart-Davis (1962), p. 218, May, 1888.
29 W. B. Yeats, 'The Trembling of the Veil', in *Autobiographies* (1955), p. 130.
30 See n. 182 below.
31 *Walter Pater: Essays on Literature and Art*, p. 142.
32 Richard Ellmann, *Golden Codgers: Biographical Speculations* (1973), p. 53.
33 *The Oxford Book of Modern Verse, 1892–1935*, ed. W. B. Yeats (1936), p. ix.
34 Wilde, *Works*, pp. 977–8.
35 *The Renaissance*, p. viii.
36 Wilde, *Works*, p. 1030.
37 Williams, *Culture and Society 1780–1950*, p. 165.
38 See Ian Britain's stimulating *Fabianism and Culture: A Study in British Socialism and the Arts c. 1884–1918* (1982).
39 Wilde, *Works*, pp. 1079–89.
40 *Ibid.*, p. 1088. This emasculated idea of the State points to an important difference between Wilde's Socialism and Fabian Socialism.
41 F. Darwin, *The Life and Letters of Charles Darwin* (3 vols., 1887), Vol. I, p. 309, quoted in Forsyth, *The Lost Pattern*, p. 102.
42 Herbert Spencer, *First Principles* (1863), p. 148. The substance of Chapter 2, 'The Law of Evolution', is nearly identical with the first half of the essay entitled 'Progress: Its Law and Cause', the *Westminster Review* (April 1857). NB: Sidney Webb believed Socialism to be the inevitable result of the evolution of democracy – an interesting example of the political appropriation of evolutionary principles. For a full discussion of the 'Age of Evolutionism' see Tom Gibbons, *Rooms in the Darwin Hotel: Studies in English Literary Criticism and Ideas 1880–1920* (1973). Cf. also J. W. Burrow, *Evolution and Society: A Study in Victorian Social Theory* (1966).
43 Wilde, *Works*, p. 1058.
44 *Plato and Platonism*, pp. 19–21.
45 *The Renaissance*, p. 233.
46 *Ibid.*, p. 234.
47 *Ibid.*, p. 235.
48 *Ibid.*, p. 235.
49 *Ibid.*, pp. 236–8.

50 *Ibid.*, p. viii.
51 Pater, *Uncollected Essays* (1903), p. 108.
52 *Appreciations*, p. 55.
53 *Ibid.*, p. 8.
54 *Ibid.*, pp. 9–10.
55 *Plato and Platonism*, pp. 124–5.
56 *The Renaissance*, p. 71.
57 *Appreciations*, p. 43.
58 *The Renaissance*, p. 51.
59 *Appreciations*, p. 10.
60 *Ibid.*, p. 35.
61 *The Renaissance*, p. 211.
62 Harold Bloom, *The Ringers in the Tower: Studies in Romantic Tradition* (1971), p. 190.
63 Wilde, *Works*, p. 1090.
64 *Ibid.*, pp. 991, 1049.
65 *Ibid.*, p. 1045.
66 *The Artist as Critic: Critical Writings of Oscar Wilde*, ed. Richard Ellmann (1969 (1968)), p. 248. From a letter to the Editor of the *Scots Observer*.
67 Wilde, *Works*, p. 1029.
68 *Ibid.*, pp. 1047, 1078.
69 *Ibid.*, p. 1028.
70 *Ibid.*, p. 874.
71 Coleridge, *Biographia Literaria*, Vol. I, p. 304.
72 *Walter Pater: Essays on Literature and Art*, p. 143.
73 Quoted in Wilde, *The Artist as Critic*, p. 237.
74 *Ibid.*, p. 245.
75 *Ibid.*, p. 248.
76 Wilde, *Works*, p. 1007.
77 *Ibid.*, p. 1018.
78 *Ibid.*, p. 1060.
79 *Ibid.*, p. 1048.
80 *Ibid.*, p. 1042.
81 Wilde, *The Artist as Critic*, p. xxvii.
82 *Ibid.*, p. 240.
83 *Ibid.*, p. 246.
84 Wilde, *Works*, p. 934.
85 Cf. his explanation of why he had suppressed the Conclusion in the 2nd edition of *The Renaissance* (1877): 'I conceived it might mislead some of those young men into whose hands it might fall' (Preface to 1888 edition of *The Renaissance*).
86 According to the notoriously unreliable Thomas Wright, in *The Life of Walter Pater* (1907), Vol. II, p. 87.
87 Cf. for example, Ruth C. Child, *The Aesthetic of Walter Pater* (1940), p. 10.

88 Eliot, 'Arnold and Pater', in *Selected Essays*, pp. 438–9. Cf. also Delaura, *Hebrew and Hellene in Victorian England*, for a more sympathetic account of Pater as a moralist.
89 Eliot, 'Arnold and Pater', in *Selected Essays*, p. 439.
90 *Miscellaneous Studies*, p. 250.
91 *Ibid.*, p. 253.
92 *Ibid.*, p. 253.
93 Jan B. Gordon, '"Decadent Spaces": Notes for a Phenomenology of the Fin de Siècle', in Stratford Upon Avon Studies, 17, *Decadence and the Eighteen-Nineties*, ed. Ian Fletcher (1979), p. 47.
94 *Journals*, p. 80.
95 *Plato and Platonism*, p. 282.
96 *The Renaissance*, p. 179.
97 Frank Kermode, *Romantic Image* (1961 (1957)), p. 20.
98 *Appreciations*, p. 59.
99 *Ibid.*, p. 62.
100 *Ibid.*, p. 184.
101 *The Renaissance*, p. xiii.
102 Newman, *The Idea of a University*, p. 276.
103 *Appreciations*, p. 22.
104 See Anthony Ward, *Walter Pater: The Idea in Nature*, pp. 43–80, for a rewarding discussion of Hegel's influence on Pater.
105 *Hegel's Aesthetics: Lectures on Fine Art*, Vol. I, p. 517.
106 *Ibid.*, Vol. I, p. 521.
107 *The Renaissance*, pp. 205–6.
108 *Ibid.*, p. 206.
109 *Ibid.*, p. 135.
110 'Mr Pater's Last Volume', in Wilde, *The Artist as Critic*, p. 234.
111 Wilde, *Works*, pp. 1031, 919–20.
112 'The Butterfly's Boswell', in Wilde, *The Artist as Critic*, pp. 65–8.
113 Wilde, *Works*, p. 1019.
114 Wilde, *The Artist as Critic*, p. 149.
115 Wilde, *Works*, p. 1030.
116 *The Renaissance*, pp. 226–7.
117 Wilde, *Works*, p. 931.
118 *Ibid.*, pp. 1085–7, 1104.
119 *The Renaissance*, p. 30.
120 Wilde, *Works*, pp. 1147–8.
121 *Ibid.*, pp. 924–5.
122 Cf. David Anthony Downes, *The Temper of Victorian Belief: Studies in the Religious Novels of Pater, Kingsley, and Newman* (1972), p. 8.
123 Wilde, *Works*, p. 1052.
124 *The Letters of Oscar Wilde*, pp. 31–3, March 1877. NB: it is perhaps significant that St Stephen's was a Conservative club.
125 *Ibid.*, p. 34, late March 1877, 2 April 1877.
126 *Ibid.*, p. 819, late March 1900.

127 *Ibid.*, p. 821, 16 April 1900.
128 *Ibid.*, p. 823, 21 April 1900.
129 *Ibid.*, p. 828, 14 May 1900.
130 For example, Archibald Noel Locke MacCall, David Hunter-Blair, Alexander Dennistoun Lang, Archibald Claude Dunlop were converted, while others, like Dean Miles, were 'very advanced' Anglicans.
131 See *The Letters of Oscar Wilde*, pp. 14 n, 43.
132 *Ibid.*, pp. 32, 12.
133 *Ibid.*, p. 831, 29 June 1900.
134 H. Montgomery Hyde, *Oscar Wilde* (1977 (1976)), p. 470.
135 *The Letters of Oscar Wilde*, p. 43, 16 June 1877.
136 Wilde, *Works*, p. 915.
137 Hyde, *Oscar Wilde*, p. 458.
138 Cf. *Oscar Wilde: Interviews and Recollections*, ed. E. H. Mikhail (2 vols., Macmillan, 1979), Vol. II, p. 473, and Hyde, *Oscar Wilde*, p. 477.
139 Cf. Arthur Symons and T. S. Eliot for the former view, and James Joyce, Hart Crane, and most notably G. Wilson Knight for the latter.
140 Wilde, *Works*, p. 728. NB: there is evidence to suggest that these lines were a later interpolation. See Aatos Ojala, *Aestheticism and Oscar Wilde*, Part 1 (1954), pp. 158–71.
141 Wilde, *Works*, p. 727.
142 *Ibid.*, p. 801.
143 See Ellmann, *Golden Codgers*, for an interesting discussion of the opposing spirits in these three works.
144 Cf. Hesketh Pearson, *The Life of Oscar Wilde* (1946), pp. 136, 217.
145 W. B. Yeats, *Autobiographies* (Macmillan, 1955), p. 286.
146 Michael Levey, *The Case of Walter Pater* (1978), p. 85.
147 'Poems by William Morris', the *Westminster Review*, N.S. Vol. XXXIV (1868), 302. Greek translation from Theocritus, *Works*, trans. A. F. S. Gow (2 vols., Cambridge University Press, 1952 (1950)), Vol. I, Idyll 2.17.
148 Pater, 'Coleridge's Writings', the *Westminster Review* (January, 1866), 126–7.
149 William Sharp, 'Some Personal Reminiscences of Walter Pater', *Atlantic Monthly*, Vol. LXXIV (1894), 881. Pater himself, in a letter to Violet Paget of 22 July 1883, refers to *Marius the Epicurean* as an 'Imaginary Portrait'. Marius is a fictional character, and cannot, therefore, always be assumed to speak for Pater. Nevertheless, most critics agree in finding autobiographical elements in the novel: 'No one can fail to catch the autobiographical note of *Marius* who will compare the present book with its predecessors' (Mrs Humphrey Ward, '*Marius the Epicurean*', *Macmillan's Magazine*, June 1885, 134); 'The book bears from first to last a strong personal, almost autobiographical impress' (A. C. Benson, *Walter Pater* (1906),

p. 91); 'We may safely conclude, I suppose, that the final position of Marius was also that of his creator' (Hough, *The Last Romantics* (1961 (1949)), p. 154); and Lawrence Evans, in his introduction to the *Letters of Walter Pater*, refers to *Marius the Epicurean* as a part of Pater's '*Apologia Pro Vita Sua*' and 'the indirect statement of his mature philosophy of life'. The best and most recent account of the autobiographical nature of Pater's work is Gerald Monsman's *Walter Pater's Art of Autobiography* (1980).

150 Eliot, *Selected Essays* (1972 (1932)), p. 441.

151 Wright, *The Life of Walter Pater*, Vol. I, p. 201. NB: as mentioned in n. 86 above, this biography is widely regarded as unreliable.

152 'Marius, far from being drawn to Christianity by ceremony...was drawn to it precisely by the sense of a community bound together in charity' (Hough, *The Last Romantics*, p. 154). 'There is more to the religion of this chapter ['The Minor Peace of the Church'] than Winckelmannian or Goethean Hellenism in blasphemous disguise for this is not merely Arnold's culture in its more religious mood. I believe that when Pater makes "a cheerful temper" the special quality of Christian character [*ME* II, 123], he is reflecting Arnold's more deeply moral conviction, in the religious writings, that "Christianity is, first and above all, a temper, a disposition"' (Delaura, *Hebrew and Hellene in Victorian England*, p. 282).

153 I am aware that David Delaura proposes that 'the religion of *Marius* represents...a merger of Arnold's Hellenism and his Christianity of mildness and sweet reasonableness' (*Hebrew and Hellene in Victorian England*, p. 284). Yet even here the argument is for a somewhat uneasy coexistence of two essentially unrelated qualities in Pater's Christianity, rather than for a deeper unity.

154 *Appreciations*, pp. 103–4. Pater preferred the 'scientific truth' of Winckelmann and da Vinci to the less tangible metaphysics and 'absolute formulas' of Coleridge. Cf. Jan B. Gordon, '"Decadent Spaces"', in *Decadence and the Eighteen–Nineties*, ed. Fletcher, p. 41.

155 *The Renaissance*, p. 33.

156 *Ibid.*, p. 203.

157 *Appreciations*, p. 103.

158 Newman, *Apologia Pro Vita Sua*, p. 377.

159 *Marius*, I, pp. 155–6.

160 *Ibid.*, II, p. 126.

161 Benson, *Walter Pater*, p. 111.

162 *Marius*, I, pp. 138–9.

163 Newman, *An Essay on the Development of Christian Doctrine*, pp. 55–6.

164 Hopkins, *Poems*, 28.

165 *Sermons*, p. 123.

166 *Marius*, I, p. 52.

167 *Ibid.*, I, p. 53.

168 *Ibid.*, I, p. 234.
169 *Ibid.*, I, p. 155.
170 *Ibid.*, I, p. 123.
171 *Ibid.*, I, p. 132.
172 Tennyson, 'In Memoriam A.H.H.', LVI.
173 Hopkins, *Poems*, 72.
174 *Marius*, II, p. 14.
175 *Ibid.*, I, p. 233.
176 *Ibid.*, II, pp. 66–70.
177 *Sermons*, p. 154.
178 *Marius*, II, pp. 11–12.
179 *Miscellaneous Studies*, p. 187.
180 *Appreciations*, p. 212.
181 *Marius*, II, p. 123.
182 There are of course significant distinctions between Pater's and Arnold's Hellenism. See Delaura, *Hebrew and Hellene in Victorian England*, pp. 171–81, 281–3, for a detailed account. See also Jenkyns, *The Victorians and Ancient Greece* for a wider discussion of Hellenism in the nineteenth century.
183 *Marius*, II, pp. 120–1.
184 *Ibid.*, II, p. 115.
185 *Ibid.*, II, p. 122.
186 *Ibid.*, II, p. 123.
187 *Ibid.*, II, p. 128.
188 *Ibid.*, II, p. 189.
189 *Ibid.*, II, pp. 219–20.
190 Eliot, *Selected Essays*, p. 442.
191 Cf. Jenkyns, *The Victorians and Ancient Greece*, p. 294.
192 Chris Snodgrass, 'Swinburne's Circle of Desire: A Decadent Theme', in Stratford Upon Avon Studies, 17, *Decadence and the Eighteen-Nineties*, ed. Fletcher (1979), p. 55.
193 Wilde, *Works*, p. 922.
194 Cf. Hopkins' distinction in *Letters I*, p. 225.
195 For example, James Joyce, Hart Crane, G. Wilson Knight.
196 Wilde, *Works*, p. 924.
197 *Ibid.*, pp. 922–3.
198 *Ibid.*, pp. 925–6.
199 *Ibid.*, p. 931.
200 *Ibid.*, p. 929.
201 *Ibid.*, p. 925.
202 *Ibid.*, p. 933.
203 *Ibid.*, p. 924.
204 *Ibid.*, p. 924.
205 *Ibid.*, p. 925.
206 *Ibid.*, p. 884.
207 *Ibid.*, p. 920.

208 *Ibid.*, p. 927.
209 *Ibid.*, p. 927.
210 *Ibid.*, p. 928.
211 Wilde, 'Mr Pater's *Appreciations*', in *Critics of the 'Nineties*, ed. Derek Stanford (1970), p. 86.
212 *Selected Writings of Walter Pater*, ed. Harold Bloom (1974), p. xvii.
213 *Ibid.*, p. xxiii.
214 *Imaginary Portraits*, pp. 106–7.
215 *Ibid.*, p. 110.
216 Gerald Monsman cites the following critics who describe Pater as wearing a 'mask': Edmund Gosse, *Critical Kit-Kats* (Heinemann, 1913 edn), p. 266; George Moore, *Avowals* (Boni & Liveright, 1919), p. 193; Arthur Symons, *Figures of Several Centuries* (Constable, 1916), p. 331 n. 1; Henry James, *The Letters of Henry James*, ed. P. Lubbock (Scribner's, 1920), Vol. I, p. 222. See *Walter Pater's Art of Autobiography*, p. 13.
217 Wilde, *Works*, p. 1045.
218 *Ibid.*, pp. 1046–7.
219 *Ibid.*, p. 1045.
220 *Ibid.*, p. 934.
221 Monsman, *Walter Pater's Art of Autobiography*, p. 14.
222 *Ibid.*, p. 64. Quotations are from two fragmentary essays by Pater: 'Art and Religion', Houghton Library, Harvard University: b MS Eng 1150 (11); 'Moral Philosophy', b MS Eng 1150 (17).

CONCLUSION

1 Graham Hough, in *The Last Romantics*, explores this tradition as it develops from Ruskin through the Pre-Raphaelites and Pater to Yeats.
2 Arthur Symons, *The Symbolist Movement in Literature* (1958), p. 5.
3 Cf. *The Oxford Book of Modern Verse, 1892–1935*, ed. W. B. Yeats (1936), p. ix. Yeats, as Symons, saw modern poetry as 'in reaction against everything Victorian'. 'Swinburne, Tennyson, Arnold, Browning, had admitted so much psychology, science, moral fervour', he said in 'Modern Poetry: A Broadcast', *Essays and Introductions* (1961), pp. 494–5.
4 *The Wild Swans at Coole*, 'Ego Dominus Tuus'.
5 *The Tower*, 'The Tower'.
6 The resemblance between this statement, from the Preface to *Nigger of the 'Narcissus'*, and Ruskin's frequently expressed strictures about the importance of 'seeing' (cf. for example *Works*, VI, p. 49) is very striking. Cf. Ford Maddox Ford, *Joseph Conrad: A Personal Remembrance* (Duckworth, 1924), p. 167, for Conrad's belief in the moral function of art.

7 Joseph Conrad, *Heart of Darkness*, ed. Robert Kimbrough (Norton, 1971 (1963)), pp. 13–14.
8 *Four Quartets*, 'Burnt Norton', v.
9 *Ibid.*, 'Little Gidding', III.
10 *Ibid.*, 'Little Gidding', v.
11 Eliot, *Selected Essays*, p. 388.
12 Eliot, *After Strange Gods: A Primer of Modern Heresy* (1933), p. 21.
13 Cf. Buckley, *Poetry and Morality* for a full discussion of Eliot's moral poetics.
14 Eliot, *After Strange Gods*, pp. 11, 38, 51–2.
15 Buckley, *Poetry and Morality*, p. 131.
16 'Tom Wolfe on Art: An Elitist Religion', the *Weekend Australian* (20–1 October 1984).

Select bibliography

Abbott, E. and Campbell, L. *The Life and Letters of Benjamin Jowett, M.A.* 2 vols., John Murray (1897).

Abrams, M. H. *The Mirror and the Lamp: Romantic Theory and the Critical Tradition.* Oxford University Press (1953).

Natural Supernaturalism: Tradition and Revolution in Romantic Literature. Norton (1971).

Allott, Kenneth. 'Matthew Arnold's Reading Lists in Three Early Diaries', *Victorian Studies* (March 1959).

'A Background for "Empodocles on Etna"', *Essays and Studies by Members of the English Association* (1968).

Anthony, P. D. *John Ruskin's Labour: A Study of Ruskin's Social Theory.* Cambridge University Press (1984).

Arnold, Matthew. *The Letters of Matthew Arnold, 1848–1888,* ed. G. W. E. Russell. 2 vols., Macmillan (1895).

Unpublished Letters of Matthew Arnold, ed. Arnold Whitridge. Yale University Press (1923).

The Letters of Matthew Arnold to Arthur Hugh Clough, ed. Howard Foster Lowry. Oxford University Press (1932).

The Notebooks of Matthew Arnold, ed. Howard Foster Lowry, Karl Young, and Waldo Hilary Dunn. Oxford University Press (1952).

Ball, Patricia M. *The Science of Aspects: The Changing Role of Fact in the Work of Coleridge, Ruskin and Hopkins.* University of London, The Athlone Press (1971).

Battiscombe, Georgina. *John Keble: A Study in Limitations.* Constable (1963).

Beek, W. J. A. M. *John Keble's Literary and Religious Contribution to the Oxford Movement.* Centrale Drukkerij N.V.-Nijmegen (1959).

Bellasis, Edward. *Cardinal Newman as a Musician.* Kegan Paul, Trench, Trübner & Co. (1892).

Benn, A. W. *The History of English Rationalism in the Nineteenth Century.* 2 vols., Longmans, Green & Co. (1906).

Benson, A. C. *Walter Pater.* Macmillan (1906).

Biswas, R. K. *Arthur Hugh Clough: Towards a Reconsideration.* Clarendon Press (1972).

Select bibliography

Bloom, Harold. *The Ringers in the Tower: Studies in Romantic Tradition.* University of Chicago Press (1971).

Britain, Ian. *Fabianism and Culture: A Study in British Socialism and the Arts c. 1884–1918.* Cambridge University Press (1982).

Brooks, Roger L. 'Some Unaccomplished Projects of Matthew Arnold', *Studies in Bibliography*, XVI (1963).

Buckley, Vincent. *Poetry and Morality: Studies on the Criticism of Matthew Arnold, T. S. Eliot, and F. R. Leavis.* Chatto & Windus (1959).

Burd, Van Akin. 'Another Light on the Writing of *Modern Painters*', *PMLA*, LXVIII (1953).

Burrow, J. W. *Evolution and Society: A Study in Victorian Social Theory.* Cambridge University Press (1966).

Butler, Joseph. *The Analogy of Religion, Natural and Revealed, to the Constitution and Course of Nature.* James, John & Paul Knapton (1736).

Butler, Marilyn. *Romantics, Rebels and Reactionaries: English Literature and its Background 1760–1830.* Oxford University Press (1981).

Cameron, J. M. 'The Night Battle: Newman and Empiricism', *Victorian Studies*, Vol. IV, No. 2 (December 1960).

Cecil, Algernon. *Six Oxford Thinkers: Gibbon, Newman, Church, J. A. Froude, Pater, Lord Morley of Blackburn.* John Murray (1909).

Chadwick, Owen. *From Bossuet to Newman: The Idea of Doctrinal Development.* Cambridge University Press (1957).

An Ecclesiastical History of England: The Victorian Church. 2 vols., Adam & Charles Black (1966).

Chandler, Edmund. *Pater on Style, Anglistica*, Vol. XI. Rosenkilde & Bagger, Copenhagen (1958).

Child, Ruth C. *The Aesthetic of Walter Pater.* A Wellesley College Publication. Macmillan (1940).

Church, R. W. *The Oxford Movement: Twelve Years, 1833–1845,* ed. Geoffrey Best. University of Chicago Press (1970).

Cockshut, A. O. J. *Anglican Attitudes: A Study of Victorian Religious Controversies.* Collins (1959).

The Unbelievers: English Agnostic Thought, 1840–1890. Collins (1964).

Coleridge, J. T. *A Memoir of the Rev. John Keble, M.A., Late Vicar of Hursley.* James Parker & Co. (1870).

Coleridge, M. E. *Non Sequitur.* Nisbet (1900).

Coleridge, S. T. *Letters, Conversations and Recollections of S. T. Coleridge,* ed. Thomas Allsop. Edward Moxon (1836).

Confessions of an Inquiring Spirit: Letters on the Inspiration of the Scriptures, ed. Henry Nelson Coleridge. William Pickering (1840).

Lectures 1795 On Politics and Religion, ed. Lewis Patton and Peter Mann. Routledge & Kegan Paul (1971).

Lay Sermons, ed. R. J. White. Routledge & Kegan Paul (1972).

On the Constitution of the Church and State, ed. John Colmer. Routledge & Kegan Paul (1976).

Select bibliography

Biographia Literaria, or Biographical Sketches of My Literary Life and Opinions, ed. James Engell and W. Jackson Bate. 2 vols., Routledge & Kegan Paul (1983).

Collingwood, R. G. *Ruskin's Philosophy*. Titus Wilson & Son (1922).

Copleston, Frederick. *A History of Philosophy*. 9 vols., Burns, Oates & Washbourne (1946–75).

Coulling, Sidney M. B. 'Matthew Arnold's 1853 Preface: Its Origin and Aftermath', *Victorian Studies* (1964).

Coulson, John. *Newman and the Common Tradition: A Study in the Language of Church and Society*. Clarendon Press (1970).

Religion and Imagination. Clarendon Press (1981).

Coulson, John and Allchin, A. M., eds. *The Rediscovery of Newman: An Oxford Symposium*. Sheed & Ward (1967).

Culler, A. Dwight. *The Imperial Intellect: A Study of Newman's Educational Ideal*. Yale University Press (1955).

Imaginative Reason: The Poetry of Matthew Arnold. Yale University Press (1966).

Darwin, Charles. *The Origin of Species by Means of Natural Selection*. John Murray (1872 (1859)).

Delaura, David J. *Hebrew and Hellene in Victorian England: Newman, Arnold and Pater*. University of Texas Press (1969).

Victorian Prose: A Guide to Research. Modern Language Association of America (1973).

Devlin, Christopher. 'The Image and the Word', *The Month*, N.S. Vol. III (February and March 1950).

Downes, David Anthony. *Victorian Portraits: Hopkins and Pater*. Bookman Associates (1965).

The Temper of Victorian Belief: Studies in the Religious Novels of Pater, Kingsley, and Newman. Twayne Publishers (1972).

Duns Scotus, John. *Duns Scotus: Philosophical Writings, a Selection*, ed. and trans. Allan Wolter, O.F.M. Nelson (1962).

Eliot, T. S. *Selected Essays*. Faber & Faber (1972 (1932)).

After Strange Gods: A Primer of Modern Heresy. Faber & Faber (1933).

The Use of Poetry and the Use of Criticism: Studies in the Relation of Criticism to Poetry in England. Faber & Faber (1948 (1933)).

The Complete Poems and Plays of T. S. Eliot. Faber & Faber (1969).

Ellmann, Richard. *Oscar Wilde: A Collection of Critical Essays*. Prentice-Hall (1969).

Golden Codgers: Biographical Speculations. Oxford University Press (1973).

Fairchild, Hoxie Neale. 'Romanticism and the Religious Revival in England', *Journal of the History of Ideas*, Vol. II, No. 3 (June 1941).

Religious Trends in English Poetry, Vol. IV, *Christianity and Romanticism in the Victorian Era, 1830–1880*. Columbia University Press (1957).

Fishman, Solomon. *The Interpretation of Art: Essays on the Art Criticism of John Ruskin, Walter Pater, Clive Bell, Roger Fry, and Herbert Read.* University of California Press (1963).

Fletcher, Ian, ed. *Decadence and the Eighteen-Nineties,* Stratford Upon Avon Studies, 17. Edward Arnold (1979).

Forsyth, R. A. *The Lost Pattern: Essays on the Emergent City Sensibility in Victorian England.* University of Western Australia Press (1976).

Froude, James Anthony. 'The Oxford Counter-Reformation', in *Short Studies on Great Subjects.* 4 vols., Longmans, Green & Co. (1899 (2 vols., 1867)).

Fuller, Peter. 'Radical Toryism', *New Society,* Vol. LXVII (1 March 1984.)

Fulweiler, Howard W. *Letters from the Darkling Plain: Language and the Grounds of Knowledge.* University of Missouri Press (1972).

Gardner, Helen. *The Business of Criticism.* Clarendon Press (1959).

Gibbons, Tom. *Rooms in the Darwin Hotel: Studies in English Literary Criticism and Ideas 1880–1920.* University of Western Australia Press (1973).

Gilson, Etienne. *Jean Duns Scotus: Introduction à ses positions fondamentales.* Librairie Philosophique J. Vrin (1952).

Gosse, Edmund. *Critical Kit-Kats.* William Heinemann (1896).

Gottfried, Leon. *Matthew Arnold and the Romantics.* Routledge & Kegan Paul (1963).

Hamilton, Paul. *Coleridge's Poetics.* Basil Blackwell (1983).

Hartman, Geoffrey H. *The Unmediated Vision: An Interpretation of Wordsworth, Hopkins, Rilke and Valéry.* Harbinger-Harcourt, Brace & World (1966 (1954)).

Hegel, G. W. F. *Hegel's Aesthetics: Lectures on Fine Art,* trans. T. M. Knox. 2 vols., Clarendon Press (1975).

Heuser, Alan. *The Shaping Vision of Gerard Manley Hopkins.* Oxford University Press (1958).

Hewison, Robert. *John Ruskin: The Argument of the Eye.* Thames & Hudson (1976).

Hewison, Robert, ed. *New Approaches to Ruskin: Thirteen Essays.* Routledge & Kegan Paul (1981).

Hirsch, E. D., Jr. *Wordsworth and Schelling: A Typological Study of Romanticism.* Yale University Press (1960).

Honan, Park. *Matthew Arnold: A Life.* McGraw-Hill (1981).

Hooker, Richard. *The Works of that Learned and Judicious Divine Mr. Richard Hooker,* with an account of his life and death by Isaac Walton, ed. the Rev. John Keble. Oxford University Press (1836).

Hough, Graham. *The Last Romantics.* Duckworth (1961 (1949)).

Houghton, Walter E. *The Art of Newman's 'Apologia'.* Oxford University Press (1945).

The Victorian Frame of Mind, 1830–1870. Yale University Press (1957).

House, Humphry. *Coleridge,* Clark Lectures, 1951–2. Rupert Hart-Davis (1953).

Hyde, H. Montgomery. *Oscar Wilde.* Methuen (1977 (1976)).

Select bibliography

James, David G. *Matthew Arnold and the Decline of English Romanticism.* Clarendon Press (1961).

Jamison, W. A. *Arnold and the Romantics, Anglistica,* x. Rosenkilde & Bagger (1958).

Jenkyns, Richard. *The Victorians and Ancient Greece.* Basil Blackwell (1980).

Kant, Immanuel. *Critique of Pure Reason,* trans. Norman Kemp Smith. Macmillan (1929).

The Critique of Judgement, trans. James Creed Meredith. 2 vols., Clarendon Press (1952).

Keble, John. 'Of the Mysticism attributed to the Early Fathers of the Church', *Tracts for the Times.* 6 vols., J. G. & F. Rivington (1839), Vol. VI, No. 89.

Lyra Innocentium: Thoughts in Verse on Christian Children, Their Ways and Their Privileges. Wiley & Putnam (1846).

Sermons Academical and Occasional. F. & J. Rivington (1847).

On Eucharistical Adoration. John Henry & James Parker & Co. (1857).

Letters of Spiritual Counsel and Guidance, ed. R. F. Wilson. James Parker & Co. (1870).

Sermons for the Christian Year. 11 vols., James Parker & Co. (1875–80).

Occasional Papers and Reviews. James Parker & Co. (1877).

The Christian Year: Thoughts in Verse for the Sundays and Holydays Throughout the Year. Kegan Paul, Trench, Trübner & Co. (1895 (1827)).

Lectures on Poetry, 1832–1841, trans. E. K. Francis. 2 vols., Clarendon Press (1912).

Kermode, Frank. *Romantic Image.* Routledge & Kegan Paul (1961 (1957)).

Knights, Ben. *The Idea of the Clerisy in the Nineteenth Century.* Cambridge University Press (1978).

Lahey, G. F. *Gerard Manley Hopkins.* Oxford University Press (1930).

Landow, George. *The Aesthetic and Critical Theories of John Ruskin.* Princeton University Press (1971).

Leon, Derrick. *Ruskin: The Great Victorian.* Routledge & Kegan Paul (1949).

Levey, Michael. *The Case of Walter Pater.* Thames & Hudson (1978).

Lock, Walter. *John Keble: A Biography.* The Riverside Press (1893).

Madden, William A. *Matthew Arnold: A Study of the Aesthetic Temperament in Victorian England.* Indiana University Press (1967).

Martin, Brian. *John Keble: Priest, Professor and Poet.* Croom Helm (1976).

Martz, Louis L. *The Poetry of Meditation: A Study in English Religious Literature of the Seventeenth Century.* Oxford University Press (1954).

Miller, J. Hillis. *The Disappearance of God: Five Nineteenth-Century Writers.* The Belknap Press of Harvard University Press (1975).

Monsman, Gerald. *Walter Pater's Art of Autobiography.* Yale University Press (1980).

Select bibliography

Newman, John Henry. *The Arians of the Fourth Century.* J. G. & F. Rivington (1833).

Lectures on the Prophetical Office of the Church, viewed relatively to Romanism and Popular Protestantism. J. G. & F. Rivington (1837).

Tracts for the Times. 6 vols., J. G. & F. Rivington (1839), Vol. VI, No. 90.

Sermons, bearing on Subjects of the Day. J. G. F. & J. Rivington (1843).

Sermons, Chiefly on the Theory of Religious Belief, preached before the University of Oxford. J. G. F. & J. Rivington (1843).

An Essay on the Development of Christian Doctrine. James Toovey (1845).

'*Lyra Innocentium.* By the Author of the Christian Year', the *Dublin Review*, Vol. XX, No. XL (June 1846).

Loss and Gain: The Story of a Convert. James Burns (1848).

Discourses Addressed to Mixed Congregations. Longman, Brown, Green & Longmans (1849).

Lectures on Certain Difficulties felt by Anglicans in Submitting to the Catholic Church. Burns & Lambert (1850).

Apologia Pro Vita Sua. Longman, Green, Longman, Roberts, & Green. (1864).

Parochial and Plain Sermons. 8 vols., Rivingtons (1868).

An Essay in Aid of a Grammar of Assent. Burns, Oates & Co. (1870).

Discussions and Arguments on Various Subjects. Basil Montagu Pickering (1872).

Essays Critical and Historical. 2 vols., Basil Montagu Pickering (1872).

The Idea of a University defined and illustrated. Basil Montagu Pickering (1873).

The Via Media of the Anglican Church. 2 vols., Basil Montagu Pickering (1877).

Letters and Correspondence of John Henry Newman during his Life in the English Church, with a brief autobiography, ed. Anne Mozley. 2 vols., Longmans, Green & Co. (1898 (1891)).

Historical Sketches. 3 vols., Longmans, Green & Co. (1899 (1872–3)).

Essays and Sketches, ed. Charles Frederick Harrold. 3 vols., Longmans, Green & Co. (1948).

Letters of John Henry Newman, ed. Derek Stanford and Muriel Spark. Peter Owen (1957).

The Letters and Diaries of John Henry Newman, ed. Charles Stephen Dessain *et al.* Nelson (1961–72); Clarendon Press (1973–).

The Philosophical Notebooks of John Henry Newman, ed. Edward Sillem. 2 vols., Nauwelaerts Publishing House (1969–70).

Newsome, David. *The Parting of Friends: A Study of the Wilberforces and Henry Manning.* John Murray (1966).

Two Classes of Men: Platonism and English Romantic Thought. John Murray (1974).

Select bibliography

Ojala, Aatos. *Aestheticism and Oscar Wilde*. Suomalaisen Tiedeakatemian Toimituksia (Part 1, 1954; Part 2, 1955).

Pater, Walter Horatio. 'Coleridge's Writings', the *Westminster Review*, Vol. XXIX (January 1866).

Uncollected Essays. Thomas B. Mosher (1903).

Letters of Walter Pater, ed. Lawrence Evans. Clarendon Press (1970).

Walter Pater: Essays on Literature and Art, ed. Jennifer Uglow. Dent (1973).

Selected Writings of Walter Pater, ed. Harold Bloom. New English Library (1974).

Pearson, Hesketh. *The Life of Oscar Wilde*. Methuen (1946).

Peters, W. A. M., S.J. *Gerard Manley Hopkins: A Critical Essay towards the Understanding of his Poetry*. Oxford University Press (1948).

Prickett, Stephen. *Romanticism and Religion: The Tradition of Coleridge and Wordsworth in the Victorian Church*. Cambridge University Press (1976).

Proust, Marcel. *Pastiches et Mélanges*. Gallimard (1947 (1919)).

Pusey, Edward Bouverie. 'A Letter on the Catholic Position of the English Church and the Duty of remaining in her Communion', *English Churchman* (30 October 1845).

Raynal, Dom Wilfred. *A Letter on the Validity of Anglican Orders; or, a few suggestions submitted to the Rev. F. G. Lee*. James Richardson & Son (1870).

Reilly, Joseph J. *Newman as a Man of Letters*. Burns, Oates & Washbourne (1927).

Ricks, Christopher. 'Pater, Arnold, and Misquotation', *The Times Literary Supplement* (25 November 1977).

Ritz, Jean-Georges. *Robert Bridges and Gerard Hopkins, 1863–1889: A Literary Friendship*. Oxford University Press (1960).

Robbins, William. *The Ethical Idealism of Matthew Arnold: A Study of the Nature and Sources of his Moral and Religious Ideas*. Heinemann (1959).

Robinson, John. *In Extremity: A Study of Gerard Manley Hopkins*. Cambridge University Press (1978).

Rosenberg, John D. *The Darkening Glass: A Portrait of Ruskin's Genius*. Routledge & Kegan Paul (1963 (1961)).

Ruskin, John. *The Diaries of John Ruskin*, ed. Joan Evans and J. H. Whitehouse. 3 vols., Clarendon Press (1956–9).

Ryan, J. K. and Darvil, E., eds. *American Essays for the Newman Centennial*. Catholic University of America Press (1947).

Schenk, H. G. *The Mind of the European Romantics: An Essay in Cultural History*. Doubleday (1969).

Scruton, Roger. *Kant*. Oxford University Press (1982).

Selby, Robin C. *The Principle of Reserve in the Writings of John Henry Cardinal Newman*. Oxford University Press (1975).

Spencer, Herbert. *First Principles*. Williams & Norgate (1863).

Select bibliography

Stanford, Derek, ed. *Critics of the 'Nineties*. Roy Publishers (1970).

Stein, Richard L. *The Ritual of Interpretation: The Fine Arts as Literature in Ruskin, Rossetti, and Pater*. Harvard University Press (1975).

Sulloway, Alison. *Gerard Manley Hopkins and the Victorian Temper*. Routledge & Kegan Paul (1972).

Swinburne, A. C. *Swinburne as Critic*, ed. Clyde K. Hyder. Routledge & Kegan Paul (1972).

Symons, Arthur. *The Symbolist Movement in Literature*. Dutton (1958).

Tennyson, G. B. *Victorian Devotional Poetry: The Tractarian Mode*. Harvard University Press (1981).

Tierney, Michael, ed. *A Tribute to Newman: Essays on Aspects of his Life and Thought*. Browne & Nolan (1945).

Timco, Michael. 'Corydon Had a Rival', *Victorian Newsletter* (1961).

Tinker, C. B. and Lowry, H. F. *The Poetry of Matthew Arnold: A Commentary*. Oxford University Press (1940).

Trilling, Lionel. *Matthew Arnold*. Unwin (1949 (1939)).

Turner, Frank M. *The Greek Heritage in Victorian Britain*. Yale University Press (1981).

Ward, Anthony. *Walter Pater: The Idea in Nature*. MacGibbon & Kee (1966).

Ward, Wilfred. *The Life of John Henry Cardinal Newman*. 2 vols., Longmans, Green & Co. (1912).

Warnock, Mary. *Imagination*. University of California Press (1976).

Warren, Alba H. *English Poetic Theory, 1825–1865*. Princeton University Press (1966 (1950)).

Weatherby Harold L. *Cardinal Newman in his Age: His Place in English Theology and Literature*. Vanderbilt University Press (1973).

Wilde, Oscar. *The Letters of Oscar Wilde*, ed. Rupert Hart-Davis. Rupert Hart-Davis (1962).

The Artist as Critic: Critical Writings of Oscar Wilde, ed. Richard Ellmann. Random House (1969 (1968)).

Williams, Raymond. *Culture and Society, 1780–1950*. Penguin (1961 (1958)).

Wolfe, Tom. 'Tom Wolfe on Art: An Elitist Religion', the *Weekend Australian* (20–1 October 1984).

Woolf, Virginia. *Roger Fry: A Biography*. Hogarth Press (1940).

Wordsworth, William. *The Prelude, or Growth of a Poet's Mind*, ed. Ernest de Selincourt. 2 vols., Clarendon Press (1926).

The Prose Works of William Wordsworth, ed. W. J. B. Owen and Jane Worthington Smyser. 3 vols., Clarendon Press (1974).

Wright, Thomas. *The Life of Walter Pater*. 2 vols., Everett & Co. (1907).

Yeats, William Butler. *Autobiography*. Macmillan (1916).

Essays and Introductions. Macmillan (1961).

Yeats, William Butler, ed. *The Oxford Book of Modern Verse, 1892–1935*. Oxford University Press (1936).

Index

References to concepts and adjectives based on proper names are listed under the proper name.

Index

Index

Index

Index